Institutionalization of the Parliament in Bangladesh

A. T. M. Obaidullah

Institutionalization of the Parliament in Bangladesh

A Study of Donor Intervention for Reorganization and Development

A. T. M. Obaidullah
Public Administration
University of Rajshahi
Dhaka, Bangladesh

ISBN 978-981-10-5316-0   ISBN 978-981-10-5317-7 (eBook)
https://doi.org/10.1007/978-981-10-5317-7

Library of Congress Control Number: 2018939757

© The Editor(s) (if applicable) and The Author(s) 2019
This work is subject to copyright. All rights are solely and exclusively licensed by the Publisher, whether the whole or part of the material is concerned, specifically the rights of translation, reprinting, reuse of illustrations, recitation, broadcasting, reproduction on microfilms or in any other physical way, and transmission or information storage and retrieval, electronic adaptation, computer software, or by similar or dissimilar methodology now known or hereafter developed.
The use of general descriptive names, registered names, trademarks, service marks, etc. in this publication does not imply, even in the absence of a specific statement, that such names are exempt from the relevant protective laws and regulations and therefore free for general use.
The publisher, the authors and the editors are safe to assume that the advice and information in this book are believed to be true and accurate at the date of publication. Neither the publisher nor the authors or the editors give a warranty, express or implied, with respect to the material contained herein or for any errors or omissions that may have been made. The publisher remains neutral with regard to jurisdictional claims in published maps and institutional affiliations.

Cover credit: ROBERTO SCHMIDT/Staff/Getty Images

Printed on acid-free paper

This Palgrave Macmillan imprint is published by the registered company Springer Nature Singapore Pte Ltd.
The registered company address is: 152 Beach Road, #21-01/04 Gateway East, Singapore 189721, Singapore

Preface

Democracy is a form of government that is never completely achieved. The people of Bangladesh have engaged in the struggle to establish it and have faced obstacles at regular intervals. Bangladesh achieved its independence in 1971 at the onset of a nine-month-long liberation war and framed its Constitution in a single year. However, in the forty-five years since it has failed to consolidate democracy and establish an acceptable mechanism for holding regular parliamentary elections in a free, fair, and participatory environment—the first step in establishing any democratic system. The first four parliaments elected under civil and military dictators suffered legitimacy problems due to flawed electoral processes. The elected parliaments were dominated by chief executives and were largely relegated to merely rubber-stamp policies and laws. It was only after the fall of military autocracy at the end of 1990, and the restoration of parliamentary democracy the following year, that the four parliaments subsequently elected under neutral caretaker governments would be considered free, fair, and credible by national and international observers.

When academics and policy analysts in Bangladesh debated the importance of parliament and the decline of the Westminster system, the development community, academics, think tanks, and civil society organizations became vigorously involved in empowering parliament as the central institution of democracy. Multilateral and bilateral development partners diagnosed problems, assessed needs, and recommended measures to improve the institutional and operational capacity of the Bangladesh Parliament to shoulder the onerous responsibility of maintaining the Westminster democratic model in an effective manner.

At this phase of parliamentary reorganization, I took part in the development process in a number of different capacities for nearly a decade. During that time, I got closer to the senior leadership, members of parliament (MPs), and officials of the Bangladesh Parliament Secretariat. This provided me with the opportunity to interact with donors and parliamentarians from close quarters and witness personally the organizational and institutional problems at the heart of the Bangladesh Parliament. This book is a reflection of the reform initiatives introduced by UNDP and USAID in Bangladesh and the hands-on experience I gained mainly as an organization development consultant to the Parliament Secretariat, and project implementation specialist and parliamentary adviser during 2001–2010 of the 'Strengthening Parliamentary Democracy' (SPD) and 'Promoting Governance Accountability, Transparency and Integrity' (PROGATI) projects respectively. The main thrust of this book is an analysis of the situation of Parliament in the pre-restoration period (1972–1990) and an assessment of the implementation and impact of reforms in the post-restoration period (1991–2015).

In writing this book I have incurred immense debt to innumerable people in the Bangladesh Parliament, UNDP, and USAID, who supervised and facilitated implementation of projects during my tenure as project implementation specialist and parliamentary advisor in the SPD and PROGATI projects respectively.

Among many MPs who I am profoundly indebted to the Honorable Speaker Barrister Jamiruddin Sircar, MP, without whose wholehearted support, passion for the project, and effective directives to the higher echelons of bureaucracy it would have been impossible for me to navigate the bureaucratic maze that is the Bangladesh Parliament Secretariat. I am also beholden to Advocate Abdul Hamid, MP, for allowing me easy access to his good office and offering strategic guidance for making the Parliament effective while he held the position of Honorable Speaker of the Bangladesh Parliament before assuming the office of the presidency of the People's Republic of Bangladesh. At UNDP, UN Coordinator and UNDP Resident Representative Mr. Jorgen Lissner, project manager Mr. A.H.M. Monjurul Kabir, and later Assistant Country Director Mr. Nojibar Rahman is former Assistant Country Director of UNDP, Dhaka and currently Principal Secretary to the Prime Minister. I am highly grateful to Mr. Lissner who, despite his hectic daily schedule, always agreed to discuss any critical issue and offer pertinent solutions. The friendly approach and open-door management style of Mr. Kabir and Mr. Rahman helped me expedite project implementation on time and meet the expectations of Parliament's leadership under time pressures. As parliamentary adviser of the USAID-funded and DAI-administered PROGATI project my debts are due to Dr. Rezaul Haque, Ms. Sherina Tabassum, Dr. David A. Pottebaum, and Mr. Jeremy Kanthor for their constant support and technical advice on different aspects of fiscal oversight issues to discharge my responsibilities during my two-year stay on the project.

In writing this book those names I cannot but gratefully mention include Mr. Kamrul Islam, Director of Editing of Debates and Printing, Ms. Rehana Akhtar, Deputy Director of Reporting, and Mr. Faisal Morshed, Senior Committee Officer of the Parliament Secretariat, all of whom always generously extended their cooperation for finding the necessary data for completing this book. I am greatly indebted to the Rajshahi University authority who granted me sabbatical leave for undertaking this project. Finally, I incurred huge debt to David Butcher who meticulously read the first draft of the manuscript and gave necessary corrections. My immense gratitude and indebtedness go to the authors of all those books, articles, and reports whose scholarly writings I have referred and quoted to bolster my point of view and contribute to discussions in their proper contexts. Last but not least my final gratitude goes to my family members—particularly, my son-in-law, Nasim Hasan who greatly inspired me to take up this arduous venture, wife Mana and only daughter Dr. Sabreena Obaid who gracefully lent time that rightfully belonged to them. Their support sustained me throughout the arduous journey to finish this book. No one but me bears the responsibility for any omissions or mistakes, inadequacy or inaccuracy of interpretation of facts and information presented in this book.

Dhaka, Bangladesh   A. T. M. Obaidullah

Contents

1 **Introduction** 1
  Introduction 10
  Political Landscape and Growth of Bangladesh Parliament:
  A Glimpse 10
  Understanding Parliamentary Democracy 11
  Reorganization of Parliament Secretariat 11
  Making Parliamentary Standing Committees Effective:
  Minimizing Systemic Constraints 12
  Parliamentary Oversight: A Conceptual Framework 13
  Comparative Budget Process in Westminster Parliaments:
  A Lesson for Effective Fiscal Oversight 13
  Human Resource Management and Development
  in the Parliament Secretariat: An Overlooked Agenda 14
  Gender Mainstreaming in Bangladesh Parliament 15
  Present State of Parliament and Democracy 16
  Concluding Observations and Recommendations 16
  References 18

2 **Political Landscape and Parliamentary Development** 21
  British Colonial Rule (1861–1947) 21
  The Pakistani Period (1947–1971) 24

    Nature of Polity and Parliamentary Development
    in Bangladesh   27
        The Short Life of Democracy (1972–1975)   28
        Ascendancy of Military Rule (1975–1990)   33
        Restoration of Democracy from 1991   39
    References   56

3 **Parliament in Parliamentary Democracy: Theoretical-Institutional Framework (Understanding the Westminster Parliament System)**   61
    What Makes a Government Parliamentary?   61
    How the Westminster Model Differs from the Presidential System   63
    Functions of Parliament   65
    The Debate on Parliament's Influence on Policy   68
    Regaining Parliamentary Influence   70
    Colonial Legacy of Weak Parliaments   71
    Pre-requisites for Institutionalization   72
    Parliamentary Autonomy   74
    Parliamentary Culture   76
    References   77

4 **Reorganization of Parliament Secretariat Barriers to the Capacity Development**   81
    The Imperatives of Reorganization   81
    The Meaning of Operational Efficiency   83
    The Situation of the Secretariat Before 1994   84
    Select Studies on Reorganizing the Secretariat   85
    The Asia Foundation, 1991   85
    Legislative Drafting   90
    Library Services   90
    Research and Documentation   92
    Member Liaison   95
    DFID Bangladesh Report, 2000   96
    UNDP Organizational Review Report, 2002   97
    Shortcomings of the Existing Secretariat   97
    Main Recommendations of the Organizational Review Report   99
    Implementation and Impact of Reform Measures   100
    References   105

5 Making Parliamentary Standing Committees Effective: Minimizing Systemic Constraints — 107
Origin of Standing Committees — 107
Imperatives of Parliamentary Committees — 109
Legacy of Weakened Accountability — 111
Constitutional and Legal Basis for Parliamentary Committees — 113
Organization of Parliamentary Committees — 115
Increased Scope and Revision of the Rules — 116
Secretarial Services to Parliamentary Committees — 118
Systemic Weaknesses in the Committee System — 121
Adoption of the Cluster System — 123
Modus Operandi of the Clusters — 125
Proposed Reorganization of Clusters — 128
   Regrouping of Clusters — 128
   Reducing the Number of Standing Committees — 131
   Developing Resources to Support Clusters — 132
Concluding Observations — 134
Note — 135
References — 136

6 Parliamentary Oversight: A Conceptual Framework — 139
Why Parliamentary Oversight — 139
Types of Parliamentary Oversight — 142
Oversight Tools and Form of Government — 144
Bangladesh Parliament and Oversight Tools — 147
Constitutional and Procedural Sanctions — 148
Individual Oversight Methods — 148
Enforceability of Individual Methods — 149
Collective Oversight Methods — 151
Barriers to Effective Accountability — 152
References — 154

7 Comparative Budget Process in Westminster Parliaments: A Lesson for Effective Fiscal Oversight — 157
Budget as an Instrument of Fiscal Policy — 157
Budget Process in Parliaments in the Developed World — 158
Why Parliament Should Be Involved in the Budget Process — 161
The Move Toward Budget Openness — 162

Budget Process in British Parliament 164
   Pre-budget Discussion 164
   Budget Process in the House of Commons 165
Budget Process in New Zealand Parliament 167
Budget Process in Canadian Parliament 171
   The Budget and National Priorities 171
   The Expenditure Management System 172
Budget Process in Bangladesh 175
   Constitutional Legal Framework 175
Executive Phase of the Budget 176
   Budget Structure 176
The New Trend in Bangladesh Budgeting 179
Procedures of Budgeting under MTBF 181
Parliamentary Phase of the Budget Process 183
Financial Accountability System: A Triangular Relationship 185
Ex-post Oversight of the National Budget 187
Improving Bangladesh Parliament's Fiscal Oversight Capacity 194
Strengthening the Public Accounts Committee 195
Pre-requisites for Effective Budget Debates 196
Strengthening Financial Committee Control on Public Expenditure 198
Promote Transparency, Strict Oversight, and Public Disclosure 201
Lessons for Bangladesh 202
References 204

8 Human Resource Development in Parliament Secretariat: An Overlooked Agenda 207
Conceptual Definition of HRM and HRD 207
Scope of Human Resource Development 209
HRM and HRD in the Secretariat 210
Legal Foundation of Parliament Secretariat's HRD Policy 211
Recruitment Policy and Staffing 211
Staff Development and Training in the BCS 215
Training for Secretariat Staff 217
Donor-Funded Staff Development Programs 219
Seminars and Workshop for MPs 221
Training Programs 221

	Promotion	225
	Indifference to Promotion Rules	226
	Motivation and Employee Morale	228
	Final Observations	230
	References	233
9	**Gender Mainstreaming in Parliament**	**237**
	Concept of Gender	237
	Gender Equality	238
	Gender Mainstreaming	241
	Gender Responsiveness and Gender Sensitiveness	242
	Importance of Gender Equality in Parliaments	243
	Barriers to Gender Mainstreaming in Parliaments	247
	Gender and Bangladesh Parliament	249
	Constitutional Commitments	249
	Gender Makeup of Ninth Parliament	249
	Tackling Underrepresentation	252
	Resourcing Parliament	253
	Gender Consideration in Rules and Procedures	254
	Gender Consideration in Legislation	255
	Gender Legislation Review	258
	Parliamentary Oversight of Gender Issues	259
	Gender Responsive National Budget	265
	Recent Trends in Bangladesh Budgeting	266
	Gender Equality in the Staffing of the Secretariat	267
	The Way Forward	268
	Barriers to Implementation of Gender Mainstreaming Programs	269
	Conclusion	270
	References	271
10	**Paradox of Reforms: A Reflection on Present State of Democracy and Parliament**	**275**
	Institutionalization of Parliament	275
	Democratic Consolidation	284
	Why Democratization Has Failed in Bangladesh	286

Where Bangladesh Stands	288
Democracy Type	289
Facade Democracies	289
Illiberal Democracies	290
Electoral Democracies	290
Full/Liberal Democracy	291
Rule of Law	292
Extra-Judicial Killings and Torture	292
Torture	296
Attacks on Civil Society	296
Political Violence	297
Independence of Judiciary	299
Neutrality of Civil Service	301
Conclusion	305
References	307
11 Concluding Observations and Recommendations	313
References	321
Annex 1	323
Annex 2	329

Acronyms

AD	Appelate Division
ADP	Annual Development Plan
AL	Awami League
APS	Assistant Private Secretary
ASTD	American Society for Training and Development
BAKSAL	Bangladesh Krishak Sramick Awami League
BAMU	Budget Analysis and Monitoring Unit
BAU	Budget Analysis Unit
BIPS	Bangladesh Institute of Parliamentary Studies
BNP	Bangladesh Nationalist Party
BNPP	Bangladesh Nationalist Party Parliamentary
BPS	Budget Policy Statement
BRAC	Bangladesh Rural Advancement Committee
C&AG	Comptroller and Auditor General
CA	Constituent Assembly
CCTV	Close Circuit Television
CHT	Chittagong Hill Tracts
CEC	Chief Election Commissioner
CEDAW	Convention on the Elimination of all Forms of Discrimination Against Women
CJ	Chief Justice
CS	Committee Support
CSO	Civil Society Organization
CW	Chief Whip
CWO	Chief Whip of the Opposition

DFID	Department for International Development
DSCs	Departmental Select Committees
EC	Bangladesh Election Commission
ECOSOC	United Nations Economic and Social Council
EMS	Expenditure Management System
ERD	External Resources Division
FH	Freedom House
FPTP	First Past the Post
FTC	Foundation Training Course
GAD	Gender and Development
GAG	Comptroller and Auditor General
GRB	Gender Responsive Budgeting
HCD	High Court Division
HRD	Human Resource Development
HRM	Human Resource Management
ICS	Indian Civil service
ICT	Information Communication Technology
ILI	International Law Institute
IPD	Improving Democracy through Parliamentary Development
IPU	Inter-Parliamentary Union
KPI	Key Performance Indicator
LAN	Local Area Network
LGRD	Local Government and Rural development
LIC	Legislative Information Center
LS	Legislative Support
MDG	Millennium Development Goals
MP	Member of Parliament
MLSS	Member of Lower Subordiate Staff
MTBF	Medium Term Budgetary Framework
MWCA	Ministry of Women and Children Affairs
NA	National Assembly
NBR	National Bureau of Revenue
NDI	National Democratic Institute
NSAPR	National Strategy for Accelerated Poverty Reduction
P&D	Planning & Development
PAC	Public Account Committee
PEC	Public Estimates Committee
PMQT	Prime Minister's Question Time
PRODIP	Promoting Democratic Institutions and Practices

PROGATI	Promoting Governance, Accountability, Transparency, and Integrity
PRSP	Poverty Reduction Strategy Paper
PSA	Parliament Secretariat Act
PSC	Public Service Commission
RI	Republican Institute
RIPA	Royal Institute of Public Administration
ROP	Rules of Procedure
SCM	Standing Committee on Ministry
SPCPD	Strengthening Parliament's Capacity in Integrating Population Issues into Development
SPD	Strengthening Parliamentary Democracy
SPO	Strengthening Parliamentary Oversight
TAF	The Asia Foundation
TIB	Transparency International, Bangladesh
UNDP	United Nations Development Programme
UNESCO	United Nations Educational, Scientific and Cultural Organization
UNFPA	United Nations Population Fund
USAID	United States Agency for International Development
UWOPA	Uganda Women's Parliamentary Association
VIP	Very Important Person
WID	Women in Development

List of Figures

Fig. 4.1	Establishing a parliamentary research service: key phases. (Guidelines for parliamentary research services, www.ipu.org)	94
Fig. 5.1	Existing functional staff support provided by the Secretariat to committee chairs	120
Fig. 5.2	Proposed functional support to committee chairmen	124
Fig. 7.1	Budget cycle in parliaments in the developed world	159
Fig. 7.2	Key phases of the New Zealand budget. (Source: http://www.treasury.govt.nz/budget/process)	169
Fig. 7.3	Expenditure management systems	172
Fig. 7.4	Roles of the expenditure management system	173
Fig. 7.5	Medium-term strategic objectives and key activities. (Source: GOB, Ministry of Finance, Budget Circular I, 2009 cited in PROGATI/BAMU: note No. 2, 2012, Medium Term Budget Framework, USAID-PROGATI)	180
Fig. 7.6	MTBF and annual budget preparation. Integration of budgeting under MTBF. (Source: PROGATI/BAMU: note No. 2, 2012, Medium Term Budget Framework, USAID-PROGATI)	182
Fig. 7.7	Triangular system of financial accountability	186
Fig. 7.8	Frameworks of accountability and transparency. (Source: Md. Shahidul Islam (2010) BRAC University Dhaka)	190
Fig. 7.9	Delays in ministry response to audit objections. (Sources: Rahman (2008) and 1st report of PAC in 8th parliament)	200

Fig. 9.1	Representation of women and level of trust. (Source: Women in Parliament: www.parl.gc.ca/content/lop/researchpublications/prb0562-e.htm)	245
Fig. 9.2	Proportion of seats held by women in national parliament (%)	246
Fig. 10.1	Law and order situation in Bangladesh and other South Asian countries	293

List of Tables

Table 2.1	Party composition and electoral performance in First–Fourth Parliament	45
Table 2.2	Party composition and electoral performance in Fifth–Tenth Parliament	46
Table 5.1	Standing committees at Bangladesh Parliament	114
Table 5.2	Organizational profile of the present cluster system of standing committees	129
Table 6.1	Accountability, value emphasis, and behavioral expectations	143
Table 6.2	Number of oversight tools by form of government	146
Table 6.3	Number of oversight tools by level of democracy	146
Table 6.4	Use of interpellations by income level	147
Table 6.5	Summary of individual oversight methods practiced in Bangladesh Parliament	150
Table 7.1	Budget transparency in South Asian countries	163
Table 7.2	Budget calendar	178
Table 7.3	Timelines of Parliament sitting and Public Accounts Committee formation	191
Table 7.4	Composition and output of Public Accounts Committees	192
Table 7.5	Parliament's ability to use its authority and resources	194
Table 8.1	Profile of Class 1 staff in parliament secretariat	213
Table 8.2	Nature of appointment in the Secretariat	214
Table 8.3	Heads of expenditure for secretariat training	223
Table 9.1	Proportion of women in world parliaments	248
Table 9.2	Gender makeup of the Ninth Parliament	250
Table 9.3	Women members in Bangladesh Parliament from 1973 to 2012	251

Table 9.4	Standing committees of Ninth Parliament	260
Table 9.5	Oversight tool	262
Table 9.6	Gender-based staff profile of the Bangladesh Secretariat (Class 1–4)	267
Table 10.1	Legislative measures limiting human rights adopted under elected civilian governments in the pre- and post-democratic period	280
Table 10.2	OSDs in the Bangladesh Secretariat	303

CHAPTER 1

Introduction

The Indian subcontinent achieved independence at the beginning of the second wave of democracy shortly after the Allied victory in World War II. While Pakistan failed to establish democracy even when the second wave was at its peak, Bangladesh became independent in December 1971 as the second wave ebbed and before the rush of the third wave which swept across the world from the mid-1970s (Huntington 1991). Bangladesh began its democratic journey under the Westminster system as soon as its founder, Bangabandhu Sheikh Mujibur Rahman, returned from prison in Pakistan and passed the Constitution in December 1972. Within three years, the democratic system was substituted by the Bangladesh Krishak Sramik Awami League (BAKSAL), which established a one-party authoritarian system. From 1975, the people of Bangladesh struggled to re-establish democracy in the face of a succession of civil and military autocracies that ended in 1990, at a time when the third wave of democracy was sweeping over most of the third-world countries of Asia, Africa, and Latin America. Bangladesh restored democracy in 1991. By and large, the last part of the twentieth century was marked by the global triumph of democracy as an ideal system of government, with world power reaching a consensus to dispense with any form authoritarianism.[1] The end of the Cold War and rise of the third of wave of democracy allowed for the expansion of democratic government to the former communist bloc and the non-aligned group of states and eliminated the rationale for tolerating autocratic practices worldwide (Magen 2009: 5–6). All over of the

© The Author(s) 2019
A. T. M. Obaidullah, *Institutionalization of the Parliament in Bangladesh*, https://doi.org/10.1007/978-981-10-5317-7_1

world, the numbers of democracies increased significantly. The exact tally varies depending on the criteria used to assess democratic consolidation (https://en.wikipedia.org/wiki/Third_Wave_Democracy). By 2006, the number of democratic states in the world rose to 121 from forty in 1974 (Diamond 2008 cited by Magen 2009: 6). However, the majority of independent countries emerging from colonial rule could not achieve a reasonable degree of success in establishing liberal democracy.[2] Bangladesh is a case in point.

Bangladesh emerged as a sovereign state on December 16, 1971, having fought a war of independence against Pakistan for the right to establish a true democracy—to build a country where people would enjoy civil and political liberties without suffering economic and social exploitation. The partition of British India in August 1947 gave birth to Pakistan but Bangladesh, which constituted its eastern province, would experience internal colonialism for the following twenty-three years until its dismemberment in 1971. Bangladesh is built on the premise of 'Sonar Bangla' (Golden Bengal)—a totally different polity that would ensure an economically prosperous, democratically governed society, free of exploitation and respectful of the rights of the people. The country made a spectacular stride toward establishing a democratic state within one year, adopting its Constitution in 1972 with a Westminster-style parliamentary form of government and the provision of an elaborate suite of fundamental rights and an independent judiciary. Article 11 of the Constitution unequivocally stated that "Bangladesh shall be a democracy in which fundamental human rights and freedoms and respect for the dignity and worth of human person shall be guaranteed" (GOB Constitution of Bangladesh). The government held the first parliamentary elections the following year, 1973, in which the ruling Awami League (AL) party won a landslide and formed a government with Bangabandhu Sheikh Mujibur Rahman as prime minister. Sheikh Mujib had been the chief architect of an independent Bangladesh, and at the advent in 1973 of parliamentary democracy based on the Westminster model, there were high hopes that under his leadership the country could realize the spirit of the liberation war.[3]

At the very dawn of independence, Sheikh Mujib was faced with the gigantic task of restoring a war-ravaged economy and combating a declining law and order situation across the country, all with a very inexperienced and inept administration. Within months of winning a landslide victory, the AL was plunged into factional politics. A deep schism opened between militant youth leaders and the older moderate members who disagreed over the modus operandi of governance. In this spell of political listlessness, the personal discretion of Sheikh Mujib reigned over the entire machinery of government and thus weakened democratic institutions in the country at the very beginning of its democratic journey. Instead of accommodating dissenting views and showing tolerance, Sheikh Mujib preferred to exercise undisputed authority, demanding unconditional submission from all members. Any opposition to Mujib inside and outside Parliament was considered tantamount to sedition. The administration was managed by people who were close and loyal to Mujib, who placed his relatives in strategic administrative positions: "Many appointments were made on the basis of nodding acquaintance with Mujib or on the recommendations of his close friends. Some even took commission for a chit" (Mascarenhas 2013: 14). The Bangladeshi public, by and large, resented this nepotism and favoritism which opportunists and conspirators successfully exploited to their favor (Jahan 2005: 167–173). In 1974, the situation worsened due to rampant corruption, excessive price hikes of essential commodities, and terrible flooding. The civil and military bureaucracy proved inefficient to deliver services to the population or counteract corruption and lawlessness across the country. Far-left political parties vehemently criticized Sheikh Mujib and conspired to oust him from power. Anthony Mascarenhas observes:

> Eight months after he had taken over as prime minister, the tide of popularity had begun to run out for Mujib. The great agitator, the champion of the people's grievance, the beloved Bangabandhu on whom the most fulsome praise had been lavished, had now become the target of criticism from an outraged public. (Mascarenhas 2013: 19)

The situation was further worsened by a deadly famine in 1974 in which some 26,000 people starved to death according to an official government estimate, although "one scholar estimates 1.5 million deaths as a reasonable estimate" (https://en.wikipedia.org/wiki/Bangladesh_famine_of_1974, retrieved on September 24, 2016). Whatever the true figure, this claimed a heavy toll on the popularity of Sheikh Mujib. The people of Bangladesh felt ashamed, insulted, and demoralized as a nation since this famine was not due to a food crisis but rather maldistribution and mismanagement. The scarcity of food was due to corrupt and inefficient management in the nationalized public sector (Jahan 2005: 167). Faced with growing starvation, every village heard stories about fantastic smuggling and profit being made from the illegal shipment of rice and jute to India (Lifschultz 1979; Mascarenhas 2013). The Jatiya Samajtantrik Dal (JSD) launched a vigorous movement to bring an end to the regime, collaborating with other left-wing parties to take up arms and fight an underground insurgency to oust the AL from power. The JSD leaders openly denounced the AL as more corrupt and much worse than the Pakistani leaders ever were (Mascarenhas 2013). The top brass of the pro-left leadership, including Major M.A. Jalil and JSD founder A.S.M. Abdur Rab, as well as innumerable activists, were imprisoned (Huq 1985).[4] Sheikh Mujib, increasingly desperate at the deteriorating situation, conceded to suggestions by the AL militant youth leaders to introduce the Constitution (Fourth Amendment) Bill in 1975 in order to consolidate his power absolutely. This amendment replaced the parliamentary system with a presidential one, introduced a monolithic one-party system under the BAKSAL, and concentrated all political power in the hands of the president. Lifscultz observes the painful tragedy of the once-revered leading architect of Bangladeshi independence overturning parliamentary democracy and emerging as a dictator in a one-party system (Lifschultz 1979: 87).

This kind of reversal to authoritarianism is not unique to Bangladesh. In fact, a large number of democracies that emerged from internal or external colonialism in Africa and Latin America during the third wave of democracy failed to consolidate their democracies (Magen et al. 2009; Haynes 2001). Before independence, nationalist leaders organized liberation movements against colonial powers and spoke of Western values of democracy such as liberty, equality, and popular participation. But following independence, many questioned whether the liberal values the same leaders had espoused were in fact more of a tactic for gathering mass support than a true commitment to liberal ideology. The people of these countries witnessed a sharp contrast between what was promised and what actually came about after independence. This is what David Beetham (2006) describes in the guide to good parliamentary practice published by the Inter-Parliamentary Union (IPU) as the 'paradox of democracy.' Another commentator makes the observation that their initial experiments with western style constitutional government were soon discarded in favor of either a one-party system or military dictatorship (Jahan 1987: 95). Moreover, popular nationalist leaders realized that liberal democratic values such as liberty, equality, and participation were mutually conflicting and ran counter to their political interests, which led them to revert to authoritarianism for their political survival (Jahan 2005: 1–3). However, Sheikh Mujib's experiment with the BAKSAL was crushed before it could be given a trial by the August coup of 1975 staged by Lt. Col. Abdur Rashid and Lt. Col. Farooq Rahman.[5] Sheikh Mujib and most of his family were brutally assassinated on August 15, 1975 and thus brought the end of the first phase of Awami League rule (1972–1975).[6]

After Sheikh Mujib's assassination, Bangladesh underwent prolonged military and pseudo-military rule, led in succession by Generals Zia and Ershad until 1990. This period was characterized by a plethora of successful and abortive military coups and countercoups; the rise of civil and military authoritarianism, and mock democracy under the presidential system of government; intermittent attempts to restore a democratic system through elections that were farcical and rigged; political institutions subservient to the whims of the chief executive; and ineffective Parliament—to mention but a few. Democracy was restored after a tremendous mass uprising in 1990 (Lifschultz 1979; Mascarenhas 2013).

From 1972 to 1990, the Bangladeshi Parliament, when it existed, was constituted through flawed elections designed to legitimize the regime and serve the desires of the chief executives and autocrats, be they military or civil. Each parliament suffered a legitimacy crisis, since none of them were elected democratically or attained public confidence. Any supremacy of Parliament over the executive was too much to expect during this period in Bangladesh.[7] Parliament was ever prepared to approve whatever resolutions the executive had brought before them.

From the election of the First Parliament in 1973 to the end of military rule at the close of 1990, all four parliamentary elections (1973, 1979, 1986, and 1988) were flawed under the politicized Bangladesh Election Commission (EC) (Tim Meisburger, asiafoundation.org/resources/pdfs/OccasionalPaperNo11FINAL.pdf) that set out to manipulate elections in favor of the incumbent government by exerting influence on constituencies through government machinery at the field administration level.[8] In order to prevent election rigging by the ruling party, the Thirteenth Amendment to the Constitution, made in the run-up to the 1996 parliamentary elections, institutionalized the unique system of non-party caretaker government (NCG) election oversight. Under the new system the party government had to cede power to an interim, unelected NCG, usually headed by the Chief Justice, ninety days before an election to ensure a level playing field for all political parties to contest elections (Arafat Kabir 2015). The system gained public confidence at home and abroad and worked well for years; power changed hands in four successive elections held in 1991, 1996, 2001, and 2008. "In four electoral contests, the caretaker government ensured that political foxes did not guard the electoral hen houses" (Landry 2016). The EC was perceived as neutral and unbiased, and the electoral process was believed transparent and credible. The voter list was considered reliable following a comprehensive voter registration exercise. As a matter of fact, the whole election management reached such a level of excellence that it was held up as a model for other emerging democracies. These elections were believed to be ushering in a new era for making the transition to an effective democracy (Arafat Kabir 2015).

After the fall of the military dictatorship in 1990, subsequent parliaments popularly elected under NCGs were expected to be institutionalized, assert their supremacy over the executive, and hold it to account for its actions and policies—as is parliament's role in the Westminster model.[9] However, that remained a dream for Bangladesh. Of all the problems that thwarted true democracy in the country, the most fundamental challenge was successfully holding credible and participatory parliamentary elections. In addition, other challenges Bangladesh confronted in its journey toward establishing a democratic system since its independence may be summarized as:

1. holding free, fair, and credible elections to Parliament by an impartial EC;
2. lack of continuity in constitutional rule;
3. lack of enforcement of the rule of law;
4. lack of resources to make Parliament independent of the executive;
5. unwillingness of the chief executive to be accountable to the legislature;
6. weak political opposition;
7. lack of assertion from Parliament to hold the powerful executive to account;
8. highly confrontational politics stemming from fear of defeat and consequent risk of life and property.

Parliaments in countries emerging from a long spell of colonial rule frequently fail to serve the requirements of an independent nation and are thus held in low esteem because of a wide gap between what political leaders promised and what they actually delivered. The IPU study (Beetham 2006: 109–110) holds that parliaments often struggle to meet the challenges they face but, in general, have become more open and responsive to the needs of the electorate in a rapidly changing world. There is, of course, variation in the overall record of parliamentary performance. During the colonial era, when governance was oriented to a subject–ruler relation, the development of representative institutions such as parliament was never given priority. Rather, the priority was the development of control mechanisms. Many parliaments have still not taken significant steps to improve their performance. In some cases, instead of progress there has been stagnation or further deterioration (Beetham 2006 cited by Jahan and Amundssen 2012). The poor governance, political instability, corruption, and violation of democratic rights that are very often reported features of these countries are in part due to the absence of a truly representative parliament with robust political opposition that can enforce strong accountability and act as a check on the caprice of the ruling majority party. Parliaments in post-independence countries that struggle to assert supremacy over the executive are constrained by power, resources, and a lack of independence. This weakness is further worsened by lack of parliamentary and democratic culture; a consensual politics between the treasury and opposition benches and proper use of the existing accountability mechanisms – both horizontal and vertical (Jahan, R 2015) under the constitutional and legal system Jahan (2015). Parliaments in nascent democracies only rarely have these provisions (Beetham 2006, Chap. 6). The Bangladesh Parliament is no exception.

After ousting autocratic rule, policy-makers and think tanks quickly realized that if democracy was to be institutionalized in Bangladesh, the institutional and operational reforms of Parliament would have to be made simultaneously. Institutional reforms included necessary constitutional reforms to the parliamentary government, the revision of the anachronistic Rules of Procedure (ROP), and the strengthening parliamentary oversight. Operational reforms called for legal enactments to empower the Parliament Secretariat and streamline its organizational structure, rejuvenate the parliamentary committee system, and strengthen the provision of research and training facilities to increase human capacity in Parliament. In the situation where Parliament had no independence, the Secretariat was unorganized and weak and the committees were in chaos, their structure haphazard and lacking institutional memory (Watson and Williams 2000). Rules were inadequate to support backbench members and committees to perform their legislative and oversight responsibilities (Siddiqi et al. 1994; Obaidullah 2011). In such an environment, the fact that the Bangladesh Parliament was not functioning effectively is hardly surprising.

Against this backdrop, the Bangladesh government and the international community implemented a series of reorganization programs in the post-restoration period to address the parliamentary inadequacies that existed during the previous two decades of autocratic rule. With this end in view, the Constitution was amended to enable effective political changeover and revise anachronistic rules of for procedures in the presidential system. The Parliament Secretariat was made independent of the president's control, reorganized and resourced to ensure that it could respond quickly and effectively to the needs of members and committee chairs. The committee wing was comprehensively reorganized with adequate logistics and trained human resources to strengthen support services to MPs to discharge their onerous responsibilities in respect of legislation and oversight (Obaidullah 2011). All these changes were geared toward strengthening the hitherto rubber-stamp Parliament into a properly representative body that would hold the traditionally omnipotent executive to account for its actions and policies.

However, these major reforms did not have the desired impact on Bangladesh's democracy. This is largely because alongside Parliament's organizational and institutional reforms there was no corresponding political development and work to improve the rule of law, which are both necessary if democracy is to thrive. After the immediate target of deposing General H.M. Ershad had been achieved, the old rivalry between the AL and the Bangladesh Nationalist Party (BNP) resurfaced, despite their having worked hand in hand in the pro-democracy movements. The rivalry has its roots in differences in ideological conviction about the fundamental principles of state policy and the place of religion in politics. The basic difference is constituted on the issues of nationalism and attitude toward India. The AL believes in 'Bengali nationalism' whereas the BNP believes in Bangladeshi nationalism or, in other words, 'territorial nationalism.' The AL is perceived as 'pro-Indian' and the BNP 'anti-Indian.' In addition, the AL claims to be secular whereas the BNP leans toward the right; the AL undermines the role of Zia, the founder of the BNP, in national politics while the BNP questions Sheikh Mujib's role in first three years of his rule (Islam 2015). In this polarized political milieu, the AL and the BNP were never seen to be cooperating with each other in Parliament. Rather, both parties, when on the opposition bench, seemed to consider their main responsibility as overthrowing the incumbent government by any means. Against this backdrop, popularly elected parliaments with improved legal provisions and organizational support could hardly function as an effective national forum of deliberations for policy-making and resolving political conflicts. In 2011, the AL-led government abolished the NCG system through passing the Fifteenth Amendment to the Constitution and in doing so totally overturned the political landscape. Three years later, in the tenth and most disputed parliamentary elections the country has witnessed, almost all major opposition parties, including the BNP, boycotted the polls, citing unfair election conditions, and 154 of the total 300 seats went uncontested, meaning almost half of all MPs were elected unopposed. The country again plunged into a 'black hole' of electoral crisis and thus the question of how to hold peaceful, participatory, and credible parliamentary elections remains a significant one for Bangladesh's future.

This book intends to focus on three main areas. First, the institutional and operational weaknesses that obstructed Parliament's functional efficacy in the pre-restoration period (1972–1990); second, the reform measures offered by the development partners to overcome those weaknesses in the post-restoration period (1991–2015); third, the extent to which the Bangladesh Parliament adopted the recommendations of the development partners; and fourth, the extent to which the Bangladesh Parliament has been institutionalized consequent to the adoption of the reform measures.

The present study seeks to visualize Parliament's problems with institutionalization through a holistic approach that focuses on its institutional, organizational, procedural, and human features. It will ask the following three fundamental questions:

1. To what extent has the Bangladesh Parliament been institutionalized?
2. Has Parliament played a significant role in democratic transition in Bangladesh?
3. To what extent has democracy been consolidated following parliamentary reform?

In order to properly understand Parliament's functional effectiveness and its growth as an institution, Chap. 2 will shed light on its evolution and the present political landscape in which Parliament must evolve and function. This book is exploratory in nature, based predominantly on secondary data, and qualitative in analysis. Yet, primary data is incorporated through structured questionnaires and interviews with senior AL MPs and former BNP MPs to gather a comparative picture of the pre-restoration and the post-restoration parliaments.[10] In addition, a handful of permanent officials of the Parliament Secretariat were interviewed on the core issues of this study and their insights gathered through consultations. Secondary data has been collected from available books, research reports, diagnostic studies, articles, newspapers, and web sources. The book has been divided into eleven chapters and a synopsis of each is given below.

Introduction

This chapter presents a synoptic view of this book. It briefly outlines the global perspectives of the nascent democracies that emerged after independence from colonial power or democratization after the overthrow of autocratic regimes, with special reference to Bangladesh. This chapter identifies the objectives of this study, its research questions and methodology, and an outline of the rest of the book.

Political Landscape and Growth of Bangladesh Parliament: A Glimpse

This chapter traces the growth of Bangladesh Parliament since its germination in British India up to the turn of the twenty-first century. After discussing its roots in British India and the Pakistan period, it analyzes Parliament's development in response to regime change and an evolving political landscape in Bangladesh since independence. In particular, it describes Parliament's position vis-à-vis the executive in both the parliamentary and presidential systems and under civilian autocracy and military authoritarianism in pre- and post-restoration periods. Since independence in 1971, Bangladesh has undergone ten parliamentary elections, six of which were held under party government and considered flawed, allegedly rigged, or suffering legitimacy crises. The post-restoration parliamentary elections since 1991, however, were fair, free, and highly contested for two decades. But the fact remains that despite receiving a popular mandate none of the four parliaments can be described as components of a full-fledged and functioning electoral democracy. And with the Fifteen Amendment to the constitution enacted in 2008 and parliamentary elections due in 2018, the country again faces the foundational challenge of how to hold credible and participatory national elections. Despite the success of the four elections under NCGs, Parliament has never been a focal point for policy decision-making or a forum for debating national and international issues and resolving national crises through deliberations. Executive dominance is a colonial legacy that still persists in state affairs and continues to be one of the core obstacles to parliamentary institutionalization in Bangladesh (Jahan 2004). This chapter presents a brief portrait of Bangladesh's efforts to make the transition to democracy, the constraints it encountered, and continues to encounter, in the institutionalization process, and the measures taken to overcome them.

Understanding Parliamentary Democracy

This chapter outlines the conceptual framework of parliamentary democracy and what is popularly called the 'Westminster system.' It presents the pivotal position of parliament in the Westminster model as compared with the presidential system. The main feature that characterizes the parliamentary system is its ability to hold the executive to account for its actions and policies. The executive can remain in power so long as it enjoys the support of the majority of MPs. This chapter also asks why parliaments in most developing countries cannot discharge their expected role and assert supremacy over the executive and why parliaments in post-colonial countries do not institutionalize or contribute to the consolidation of their democracies. By contrast, parliaments that have been institutionalized and consolidated in developed countries can assert their supremacy and play the role expected by the Westminster model. A parliament that is not yet institutionalized can hardly exercise its constitutional authority over the executive. This chapter presents the IPU framework of institutionalized parliament against which the post-restoration reform initiatives of Bangladesh Parliament have been analyzed in order to ascertain the present institutional capacity of the Bangladesh Parliament.

Reorganization of Parliament Secretariat

The secretariat is an integral part of any parliament. It is now widely recognized that an independent and strong secretariat is a pre-condition for a strong and effective parliament. From this point of view, the Bangladesh Parliament happened to be in an advantageous position due to the constitutional sanction of its Secretariat under Article 76 of the Constitution. The Parliament Secretariat would provide independent, impartial, and efficient support services to members and committee chairs in the discharge of their responsibilities of law-making and oversight of the executive. However, until the restoration of parliamentary democracy in 1991, the Secretariat was a subservient body to the executive/president's secretariat, and unaccountable to Parliament. In 1994 the Parliament Secretariat Act (PSA) was passed which accorded the Secretariat independent status in respect of its budget preparation, manpower planning and undertaking any development plan without the endorsement of the executive. In the years immediately following the change in the political landscape, however, the Secretariat was ill-prepared to shoulder the onerous responsibilities of what parliamentary government is called upon to perform. Thus, the Secretariat has undergone massive reorganization in the last two decades in its organizational and human resource development. This chapter makes an attempt to assess the present state of the Secretariat as a prime political organization to support Parliament and to examine whether it is in a position now to render effective services to MPs and parliamentary committees to perform their mandated roles in legislation and oversight. Stakeholder views suggest that the Secretariat is yet to attain that required level and that this is due largely to the adoption of inappropriate human resource policies.

Making Parliamentary Standing Committees Effective: Minimizing Systemic Constraints

Each and every MP, as a representative of the people, must have equal opportunity to participate in the legislative and oversight duties of parliament (Lindley 1991). As a matter of fact, the National Parliament House (House hereafter) cannot provide this opportunity to its members. This is now provided by expanding the role of parliamentary committees. This chapter briefly traces how standing committees in Britain and Bangladesh evolved as watchdogs. Globally, standing committees are today considered the main center of legislation and oversight of the executive irrespective of the form of government (Obaidullah 2011). A standing committee is regarded as a microcosm of parliament itself. Moreover, the effectiveness of committees in performing oversight functions can be the difference between an effective parliament and an ineffective one. Just how successful they are depends to a great extent on the functional ability of the system in which they operate. Since parliaments in the pre-restoration period in Bangladesh served under authoritarian regimes, committees were neither systematically organized nor provided with resources to carry out effective oversight of legislation or hold the executive to account. With the change in political landscape in 1991, parliament's mandates changed. The existing committee system was considered weak, chaotic, and unable to perform its role, and called for a major overhaul both in respect of its operating system and scope of work. Against this backdrop, the parliamentary committee system was thoroughly refurbished to shoulder its mandate. This chapter focuses on the inherent constraints that hindered parliamentary committees in discharging their oversight functions effectively and discusses the reform measures that were adopted to remove this bottleneck.

Parliamentary Oversight: A Conceptual Framework

In the parliamentary system of democratic governance, the executive branch is the organ exercising authority in governing the state, executing and enforcing laws and policies. Its members originate from parliament and it derives its democratic legitimacy from being able to command the confidence of parliament, the legislative branch, and is also held accountable to that parliament. It is parliament's principal responsibility to make sure that the executive administers the country in line with the policies it sets out. Parliamentary oversight thus takes into account all activities undertaken by the executive. For the citizen it is vital that all powers of the government should be exercised fairly and with their expectations of good administration (Wade 1971: 1). The legitimacy of parliament comes into question if it fails to hold the executive to account. Parliaments in developed and developing countries adopt various means and exercise various types of oversight of the executive. The parliament of each country outlines tools and oversight mechanisms in its rules of procedure or standing orders. The rules are divided into two groups—individual and collective methods. However, their degree of success varies depending on the type of government, the form and level of democracy, and prevailing political culture. This chapter presents a conceptual understanding of parliamentary oversight: what it is and what it is for; what are its types; what are the tools used in different types of government; and their limitations and enforceability vis-à-vis the Bangladesh Parliament.

Comparative Budget Process in Westminster Parliaments: A Lesson for Effective Fiscal Oversight

Parliament holds the constitutional power of the purse. As the guardian of the public purse, parliaments have the right to oversee the budget process in its totality. Parliament must ensure that the revenue and spending measures it authorizes in the budget are fiscally sound, match the needs of the population with the available resources, and are implemented properly and efficiently. Legislatures in both developed and developing countries are seeking to strengthen their role in the budget process. Parliament is responsible for monitoring how the government raises money, how much and on what it spends that money, and what consequences that brings forth to the economy of the country. In this context, parliament must exercise oversight before the money is appropriated (*ex-ante* control) and monitor public expenditure after money has been spent by the executive agencies (*ex-post* control). A token involvement in the budget process relegates the legislative power of the purse to the realm of constitutional fiction. Is it possible for parliaments in the Westminster system to exercise this continuous oversight throughout the entire budget process? It was once common wisdom in systems derived from the Westminster model that budget-making was an executive function and parliament had to simply approve it, with or without amendment. In the early decades of the twenty-first century, however, this conception has widely changed. Some parliaments exercise significant oversight throughout the process, while others exercise minimal oversight. This chapter analyzes the budget-making process of a few developed Westminster democracies and compares it to the case of Bangladesh. The findings suggest that the budget process in Bangladesh is less open and *ex ante*, and that Parliament has little scope to be involved in it. *Ex-post* oversight is also limited by systemic constraints. Changes in the ROP could make a substantive improvement in the budget process and create room for exercising effective fiscal oversight on the public purse.

Human Resource Management and Development in the Parliament Secretariat: An Overlooked Agenda

The secretariat can be no more effective than the personnel who administer it. An effective parliament is too much to expect without strong parliamentary secretarial support. Various diagnostic studies reveal that in post-political transition societies there is an unpreparedness of the secretariat to shoulder the massive responsibilities of parliamentary governance. It was recognized in Bangladesh that if members and committee chairs were to make quality legislation and retain effective oversight of the executive, the Bangladesh Secretariat's organizational and human capacity would have to be increased and improved. Thus, since the turn of the century, the Secretariat has been significantly reorganized in legal and organizational aspects. Measures include the enactment of the PSA 1994, the Institute of Parliamentary Studies Act 2000, and the Recruitment and Promotion Rules 2001. All three measures were geared toward making the Secretariat better resourced and independent of the executive. The Recruitment and Promotion Rules 2001 opened up the opportunity for career progression among the Secretariat's staff with the view that they could assume the main responsibility of administering the Secretariat and gradually remove the officials on deputation from line ministries. The Institute of Parliamentary Studies Act 2000 was intended to provide year-round training to Secretariat staff to ensure the regular supply of competent personnel and extend research services to MPs to improve to a global standard their capacity to discharge their mandated role effectively. This chapter traces the extent to which the measures recommended by the reformers have been implemented and aims to determine their present standing in supporting the current demands of Parliament following long and drawn-out human resource development programs.

Gender Mainstreaming in Bangladesh Parliament

Parliament is the apex representative body in a democratic country. A parliament cannot be said to be democratically elected and legitimate if it is not an inclusive institution that represents the citizens of the country, with all its diversity across gender, social class, and ethnicity. The international community holds the view that promoting a gender balance in parliament is essential for increasing legislative capacity, performance, and legitimacy (http://iknowpolitics.org/en/discuss/e-discussions/parliamentary-oversight-gender-equality). Democratic parliaments derive their legitimacy from their ability to represent all the citizens of their country. Therefore, where the role of women is hampered or limited, overall institutional legitimacy suffers as a result. The larger the presence of women in parliament, the greater the benefit to the nation. Parliaments with a greater gender balance are more representative, more responsive, and more effective in overseeing the executive, and enjoy higher levels of trust (http://iknowpolitics.org/en/discuss/e-discussions/parliamentary-oversight-gender-equality). However, women have faced inequality in most parliaments throughout the world in the past and even today. Against this backdrop, this chapter analyzes gender equality in the Bangladesh Parliament in relation to its organization, representation, legislation, budgeting, and oversight functions.

Present State of Parliament and Democracy

In the first two decades of independence, the Bangladesh Parliament did not enjoy the confidence of the public because of fraudulent electoral processes under civil and military authoritarianism. Parliament could not be institutionalized due to frequent breaches of constitutional rule. After deposing the military autocracy in 1990, Bangladesh underwent significant constitutional and political transformation. Elections to Parliament in the post-restoration period were highly contested, and the participatory electoral process was considered transparent and credible (Jahan 2008). A series of reforms to Parliament and the Secretariat were carried out to address shortcomings that continued to prevent a fully functioning and institutionalized parliamentary democracy from being a reality in Bangladesh. Institutionalization of parliament and consolidation of democracy in any country are long and complicated processes, requiring decades or sometimes longer (for the requisites of institutionalization see Diamond and Morlino 2004; Jahan 2008). Free and fair elections in themselves do not guarantee the success of these processes if simultaneous development does not take place in other areas. This chapter evaluates the extent to which the institutionalization of Parliament and consolidation of democracy in Bangladesh have been successful in the two decades that have passed since the reform initiatives. It discusses the opinions of a selection of MPs from the current ruling party AL, as well as former BNP MPs, on the issue of Parliament's level of institutionalization and its contribution to democratic consolidation. Exponential analysis reveals that popularly elected governments in Bangladesh did not pay attention to safeguarding the civil liberties of their citizens or enforcing the rule of law, which has a telling effect on democracy. This chapter locates the present standing of Bangladeshi democracy within the framework of global democratic categorization.

Concluding Observations and Recommendations

This chapter briefly summarizes the issues and problems around institutionalization confronted by the Bangladesh Parliament since the early days of independence and especially after the restoration of parliamentary democracy in 1991. It also discusses the measures adopted to make the successful transition to a functional democracy. Finally, the author presents a few observations on what he thinks constitute the main hurdles in institutionalizing parliament and consolidating democracy in Bangladesh and offers some modest recommendations for policy-makers to consider.

Notes

1. Here 'world power' refers not to a single state, but rather to a group of the states that are industrialized and democratically far advanced like the USA, the UK, Germany, France, Canada, and Australia and that have significant influence on the democratic politics of third world countries. They followed different policies for different parts of the world, yet all agreed that Hobbesian states which seemed to be breeding grounds for terrorists and a threat for world peace needed to be democratized. Following this agreement there was a sharp rise in the number of democracies in Asia, Africa, and Latin America.
2. 'Reasonable degree' refers to the establishing of a political environment for holding regular free and fair elections as the first step to democracy and enforce rule of law.
3. "We, the elected representatives of the people of Bangladesh ... in order to ensure for the people of Bangladesh equality, human dignity and social justice, [we] declare and constitute Bangladesh to be a sovereign People's Republic and thereby confirm the declaration of independence already made by Bangabandhu Sheikh Mujibur Rahman. We further resolve that this Proclamation of Independence shall be deemed to have come into effect from [the] 26th day of March 1971." Appendix 1 of the Bangladesh Constitution," p. 91
4. Major M. A. Jalil, a freedom fighter and an ex–army officer, was the first president of the JSD and a violent opposition leader after the independence of Bangladesh.
5. Khandaker Abdur Rashid was a major at the time of the coup and subsequently promoted to Lt. Col in Khondaker Mostaq Ahmed's short-lasting government.
6. "Although many details of this event are still obscure and remain to be unearthed the political organizers of the August coup were the circle within Mujib's own ruling Awami League which for the years had been considered a pro-American faction" (Lifschultz 1979: 5).
7. 'Supremacy' refers to Parliament's independence and authority over the executive not only in the share of enactments but also in respect of holding them to account for their policies and administration.

8. An election commission that is politicized is composed of officials who are politically aligned to the regime in order to maneuver the election result through field administration functionaries where elections take place. And politically aligned officials get appointed at the strategic position from where they can oversee and manipulate the situation in favor of the incumbent government during election day.
9. In autocratic regimes parliaments were subservient to the executive—ever ready to approve whatever legislative proposals were placed before them by the executive. After the fall of the military dictatorship, it was expected that parliament would play their real expected role in legislation and oversight by vibrant debates on the floor and scrutiny in the parliamentary standing committees and hold the executive to account for any excess of power. Constitutionally they are mandated to assert their legitimate authority over the executive to ensure accountability of the government. Here 'supremacy' refers to legislation and oversight—the core functions that parliament is vested with in the Westminster democracy.
10. The author initially planned to gather information on the three fundamental questions outlined above from at least 10% of MPs in Bangladesh. For this purpose, more than 100 structured questionnaires were circulated among different level of MPs. After three months of sustained effort, only a few (fifteen) questionnaires were returned completed. In the present political context, most members felt reluctant to fill in the questionnaire due to the political sensitivity of some of its content. To address this, the author made recourse to party stalwarts of both the ruling party AL and former members of BNP to gain substantive and knowledge-based information about Parliament as such and the democratic development of the country. In order to secure the necessary information, a good number of senior MPs from the AL and BNP were interviewed. In addition, the author consulted ten Secretariat staff in order to obtain their opinions on the institutionalization of Parliament and the present state of the Secretariat in respect of discharging its role.

References

Arafat Kabir (2015) http://thediplomat.com/2015/05/democracy-departs-from-Bangladesh

David Beetham (2006) Parliament and Democracy in the Twenty First Century: A Guide to Good Practice, IPU

David G. Landry, "Downfall of Democracy in Bangladesh" http://thediplomat.com/2016/07/the-downfall-of-democracy-in-bangladesh/

David Watson and Deborah Williams (2000) Support to Parliamentary Committees in Bangladesh, DFID Bangladesh. Dhaka

Diamond, L. (2008) The Spirit of Democracy: The Struggle to Build Free Society Throughout the World. New York: Times Book

Diamond, L. and Morlino, L. (2004) "The Quality of Democracy: An Overview", Journal of Democracy, 15(4), pp. 20–31. http://iknowpolitics.org/en/discuss/e-discussions/parliamentary-oversight-gender-equality; http://thediplomat.com/2015/05/democracy-departs-from-Bangladesh; https://en.wikipedia.org/wiki/Third_Wave_Democracy

Huq, A. F. (1985) Constitution and Politics in Bangladesh (1972–1982): Conflict, Change and Stability. Department of Political Science University of Rajshahi, Rajshahi, Bangladesh (unpublished PhD dissertation)

Islam, M. M. (2015) "Electoral violence in Bangladesh: Does a Confrontational Bipolar Political System Matter?" Pages 359–380 | Published online: 21 Oct 2015

Jahan, R. (2015) The Parliament of Bangladesh: Representation and Accountability, The Journal of Legislative Studies, 21:2, 250–269, https://doi.org/10.1080/13572334.2014.975470

Jahan, R. (2004) "Why Are We Still Continuing With a 'Viceregal' Political System?" *The Daily Star*, 31 January 2004

Jahan, R. (2005) Bangladesh Politics Problems and issues The University Press limited: Dhaka

Jahan, R. (1987) Bangladesh Politics: Problems and Issues, University Press Limited, Dhaka

Jahan, R. and I. Amundssen (2012) The Parliament of Bangladesh, CPD-CMI Working Paper 2

Jahan, R. (2008) The Challenges of Institutionalizing Democracy in Bangladesh, ISAS Working Paper No. 39

Lifschultz, L. (1979) Bangladesh: The Unfinished Revolution, London: Zed Books

Lindley, J. A. (1991) An Assessment of the Institutional Development: Needs Assessment of the Parliament of Bangladesh, The Asia Foundation, Dhaka

Magen, A. (2009) "The Rule of Law and its Promotion Abroad: Three Problems of Scope", Stanford Journal of International Law 45/1:51

Magen, A. Thomas Risse and Michael A. McFaul (2009) Promoting Democracy and the Rule of Law. American and European Strategies, Palgrave Macmillan

Mascarenhas, A. (2013) Bangladesh: A legacy of Blood, Hodder and Stoughton, London

Obaidullah, A. T. M. (2011) "Standing Committees on Ministries in the Bangladesh Parliament: The Need for Reorganisation", South Asian Survey, Vol. 18, No. 2

Samuel P. Huntington (1991) "Democracy's Third Wave", Journal of Democracy, Vol. 2, No. 2, Spring, pp. 12–34

Siddiqi, L. K. et al. (1994) Making Parliament Effective: A British Experience, Dhaka

Tim Meisburger, Strengthening Democracy in Bangladesh (asiafoundation.org) Tim Meisburger, asiafoundation.org/resources/pdfs/OccasionalPaperNo11 FINAL.pdf

Wade H. W. R. (1971) Administrative Law, Oxford: Clarendon Press

CHAPTER 2

Political Landscape and Parliamentary Development

The People's Republic of Bangladesh emerged as an independent nation in 1971 after fighting the cause of establishing liberal parliamentary democracy and achieving independence from Pakistan in the Bangladesh Liberation War. The people of this territory were already acquainted with the concept of parliament and some kind of democratic practice long before its independence as a modern state. However, the parliamentary democracy they experienced under British rule in India and the domestic colonial rule of Pakistan that ensued after partition were the very mockery of democracy. In 1972, Bangladesh formally established its parliament, known as the House of the Nation, on the Westminster model. Its constitution, adopted the same year, affirms that all powers of the Republic belong to the people and that power should be exercised by the government on behalf of the people by or under the authority of the constitution. The constitution vests all legislative powers of the Republic in the parliament. This chapter will trace the growth and evolution of the Bangladesh Parliament as an apex representative institution and pivotal organ of government in the Westminster system.

BRITISH COLONIAL RULE (1861–1947)

The people of this subcontinent were first introduced to some form of democratic rule in 1861 when the Bengal Legislative Council was set up under the Indian Councils Act and created for the first time the opportunity for ordinary Indians to participate in the legislative process along with British representatives. This legislative mechanism, however, had little implication in reality since colonial government maintained complete control of the Council (Hussain 1991: 9). Between 1861 and 1891, the Bengal Legislative Council resembled a law-making committee rather than a deliberative body with the capacity to influence the executive through its actions (Rashiduzzaman 1967: 2). In reality, the laws passed were nothing more than the orders of the British colonial government (Subramania cited by Rashiduzzaman 1965: 3). The Indian Councils Act 1909 empowered the central legislative council to move resolutions and ask supplementary questions (en.wikipedia.org). Indian people were introduced to the concept of 'responsible government' with the passage of the Government of India Act 1919. Edwin Samuel Montague, the Secretary of State for India, stated in the House of Commons in August 1917:

> The policy of his Majesty's Government, with which the government of India are in complete accord, is that the increasing association of Indians in every branch of the administration and the gradual development of self–governing institutions with a view to the progressive realization of responsible government in India as an integral part of the British Empire.[1]

Under the 1919 Act, a bicameral legislative system was established at the center with two Houses—Council of State and Legislative Assembly. The Governor-General was empowered to dissolve both Houses at any time. Elections to the new councils were held in 1920, 1923, 1926, and 1929. The powers and privileges of these councils included asking questions, moving resolutions and other motions, legislation and appropriating supplies (en.wikipedia.org; Rashiduzzaman 1967: 19).

The Government of India Act 1919 attempted to introduce a partial responsible government in the Indian provinces through a peculiar system of 'diarchy' in which provincial subjects were divided into 'reserved and 'transferred' ones (Chowdhury 1968). The responsibility of administering transferred subjects (such as like education, health, public works, and local self-government) was entrusted to the legislative council accountable to voters in the province. In administering these transferred subjects, the governor of a province "was expected to be guided by the advice of his ministers, unless he saw sufficient cause to dissent from their opinion in which he might require action to be taken otherwise in accordance with the advice of the council of ministers" (cited by Hakim 2002: 14). The reserved subjects such as policing, finance, land revenue, and justice were to be administered by the governor in council responsible to the British electorate. The system of diarchy failed due to inherent shortcomings : under responsible government the cabinet should be a unit accountable to the legislature for policy and administration. It cannot be divided into two watertight compartments. Division of the executive branch into two distinct entities rendered overall coordination difficult. The particular reasons underlying failure of diarchy were: Provincial ministers and law makers were inexperienced in self-rule; provincial administration had to depend on central government as the finance was retained in reserved half; and the governor had the right to reject the advice of his ministers. In this situation it is unlikely for the provincial government to administer their business and make diarchy work. However, the Mont-Ford Reforms embodied in the 1919 Act provided for the first time in the Indian provinces an (albeit very restricted) level of executive accountability to the legislature and encouraged a spirit of competitive politics among the forces active in colonial India. Above all, it generated an urge for absolute autonomy for the provinces.

The Government of India Act 1935 replaced diarchy in the Indian provinces with some measure of autonomy and responsible government. The Act envisaged a parliamentary system of government in the provinces. Unlike in the diarchy system, in the new scheme, the governor and council of ministers were empowered to administer all provincial subjects, being responsible only to the provincial legislature and indirectly to provincial electors. However, autonomy granted to the provinces was not unfettered; it had considerable limitations which made the working of the parliamentary system in the provinces quite difficult. The 1935 Act granted the provincial governor enormous discretionary powers and the right to assume all powers, and outright reject the advice of the council of ministers if he deemed it necessary to protect the wider interests of the province. Provincial elections were held in eleven provinces in early 1937 as mandated by the Act. Both the Indian National Congress and the All-India Muslim League participated, with the Congress winning a clear majority in six provinces and plurality in three others, and the Muslim League failing to form a government in any. Coalition ministries were formed in Bengal, Punjab, Sind, and Assam but could not operate for long. Congress ministries resigned from the provinces under the instruction of the party high command in October 1939, making the participation of the Indian people in World War II an issue. Although responsible government in the provinces did not work the way it was expected to, the fact remains that the Act of 1935 was the first exposure Indian politicians and legislators had to some sort of autonomous government.

In August 1940, Viceroy Lord Linlithgow appealed to the Indian people for their fullest possible contribution in World War II and pledged to frame a new constitution after the war. The Congress rejected cooperation with the British since India was under "an arrogant imperialism indistinguishable from fascist authoritarianism" (Palmer cited by Hakim 2002: 18). The Lahore Resolution adopted by the All-India Muslim League in March 1940 further complicated the political situation. The resolution stated:

> No constitutional plan would be workable or acceptable to the Muslims unless geographical contiguous units are demarcated into regions which should be so constituted with such territorial readjustments as may be necessary. That the areas in which the Muslims are numerically in majority as in the North-Western and Eastern zones of India should be grouped to constitute independent states in which the constituent units shall be autonomous and sovereign. (Sayeed 1968; http://storyofpakistan.com/lahore-resolution)

Meanwhile, the British government tried to appease the Indian people by formulating the Cripps Mission Plan 1942[2] and the Cabinet Mission Plan 1946,[3] both of which were found to be unacceptable to the Indian people. Thus, the British effort to keep the country united failed. In the face of the irresistible movement by nationalist forces for independence, the British relinquished their sovereignty over India and established through the Indian Independence Act 1947 two separate sovereign states—India and Pakistan (Hakim 2006). Pakistan comprised of eastern part called East Pakistan and western part that constituted West Pakistan consisting of four provinces—Punjab, Baluchistan, Sind, and North West Frontier Province.

The Pakistani Period (1947–1971)

With the end of colonial rule, the new Pakistani government faced the major challenge of writing its constitution. The new leaders of different provinces were not guided by a spirit of compromise, accommodation, and consensus to resolve the deadlock. Rather, they were locked in acrimonious relations and reluctance due to their geographical, topographical, cultural, ethnic, and linguistic diversities (Hakim 2000: 20). The Government of India Act 1935 and the Indian Independence Act 1947 served as the interim constitution of the country for nine years (Hakim 2006). The issue at the center of dispute among the provinces was striking an acceptable balance in the distribution of seats in the Constituent Assembly (CA). The CA of Pakistan adopted its first constitution on March 23, 1956, which selected the Westminster model of parliamentary democracy for its system of government. Notwithstanding the constitution in place, the country faced tremendous political instability due to very frequent changes of government. Seven cabinets with an average duration of nineteen months each administered the country between 1947 and 1958. In addition, the unfettered authority exercised by the Governor-General at the helm of state authority hindered the normal way of administering state affairs in a Westminster democracy. The situation was further worsened by the political vacuum created by the untimely death in September 1948 of M.A. Jinnah, leader of the All-India Muslim League until independence and first Governor-General of Pakistan, and the assassination three years later of Pakistan's first prime minister L.A. Khan (Gorvine 1966; Ahmed Nizam 1998). During the presidency of General Ayub Khan (1958–1969), politicians remained seriously disadvantaged vis-à-vis other sources of power, especially in the military and the bureaucracy (Nizam 2002). Right from the inception of Pakistan, the pivotal positions in the management of state affairs, such as Governor-General or governors of provinces, were generally held by former officials of the Indian Civil Service (ICS). These senior leaders often presided over cabinet meetings (one was able to reallocate portfolios without the formal approval of the chief minister) and exercised authority and control over the administration on a par with that of the viceroys of British India. This tendency in the Governor-General and governors of provinces to exercise unfettered authority hindered from the very beginning the operation and development of a parliamentary system of government (Hakim 2000: 28–31).

The assumption of state authority by General Ayub Khan through a bloodless coup in 1958 brought some respite and stability to Pakistan for several years. One of his first major steps was to form a Constitution Commission on February 17, 1960, with Chief Justice Muhammad Shahabuddin as chair and officials of his own choice as members. The Commission was entrusted with the responsibility of making recommendations about the future constitution of Pakistan that would stabilize the political situation and help build a strong government capable of contributing to national progress and prosperity. The Commission submitted its report in May 1961 which, after due alteration and extensive debate in the cabinet and at the governor's conference, was the basis of the constitution granted in June 1962.

The 1962 Constitution substituted a presidential system for the parliamentary system introduced under the 1956 Constitution. The new constitution, in effect, produced a constitutional autocracy that revolved around the president who was an integral part of the legislature known as the National Assembly (NA) of Pakistan. The president could appoint a council of ministers to assist him in the discharge of his functions and held office during his pleasure—a striking parallel to the viceroy's executive council during British rule in India (Rashiduzzaman 1967: 171; see also Hakim 2000: 34). Unlike the American system, the president did not require the approval of the NA to appoint ministers. The provincial governors in Pakistan at this time served the president as long as they enjoyed his confidence and wielded power in the provinces comparable to the president at national level. More importantly, members of the NA were elected by the local councilor, not by the public. As a consequence, it also lacked legitimacy to a great extent. The AL successfully mobilized the public against the Ayub regime, which adopted a discriminatory policy of enriching West Pakistan at the expense of East Pakistan (Haque 2011).[4] The AL leader Sheikh Mujib presented a strong argument in 1966 that after the seventeen-day war between India and Pakistan in the September of the previous year, it was now abundantly clear to the people of East Pakistan that their defense was not safe in the hands of West Pakistan. Rather, East Pakistan should be made self-sufficient for defending itself from external aggression. "He then propounded a 'six-point charter of survival' program for East Pakistan" (Maniruzzaman 1967). On the basis of the six-point program, the AL demanded greater autonomy for East Pakistan and the reintroduction of the parliamentary system of government that Ayub had abolished in 1958.

The people of East Pakistan gathered behind the AL on the premise of building a 'Sonar Bangla'—a land replete with the ideals of democracy, human rights, personal dignity, and economic affluence. The AL won a decisive majority (167 out of 313 seats) in the 1970 Pakistan parliamentary elections, the first to be held on the basis of universal adult suffrage and secured all but twelve seats in the provincial assembly. However, with the Bengali population expecting a swift transfer of power to the AL based on the six-point program, the central government in West Pakistan ordered the Pakistani Army to launch 'Operation Searchlight' on March 25, 1971—a vicious military crackdown that would last two months (Salik 2017) and plunge East Pakistan into a liberation war (Rahman 2007). Following nine months of bloodshed, Bangladesh emerged as an independent state on December 16, 1971.

Nature of Polity and Parliamentary Development in Bangladesh

In the forty-five years since independence, Bangladesh has experienced ten parliamentary elections and the government of three major political parties—the AL, the BNP, and the Jatiya Party (JP). During the same period, Bangladesh has passed through four stages of political transformation. The first phase of independence (1972–1975) was marked by several political turnarounds—a flawed first parliamentary election, unwarranted constitutional amendments, the ascendancy of civil autocracy, demise of democracy, change in the forms of government, the tragic assassination of the founding father of the nation, and a military coup and countercoup. The second phase (1975–1990) was characterized by the ascendancy of military dictators, flawed parliamentary elections, the tragedy of democracy, pro-democracy movements for ousting military autocracy, and demands for fair, credible, and participatory parliamentary elections. The third phase is best known for consensual politics between the arch-rivals in Bangladeshi politics the AL and the BNP, the deposition of a military autocrat, the restoration of parliamentary democracy, the movement for NCG-supervised elections and innovations of the NCG idea, free, fair, credible, and highly contested parliamentary elections, and the rotation of power. The fourth phase of Bangladesh politics is characterized by confrontational politics; attempts to politicize the NCG, the Fifteenth Amendment scrapping the NCG, unprecedented violence, and the hugely disputed election to the Tenth Parliament in which 154 members were elected unopposed and the majority of the political parties boycotted the polls.

In the same time period, fifteen constitutional amendments have been made (see Annex 1), some by executive order (e.g. by martial-law proclamation orders) and others through parliament. With the exception of perhaps the Twelfth and Thirteenth Amendments, governments winning a supermajority in parliament made constitutional amendments to their own political benefit. Repeated constitutional amendment and changes in the form of government meant that the principles of state policy and the nature of parliament were never settled very long. The ruling party in each government manipulated the constitution as a political tool, rather than a guide to the nation (Riaz 2015: 3). This constant disruption inevitably held back the institutionalization of parliament and slowed the transition in Bangladesh to a stable democracy even after nearly half a century since independence. The following section will present the paths along which parliament and democracy in Bangladesh arrived here.

The Short Life of Democracy (1972–1975)

Bangladesh's journey toward Westminster democracy started on January 11, 1972, with the promulgation of the Provisional Constitutional Order by Sheikh Mujib just one day after his return from a Pakistani jail. Two months later, on March 22, he passed an Order to establish the CA with a thirty-four-member constitution drafting committee. The CA approved the draft constitution after seventy-four sittings on November 4 and it came into effect on December 16 (Jahan and Amundsen 2012), a day that is observed in Bangladesh as 'victory day.' As soon as the constitution came into effect the CA became the provisional Parliament of Bangladesh, which remained in operation until the government held the country's first parliamentary elections in 1973 (en.wikipedia.org/wiki/Constituent_Assembly_of_Bangladesh).

The constitution provided for a Westminster democracy with executive power vested in the prime minister as head of the cabinet/government and the president as titular nominal head of the state. The cabinet is collectively responsible to the parliament. A unicameral Parliament was vested with all legislative power of the Republic under Article 65 of the Constitution. Parliament comprised 300 general seats elected directly from single territorial constituencies through the 'first past the post' (FPTP) system (Jahan and Amundsen 2012: 4). The president would be elected by MPs and act in accordance with the advice of the prime minister commanding the support of the majority party in parliament. Nationalism, democracy, secularism, and socialism were enshrined (see Articles 8–25) as fundamental principles of state policy and fundamental rights were guaranteed by Part III of the Constitution (GOB Articles 26–47). The first constitution made the provision for fifteen seats would be reserved for women for a period of ten years, to be indirectly elected by the 300 general members.

The first parliamentary election was held on March 7, 1973. The AL won 307 seats out of 315, in which eleven were elected unopposed without a vote (en.wikipedia.org/wiki/Bangladeshi_general_election, 1973). Voter turnout was 54.9%. The remaining parties could not win enough seats to even constitute a formal opposition in the House—there were a mere two opposition and five independent MPs (Ahmed 2002). Some of the defeated candidates alleged that votes were rigged. Professor Muzaffar Ahmed of the National Awami Party (NAP) accused the AL of intimidation, false votes, and fraud activity such as hijacking the ballot box and rigging the vote counting. Ahmed claimed that had the election been fair, his faction would have won twenty-five seats. Mascarenhas records that during vote counting Sheikh Mujib's minister, Mr. Mannan, had trailed all day until a mysterious upsurge of votes for him were recorded at the close of day (1986: 33). The JSD alleged that they would have won in all the cantonment areas but were defeated by riggings (Choudhury 2012: 54). Whatever may have been the case, at the dawn of independence, the AL set the trend for flawed parliamentary elections and provided grounds for public skepticism of the electoral system and a lack of confidence in any election under an incumbent government (Islam 2015). This trend continued until the Thirteenth Amendment incorporated the provision for holding parliamentary elections under an NCG.

Despite securing an overwhelming majority, the AL did not institutionalize parliamentary politics. Parliament was not permitted to grow as an effective forum of deliberation and perform its scrutiny functions since the ruling party's presence was so overbearing and intolerant of dissenting views and the presence of an opposition minuscule. Moreover, the party, cabinet, and parliament were all overshadowed by the towering personality of the independence hero Sheikh Mujib. Any opposition was considered to defy his authority and thus tantamount to sedition (Mascarenhas 2013).

Not long after independence was achieved, a deep schism within the AL leadership plunged the party into factionalism. A rift surfaced between militant youth leaders and the elder more moderate leadership on the issue of the nature of governance and the form of government. Prior to independence, there had been a consensus in the AL leadership on parliamentary government, but after 1971 an increasing number of the more militant leaders rejected it. Sheik Mujib himself became increasingly skeptical that the parliamentary model was the most suitable for government to be collectively responsible to parliament in the prevailing conditions. He needed more power; and power became an end in itself (Jahan 1980: 97; Mascarenhas 2013: 45). His charisma and personal popular support was the bridge between the factions that threatened to tear AL apart. His decisions and discretion reigned over the entire machinery of government and risked weakening democratic institutions with the rise of a personality cult (Jahan 2005: 275). A.S.M. Abdur Rab, who formed the JSD shortly after independence, recently argued in a television talk show that the experience of countries like Cuba, Algeria, Russia, and Vietnam, demonstrated that authoritarianism was the inevitable result of a revolutionary party becoming a constituted government. And so it was in Bangladesh's case, where, Rab holds, it was a mistake to permit the AL to form a government and allow Sheikh Mujib to emerge as an all-powerful leader.[5] He argues that rather than consisting of a single party, a revolutionary national government should be a coalition formed from all parties that participated in the liberation war (A.S.M. Abdur Rab, Channel 1).

The newly elected AL government was confronted with the huge challenge of restoring a dwindling economy and rebuilding a war-ravaged country with devastated infrastructure and an inefficient and corrupt administration—all this in the context of a rapidly deteriorating law and order situation. By the end of 1973, the country was bankrupt despite more than US$2 billion foreign aid pumped into its economy (Mascarenhas 2013: 28). In order to restore law and order, Sheikh Mujib adopted a number of measures which included establishing a private force, Lal Bahini, to restore law and order in the countryside because the police had failed to do so. He also created the new national security guard Jatiya Rakshi Bahini (JRB). Both measures would prove counterproductive. The creation of JRB, in particular, caused serious resentment among the regular army (http://www.londoni.co/index.php/history-of-bangladesh?id=22).

After independence, both civil and military bureaucracies proved inept to handle the political and economic crisis in Bangladesh. Many senior members of both were imprisoned in West Pakistan and several civil servants who had remained in East Pakistan during the liberation war were subsequently removed from office under President's Order No. 9 under suspicion of collaborating with the Pakistani Army. Under this Order, the AL government screened 900 civil servants who were not permitted a defense. These included Shafiul Azam, the former chief secretary of East Pakistan (Maniruzzaman 1979). Only Mujibnagar-based officials were rewarded, gained promotion and better placement, and received undue favor. In contrast, those who remained in West Pakistan during the war were harassed, humiliated, and inconvenienced by inquiries into their links with the Pakistan military junta, delays in clearance and placement, and even by suspension and termination of their contracts (Obaidullah 1991; Mamoon and Roy 1987). Thus, the civil bureaucracy was in disarray and riven by factionalism in the years following independence but things soon worsened in 1974 with an unprecedented famine, which claimed approximately 1.5 million lives of predominantly wage laborers and landless farmers in the months between March and December 1974—"which has become known as the 'mass starvation period'" (https://en.wikipedia.org/wiki/Bangladesh_famine_of_1974). It is worth mentioning that despite early warnings of this famine in March 1974, the government failed to prevent it; not due to the unavailability of food but, rather, the mismanagement of food grain stocks, legislation restricting the movement of food between districts, rampant grain smuggling to neighboring countries, and so-called distributional failures. Industrial production continued to fall, as did food production, and some people began to feel nostalgic for the time before independence. It was a moment when many remembered Sheik Mujib's promise that after independence rice would be sold at half its previous cost (ibid.). In fact, it turned out to be ten times that.

In desperation at the situation, Sheikh Mujib conceded to the suggestions of the young militant leaders in the AL to pass the Fourth Amendment to the Constitution in January 1975 and introduce all-powerful presidential rule and monolithic one-party system. In the February, Mujib formed a new party, BAKSAL, which all MPs were required to join. Lifschultz has observed the painful tragedy of seeing Sheikh Mujib, once the leading personality among the founders of the state, emerge as a dictator just a few years after independence was won (Lifschultz 1979: 87). Under the new system, Sheikh Mujib made himself president for next five years without holding any elections; civil liberties were curtailed, political institutions like parliament and the judiciary were subjugated to the all-powerful executive, and freedom of the press was denied. Sheikh Mujib described this constitutional overturn as a 'second revolution' and necessary for bringing democracy for the 'Sorbo Hara' (Jahan 1980; Maniruzzaman 1980).[6] Mascarenhas argues that by this amendment Mujib sought to legitimize his assumption of supreme power by stating it necessary for future democracy. However, "in fact it was nothing more than a palace coup which removed the last vestige of democracy, justice and hope from a country whose founding was intended to epitomize these virtues" (Mascarenhas 2013: 57). The Bangladeshi people, who had fought for liberation and democracy, now looked on in dismay as the hero of independence himself put the final nail into the coffin of democracy.

On January 25, 1975, Sheikh Mujib declared a state of emergency and of war against enemies of the new nation and fell back onto the military to deal with left-wing dissidents and opposition politicians and clean up the traders and smugglers who hoarded food or smuggled it to India (Mascarenhas 2013). Sheikh Mujib avowed that all guilty parties would be brought to justice; nobody could escape it (Mascarenhas 2013: 20). However, this promise was found somewhat wanting since many of the hoarders and smugglers were in fact members of the AL; once arrested, they would make a few phone calls and be released, much to the dismay of an increasingly demoralized officialdom (Tripathi 2014: 232). Among the kingpins of the unlawful trade were the prime minister's own people. Rampant black marketing across the border was a fact, argues Lifschultz (1979: 7–8). Lt. Col. Farooq Rahman, later the chief organizer of Mujib's assassination, was at this time one of the senior officers charged with combating the outlaws and conducting combing operations to identify smugglers and hoarders. He soon discovered that all these offenders found protection at the behest of Sheikh Mujib, including the case of Muzammil, chairman of the Tongi branch of the AL, who managed to escape arrest for his involvement in a sensational three-murder case.[7] Some have claimed that this event was the trigger for Lt. Col. Farooq Rahman's decision to take drastic action to "to eliminate Sheikh Mujib no sooner" (Mascarenhas 2013: 48). In the early hours of August 15, 1975, Lt. Col. Farooq Rahman and Col. Abdur Rashid, along with a group of other disgruntled military officers, assassinated Sheikh Mujib and most of his family members (Jahan 1976). The coup leaders apprehended a countermove from Mujib's loyal forces like the JRB, Lal Bahini, and a faction of the army who were known to be very loyal to the regime. For example Col. Shaffayat Jamil, Dhaka Brigade Commander, planned to organize a countermove. However, he left the plan to avoid likely bloodshed. On the day of the coup the overall situation was calm. A day after, Mujahidul Selim brought out a procession in some part of the Dhaka city in protest. And Bangabeer Qader Siddiqui registered a protest of this heinous killing from outside the country. The majority of Sheikh Mujib's cabinet ministers, except four founding AL leaders who were detained by the coup leaders in Dhaka central jail, joined the new government led by Khondakar Mushtaq Ahmed. Many of the AL leaders went into hiding, and the leading conspirators all received the highest ranks. After Col. Rashid's appearance at his house and telephone calls from the distraught chief of staff, General Shafiullah, informing him of Mujib's assassination, Col. Shaffayat Jamil walked to General Zia's residence in the early morning and asked for his orders. Zia is reported to have said "so what, President is dead? Vice president is there. Get your troops ready. Uphold the constitution" (Shaffayat Jamil 2016: 103). Meanwhile, General Shafiullah's expression of allegiance to the Mushtaq government in a national radio broadcast later the same morning foiled all possible attempts to counter the coup (Shaffayat Jamil 2016: 107).

As to why Sheikh Mujib was brutally killed along with most of his family, there are several views advanced by different groups. AL calls it the heinous revenge of anti-liberation forces that were defeated in the liberation war and wanted to turn Bangladesh into a mini Pakistan. Another theory is that it was a palace coup orchestrated by a pro-USA faction the AL. Another view is that Sheikh Mujib's end was the outcome of the hotly disputed Fourth Amendment scrapping the democratic system and installing the BAKSAL. Some AL stalwarts, for example M.A.G. Osmani and Mainul Husein, protested the Fourth Amendment and the formation of BAKSAL and resigned from Parliament. Despite their protests, they could not resist it. Many of Mujib's cabinet members were opposed to the BAKSAL system yet did not dare to challenge it or oppose Sheikh Mujib. Some later engaged in the conspiracy to assassinate him. A fourth position holds that the overall situation prevalent in the country from 1974 onward was responsible for this tragic massacre. Shaffayat Jamil was of the opinion that previous mutinous (but miscarried) actions within the military went unpunished despite being outside the chain of command, against army discipline, subversive, and justifiably punishable, and that this only encouraged the conspirators to kill Mujib (Shaffayat Jamil 2016: 118). Whatever the cause, it still needs serious academic inquiry. Years after the coup, it was revealed that Sheikh Mujib was in fact informed about the potential military threat against his regime by national and international sources. Yet he made no countermove because he genuinely did not believe anybody in an independent Bangladesh could kill him.

Ascendancy of Military Rule (1975–1990)

With the assassination of Sheikh Mujib, his political experimentation with a one-party BAKSAL system was crushed before it could even take off. Khondakar Mushtaq Ahmed, a veteran of the AL, assumed the presidency. He did not dissolve Parliament, nor suspend the Constitution, but did halt political activities (Jahan 2008). He pledged to hold parliamentary elections in February 1977 and revert to parliamentary democracy. Mushtaq replaced Major General Shafiullah with Major General Ziaur Rahman (Zia hereafter) as the chief of army staff. But Mushtaq was ousted by a countercoup led by Brigadier Khaled Mosharraf on November 3, 1975, who installed Chief Justice Abu Sadat Mohammad Sayem as the president and placed General Zia under house arrest. Just four days later, Mosharraf was toppled by another countercoup and mutiny spearheaded staged by the JSD under Col. Abu Taher. General Zia was freed from house arrest and eventually emerged as the strongman of the regime (Lifschultz 1979).

Shaffayat Jamil, a key figure in the November 3 coup who was arrested four days later in the countercoup, has remarked that the November 7 coup was nothing more than a naked attempt by the JSD to capture state power by using the honest image of General Zia to manipulate and provoke the non-officer section of the military into taking action against Mosharraf. According to Jamil, the twelve demands laid out by the JSD that the coup leaders placed before General Zia for approval was nothing but exploitation of the sentiments of non-officer soldiers under the cover of 'class struggle' (Jamil 2016: 107–122). General Zia soon realized the true motivations of the JSD and put an end to them. Yet, to this day the BNP, the political party he later founded, continues to observe November 7 as a 'day of revolution and national integration'.

Following a meeting at army headquarters, an interim government was formed with Chief Justice A.S.M. Sayem as chief martial law administrator and General Zia as one of his deputies. However, with army discipline having collapsed and mutiny rife, General Zia cracked down on the JSD and Col. Abu Taher was arrested and executed in July 1976. Four months later, General Zia became chief martial law administrator (CMLA) with Sayem's elevation to the presidency. Zia subsequently became Bangladesh's seventh president on April 22, 1977 (Jahan and Amundsen 2012). Assuming full control of the state, Zia lifted martial law and introduced sweeping reforms. Key features of Zia's presidency until his assassination in May 1981 include scrapping BAKSAL and reintroducing the multi-party system, fundamentally changing the principles of state policy, continuing the presidential system, launching the BNP, holding referenda to secure public approval of his actions and policies, electing himself to the position of president, and holding elections to the Second Parliament.

Second Parliament under President Zia

On assuming the presidency, General Zia brought about fundamental changes in the principles of state policy enshrined in the Constitution of 1972 through a martial law ordinance. "Trust and faith in Almighty Allah" substituted 'secularism' as a core principle, while socialism was soft-peddled in favor of economic and social justice (Ahmed 2002: 40). On May 30, 1977, he organized a nationwide referendum to demonstrate public support for his policies and managed to secure a 99% 'yes' vote in his favor with an 87% voter turnout (Jahan 1980: 235). After winning public confidence, Zia lifted the ban on political party activities and restored a multi-party democratic system in April 1978. He held a presidential election on June 3, 1978, while the country was still under martial law with him as

CMLA Zia and got himself elected president by a direct vote. Zia launched his own political party, the BNP, in September 1978 drawing both from the far-left and far-right (Jahan 1980). Zia's regime was composed of at least three different streams of political forces:

1. his own factional supporters in the army and bureaucracy;
2. the right-wing Bangladesh Muslim League and other Islamic fundamentalists who were either eliminated or suppressed by the secularist government led by Sheikh Mujib;
3. a major chunk of radical forces who were opposed to Sheikh Mujib. (Zaman 1984: 108; Huq 1985)

Zia held parliamentary elections on February 18, 1979, in which most of the political parties participated. The BNP won a two-thirds majority (207 out of 300 seats). The AL secured thirty-nine seats, and the Bangladesh Muslim League (banned after independence in 1971 but revived in 1976) and Islamic Democratic League won twenty seats. The JSD won eight seats. Thus, the Second Parliament had within it significant opposition to the ruling party, unlike the AL-whitewashed first one. There were seventy-seven opposition and sixteen independent MPs. The House ratified the Fifth Amendment to the Constitution to validate all acts of the Martial Law Administration between August 15, 1975, and April 9, 1979 (Ahmed 2002: 80). The opposition parties, however, made serious allegations against the BNP of vote-rigging but were unable to organize any strong mass movement against the government (Hakim 2000: 51). The second parliamentary elections, as Ziring observes, helped Zia to isolate the AL and simultaneously neutralize the extreme left' the JSD, in particular, was at serious odds with the regime (Ziring 1993). Zia followed the track of presidential rule vested with real executive power unaccountable to Parliament. Yet, he restored Parliament with a prime minister enjoying the confidence of the majority in the House (Jahan 1980). Zia's experimentations, much like Mujib's, did not last long. During five and a half years in office, he suffered twenty mutinies, several attempted coups and assassination attempts, a statistical average of one military uprising every 3.3 months, and certainly a record that no general could be proud of (Lifschultz 1979: 121). He was ultimately assassinated by a group of discontented military officers on May 30, 1981, at a rest house in Chittagong. Lifschultz points out that "it is ironical that the troops who literally carried Zia to power on their shoulders during the Sepoy Mutiny in November 1975, would later try so many times to kill him" (Mascarenhas 2013: 121).

Zia's assassination did not cause his regime to fall immediately. He was succeeded by Abdus Sattar, who had served as his vice president, after a landslide victory in the presidential election held on November 15, 1981. However, the chief of the army staff, Lt. Gen. H.M. Ershad staged a bloodless coup on March 24, 1982, and ousted Sattar on the grounds of his incapacity and inefficacy as president. Ershad became CMLA, suspended the Constitution, dissolved Parliament, and abolished political parties—and eventually became president over time (www.cpd-cmi.org.bd; Jahan and Amundsen 2012).

After assuming office, Ershad remained the sole source of legislation for more than four years as CMLA. However, like his predecessor, Ershad recognized the importance of civilianizing his rule early on. He followed a similar strategy to that adopted by General Zia. But he failed miserably. He also floated a state-sponsored political party, the JP, composed of various factions from leftist and rightist political parties to support his regime. He carried out various experiments with democratization and elections to Parliament that compounded his legitimacy crisis (Kabir 1999; Hakim 1998). The centrist and center-right parties led by the BNP and an AL-led alliance of fifteen parties of the left and center-left successfully resisted Ershad's attempts to hold presidential elections before the parliamentary polls. The Jamaat-i-Islami Bangladesh (JIB) also opposed to Ershad regime but did not join any alliance. The opposition demanded that elections to a sovereign parliament be held first. Despite Ershad's initial unwillingness to comply, he was forced to succumb and shifted the parliamentary elections to May 1986, five months before the presidential election.

Parliamentary Elections under Ershad
The third national parliamentary elections were held under martial law on May 7, 1986. Twenty-eight parties contested it and the government-sponsored JP headed by Ershad secured 153 seats and emerged as the majority party in the Third Parliament (Ahmed 2010: 33–36). There was 115 opposition and thirty-two independent members (ibid.), the majority of whom subsequently joined the JP (Ahmed 1998). Voter turnout (61.1%) was higher than in previous elections. Unsurprisingly, the elections were controversial, with the BNP choosing to boycott and the AL convinced they had won before vote counting was suspended for several days and the JP subsequently declared as winners (http://nvdatabase.swarthmore.edu/content/bangladeshis-bring-down-ershad-regime-1987-1990). One

British observer described the election as a 'cynically frustrated exercise' and 'tragedy for democracy' (Islam 1987: 166, cited by Ahmed 2002: 47). In his bid to cling to power, Ershad had manipulated and systematically destroyed the whole electoral process. He refused to summon the session of the Third Parliament for several months during which he held the presidential elections which he won with 84.1% of the vote on October 15. None of the three alliances nor JIB took part in the presidential polls. Herein lies the basic difference between the Zia and Ershad regimes. Zia succeeded in convincing almost all registered parties to participate in the presidential elections as well as the second parliamentary polls. For the reason, the Second Parliament was more legitimate, at least formally so, than the third.

The Third Parliament approved the Seventh Amendment to the Constitution on November 10, 1986, which ratified all the actions of Ershad's Martial Law Administration. Martial Law was then withdrawn and the Constitution restored. However, Ershad faced increasing mass demonstrations on the streets mobilized by both the AL and the BNP. The BNP had boycotted the 1986 parliamentary elections, while the AL contested it but subsequently resigned from Parliament. Ershad dissolved the Third Parliament on December 6, 1987 and called for elections to a Fourth Parliament. The fourth national parliamentary elections were held the following year on March 3; this time, both the AL and the BNP boycotted it. Ershad's JP won 251 out of 300 seats by default in the absence of the other major political parties (www.cpd-cmi.org.bd; Ahmed 2002: 61; Jahan and Amundsen 2012). There were twenty-four opposition and twenty-five independent MPs in the Fourth Parliament. The Third and Fourth Parliaments elected in 1986 and 1988 respectively were both unrepresentative and grossly ineffective due to a lack of legitimacy and support from the public (Ahmed 2011). The Fourth Parliament made three constitutional amendments: the Eighth Amendment in 1988 declared Islam the state religion; the Ninth Amendment in 1989 provided for the direct election of vice president; and the Tenth Amendment in 1990 reinserted Clause (3) to Article 65 providing thirty reserved seats for women for a ten-year period.

Opposition parties denied legitimacy to the Ershad regime and demanded his resignation and transfer of power to an NCG to hold elections to the Fifth Parliament (Ahmed 1998). Skeptical members of the public also lost faith in elections under party governments and called for an NCG-held election. Ershad publicly rejected the opposition's demand

and made it clear that he would remain in office for the remaining years of his term of presidency. He declared a state of emergency on November 29, 1987 and arrested the chief agitators: the AL leader Sheikh Hasina (daughter of Sheikh Mujib), the BNP leader Khaleda Zia (widow of General Zia), and other main opposition leaders. Ershad also suspended all fundamental rights, barred courts from trying any cases related to the violation of citizens' rights, and banned the publication of any news or commentary against the government. He also resorted to massive repressive measures to clamp down on protesters and clashes between protestors and the police led to several casualties (http://nvdatabase.swarthmore.edu/content/bangladeshis-bring-down-ershad-regime-1987-1990).

Civil unrest and popular protest rattled the Ershad regime, but it could not dismantle it. Instead, opposition parties began to reorganize in an effort to achieve the common goal of bringing Ershad down. Diverse segments of the Bangladeshi population including workers, doctors, lawyers, and intellectuals joined hands with the opposition movement. Strikes and public demonstrations paralyzed Dhaka and other major urban areas of Bangladesh. In the face of rapidly losing control of Dhaka and other major cities, Ershad publicly announced on December 3, 1990, his willingness to make concessions with the opposition. The following day the opposition rejected Ershad's proposal. Over 100,000 people marched in the streets of Dhaka demanding the president's immediate resignation. Ershad realized he was losing control over the law enforcers—the Bangladeshi police refused to comply with his order to fire on demonstrators—and later that day he was forced to step down (http://nvdatabase.swarthmore.edu/content/bangladeshis-bring-down-ershad-regime-1987-1990). On resigning, Ershad promised to hand over to an acting president agreeable to his political opponents.

> For the first time a regime was changed not through bullet but through a citizen's movement. Ershad's resignation in the face of 8 years continuous political movement against military rule marked a grand victory of the people in Bangladesh's political history. It was perceived as a victory of democracy and constitutional rule. (Jahan 2005: 285)

The transition to democratic rule was marked by dialogue and reaching a consensual joint declaration among contending political parties on the basic outlines of democratic governance including ground rules for future regime changes (ibid.). All opposition parties associated with the pro-democracy movement reached an agreement about the modal of future parliamentary elections. Chief Justice Shahabuddin Ahmed was chosen as acting president to oversee a free and fair election. Military takeovers had caused the dissolution of the first two parliaments, and the Third and Fourth Parliaments were dissolved in the face of irresistible pressure from political opposition who supported the restoration of democracy. Not one of the four parliaments completed their five-year term.

In the new political climate, three political alliances emerged: one led by the AL comprising eight parties, another consisting of seven parties backed by the BNP, and a third formed from five leftist parties. According to a joint declaration these three alliances signed after Ershad's fall, an interim caretaker government must hand power to the sovereign Parliament, elected through free and fair elections (Jahan and Amundsen 2012). There existed a general consensus that a democratic government would not follow the path of assassination and state-controlled elections, the two dominant methods of gaining and holding on to state power during military rule. Rather, "in future winning free and fair elections will be the legitimate means of gaining and continuing in state power" (Jahan 2005: 285). It was in this way that the political parties rallied together to bring an end to military dictatorship and restore democracy to Bangladesh.

None of the four parliaments led by Sheikh Mujib, General Zia, and General Ershad had any scope or disposition to assert its supremacy over the executive. As chief executives of state power, all three leaders enjoyed the unquestionable loyalty of ruling-party MPs inside and outside Parliament and this combined with the severe numerical weakness of opposition parties made successive parliaments mere rubber-stamp bodies (Ahmed 1998). Moreover, they lacked legitimacy, to a great extent, mainly because of the ways in which they were elected (Ahmed 1998; Jahan 2014). From 1975 onward, parliaments in Bangladesh worked under a presidential system in which the president had effective formal and informal mechanisms at their disposal to make the parliament behave the way they desired until the mass uprising and restoration of democracy in 1991 (Hakim 2002: 103). Indeed, as Hakim points out: "The parliaments seemed ever prepared to give legislative approval even to the most authoritarian policy proposals and constitutional amendments" (Hakim 2000: 104).

Restoration of Democracy from 1991

Fifth Parliament (1991–1996) under the BNP
Bangladesh returned to democracy at a time when around three-quarters of the world had democratically elected governments, as a result of what Samuel

Huntington called the "third wave" of democracy (Huntington 1991). With Chief Justice Shahabuddin Ahmed installed as acting president and head of the NCG, elections to Bangladesh's Fifth Parliament were held on February 27, 1991 (Jahan and Amundsen 2012). The NCG had two mandates. First, to conduct the routine administration of the country without taking major policy decisions before a new parliament was elected. Second, to organize and conduct the election in a free and fair manner on a level playing field for all political parties (https://en.wikipedia.org/wiki/Caretaker_government_of_Bangladesh). Although there were some mutterings from the BNP that the council of 'advisers' (not ministers) appointed by the president to assist him was biased toward the AL, it is largely agreed that Shahabuddin Ahmed carried out his assigned tasks admirably (Baxter 1992: 162). The BNP secured 140 seats and emerged as the single largest majority in the Fifth Parliament (Jahan and Amundsen 2012), although it needed the support of eighteen JIB MPs to form a government. Khaleda Zia was thus sworn in as the first woman prime minister of Bangladesh—analysts have attributed her victory largely to her uncompromising battle against military rule. The Fifth Parliament was characterized by a healthy opposition presence with the AL winning eighty-eight seats, JP thirty-five,

> Soon after the BNP's victory in the fifth parliamentary elections, the remaining members of the three alliances' joint declaration to oust Ershad renewed their commitment to establishing a sovereign parliament. While addressing the inaugural session of the Fifth Parliament, Acting President Shahabuddin Ahmed emphasized the need to consider the promises of this declaration, stating that "though the joint declaration does not bear any constitutional validity, it has sufficient political significance" (Bangladesh Observer, April 6, 1991). Sheikh Hasina, the Leader of the Opposition, promised immediately after the election that "she would not allow the government to work peacefully even for a day" (cited by Islam 2002: 138). In the inaugural session, her deputy leader, Abdus Samad Azad, submitted a constitution amendment bill for the establishment of parliamentary democracy. The Leader of the House outright rejected the bill on the grounds that a parliamentary system might give rise to instability at the nascent stage of democratic development. However, amidst

mounting pressure to revert to a parliamentary system, the BNP parliamentary party conceded to the demand. Hakim observes a number of factors that influenced the ruling party to depart from its original stance of ensuring the continuity of presidential government.

1. First, signing the joint declaration when opposing Ershad placed the ruling party under moral obligation to keep its commitment. The party wanted to score points by being seen to live up to its commitments.
2. Second, the ruling party could visualize that ignoring the oppositions' demands could lead to political unrest and turmoil.
3. The BNP treated the consensus on this issue as a gesture of its willingness to achieve consensus on issues of national importance.
4. Finally, and most importantly for the BNP, it was the easiest means to avoid a risky presidential election. It should be noted here that the percentages of BNP and AL votes in the fifth polls were very close; while the BNP polled 30.81% votes, the AL bagged 30.08%. (Bangladesh Election Commission 1991: 48; see also Hakim 2002: 109).

The Fifth Parliament ratified all actions of the NCG led by Shahabuddin Ahmed through the Eleventh Amendment to the Constitution. The Twelfth Amendment restored the parliamentary system of government. Eighty-four percent of voters endorsed this return to parliamentary democracy in a nationwide referendum held on September 15, 1991. This is "for the first and the last time an amendment was passed with bi-partisan support, which also had overwhelming popular support" (www.cpd.org.bd; Jahan and Amundsen 2012: 2).

and seats also going to three independents. The AL, although faring worse than expected with approximately 30% of seats, were nevertheless comfortably ahead of the previously ruling JP. Both domestic and international observers certified the election to be free, fair, and participatory. Although conducting the fifth parliamentary elections in 1991 under an NCG was an ad hoc arrangement, the caretaker system was later institutionalized through the Constitution (Thirteenth Amendment) Act passed in March 1996 by the BNP-controlled Parliament which, as an effect of the Act, dissolved itself for fresh elections to be held (Jahan and Amundsen 2012).

It was largely expected that through this historic event a two-party system resembling that in the UK or other parliamentary democracies would emerge in Bangladesh and contribute to the development of a vibrant and stable parliamentary democracy that people could cherish (Jahan and Amundsen 2012: 11). But the consensual politics of the Fifth Parliament did not last long and Bangladesh again faced a political crisis for two years from 1994 until fresh elections were held in June 1996 under an NCG. The initial bipartisan approach to compromise that had seemed to have been established between the AL and BNP after the restoration of parliamentary government gradually disappeared and the two parties went head-to-head over disagreements about the results of several by-elections. The political deadlock that followed began in March 1994 with the Magura parliamentary by-election. The main opposition party, the AL, charged the BNP government with vote-rigging and claimed its victory was 'snatched away' in what had been a safe constituency since 1954 by a massive demonstration of hooliganism and fraudulent electoral practices in collaboration with local administration. Subsequently, widespread allegations of electoral rigging in by-elections provided room for opposition parties to unite against the BNP and launch a concerted movement for the installation of an NCG to supervise future parliamentary elections. Initially, the BNP refused and even ridiculed the opposition demand by saying no one except for children and the insane could be truly politically neutral. However, the political crisis deepened later that year when in the face of BNP's refusal to budge on the NCG issue, all 147 members of Parliament of the three opposition groups (the AL, JP, and JIB) resigned en masse on December 28. Opposition-sponsored *hartals* (nationwide strikes) and violence became a feature of the day. Parliament performed only constitutional rituals as a one-party legislature. The Speaker of the House declared the 147 seats vacant due to unauthorized absence for ninety consecutive sittings (GOB Article 67(1)(a).[8] The BNP dissolved Parliament in November 1995 and scheduled the sixth parliamentary polls for February 1996.

The Rise of Confrontational Politics

On February 15, 1996, elections to the Sixth Parliament were held without the participation of any major opposition parties, all of whom boycotted the vote. Thus, the BNP won a landslide victory (289 of 300 seats). However, voter turnout was just 15% and most independent observers concluded that the BNP rigged the vote. The election failure added to the opposition demand for NCG-led elections and the BNP finally gave in and Parliament unanimously passed the Constitution (Thirteenth Amendment) Bill on March 26, 1996. The Amendment incorporated Articles 58B to 58E of the Constitution, which provides that the incumbent government hand over power to an NCG to conduct parliamentary elections within three months. Had the BNP accommodated this earlier, it would have saved the Fifth Parliament a political impasse that had lasted twenty months and rendered it wholly ineffective.

In the seventh parliamentary elections held on June 12, 1996, with Chief Justice Muhammad Habibur Rahman as the chief adviser of the NCG, the AL emerged as the single largest party in Parliament with 146 seats and formed a government with the support of the JP (thirty-two seats) and the JSD (one seat) (Jahan and Amundsen 2012: 11). After twenty years in opposition wilderness, an AL-led alliance headed by Sheikh Hasina now took power. In the November, just five months after taking power, the AL government repealed the Indemnity Ordinance, which prohibited the trial of Sheikh Mujib's killers and which had been incorporated in the Constitution by Martial Law Proclamation Order passed by Mushtaq in September 1975. For two decades it had prevented bringing the Mujib's to justice and the government led by his daughter Sheikh Hasina now moved quickly to arrest the self-confessed coup leaders, many of whom had reportedly gone into hiding abroad. The lower court awarded the death sentence to fifteen ex-military personnel, five of whom were executed in 2010 on the verdict of the Supreme Court. Acrimony and revenge would set the tone going forward and hopes for a smooth journey to democracy were very soon dashed as the political parties failed to honor the commitments they had made when in alliance against military rule or work to make Parliament effective (Jahan and Amundsen 2012). The acrimony between the AL and the BNP soon reappeared with vengeance and retribution. The AL had inflicted huge damage to the BNP when in opposition with boycotts, mass resignation, and forcing the installation of the NCG system, and it is hardly surprising that the BNP followed the same track at the beginning of the Seventh Parliament. It vowed not to return to session until various demands—such as ensuring a non-partisan role of the speaker in the House, providing and safeguarding BNP members' right to speak in the House, including BNP members in the parliamentary standing committees, and withdrawing politically motivated cases against BNP lawmakers—were given proper attention. Consequently, Parliament again turned into a ritual-performing body without major opposition. Political opposition in this period preferred extra-parliamentary tactics like *hartals*, street agitation, and violence to negotiating and settling issues in the House.

After frantic efforts, the AL succeeded in bringing the BNP back to the House to resolve parliamentary deadlock at the negotiation table through the mediation of the Speaker of the House. After three days of hectic discussions, the BNP signed an accord and rejoined Parliament for its eighth session on March 8, 1998. The accord provided, inter alia, for an arrangement to include 113 BNP MPs in thirty-five standing committees, to reconstitute previously formed committees, withdraw all pending cases against BNP law-makers (subject to an examination of the nature and merit of each case) and institute impartiality of state-controlled media in its coverage of the proceedings in parliament (The Independent, March 3, 1998).

Notwithstanding a hard-earned accord of cooperation between the Treasury and opposition benches, rivalry and adversarial relations continued over the issue of two rebel BNP MPs joining the AL cabinet as ministers. The BNP demanded its seats be declared vacant in Parliament in accordance with Article 70 of the Constitution. However, the Speaker ruled on April 21, 1998, that since they did not resign from their party, nor vote against it, Article 70 did not apply to their case. The Speaker's ruling antagonized the BNP who declared that the situation would lead to the sort of large-scale horse trading reminiscent of the instability of governments in post-independence Pakistan (Rahman 2014). Ultimately, the Appellate Division of the Supreme Court directed the Speaker to refer the dispute to the EC. The EC, of course, declared in its verdict on October 11, 1999, that the BNP demand that its seats be declared vacant violated the spirit of Article 70. The BNP, however, continued to boycott parliamentary sessions on trifling issues, organized street demonstrations and even managed to shut down the country with prolonged strikes (Jahan 2005: 189). To put it bluntly, the AL, when in opposition, boycotted 135 sittings out of 400 during the Fifth Parliament. In retaliation, the BNP in opposition boycotted 163 of 382 between 1991 and 1996 over predominantly petty political rows (Haque 2009). According to norms of democracy and rules of procedure, problems of any magnitude should be settled on the floor of the

House. Unfortunately, both the AL and the BNP flouted these norms and rules when sat on the opposition bench (Chowdhury 2013).

Mudslinging from both the Treasury and opposition benches continued to violate the 'March Accord' and the situation largely remained as it is (Hakim 2002: 120). The ruling and pro-government parties (the AL, JP, and JSD) became intolerant toward the opposition and adopted a 'winner takes all' policy, thus forgetting the spirit of shared governance. The opposition equally counteracted not only by boycotting parliamentary sessions but also calling repeated *hartals* and street demonstrations with vengeance (See Moniruzzaman 2009 he explained how policies and ideologies engendered confrontations and violence in politics; Jahan and Amundsen 2012: 11). Thus, the spirit of consensus and compromise demonstrated by the two major political adversaries at the dawn of the post-restoration period gradually disappeared and the accords were flouted. The adversarial attitude of the two major political parties was such that on many occasions they failed to adopt unanimous resolutions in Parliament, although they may have held almost identical views (Riaz 2015).

Under party government in the period of 1973–1990, the incumbent ruling party always won elections with overwhelming majorities in Parliament. In contrast, the parliamentary elections held after the introduction of the NCG system demonstrated three clear trends. The EC played a neutral role ensuring a level playing field for all contestants, elections were closely contested, and power rotated between the AL and the BNP. Both the parties secured near equal popular vote share though big differences in seat share under the FPTP system (Jahan and Amundsen 2012). The tables below demonstrate data on the vote and seat shares of the government and opposition parties/alliances from the First to the Ninth Parliament (Tables 2.1 and 2.2).

Table 2.1 Party composition and electoral performance in First–Fourth Parliament

Electoral performance of the government and opposition: number of seats

Parliament	Ruling party Vote share (%)	Ruling party	Government MPs	Opposition MPs	Independent MPs
First	73.2	AL	292	2	5
Second	41.2	BNP	207	77	16
Third	42.3	JP	153	115	32
Fourth	NA	JP	251	24	25

Source: Jahan and Amundsen (2012)

Table 2.2 Party composition and electoral performance in Fifth–Tenth Parliament

Electoral performance of the government and opposition: number of seats

Parliament	Ruling party coalition Vote share %	Ruling party coalition	Government MPs and supporters	Opposition MPs	Independent MPs
Fifth	30.8	BNP	158	139	3
Seventh	37.4	AL	179	120	1
Eight	47.2	BNP four-party alliance	216	78	6
Ninth	57.1	AL Grand Alliance	262	34	4
Tenth	79.14		289	43	16 and other pro-left parties 17

Source: Jahan and Amundsen (2012)

Note: The sixth parliament elections were controversial and flawed; AL along with other political parties including JIB did not participate in the polls. Voter turnout was extremely low. It sat only in one session to pass 13th amendment of the constitution. After passage of the 13th amendment bill, the parliament was dissolved on March 31, 1996. As this parliament was not representative and legitimate and did not work beyond passing one constitutional amendment, its party composition and electoral performance are not included in the table.

With the eighth parliamentary elections, however, the trend was reversed. In July 2001, the AL stepped down and handed over power to the NCG headed by former Chief Justice of the Supreme Court, Latifur Rahman, who held the elections in October 2001. A remarkable change was noticed in the composition of seats between the two major parties. The result of the eighth elections saw a reversal of fortunes for the AL. The BNP-led four-party alliance won 216 seats in parliament—more than a two-thirds majority—while opposition strength dropped to seventy-eight seats. The AL alleged blatant rigging in the polls while international observers hailed the elections free and fair. The Eighth Parliament was once again beset with the same gestures from the opposition in and out of parliamentary sessions that had dogged previous parliaments. The opposition boycotted 60% of parliamentary working days and observed 270 days of *hartals* (Liton 2011 cited by Jahan and Amundsen 2012: 12). The Eighth Parliament passed one constitutional amendment (TIB 2011), approving the Fourteenth Amendment on May 16, 2004, which, among other provisions, increased the retirement age of Supreme Court judges from 65 to 67. The opposition rejected this change as a political move to ensure the appointment of Chief Justice K.M. Hasan, who earlier in his career had been a BNP supporter, as the chief adviser of the next NCG. It was also argued by the opposition and by civil society that raising the retirement age of Supreme Court judges would make both the judiciary and the NCG controversial. Thus, with the Thirteenth Amendment, another political crisis ensued and Bangladesh's hard-fought democratic development and political stability began to move in the reverse direction. The BNP government's attempt to politicize the NCG added extra fuel to confrontational party politics and invoked violent street protests by the opposition. As has been observed, "The depth of the rift was made evident when early in 2004, AL announced its intention to launch a movement and topple the government" (Jahan 2005: 290). The Fourteenth Amendment eventually proved counterproductive for the BNP alliance as it paved the way for the installation, just three years later, of a military-backed NCG headed by Dr. Fakhruddin Ahmed.

The confrontation between the AL and the BNP crested with the violation of the constitutional procedure of appointing the chief adviser of the NCG. After Justice K.M. Hasan refused the position, Khaleda Zia's government appointed the then President Iajuddin Ahmed as chief adviser of the NCG in October 2006 without exhausting the constitutional procedure. In the May of the previous year, the BNP government's appointment of Justice M.A. Aziz as the chief election commissioner (CEC) also caused serious resentment among the AL-led alliance (Jahan and Amundsen 2012). The opposition had tremendous objections about the new CEC and, upon his appointment, the AL's general secretary M.A. Jalil said: "The government's unilateral appointment of the CEC withoutconsulting the opposition political parties is part of blueprint to ensure its return to power in the coming general elections" (http://zeenews.india.com/news/south-asia/bangladesh-opposition-rejects-new-cec_218870.html). The AL criticized him as politically biased and unwilling to rectify the flawed voter's list which allegedly included 12.2 million fake voters (NDI 2006 cited by Jahan and Amundsen 2012).

Things took a turn for the worse with the refusal of Justice K.M. Hasan on October 28 to take up the reins of the NCG in the face of mounting political opposition. Four advisers of the NCG stepped down as a mark of protest against the appointment of the partisan character of the President

Iajuddin Ahmed. Against this backdrop, the AL took the momentous decision to boycott and thwart the upcoming parliamentary elections scheduled for January 22, 2007. With intensified opposition protests and the country on the brink of civil war, President Ahmed resigned as chief advisor of the NCG and declared a state of emergency. Elections were postponed indefinitely and the sitting NCG, accused by the AL of being partisan, was replaced by a new one backed by the military and headed by Dr. Fakhruddin Ahmed. (Jahan and Amundsen 2012: 13). Its task, so far as constitutional provisions were concerned, was to create a level playing field for all parties, hold credible and inclusive parliamentary elections, and hand over power to an elected government. However, it set a higher agenda for itself: to flush out the "crime and corruption" which had overrun Bangladesh's political culture (http://www.frontline.in/static/html/fl2415/stories/20070810506605900.htm).

The NCG headed by Dr. Fakhruddin Ahmed was a variant of the body previously constituted and functioned under Article 58B of the Constitution. It was essentially a military government legitimized and disguised by a civilian head, and its jurisdiction was not limited under the provisions enshrined in the Constitution. Unlike previous NCGs, it worked more as an interim government than a caretaker government (Jahan and Amundsen 2012). In this period, the government made a number of efforts to cast off the garbage amassed in the electoral process and launch a number of long overdue institutional reforms. The reforms included:

1. strengthening the EC;
2. rectification of voter list;
3. introducing tamper-proof voter ID cards with photographs together with national ID cards;
4. cutting down election-related expenses and violence;
5. cleaning up politics (Jahan and Amundsen 2012).

Both Sheikh Hasina and Khaleda Zia were arrested on charges of corruption, and it was alleged that the military-backed government had a clandestine plan to keep these two dynastic women leaders away from politics and float a new political party to usher in a new era of democracy. Several commentators branded this new party the 'King's Party' (http://www.frontline.in/static/html/fl2415/stories/20070810506605900.htm), nicknamed the 'minus 2 formula'. The chief of the army staff, General

Moeen U. Ahmed, in his first public statement since the proclamation of the state of emergency, said that Bangladesh needed efficient and honest politicians to take the country forward and that the current crop of politicians "do not understand anything beyond their self-interest" (http://www.frontline.in/static/html/fl2415/stories/20070810506605900.htm). However, Fakhruddin Ahmed's far-reaching reform plan died before it was born. The so-called reformists who pledged to push forward political reform could not muster the support from their own rank-and-file members. In contrast, both Khaleda Zia and Sheikh Hasina demonstrated the stronghold they had over their respective party rank and file, sufficient to nullify any conspiracy against them (Islam 2008 in Jahan and Amundsen 2012). However, the military-backed NCG was able to organize credible parliamentary elections (ANFREL 2009) and handed over the reins of government to the victorious AL-led Grand Alliance, which has been in office since January 2009 (Jahan and Amundsen 2012).

After two years of emergency rule, the election to the Ninth Parliament was held on December 29, 2008 with highest voter turnout in Bangladesh's history (85.26%). The AL-led Grand Alliance (comprised of fourteen parties including the JP) swept to power with an overwhelming majority and took office on January 6, 2009, with Sheikh Hasina as prime minister. Jahan and Amundsen (2012) have observed that it was the first time ever in South Asia that a de facto military government voluntarily handed over power to a democratically elected civilian government (Jahan and Amundsen 2012: 13). The Ninth Parliament took several commendable measures including the formation of all forty-eight parliamentary standing committees in its first session, the allocation of the chair of several standing committees to senior parliamentarians in the ruling alliance, and also made opposition law-makers chairmen of two parliamentary committees (Jahan and Amundsen 2012). Despite this move, the opposition's presence in the Ninth Parliament was weaker than ever before. The BNP managed to win just thirty-four seats, although the Leader of the House, of course, said that the opposition status was not to be determined by the number of seats secured in the House but rather in the manner of its participation in Parliament. No change was noted, however, in the opposition's behavior. They boycotted 74% of working days of Parliament in the first two years alone, although the frequency of calling *hartals* diminished significantly, with only eight days during 2009 and 2010 (Jahan and Amundsen 2012).

Upon assuming power, the AL government made several substantial changes to the Constitution following various court verdicts. In a significant verdict in 2011, the Appellate Division of the Supreme Court declared the Fifth Amendment Act 1979, passed by General Zia to legitimize martial law authority and remove secularism as a basic principle of state, null and void on the grounds that the declaration of martial law and seizure of state power by ousting an elected government is illegal and hence all actions taken subsequently are also illegal (DLR No. 62. P. 298). In the same year on May 10, the Appellate Division declared the NCG provision enshrined in the Thirteenth Amendment unconstitutional on the basis that as an unelected body such an interim government is undemocratic. A seven-member Supreme Court panel, headed by Chief Justice A.B.M. Khairul Hoque, reached the verdict on the basis of majority vote. However, justices also concurred with senior lawyers that there would be anarchy if the ensuing election was held under party government. They made observations that "the elections to the 10 and 11 parliament may be held under the provisions of the above mentioned 13 amendment provided parliament chooses to do so" (Riaz 2015: 108). The AL-led government did not pay heed to this observation and unilaterally amended the Constitution.

Ignoring the Court recommendation to keep the NCG provision in place for the next two parliamentary elections, the AL government pushed on with passing the Fifteenth Amendment through Parliament in 2011, thus repealing the Thirteenth Amendment and making several major changes. For example, it proposed organizing future parliamentary elections with the incumbent political government going into caretaker mode, leaving it to an independent EC to oversee the election. Two major complaints were made by the majority of political parties, even by partners in the Grand Alliance. First, the AL's decision to abolish the NCG provision ignored the unanimous resolution of a fifteen-member parliamentary special committee to retain it. The committee had been set up by the prime minister in July 2010 with Deputy Leader of the House as its chair (www.parisvisionnews.com). In this respect, Barrister Nazir Ahmed remarked that "the truth of the matter is that it was the wish of the prime minister to repeal the caretaker system" (Nazir Ahmed 2014).[9] The BNP-led opposition rejected the government's decision and held that it was a mala fide political motive to make the AL's stay in power permanent. Second, the Fifteenth Amendment reverted to secularism as the guiding principle of state while retaining Islam as the state religion, which the pro-left parties and critics considered a paradox and contradiction (Jahan 2008; Jahan and Amundsen 2012). The AL preferred to describe it as answering the reality of prevailing circumstance in the country. When, just three years later, the BNP and other opposition parties refused to participate in the tenth parliamentary elections, the country was again brought back to the prevailing political milieu of pre-1990 Bangladesh. Ali Riaz has made the remark that the scrapping of the NCG provision in the Fifteenth Amendment was the "last nail in the coffin of a fair election" (Riaz 2015: 6) This change to the Constitution not only plunged the electoral system into jeopardy; it forced democracy itself into hibernation.

After the Fifteenth Amendment was enacted, opposition parties argued for the NCH provision to be reinstated and threatened to boycott the elections. Finally, in December 2013, following weeks of protests and *hartals*, the BNP and its alliance announced that it would boycott the elections due in January 2014. The BNP left no stone unturned to thwart it. However, the rivalry between the AL and the BNP, though perennial, was to a degree functional because the victorious party/alliance formed the government and defeated party/alliance sat in opposition however much ineffective that might may be. Zia and Hasina had been at one another's throats for decades, escalated countless squabbles into political rows, and had taken part in five electoral contests. However, after the radical political changes following the abolition of the NCG provision in 2011, fierce competition turned into ferocious violence as politics in Bangladesh became a zero sum game—the victorious takes all and the vanquished loses all (http://thediplomat.com/2016/07/the-downfall-of-democracy-in-bangladesh/).

The AL government went ahead with the tenth parliamentary elections on January 5, 2014, despite weeks of strikes, *hartals*, and protests, many of which turned violent. Violence on this level, despite Bangladesh's turbulent political history, was unprecedented. Opposition leader Khaleda Zia was placed under house arrest at the end of December, with scores of policemen cordoning off her residence, but continued to coordinate efforts to scupper the government's plans. After the BNP-led alliance initiated a crippling anti-government nationwide transport blockade, the Bangladeshi authorities are reputed to have cut the power to Zia's home in a bid to force her to call it off. Khaleda Zia demanded that Prime Minister Sheikh Hasina quit and call off the polls. Hasina, on the other hand, vowed to go ahead with the election despite a boycott by all major opposition parties and refusal from the international community to send delegates to observe it.

The crux of the AL's argument for holding the election was that it was a 'constitutional necessity' to maintain democratic continuity. The issue of boycotting or not caused tension in the JP. Its leader, General Ershad, was unwilling to join in electoral alliance with the government and instructed the party's rank and file to boycott. However, a faction led by his Ershad's wife Rowshan defied orders and participated in the election. Rowshan Ershad subsequently became Leader of the Opposition when her party won thirty-four seats. What surprised many even more in the aftermath of the election was the dual role of the opposition in Parliament; a few opposition members were included in the cabinet as ministers or state ministers and H.M. Ershad himself was appointed as special envoy to the prime minister. With this state of affairs, the question is begged as to whether the current Parliament has any opposition at all and whether a party which claims to be main opposition can retain positions in the cabinet or in any other capacity? Whatever the answer, Parliament in Bangladesh is a quirk in the theory and practice of parliamentary government as it applies around the world and places the present AL government in a legitimacy crisis at home and abroad. There were several other features that made the 2014 elections unique, not just the widespread violence, boycotts, general strikes, and low turnout that marred it. Indeed, it is no small feat to consider how many anomalies Bangladeshi citizens have witnessed in the name of democracy (Riaz 2015: 107).

The election result delivered a predictably hollow victory for the incumbent regime—not only did most opposition parties boycott it but more than half of the total members (154) were elected unopposed. (Riaz 2015: 107). As a result, there is now no representation of the main opposition political parties in parliament (Riaz 2015: 107). A flawed election is not an unfamiliar experience for Bangladesh; for decades ruling regimes, especially military rulers, have stuffed ballot boxes, intimidated opposition candidates, and manipulated the results in their favor. But the elections held in January 2014 were extraordinary on various counts.

The reasons for the 2014 election's uniqueness include the tiny number of parties participating, the number of candidates elected unopposed, the percentage of voter turnout (22%), and the moral legitimacy of the election. All these are indicative of the hollowness of the exercise, as well as warnings of what was to come—a de facto one-party system (Riaz 2015: 8). The dual role of JP as a member of the cabinet and the main opposition in the House makes the entire political scenario farcical. Parliament in this system is little more than an echo chamber. The emergence of one-party authoritarianism is a likely apprehension and a very unwelcome reminder of 1975 when Sheikh Mujib introduced the one-party system under BAKSAL (Riaz 2015: 115).

The elections to the Tenth Parliament were held on the grounds of constitutional necessity and on a premise that an eleventh parliamentary election would be inclusive on the basis of compromise and consensus. In the early months of 2014, it was anticipated that, the election being over, the AL government would start negotiations with the opposition to reach a consensus on fresh elections to the Eleventh Parliament that would meet the requirements of a functioning democracy and be free, fair, and inclusive. However, upon taking office for another term, the AL quickly reneged on its pledge and shifted its stance. Prime Minister Hasina puts emphasis instead on the question of midterm elections before the completion of the government's five-year tenure—and negotiation with the BNP-led alliance in regard to the next parliamentary elections would be totally irrelevant to this context. She remarked that pro-liberation elements did vote in the elections and that those anti-liberation forces who believed in the militancy opposed it; she added that consensus is already built among the major political parties as to how future parliamentary elections would be held. The Bangladeshi people at home and abroad increasingly apprehend that the country is shifting away from a democratic path and moving back toward the regrettable scenario of de facto one-party rule. The AL should recognize that the election has not provided them with a mandate to govern for the constitutionally stipulated full term, but an opportunity to bring respite to violence, complete the war crime trials within a short period, and organize an inclusive election at the earliest opportunity (Riaz 2015: 124). "The failure of the two sides to settle their differences through peaceful dialogue and the increasingly violent confrontations between them have again put at risk the institutionalization of a system to organize parliamentary elections" (International Crisis Group 2012). If the ruling party attitude remains unchanged and continues to marginalize the opposition, deny it the space for peaceful protest and disregard the need for a political settlement for moving forward, it will encourage unwanted authoritarian elements to take over. Bangladesh cannot afford to do this. As one commentator points out, "The absence of street agitation and the apparent weakness of the main opposition should not be read as acceptance of this flawed election by all citizens" (Riaz 2015: 125). Political critics often call it the 'silence before the storm' and the prevailing political instability and uncertainty will invite potential 'violence and terrorism' (ibid.).

With the dawn of an era of fair parliamentary polls it was expected that the parliamentary actors would abide by the rules of the parliamentary game (Ahmed 2010). However, from the Fifth Parliament onward, the way successive parliaments have worked, it would not be too much to say, have substantially dashed the democratic aspirations of the nation and uncertainty now looms large on the horizon. However, we do not intend to argue that the opposition alone should be blamed for the failure of parliaments and the decay of the democratic system. Government also contributed to the process of making parliaments virtually ineffective. Making the parliament work is as much a responsibility of the opposition as it is of the Treasury. The intransigence of the Treasury bench and its lack of regard for opposition MPs, reluctance to accommodate amendments to bills proposed by the opposition, and the tendency to get bills passed by using brute parliamentary majority reduced the opposition's role in the system. Such behavior of the ruling party encouraged the opposition parties to adopt extra-parliamentary tactics to destabilize the government. As a consequence of these, the consolidation and institutionalization of parliamentary processes have remained problematic. It can be argued that the Treasury and opposition benches are equally responsible for 'illiberalism' in the democratically elected parliaments of Bangladesh in the post-restoration period. Unless the government and opposition abandon their mutual distrust and suspicion and are guided by the 'rules of the game,' it is not unlikely that the parliamentary system itself will be the price paid. Thus, at this critical juncture, it is the responsibility of legislators to decide on the future course of Bangladeshi politics. Yet, there is no agreement between the government and the opposition about the ground rules for organizing the next parliamentary elections. The dire need of the day is to take initiatives to bring the government and the opposition to the table to engage in sensible dialogue and work out a formula that can ensure inclusive and participatory elections for all political parties and help resolve the present deadlock for the consolidation of a future democratic Bangladesh (www.cpd-cmi.org.bd; Jahan and Amundsen 2012: 15).

Notes

1. The Montague Chelmsford Report (1918), cited by Norman D. Palmer, The Indian Political System, Boston: Houghton Miffin Company 1961: 48.
2. The British government, in an attempt to secure the support of the Indians in World War II, sent a mission in 1942 under the leadership of Sir Stafford Cripps, a cabinet minister, to offer a plan to set up an Indian Union within the British Commonwealth after the end of war. The plan proposed that a

constituent assembly be elected by the provincial legislatures to negotiate a treaty with the British government to frame the future constitution of India. The mission made it clear that Indian states would be free to join the Indian Union with the right of secession from the union if they so desired. Indian Congress vehemently opposed the provision of the right to secede of any state from the Union. The Muslim League too rejected the Cripps Mission because the mission did not mention the right to establish Pakistan (Mohammad Shah, en.banglapedia.org).

3. Cabinet Mission Plan 1946 proposed a federal union for India comprising the Indian provinces and Indian states with very limited power (foreign affairs, defense, and communication) in the hands of the union government and maximum autonomy for the provincial governments. Individual provinces would be able to form regional unions to which they could surrender, by mutual agreement, some of the powers. The existing provincial assemblies were to be grouped into three sections while electing the constituent assembly: the Hindu majority provinces would constitute Section A and the Muslim majority provinces of the northwest and northeast (including Assam) would constitute Sections B and C. Although the Congress and the Muslim League initially accepted the plan, they eventually rejected it on the ground of disagreement as to how an interim government was to be constituted to convene a constituent assembly to frame a constitution. The Muslim League did welcome compulsory groupings that would help establish Pakistan while the Congress rejected the compulsory grouping as they thought it would contradict provincial autonomy. In response to Congress reaction to the compulsory groupings, the Muslim League withdrew its earlier acceptance of the long-term plan and called for direct action from 16 August to create Pakistan. Lord Wavell's efforts to set up short-term coalition/interim government at the center also broke down. The British prime minister Attlee declared their intention to leave India by June 1948 resulting in the partition of India in August 1947 (Mohammad Shah, en.banglapedia.org).

4. Pakistan comprised of two parts—East Pakistan and West Pakistan—and had several provinces such as Punjab, Sind, Baluchistan, and North West Frontier province. After independence, the Pakistan government confronted the major challenge of making its first constitution. The new leaders of the different provinces were not guided by the spirit of compromise, accommodation, and consensus to resolve the deadlock. Rather, they were locked in acrimonious relations and reluctance due to the geographical, topographical, cultural, ethnic, and linguistic diversities between East Pakistan and West Pakistan.

5. A.S.M. Rab held "that any country achieving her independence though socialist movement or a liberation war constitutes a revolutionary government immediately after independence. And he reckoned that Bangladesh made an early mistake by allowing the AL to constitute a party government. It set the authoritarian trend and continues unabated in different shapes at different times (Independent Television, September 15, 2014).

6. 'Sorbo Hara' refers to a class of people who have nothing, i.e., they do not possess any personal belonging. It is a synonym of 'have-not'—what Karl Marx called 'proletariat'.
7. Muzammil was arrested by Major Nasser who took him to Dhaka civil administration for prosecution but was released within a couple of days after direct intervention from Sheikh Mujib. Mascarenhas argues that for Lt. Col. Farooq Rahman "this was not acceptable and he (Sheikh Mujib) must go. And Farooq wanted to kill him on that very day." (Mascarenhas 2013: 48). However, Shaffayat Jamil (2016) argues in his book that Farooq Rahman made another attempt to overthrow the AL government in the late March of 1973 with the support of troops from the Comilla cantonment. That attempt failed because the troops did not show up.
8. "A member of Parliament shall vacate his seat – if he fails, within period of ninety days from the date of the first meeting of Parliament after his election" Article 67(1)(a).
9. Nazir Ahmed expands thus: "[The] Fifteenth amendment had shaken the entire constitution and put the whole nation into long term political uncertainty. The history will never forgive the prime minister of her double standards and misleading role which had put the nation in deep crisis and made the democracy in Bangladesh derailed. Government did not take any mandate from the people of Bangladesh" www.parisvisionnew.com

REFERENCES

"What Is Democracy? – Democracy's Third Wave". U.S. State Department. Retrieved 2007-08-07, https://en.wikipedia.org/wiki/Third_Wave_Democracy

Ahmed, N. (2002) The Parliament of Bangladesh. Ashgate, London

Ahmed, N. (2011) "Parliament and Democratic Consolidation in Bangladesh", Parliamentary Review, Parliamentary Review, Spring, Vol. 26, No. 2, pp. 53–68

Ahmed, Nizam (1998) "In Search of institutionalisation: Parliament in Bangladesh", Journal of Legislative Studies

ANFREL (2009) Bangladesh Ninth National Parliament Election, Bangkok, Asian Network For Free Elections (ANFREL)

Bangladesh Election Commission (1991) Election Proceeding Report, Jatiya Sangsad Election, 27 February 1991

Baxter, C. (1992) "Bangladesh in 1991—A Parliamentary System", Asian Survey, Vol. 32, No. 2

Choudhury, M. H. (2012) The Silent Witness by a General: First Decade of Independence, Adorn Publication, Dhaka

en.wikipedia.org/wiki/Bangladeshi_general_election,_1973, Bangladeshi general election, 1973

Chowdhury, M. A. (1968) Government and Politics in Pakistan, Puthighar Ltd, Dhaka

Chowdhury, D. (2013) The Daily Star, "Culture of Parliamentary Boycott in Bangladesh" (http://www.thedailystar.net/news/culture-of-parliament-boycott-in-bangladesh)

GOB, Constitution of the People's Republic of Bangladesh

Gorvine, A. (1966) "Administrative Reforms: Function of Economic and Political Change", in Birkhead, G. S. (ed) Administrative Problems in Pakistan. New York: Syracuse University Press

Hakim, M. A. (2006) "Emerging Trend of Ballot-Based Succession in Bangladesh", South Asian Survey

Hakim, A. (2000) Changing Forms of Government in Bangladesh : The Transition to Parliamentary System in 1991 in Perspective, Bangladesh Institute of Parliamentary Studies (BIPS), Dhaka

Hakim, A. (2002) "Parliamentary Politics in Bangladesh in the 1990s: Consensus and Conflict" in Chowdhury, M. H. (ed) Thirty Years of Bangladesh Politics. University Press Limited, Dhaka, pp. 103–132

Haque, Masudul (2011) "Revisiting the Role of the President during Caretaker Government in Ensuring Credible Free Elections in Bangladesh", Asian Journal of Comparative Law, http://www.frontline.in/static/html/fl2415/stories/20070810506605900.htm

Nurul Haque, A. N. M. (2009) Parliament boycott also repeats, http://www.thedailystar.net/news-detail-111271

Huq, A. F. (1985) Constitution and Politics in Bangladesh (1972–82) Conflict, Change and Stability (unpublished PhD thesis, Department of Political science, University of Rajshahi, Rajshahi)

Hussain, S. A. (1991) Politics and Society in Bengal—1921–36: A Legislative Perspective, Dhaka: Bengla Academy in Chowdhury, M. H. (ed) Thirty Years of Bangladesh Politics. University Press Limited, Dhaka

International Crisis Group (2012) Bangladesh Back to the Future, www.Crisisgroup.org/

Islam, M. M. (2015) "Electoral violence in Bangladesh: Does a confrontational bipolar political system matter?", Commonwealth and Comparative Politics

Islam, M. S. (2008) Return of The Begums: A Hobson's Choice for Bangladesh, ISAS Brief No. 84, Singapore Institute of South Asian Studies (ISAS)

Islam, S. S. (1987) "Bangladesh in 1986: Entering a New Phase", AS, Vol. 27, No. 2, pp. 163–73

Islam, S. S. (2002) "Elections and Politics in the Last Decade of the Twentieth in Bangladesh" in Chowdhury, M. H. (ed) Thirty Years of Bangladesh Politics. University Press Limited, Dhaka, pp. 133–148

Jahan, F. (2006) Public Administration in Bangladesh: State of Governance, BRAC University Dhaka, Bangladesh, www.cgs-bu.com

Jahan, R. (2014) "The Parliament of Bangladesh: Representation and Accountability", The Journal of Legislative Studies, Vol. 21, No. 2, pp. 250–269, https://doi.org/10.1080/13572334.2014.975470

Jahan, R. (2008) The Challenges of Institutionalization of Democracy, ISAS Working Paper No. 39, March

Jahan, R. (1976) "Bangabandhu and After: Conflict and Change in Bangladesh", The Round Table: The Commonwealth Journal of International Affairs, Vol. 66, No. 261

Jahan, R. (1980) Bangladesh Politics: Problems and Issues University Press limited, Dhaka

Jahan, R. (2005) Bangladesh Politics: Problems and Issues University Press limited, Dhaka

Jahan, R. and I. Amundsen (2012) The Parliament of Bangladesh: Representation and Accountability, CPD-CMI Working Paper 2. Dhaka

Kabir, B. M. M. (1999) Politics of Military Rule and the Dilemmas of Democratization in Bangladesh, New Delhi, South Asian Publishers

Khondker Delwar Hossain Vs. Bangladesh Italian Marble Works Ltd., Dhaka (DLR No. 62, p. 298)

Lifschultz, L. (1979), Bangladesh: The Unfinished Revolution, Zed Books, London

Liton, S. (2011) Limping Parliament and unmet expectations. *The Daily Star*, 17 March, Available at http://www.thestar.net/supplements/2011/anniversary/section2/pg5.htm

Mamoon, M. and J. K. Roy (1987) Bangladesh, Inside Bureaucracy Calcutta, Calcutta University, Center for South Asian Studies

Maniruzzaman, T. (1979) Administrative Reforms and Politics within the Bureaucracy of Bangladesh, Journal of Commonwealth and Comparative Politics 17 (1), March

Maniruzzaman, T. (1980), Bangladesh Revolution and Its Aftermath, Bangladesh Books International, Dhaka

Maniruzzaman, National Integration and Political Development in Pakistan, Asian Survey, Vol. 7, No. 12, 1967, pp. 876–885. http://www.thedailystar.net/news-detail-40021Talukder

Mascarenhas, A. (2013) Bangladesh: A Legacy of Blood, Hodder and Stoughton, London

Moniruzzaman, M. (2009) "Party Politics and Political Violence in Bangladesh: Issues, Manifestation and Consequences". Article (PDF Available) in South Asian Survey, Vol. 16, No. 1, pp. 81–99, March 2009, https://www.researchgate.net/publication/240717337_Party_Politics_and_Political_Violence_in_Bangladesh_Issues_Manifestation_and_Co

Hakim, Muhammad (1998) "Bangladesh: The Beginning of the end of militarised politics?", Contemporary South Asia, 11

Ahmed, Nazir (2014) Legitimacy and Legality of the 15th Amendment of the Constitution of Bangladesh, www.parisvisionnews.com, 29 January 2014

NDI 2006 Report of the National Democratic Institute (NDI) Pre- Election Delegation to Bangladesh's 2006/7 Parliamentary Elections. Washington, DC: National Democratic Institute for International Affairs (NDI). Available at http//www.ndi.org/files/2054_bd_finalstatement_091106

Ahmed, N. (2010) "Party Politics Under a Non-party Caretaker Government in Bangladesh: The Fakhruddin Interregnum (2007–09)", Commonwealth and Comparative Politics, 02

Plamer, Norman D. (1961) The Indian Political System, Houghton Miffin Company, Boston

Obaidullah, A. T. M. (1991) "Problem of Administrative Reforms in Bangladesh: Institutionalization of Bureaucracy", Asian Profile, Vol. 19, pp. 39–60

Rahman, M. M. (2007) "Origins and Pitfalls of Confrontational Politics in Bangladesh", South Asian Survey

Rahman (2014) http://bv-f.org/VOL-14/16.%20BV%20Final.pdf

Rashiduzzaman, M. (1965) Central Legislature in British India: 1921–1947, Mullick Brothers, Dhaka: 4

Rashiduzzaman, M. (1967) Pakistan: A Study Government and Politics, Ideal Library, Dhaka

Riaz, A. (2015) How Did We Arrive Here? Prothoma Prakashan, Dhaka

Salik Siddiq (2017) Witness to Surrender, University Press Ltd., Dhaka

Huntington, S. P. (1991) "Democracy's Third Wave", Journal of Democracy, Vol. 2, No. 2, Spring, pp. 12–34 (also his "Third Wave: Democratization in Late Twentieth Century, Norman", Oklahoma, University of Oklahoma Press)

Jamil, S. (2016) 1971. Liberation War, Bloody Mid August and Conspiring, Shahittya Prakash, Dhaka, November

Sayeed, K. B. (1968) Pakistan: The Formative Phase, Oxford University Press, London

TIB (2011) Gonotonrer Pratishthanikeekoron: Ashtam Jatiyo Sangshad 2001–2006 (Institutionalising Democracy: Eighth National Parliament 2001–2006). Dhaka: Transparency International Bangladesh (TIB).

Tripathi, S. (2014) The Colonel Who Would Not Repent, Aleph Book Company, New Delhi

Zaman, M. Q. (1984) "Ziaur Rahman Leadership Style and Moblization Policies", Indian Political Science Review, Vol. XVIII, No. 2, July

Ziring, L. (1993) Bangladesh: From Mujib to Ershad: An Interpretive Study, Oxford University Press

CHAPTER 3

Parliament in Parliamentary Democracy: Theoretical-Institutional Framework (Understanding the Westminster Parliament System)

What Makes a Government Parliamentary?

Based on the location of sovereignty, a regime type may be either democratic or non-democratic. In all democratic systems, parliaments exist. Even countries that are not democratic have parliaments. Whatever the regime type, parliaments have always existed with varying roles and significance in different systems and at different times. In this sense, parliament is an old and ubiquitous political institution. Loewenberg (1971: vii-1) observes that assemblies have existed in all political systems and survived in all ages. Even in the medieval period, it had its place; in aristocracies and dictatorships assemblies existed, though they did not have the power and effectiveness that democratic parliaments enjoy in the twenty-first century. If the sovereignty of the state remains vested in the people, the government is elected by popular vote and stays in power with the consent of the governed, the system of government may be called democratic (Strong 1966). A political system that can be rightly called democratic needs a framework of citizen rights, institutions of representative parliament that hold the executive power to account, an active citizen body or civil society, and a number of mediating institutions between government and citizens (www.IPU.org; Beetham 2006). Not all democratic systems are parliamentary. But a political system that is not democratic lacks a parliament that represents the people in all their diversity or a parliament whose presence matters to the public. The Inter-Parliamentary Union (IPU 2006) calls parliament the central institution of democracy as it represents society and tries to solve the most pressing problems that face constituents in their daily lives.

Based on the relations between the executive and the legislature, a democratic government may be classified into two models: presidential and parliamentary/Westminster. In a parliamentary government, the party or alliance of parties that win the majority of seats in parliament in the general election forms the government. The leader of the majority party becomes the prime minister and appoints members of the party leadership to positions in the cabinet. If no party succeeds in winning a clear majority, a coalition of parties forms the government. The minority party/parties form the opposition who have the duty to regularly challenge the majority party on issues of the government's policy and performance.

The division between government and opposition is as old as political democracy itself. In Aristotle's Athenian democracy the citizens could rule by turns; they were rulers and the ruled. As such, McIver defined democracy as a 'way governing and being governed' (McIver 1950). The minority has the opportunity to impress upon the majority its point of view by peaceful reasoning, that is, by political means. All that is necessary is to have ideological supremacy in order to win majority support of the people and legitmize their rule over minority (Gramsci 1952).

> [T]he minority accepts the right of the majority to make decisions, provided that there is reciprocal respect for the minority's right to dissent from these decisions and to promote alternative policies. (Gerald Schmitz; http://www.lop.parl.gc.ca/content/lop/researchpublications/bp47-e.htm)

The absence or ineffectiveness of an opposition thus allows the executive power to become authoritarian and arbitrary (http://www.lop.parl.gc.ca/content/lop/researchpublications/bp47-e.htm). Political opposition is a necessary pre-condition and indispensable to the functioning of parliamentary democracy (Schmitz, G 1988). However, with the ever-increasing population count in virtually all countries in the world, direct citizen participation in governance has been replaced by representatives through the systems of periodic elections. What remains is the sacred principle that 'government must rest on the consent of the governed.'

In the Westminster model, the executive is made up of members of parliament and remains collectively accountable to it as a responsible government (http://study.com/academy/lesson/parliamentary-government-definition-examples-advantages-disadvantages.html). Parliament in a parliamentary system holds the power of life and death over the executive. The executive remains in office so long as it enjoys the confidence of the majority of members of the parliament. Parliamentary democracy originated in Britain and was adopted in several of its former colonies after World War II. The parliamentary system is usually known as the Westminster model throughout the world, named after the Palace of Westminster, the seat of the British Parliament. However, over the centuries parliamentary democracy has assumed various different nomenclatures. The position of parliament and its gravity in the governmental system determines its nomenclature. The system is variously known in different countries as cabinet government, responsible government, accountable government, majoritarian government, and so on. It is called 'parliamentary government' because of pre-eminent position parliament holds in relation to the executive. The concept of parliamentary democracy owes its origin to John Locke, the seventeenth-century British philosopher, who laid the foundation of responsible government through his 'theory of consent' and distinguished it from authoritarian government as propounded by his predecessor and fellow philosopher Thomas Hobbes.[1]

The classification of a democratic regime into presidential and parliamentary systems is again based on the nature of the 'separation of power.' In the presidential system, three organs of government are clearly demarcated: executive, legislative, and judicial. In the parliamentary system, however, there is an inseparable relation between the legislature and the executive, without a rigid separation of powers, which leads to it being called "organic separation and personal union" (Willoughby 1919). In John Locke's model of the separation of powers, the legislative and executive powers are to be separated and the executive is subordinate to the legislature for its actions and policies. The executive and legislative branches are linked because the executive branch gets its power from the legislative branch and is held accountable for its actions to parliament. In the presidential system, the president is a directly elected person; neither is he a member of the legislature nor does he derive his authority from the legislature.

How the Westminster Model Differs from the Presidential System

Theoretically, parliament holds more power in the parliamentary system than in the presidential one. In a parliamentary system there is a head of state, which is a ceremonial figure like the queen, who does not engage in legislation and politics. In the presidential system, the president is both the head of state and head of the executive. In the presidential system, the executive is presumed to be more powerful than in the parliamentary system. It is argued that parliamentary government is more efficient than the presidential system because of conducive relations between the executive and the legislature. In a presidential system, the executive and the legislature very often represent different parties, and the rigid separation of powers can create political deadlock instead of striking a balance of power. Disagreement between the president and parliament can lead to government shutdown http://study.com/academy/lesson/parliamentary-government-definition-examples-advantages-disadvantages.html). In a parliamentary system, this kind of situation is unlikely provided the cabinet is not coalition of parties. According to the IPU PARLINE database, there were 180 national parliaments operating in September 2002 (Rahman (2008). Today, more than two-thirds of the world's population lives in a parliamentary democracy (Copeland and Patterson 1998 cited by Rahman, 2008: 1). In parliamentary systems, the legislature has the right to move to dismiss a prime minister at any time if the majority of members of the legislature feel that he/she is not doing the job as well as expected. This is called a 'motion of no confidence' and is not a particularly long or drawn-out process. In the USA, on the contrary, the impeachment of the president is an extensive formal process in which the president is accused of doing something illegal (https://www.reference.com/government-politics/parliamentary-form-government-adbd8c11b15125).

Of all Westminster-derived parliaments, British Parliament is called 'sovereign.' The British courts cannot declare any law passed by the House of Commons *ultra vires* or unconstitutional because laws enacted by the British Parliament constitute the sovereign law of the land. There is a proverb that goes "it can do and undo whatever it likes. What it cannot do is to make a man woman and woman a man." However, the power of British Parliament is limited by its customs, conventions, and principles of natural justice. On the other hand, in the Westminster system, where the constitution is the supreme law of the land, parliament's power of legislation is subject to judicial review thereby imposing some checks on the arbitrary exercise of powers by parliament. In regard to the supremacy of the constitution in the USA, Justice Charles Evans Hughes said 'we are under a constitution and the constitution is what the judges say it is' (in Finer 1965: 145).

Lijphart identifies nine essential features of the Westminster model. These are: (a) concentration of executive power, (b) fusion of power and cabinet dominance, (c) asymmetric bicameralism, (d) two-party system, (e) one-dimensional party system, (f) plurality system of elections, (g) unitary and centralized government, (h) unwritten constitution and parliamentary sovereignty, and (i) exclusively parliamentary democracy. Significant deviations in Britain from all of the nine characteristics of the Westminster model of majoritarian democracy have also been pointed out by Lijphart (Lijphat, A. 1984; Hakim 2002: 4). The essentials of parliamentary democracy are:

1. The members of the cabinet are members of parliament.
2. They necessarily belong to the majority party or coalition of parties.
3. They remain accountable to parliament so long as they enjoy the confidence of the majority of members of parliament.
4. The cabinet acts as a unit but the system implies the predominance of the prime minister, as first among the equals (Lijphart, A. 1984; Hakim, 2002: 4).

Functions of Parliament

It is more important to understand how parliaments function in a parliamentary system than it is to define what the Westminster system is. This section describes the functions of parliament in a parliamentary democracy. The powers and functions of parliament in a democracy continue to evolve. Democratic parliaments across the world carry out certain fundamental functions like representation, legislation, oversight, and control of the public purse though its magnitude and effectiveness vary substantially in different parts of the world. Although experts may differ on the exact list of functions that parliament in a Westminster democracy performs, Beetham (2006) notes broad agreement among the parliamentary experts on the following functions:

1. law-making;
2. approval of taxation and expenditure, generally in the context of the national budget;
3. oversight of executive actions, policy, and personnel;
4. ratification of treaties and monitoring of treaty bodies;

5. debating issues of national and international moment;
6. hearing and redressing grievances;
7. approving constitutional change.

In terms of these functions, "parliament's contribution to democracy lies in carrying out these functions effectively, not only in the sense of the efficient organization of business, but of doing so in a way that serves the needs of all sections of society" (www.ipu.org; Beetham 2006: 5).

Jahan and Amundsen (2012) hold that the representative function is the primary function for which any parliament exists. Parliament performs three types of representational roles: political, social, and constituency (Jahan and Amundsen 2012). The representational function of parliament is the thread that remains unbroken throughout the process of evolution to the present day (Laundy 1995: 42). Representative assemblies are regarded as an essential forum of representation—the bedrock of democracy: "It is through the parliament's representation, the popular interest is expressed, and popular self-government is realized in practice" (Beetham 2006: 4). Parliamentarians claim the supremacy of parliament among the three organs of the government on the grounds that it houses the peoples' elected representatives (Jahan & Amundsen, cpd-cmi 2012). The legislature in its representative capacity derives its power from the will of the people, which makes its authority legitimate in all democratic countries (Stapenhurst 2003).

The legislature's core function, however, is considered to be passing legislation that includes a constitutional mandate to amend, approve, or reject government bills (Stapenhurst 2003). As the apex representative institution of all social diversity, parliament reconciles the conflicting interests and expectations of different groups and communities through the democratic means of dialogue and compromise. With this end in view, parliaments enact laws reflecting the needs of the people, adopt laws to meet the changing needs of society, remain vigilant of government policies and their execution, and make sure that the government is fully accountable to the people (Beetham 2006: 1–2).

The executive branch runs the government, formulates policies, and exercises enormous powers to deliver services to the people. But if it runs amok and infringes on the citizens' rights, it is parliament in theory that will guard against and prevent this. For the citizen, it is vital that all powers should be exercised in a way that is compatible with their aspirations for liberty, fair dealing, and good administration (Wade, 1971: 1). This dynamic gives birth to the principle of accountability. And if the legislature fails to secure accountability of the executive, the justification for having a parliament is largely rendered obsolete. In the Westminster system, parliament is mandated to hold the executive to account and, as the representative of the people in a democracy, guard citizens' rights (Staphenhurst. 2005: 2). Parliaments perform this accountability function through various tools and mechanisms that ensure that the executive implements policies and programs in accordance with the wishes and intent of the legislature (Stapenhurst et al. 2005). Accountability tools vary depending on the form of government, the geographical location, and economic status of a country (Stapenhurst et al. 2005: 2). In all parliaments, accountability tools are classified into individual categories of mechanisms and collective methods (see Chap. 6). For a parliament to be effective as an oversight agency there is a need for a combination of different tools, all of which can contribute to making the government accountable in different ways.

Parliaments exercise two types of accountability: vertical and horizontal. Vertical accountability refers to MPs' accountability to constituents. Citizens rely on their representatives to seek redress of their grievances. Parliamentarians use accountability devices like questions, hearings, and other means to hold the concerned minister or government to account for the misuse/abuse or maladministration of any policy or program of the government. In addition to MPs, pressure groups, the media, and civil society all play a role in holding elected representatives to account. In other words, vertical accountability refers to parliament's own accountability to voters, from whom members derive their authority in a democracy. It is not always possible for citizens to hold their representatives to account during the tenure of parliament, but democratic governance retains provisions in place to establish checks and balances within the three branches of government. This is what is called horizontal accountability. Horizontal accountability is achieved through the interplay of different institutions—parliament, the judiciary, the election commission, the media, and civil society—to uphold the rule of law and political and civil rights of citizens, that is, the core value of democracy. In developing countries, horizontal accountability mechanisms only rarely function effectively. It flows sideways among branches and agencies of government (Jahan and Amundsen 2012) and generally takes the form of mutual accountability among the organs of the government. Parliament has a mediating role as the representative body of citizens to engage with the other branches of government and subnational bodies to see how well they fulfill their role. Just how efficiently and satisfactorily parliaments fulfill the diversified needs of citizens through this mediating role is an important criterion to any system being considered a democratic one (Beetham 2006: 4–5). Despite the provisions for realizing the executive's accountability to citizens through vertical accountability mechanisms, parliaments in many developing countries cannot establish the reasonable checks on the executive that they should (Jahan 2014).

Irrespective of the form of government, parliament exercises control over the public purse. It has a special responsibility to ensure that the budgetary measures it authorizes are fiscally sound and in line with the needs of citizens. It can exercise oversight before the money is appropriated (*ex-ante* control). Provisions also exist for the legislative monitoring of public expenditure after it has been approved by parliament (*ex-post* control). The Westminster parliaments are often criticized for weakened oversight of the budget. Of late, budgetary reforms adopted in most developed Westminster parliaments made provisions for exercising strong oversight before and after authorization of the national budget.[2]

The Debate on Parliament's Influence on Policy

From the late twentieth century onwards, the crucial issue that Westminster parliaments face is that of its supremacy. Scholars of parliamentary studies are engaged in debates about whether parliament is losing control over the executive in a parliamentary democracy. There are some who hold that compared to the presidential system parliamentary democracy is inefficient, even unworthy of the name since it is not parliament which controls the executive in current Westminster systems (King and Crewe 2013, 361).

In some parliamentary studies, public policy critics visualizing parliament's outcome at the agenda-setting and decision-making levels, and comparing the British House of Commons with the US Congress, have concluded parliamentary democracy inefficient compared to the US presidential system. Flinders and Kelso (2011) present a gloomy picture of parliament in line with the so-called 'decline of parliament thesis' (Russell et al. 2015). The crux of their argument is that the cabinet is more powerful than parliament in a parliamentary democracy. In all parts of the world, legislatures are confronted with the problem of 'executive dominance' in the face of increasing demands of citizens for diversified services from the government (Olson 1980). With the advent of the concept of the 'administrative state' in the twentieth century, as an inevitable consequence of profound sociopolitical changes, the legislature has lost much of its initiation of legislative functions (Street and Griffith 1967). The vast majority of legislative proposals now originate in government ministries and departments (Schwartz 1962). The whole process of legislation—drafting of the bill, presentation to the cabinet, initiation to the House—is now an executive function. The elected House is no longer 'the grand inquest of the nation' it has been so frequently characterized as in British history (Urbaniak 2011). So vital is the position of the cabinet in the parliamentary system that the "whole apparatus of the government revolves round the cabinet, concentrates upon them and radiates from them—so powerful is the body, so ubiquitous that the charge of tyranny is leveled at it, and gloomy prophecies are made about the decline of the legislature" (Finer, H. 1965: 582). Parliament is thus now confronted with the question of whether its functional gravity is in decline or merely changing to cope with changes in society (Loewenberg, 1971: vii). It is often said that the executive in the UK now controls the House of Commons instead of the other way around; that British MPs are "mere obedient servant[s] of the party machine" (Russell and Cowley 2015). Knill and Tosun (2012) hold the view that parliament's role in the British Westminster model constitutes bare minimal decision-making and is unworthy of being called a 'parliamentary democracy' (in Russell and Cowley 2015). Furthermore, one critic adds that "The complaint is often heard that legislative politics has been inefficient, ineffective, and in danger of becoming obsolete" (Schmitz 1988).

Arguing against this rather gloomy picture, Russell and Cowley hold that Westminster parliaments still have significant policy influence at successive stages of the policy-making process. They arrived at this conclusion based on the findings of quantitative and qualitative methods applied in several large research projects. There are several ways of assessing the parliamentary influence on the policy process. Parliament performs diverse roles—it acts as a forum for national debates and scrutinizes legislative proposals and public spending, but not as decision-makers. However, these functions are not targeted to immediate policy change. These multiple roles are routinely acknowledged by legislative studies scholars (e.g. Loewenberg and Patterson 1979; Norton 1993 cited by Russell and Cowley 2015). The legislature's greatest influence comes through 'anticipated reactions'; when the executive can anticipate troubles with parliament and takes action in advance to avoid it (Mezey 1979 in Russell and Cowley 2015).

Government proposals often get passed in the legislative process without much opposition and often unamended simply because the government initiates proposals with much circumspection in anticipation of legislative reactions—and will dispense with proposals which may provoke legislative obstructions (Russell and Cowley 2015). Scholars who vehemently criticize the policy influence of parliament in the Westminster model prefer to see a visible impact and the defeat of legislative proposals initiated by the executive. That only rarely happens. On the other hand, if the critics broaden their view and take into account the executive's anticipated reactions (Mayhew 1974) of parliament and decisions to avoid those proposals that might create legislative resistance, they can trace the less obviously visible impact of Westminster parliaments at pre-decision and post-decision, as well as at the decision stage (John 2012 in Russell and Cowley 2015). Hence, critics interested in detecting legislative influence on agenda and policy decisions must thus explore behind-the-scenes negotiations with the executive. Russell and Cowley argue that their research demonstrates that "parliament is powerful at the decision-making stage, but much of that power is exercised through anticipated reactions, in terms of ministers facilitating last-minute negotiations to avert rebellions and defeats" (Russell and Cowley 2015). Their study reveals that in the Westminster model parliament still has significant influence on policy. Parliament exerts this influence in last-minute negotiations with the executive to avoid political deadlock. In addition, after the creation of parliamentary standing/select committees, executive proposals go through parliamentary accountability mechanisms which thoroughly scrutinize agenda setting, policy formulation, implementation, and evaluation.

> Conventional accounts have focused too much on the decision-making stage, to the exclusion of parliament's role at earlier and later policy stages. Critics have also focused disproportionately on visible influence, overlooking behind-the-scenes negotiations and the role of anticipated reactions. (Russell and Cowley 2015)

Based on an analysis of over 6000 parliamentary votes, 4000 legislative amendments, 1000 committee recommendations, and 500 interviews, Russell and Cowley came to the conclusion that Westminster's influence is still substantive at all stages of policy-making and, contrary to many of the views in the debate, may even be on the rise (Russell and Cowley 2015).

Regaining Parliamentary Influence

Many parliaments in the Westminster system have regained the primacy that was supposedly lost. Legislatures are resilient and have a strong capacity to recover from decline. Parliaments in advanced democracies made their comeback in the last quarter of the twentieth century by compensating for their loss of power to initiate legislative functions by strengthening their scrutiny of legislative bills and increasing oversight of executive policies and implementation via increasingly active parliamentary committees. Despite some decline in legislative monopoly, legislatures are still revered and decried, and their importance continues undiminished. As a matter of fact, parliament has gained a great deal globally due to their newly created or revived and strengthened committees systems (Storm cited by Longley and Davidson 1998: 5 in Ahmed 2004). Committees are microcosms of the larger assembly. It is now a realization common across the world that committees constitute the bedrock of parliament and are the main center of legislation and oversight on the executive, irrespective of the form of government (Longley and Davidson 1998: 2).

The hitherto existing belief that Westminster-derived parliaments play a comparatively weaker role in influencing policy to that of Congress in the presidential system is thus of doubtful value. Indeed, "Until recently, strong committees were mostly seen as a characteristic of the Congressional system, an alien device to parliamentary government" (Ahmed 2004: 8). Of late, Westminster parliaments have acquired greater policy roles. Part of the reason for this is their willingness to make constructive use of committees. In the twenty-first century, most Westminster-style parliaments have set up committees for government ministries with jurisdiction to scrutinize bills and laws, review government policies, and exercise administrative oversight (Siddiqi et al. (1994). In general, parliaments are now stronger than they were before.

Colonial Legacy of Weak Parliaments

Despite the increasing popularity of the parliamentary system throughout the world, in most cases where it has been applied in countries emerging from colonial rule in Asia and Africa, there has been a significant failure in institutionalizing parliament and consolidating democracy. Parliaments in countries emerging from a long spell of colonial rule experience overly dominant executives unwilling to be accountable to parliament. Colonial rulers were paternalistic in its orientation, used to maintain ruler–subject relationship, accustomed to a regulatory administration to fulfill the desire of the imperial powers, and unwilling to be accountable to the public representative institution (Obaidullah, 1991). Strengthening a representative institution like national parliament was considered to run counter to imperial interests. Consequently, with decolonization newly independent or newly created modern states were faced with the huge challenge of giving their parliament an institutional shape. After independence, parliaments in these countries did not receive due importance from their national governments to compensate for their institutional weakness. Rather, that fragility was compounded the neglect of executive power and constraints in resources. Most developing counties failed to strike a balance of power between the executive and legislature. Institutional growth requires a congenial environment and freedom for each institution to operate according to its constitutional mandate. But it was perceived that too much obstruction and resistance from parliament would handicap the executive and thus the executive's indifference was detrimental to parliament's growth and has been a significant obstacle to institutionalization or parliament in these nascent democracies. As has been widely recognized, the more institutionalized a parliament is, the greater the prospect that democracy will be consolidated (Ahmed 1998). Thus, in the mid-twentieth century, countries that emerged from colonial rule inherited as part of that legacy weak parliaments and strong executives.

Pre-requisites for Institutionalization

The mere existence of parliament does not guarantee institutionalization. The institutionalization of parliament and consolidation of democracy grow over time. Rose observes, "It takes time, a decade or more to demonstrate a regime's commitment to the rule of law and to changing control of government in response to changes in the electoral behavior'(quoted in Ahmed 2011: 241). The institutionalization process is at stake when the stability of parliament itself is threatened by extra-constitutional politics. In fact, a lack of continuity in constitutional rule is one of the important factors that hinder the institutionalization of parliament and consolidation of democracy. Parliament needs time to evolve a standard practice and procedure of work. Longevity is a necessary but not a sufficient condition for institutionalization (Ahmed 2011). The pre-requisites for institutionalization require that certain conditions are present such as autonomy, formality, uniformity, and complexity—all of which nascent democracies only rarely have. A weak legislature makes the task of democratic consolidation more difficult, if not impossible (Copeland and

Patterson 1994). The IPU holds that the degree of institutionalization of parliament is contingent upon (a) the extent of the power and authority it enjoys vis-à-vis the executive and resources it possesses, and (b) the autonomy that parliament is granted (Beetham 2006).

Parliaments are not in a position to serve the electorates effectively if they do not have sufficient power and resources to discharge their functions. The term 'power' in the context of parliament bears two meanings: capacity and relational (http://www.ipu.org/dem-e/guide/guide-6.htm). Here, the capacity of parliament is linked with power; and power is linked with legal rights. The IPU observes that parliament cannot function effectively unless it is provided with authority based on legal enactment. Second, parliament's power is relational to the power of the executive, that is, how much independence parliament enjoys in relation to the executive's power that affords it space to oversee the functions of the executive effectively.

Parliamentary institutionalization is again affected by parliament's lack of resources including financial, human, and organizational capacity will severely detriment parliament in carrying out its necessary tasks. If parliament does not have its own finance, own staff, and a well-equipped organization to carry out its mandated tasks it is unlikely to deliver efficient services to the MPs and parliamentary committees. How efficiently parliament can serve its electorate is dependent upon the adequacy of its power and resources (http://www.ipu.org/dem-e/guide/guide-6.htm). In developed countries, a well-resourced parliament necessarily has:

1. sufficient competent staff to provide impartial support to members across parliament's whole range of work;
2. a well-equipped library and information service;
3. office facilities for individual members;
4. adequate support for training and research to increase the human capacity of members and secretarial staff;
5. the commitment of dedicated facilities to the main opposition party or alliance of parties (Beetham 2006; www.ipu.org/dem-e/guide/guide-6.htm).

Sufficient power and resources can enable parliament to establish a real check on the executive. A recent comparative survey of democratization in post-communist states concluded that "the strength of the national legislature may be a—or even the—institutional key to democratization.

Countries with weak legislatures need constitutional reforms to strengthen it as a top priority" (Fish 2006: 5–20). A wide-ranging gap is noted between the parliaments of developed and developing countries in respect of the power, resources, and facilities available to them. It is not surprising that given the enormous pressure placed on the national budget of developing countries for basic development and infrastructure, there is little left to allocate to parliamentary development. This has been a chief concern for parliamentarians in developing and resource-poor countries.

Where parliament is incapacitated because of resource constraints, the executive inevitably dominates the governance process; the balance of power is tilted in its favor. Parliament becomes dependent on staff from the line ministries for their everyday business, many of which will be naturally allegiant to their parent organization, ministry, or executive. With these officials staffing parliament, it is unlikely to establish a strong oversight of government policies and performance. In such a scenario, the government can find a way around resistance or opposition in developing policy and legislation. Parliaments in most developing countries suffer from a lack of sufficiently competent staff with the appropriate expertise. In such a situation, there is a lack of understanding of the real purpose of parliament, which often contributes it being seen in low esteem. The IPU has developed strategies for compensating these limitations of resources. These include:

1. more effective training for members themselves, with encouragement to greater specialization;
2. more extensive and systematic use of experts in different fields from civil society and academia, to support the work of parliamentary committees and groups;
3. the development of internship programs to supplement scarce parliamentary resources;
4. the development of online facilities to enhance the research and information capacity of parliaments, including library provision (http://www.ipu.org/dem-e/guide/guide-6.htm).

Parliamentary Autonomy

The autonomy of parliament is defined as "non-dependence and non-subordination of assemblies in relation to the executive, and making it free from the purview of the rules of ordinary law" (Michel Couderc, 1998). As a matter of fact, all democratic states enshrine the principle of autonomy in their constitution within the framework of the separation of powers (ibid.). However, many developing countries do not establish a strong and autonomous parliament secretariat to serve the members and committees independently. In the parliamentary system the challenge is how to establish a more robust parliamentary independence or autonomy (www.IPU.org/dem-e/guide/guide-6.htm). The IPU has worked out a number of devices for giving effect to the principle of autonomy in practice. These include:

1. enact laws empowering parliament;
2. create parliaments' own staff;
3. establish control over its own budget;
4. acquire freedom of determining its own business (http://www.ipu.org/dem-e/guide/guide-6.htm).

The Parliament's institutionalization is dependent on the degree of legal independence it enjoys vis-à-vis the executive in terms of the provision of the budget, determining the required human resources, and undertaking development programs. Parliaments should be independent of the executive to determine its course of action. The IPU and many international development agencies provide external assistance in emerging democracies for human capacity development programs for MPs and secretariat staff. However, the external assistance program should not be regarded as a substitute for adequate resourcing on an ongoing basis. The 1999 IPU study revealed that "among the 52 parliaments surveyed, the share of the state budget taken by parliament ranged from 0.01% (Denmark) to 1.6% (Greece)" (www.IPU.org/dem-e/guide/guide-6.htm). Against this backdrop, the national budget should make provision for increased allocation to continue with capacity development programs on an ongoing basis.

The constitution of a country and its legal enactments usually provide for the operational independence of parliament that ensures that the secretariat and the parliament library are manned by non-partisan professional staff distinct from the public service. Government officials in the bureaucracy move from one department to another throughout their careers while parliamentary staff tend to make their career in the parliament they serve. The model of a professional parliamentary cadre with its own career structure has now been widely accepted, in both parliamentary and presidential systems. The nature of work of parliamentary staff is unlike other government departments "where given the nature of party competition, the norms of non-partisanship and professional discretion are at a special premium" (Beetham 2006; www.IPU.org/dem-e/guide/guide-6.htm). The mechanisms parliament adopts and resources it uses determines to a great extent its independence and autonomy.

Compared with the extent of power and resources the IPU considers necessary for institutionalizing parliament, parliaments of many third-world countries are totally underprepared to render their services to MPs for making quality legislation and ensuring effective oversight of the executive. Having considered this situation, after the restoration of parliamentary democracy in Bangladesh in 1991, different development partners including The Asia Foundation, DFID Bangladesh, UNDP, USAID, and the World Bank provided technical assistance for almost two decades. They undertook several diagnostic studies of the Bangladesh Parliament to unearth the weaknesses of parliament, its secretariat in general, and committees in particular. They produced invaluable reports and sponsored massive development programs to elevate the knowledge, skills, and performance of MPs and secretariat staff to enable the Parliament in Bangladesh to enact quality legislation and conduct effective oversight of the executive power—a goal that post-restoration parliaments consistently strived to achieve.

Parliamentary Culture

When institutional arrangements are in place, the survival of a democracy and institutionalization of its parliament requires the presence of parliamentary culture—that is, a degree of moderation in one's partisanship; considerable trust and minimum suspicion of rival political actors; tolerance of opposition and criticism; and readiness to compromise, accommodate, and cooperate. Parliamentary conflict within certain limits is functional and healthy in a democratic system, but too much of it is entirely dysfunctional. Any attempt by those in power to suppress dissension adds only fuel to the political conflict and thus intensifies it, which may ultimately lead to the breakdown of the system. Thus, striking a balance between conflict and consensus is one of those nagging problems intrinsic to all democracies, but particularly to emerging ones (Diamond 1993). Dissension and division in a democracy should be on a basis of consent and cohesion. Too much conflict and a lack of consensus jeopardizes the stability of a political system (Diamond, and Plattner, M.F (1993: 95–107). Making parliament work to the satisfaction of the electorate is as much a responsibility of the opposition bench as it is of the Treasury (Hakim 2002: 106).

Notes

1. In his book *Two Treatises*, John Locke propounded that consent is the basis of legitimacy of any government. The consent by which each person agrees with others to form a body politic obligates him to submit to the majority. There were two contracts, the one between individuals giving rise to community and the other between community and government. All is for the public good. Such a power can arise only by consent, and though this may be tacitly given, it must be consent of each individual for himself. (Sabine, G. H. (1973) *A History of Political Theory*, Dryden Press, Rineheart and Winston Inc. N.Y. USA, pp. 490–491). Government is not legitimate if it is not based on the consent of the governed.
2. The UK has adopted an open budget policy since Kenneth Clark and Gordon Brown were the Chancellors of the Exchequer by providing substantial information to the members of parliament in pre-budget discussion. The Indian Lok Sabha adopted the provision of referral of the budget to the standing committees for ensuring informed debates in the general discussion on the budget. Bangladesh recently adopted mid-term budget review to provide more information on the budget implantation scenario under the Medium Term Budgetary Framework (MTBF).

References

Steven Fish, M. (2006) "Stronger Legislatures, Stronger Democracy", Journal of Democracy, Vol. 17, No. 1, January, pp. 5–20

Ahmed, N. (2011) "Parliament and democratic consolidation in Bangladesh", *Parliamentary Review*, Parliamentary Review, Spring, Vol. 26, No. 2, pp. 53–68

Ahmed, N. (2004) "Parliament and Policy: The Role of the Committees" UNDP-(SPD News Letter, July–December, BIPS, Dhaka

Antonio Gramsci (1958), Passato e Presente, uran: Einaudi, 1952, p. 158 in Islam, S.S. (2002: 134). "Elections and Politics in the Last Decades of the Twentieth Century in Bangladesh" in Chowdhury, M. H (ed.) *Thirty Years of Bangladesh Politics*, University Press Limited, Dhaka

Bangladesh, The Journal of Legislative Studies, Vol. 4, No. 4, pp. 34–65 ISSN: 1357-2334 (Print) 1743-9337 (Online) Journal homepage: http://www.tandfonline.com/loi/fjls20

Beetham, D. (2006) Parliament and Democracy in the Twenty First century: A Guide to Good Practice, Published by Inter-Parliamentary Union, PO Box 330, 1218 Le Grand Saconnex, Geneva, Switzerland

David Olson (1980) *The Legislative Process: A Comparative Approach*, Harper & Row, New York, esp. Chapter 1

Diamond, L. (1993) 'Three Paradoxes of Democracy', in Larry Diamond and Mark F. Plattner (eds) The Global Resurgence of Democracy, Baltimore: Johns Hopkins University Press, pp. 95–107

"Elections and Politics in the Last Decades of the Twentieth Century in Bangladesh" in Chowdhury, M. H. (2002) Thirty Years of Bangladesh Politics, University Press Limited, Dhaka

Finer, H. (1965) The Theory and Practice of Modern Government, Methen & Co. Ltd, London

Flinders, Mathew and Alexander Kelso (2011) "Mind the Gap: Political analysis, Public Expectation and the Parliamentary Decline Thesis", British Journal of Politics and International Relations, Vol. 13, No. 2, pp. 249–268

Copeland, G. and S. Patterson (1994) 'Parliament in The Twenty First Century' in G. Copeland & S. Patterson (eds) Parliament in the Modern World, Michigan University Press, Ann Arbour, pp. 1–12

Gerald Schmitz, The Role of Opposition in Parliamentary Democracy, http://www.lop.parl.gc.ca/content/lop/researchpublications/bp47-e.htm

Hakim, A. (2002) "Parliamentary Politics in Bangladesh in the 1990s: Consensus and Conflict" in Chowdhury, M. H. (ed) Thirty Years of Bangladesh Politics, University Press Limited, Dhaka, pp. 103–132

Jahan, R. (2014) The Parliament of Bangladesh: Representation and Accountability, The Journal of Legislative Studies, Vol. 21, No. 2, pp. 250–269

Jahan, R. and I. Amundsen (2012) The Parliament of Bangladesh: Representation and Accountability, CPD-CMI Working Paper 2. Dhaka

John, P. (2012) Analysing Public Policy, London: Routledge

King, Anthony, and Ivor Crewe (2013) The Blunders of Our Governments. London: Oneworld

Knill, Christoph, and Jale Tosun (2012). Public Policy: A New Introduction. Basingstoke: Palgrave

Laundy, P. (1995) 'Members of Parliament and the Citizen', in IPU, The Functioning of a Parliament in Multi Party Democratic setting, Geneva, pp. 42–44

Lijphart, A. (1984) Democracies: Pattern of Majoritarian and Consensus Government in Twenty-One Centuries, Yale University Press, New Haven

Loewenberg, Gerhard (ed) (1971) Modern Parliaments Change or Decline? Aldine Chicago, New York

Lowenberg, G. and Patterson (1979) Comparative Legislatures, University Press of America, New York

Longley, L. and R. H. Davidson (eds) 1998 The New Roles of Parliamentary Committee, Frank Cass, London, p. 2

McIver, R. M. (1950) Ramparts we Guard, Macmillan

Mayhew, David R. (1974) Congress: The Electoral Connection. New Haven, CT: Yale University Press.

Mezey, M. L. (1979) Comparative Legislatures. Durham, NC: Duke University Press

Michel, C. (1998) 'The Principle of Parliamentary Autonomy', Constitutional and Parliamentary Information, No. 176

Nizam Ahmed (1998) In Search of Institutionalisation: Parliament in Bangladesh, The Journal of Legislative Studies ISSN: 1357–2334 (Print) 1743–9337 (Online) Journal homepage: http://www.tandfonline.com/loi/fjls20

Obaidullah, A. T. M. (1991) "Problem of Administrative Reforms in Bangladesh: Institutionalization of Bureaucracy". Asian Profile, Vol., 19. 1991. pp. 39–60

Rahman, T. (2008) Parliamentary Control and Government Accountability in South Asia, Routledge, London

Russell, M and Philip Cowley (2015) "The Policy Power of the Westminster Parliament: The Parliamentary State and the Empirical Evidence" https://constitution-unit.com/2015/11/26/the-policy-power-of-the-westminster-parliament-the-empirical-evidence/

Sabine G. H. (1973) A History of Political Theory, Dryden Press, Rineheart and Winston Inc. N.Y USA pp. 490–91.

Schmitz, G. (1988) The Opposition in a Parliament System Canada http://www.lop.parl.gc.ca/content/lop/researchpublications/bp47-e.htm

Schwartz, B. (1962) Introduction to the American Administrative law, Sir Isaac Pitman & Sons Publisher, London

Siddiqi, L. K. et al. (1994) Making Parliament Effective: A British Experience, Dhaka

Stapenhurst, R. (2003), "Accountability and Transparency in the Budgetary Process: Parliamentary Oversight of the Budget: Reading, Analyzing and Questioning Parliamentary Tools and Mechanism", Regional Seminar, Colombo

Stapenhurst, R. et al. (2005) "Scrutinizing Public Expenditure: Assessing the Performance of Public Accounts Committee" WB Policy Research Working Paper, 3613, (May, 2005)

Street, L. A. G. and H. Griffith (1967) The Principles of administrative Law, London, Sir Isac Pitman and Sons

Strong, C. F. (1966) Modern Political Constitution, Sidgwick and Jackson

Taiabbur Rahman, 2008. Parliamentary Control and Government Accountability, Routledge Advances in South Asian Studies, p. 68

Urbaniak, T. (2011) Ministerial Responsibility: A Post Mortem in Leon R.P and Ohemeng L.K. Approaching Public Administration, Edmond Montgomarey Publications, Toronto, Canada

Wade, H. W. R. (1971) Administrative Law, Oxford Clarendon Press

Willoughby, W. F. (1919) Government of Modern States, New York, Appleton Century Crofts. Willoughby http://www.universityofcalicut.info/SDE/Foundations_of_political_science.pdf

Functions of Political Science, http://www.universityofcalicut.info/SDE/Foundations_of_political_science.pdf

Rahman, http://bv-f.org/VOL-14/16.%20BV%20Final.pdf

CHAPTER 4

Reorganization of Parliament Secretariat Barriers to the Capacity Development

The Imperatives of Reorganization

In both presidential and Westminster-style political systems, parliament plays a crucial role. Yet, it can assume substantially different positions in the entire fabric of government. Irrespective of the political system, parliament enacts and amends laws, amends the constitution, passes the budget, and scrutinizes public spending. However, nowhere but in the Westminster system is the executive individually and collectively responsible to parliament for its actions and policies. What gives parliament in the Westminster system its special position is its inherent authority to hold the trump card over the life or death of the executive. By bringing a motion of no confidence against it, parliament can unseat the cabinet if it fails to secure the majority support of the House. In the Westminster system, the executive is constituted from parliament, and can ultimately be dissolved at the hands of parliamentarians if it fails to act according to its legislative intent. Notwithstanding this constitutional mandate, however, parliament can often fail to exert its legislative supremacy over the executive if it does not receive efficient administrative and logistical support from its integral part—the parliament secretariat. In the twenty-first century, it is universally recognized that effective parliaments need a strong and efficient secretariat. The Parliament Secretariat in Bangladesh was established under the authority of Article 79 of the Constitution (GPRB).[1] It is expected to provide all administrative support to the MPs and committees to discharge their

© The Author(s) 2019
A. T. M. Obaidullah, *Institutionalization of the Parliament in Bangladesh*, https://doi.org/10.1007/978-981-10-5317-7_4

legislative and oversight functions, and any other responsibilities vested on it by or under the authority of the PSA 1994 and the ROP of Bangladesh Parliament.

In the nineteen years following independence, the Bangladesh Parliament served both the parliamentary and presidential systems of government, all of which were de facto civil and military authoritarian governments, and throughout this period the notion of making the executive accountable to parliament was virtually unthought of. After the change in the political landscape and reintroduction of Westminster-style democracy in 1991, substantive parliamentary reform became an urgent concern for policy-makers. Parliament had previously enacted laws and amended the Constitution as per the desire of the chief executive (be it the prime minister or the president), thus lending those regimes legitimacy. However, after the mass uprising in December 1990 that removed General Ershad from power, the philosophy of the state underwent radical change to reflect the aspirations of the revolutionary masses. This political maelstrom as such forced upon Parliament the need to enact laws that reflected the will of the people and hold the executive to account. The restoration of parliamentary democracy pushed the issue of the accountability of the executive to the forefront and if Parliament was to fulfill the expectations of the revolutionary and pro-democracy masses, it would itself need to reform in its vision, mission, organization, and procedure. Thus, what followed was a series of attempted reforms tabled by both the national and international community designed rejuvenate Parliament and help meet the needs of a new parliamentary democracy. It is part of this overall scheme of parliamentary reform that the Secretariat was to be reorganized. It was ill-prepared to shoulder the responsibilities entrusted to it to serve MPs and committees to carry out the mandate required by the Westminster system.

Given the change of political landscape and form of government, reorganizing the Secretariat thus became a crucial issue for the post-restoration parliaments. The Secretariat's capacity to deliver efficient services to Parliament called for both organizational restructuring and fundamental changes in the methods of work that included: the mandate of each wing, branch, and section; staff job descriptions; clear line and staff relationship and reporting system; and well-conceived accountability mechanisms through setting performance standards. Yet, structural reorganization would be futile if the secretariat wasn't simultaneously provided with resources, manpower, equipment, and the constitutional and legal status for serving Parliament independently. Structural reorganization needed to be complemented by the support of professional human resources, staff with specialized knowledge of Parliament's mandate—that is, the nature of jobs, norms, and rules of procedure, skills, training, and aptitude to work with MPs at the highest level. The Parliament Secretariat, in theory, holds the same status as that of ministry, yet it is totally different from other government ministries due to its unique responsibility to support MPs. In this context, development partners along with the Bangladesh Parliament made a prolonged effort to enhance the Secretariat's organizational and operational capability.

This chapter focuses on a selection of major studies conducted by the Asia Foundation (1991), UNDP (1997), DFID (2000), UNDP (2002), and USAID (2008–2015) on the Bangladesh Parliament Secretariat. These studies diagnosed the weaknesses of the existing Secretariat, assessed the needs, and put forward recommendations to revitalize its organizational and operational capacity as the backbone of support to MPs to discharge their responsibilities effectively. The chapter discusses, in turn, the status of the Secretariat in the period leading up to the reforms that began in 1994, the findings and recommendations of the aforementioned studies, the implementation of measures designed to sustain its organizational and operational efficiency, and their impact after 1994. This chapter is based mainly on a literature review and primary data obtained from structured questionnaires and interviews with a selection of senior MPs from both the AL and the BNP and with core staff of the Secretariat.

The Meaning of Operational Efficiency

There are no universal attributes of 'operational efficiency.' Its meaning and the standards applied to it vary depending upon the nature of output a particular organization is called upon to produce. For example, in the manufacturing industry, an organization's efficiency is easily measurable by the volume of production that the industry produces and quality of the produced commodities and by sampling of the user satisfaction, while in the service sectors operational efficiency may be measured in terms of user satisfaction. In the context of the Bangladesh Parliament Secretariat, it means how effectively this body can provide support to MPs and parliamentary standing committees in enacting laws, scrutinizing bills, and conducting oversight on the policies and administration of government, as well as how effective it is in extending services to the management of the House during sessions. In a profit-making organization, efficiency is measured in relation to the output produced to input investment. In parliament, the operational efficiency of the secretariat would be measured in relation to MPs' satisfaction and achievement of the end result that parliament envisions. Operational efficiency does not grow automatically in a vacuum; it has to be nurtured over the years through trial and error, and organizational and procedural reforms are required to cope with the ever changing demands of MPs and their constituents in the twenty-first century. In this respect, increasing knowledge, updating skills, and improving procedures of work would be considered *sine qua non* to improve operational efficiency through continuous training and developing the research capability of individual staff as well as the Secretariat as an institution.

The Situation of the Secretariat Before 1994

The most conspicuous weakness of the Bangladesh Parliament Secretariat before the 1994 reforms was that it lacked autonomy, power, and resources to recruit manpower and make annual budget, which were subject to the approval of the executive and the ministry of finance. Parliament needs to be served by independent, non-partisan, and neutral staff. Until the PSA 1994 was passed, the Secretariat was an extension of the presidential secretariat; accountable only to the president. Recruitment, promotion, and transfer of the required staff were subject to sanction by the Establishment Ministry and the approval of the president after selection by the Public Service Commission (PSC). The Secretariat had no budget of its own. In the same manner as that of other ministries or government departments, the Secretariat's budget was prepared by the Ministry of Finance. The Secretariat was not accountable to Parliament; rather, to the executive branch of the government. Secretariat staff members were deputed officials from line ministries. They were the administrative arm of the executive. The Speaker of the House had no de facto control over the Secretariat's budget allocations and the recruitment and transfer of its staff. There are even instances where the Secretariat had no authority, despite the reluctance of the Speaker, to retain officials if the parent ministry had desired to withdraw them. In this handicapped situation, it was inconceivable that Parliament could possibly assert supremacy over the executive branch or the state bureaucracy.

Select Studies on Reorganizing the Secretariat

Immediately after the reintroduction of parliamentary democracy in 1991, the Asia Foundation engaged in a diagnostic study of the Secretariat which was followed by several comprehensive studies over the following two decades (1991 to 2010) by DFID Bangladesh, UNDP, and USAID with a view to diagnosing shortcomings and increasing the effectiveness of the Bangladesh Parliament in respect of legislation and oversight on the executive. In the last twenty-five years, the Secretariat has undergone massive reorganization efforts in all its dimensions designed to increase its independence, power, and legal status, and reorganize an anachronistic system, rules and procedures, and human resource management. The following pages will briefly trace the major findings and recommendations of those studies relevant to the reorganization of the Secretariat and the extent of their implementation.

The Asia Foundation, 1991

In 1991, Jane Lindley from the Asia Foundation undertook for the first time an extensive needs assessment of the Bangladesh Parliament with a focus on empowering Parliament and resourcing its Secretariat. Lindley's reform measures covered institutional and operational reforms. The former included strengthening Parliament's oversight function, reorganizing parliamentary committees, and revising the ROP. The latter focused on organizational streamlining and resourcing the Secretariat, modernizing the parliamentary library, establishing an institute of parliamentary studies, and improving human resource development (HRD) to increase the effectiveness of its services MPs and committees (Obaidullah 2011). Of the long list of recommendations to increase the operational capacity of the Secretariat, ensuring independence from the executive and its accountability to the House through the Speaker deserve special mention.

The needs assessment report (1991) underscored the need for immediate changes to the prevailing situation in alignment with Article 79 of the Constitution. The report stated that "requisite legislative action should be taken to establish the parliament secretariat's independence from the executive and to make it accountable to its parent institution through the speaker" (Lindley 1991: 5). At the same time, reasonable measures would have to be taken to ensure that employees of the Secretariat remained non-partisan civil servants and hired on competitive merit according to established professional and technical recruitment standards. It should be the prerogative of the sovereign Parliament to determine with reasonable prudence the staff strength and budget it requires for the effective administration of its Secretariat and to authorize on its own cognizance the redeployment of its staff among its various organizational units as may be desirable. Parliament would have the authority to create new posts as and when it deems necessary, without having to obtain the approval of the executive branch. During this changeover, the Secretariat should recruit and select its staff via the PSC through competitive examination under the same criteria of job classifications, pay scales, pensions, and other service benefits; all of which should be governed by the relevant statutes and regulations pertaining to the ethics and conduct of civil servants. Most, if not all, Secretariat senior staff had joined on deputation from the line ministries. However, in order to advance their careers in the civil service, they may not wish to remain in parliamentary service on a permanent basis. The report maintained that these staff should be given the option of returning to their parent ministry when the period of their deputation expires or remaining permanently in parliamentary service; but as and when they leave or retire, they should be replaced with people directly recruited to parliamentary service (Lindley 1991: 5). In order to attract and retain well-qualified and highly motivated people, the appropriate provision would have to be made for career advancement in the various cadres of the parliamentary service (ibid.).

Three years after the Asia Foundation report was published, the PSA 1994 was passed and the Bangladesh Parliament Secretariat was established under Article 79 of the Constitution to carry out its mandated tasks within the provisions of the Act. One of the distinguishing features that separates the Secretariat from other government ministries and departments is its autonomous character enshrined in the Act and the provision of a Parliament Secretariat Commission. Under the PSA 1994, the Secretariat falls outside the jurisdiction of any government ministry or division and can directly communicate with any ministry, division, department, or any other institution of government. The Parliament Secretariat Commission is the highest policy-making body in Bangladesh and is comprised of the following members:

1. the Speaker of the House, who is chairman;
2. the prime minister, or any MP nominated on his/her behalf;

3. the Leader of the Opposition, or any MP nominated on his/her behalf;
4. the minister in charge of the Ministry of Parliamentary Affairs, or any MP nominated on his/her behalf;
5. the finance minister, or any MP nominated on his behalf (Parliament Secretariat Act 1994, No. 8).

The Parliament Secretariat Commission advises with regard to determining the number of officers and employees of the Secretariat, and any enhancement or reduction to that number, preparing the annual budget, and monitoring expenditure allocated under the budget. The Commission also determines its own procedures and course of action (Parliament Secretariat Act 1994 No.8 7(3)). Parliament has authority over its own budget and fixes its priorities. The PSA 1994 made the Speaker of the House de facto and de jure head of the Secretariat in its entire management, as envisioned in the Lindley Report. There is of course provision for delegating his/her power in discharging official business (see Order, Delegation of Power for the Officials of Parliament Secretariat 2004). A permanent secretary to the government is placed as the secretary of the Secretariat as its administrative head. The Speaker makes the provision for the distribution of the work of the Secretariat by rules or standing orders and the Secretariat retains both financial and administrative autonomy. Under this Act, the Speaker has the power to make rules in consultation with the Commission and does not have to consult with or get vetting approval from the Law and Finance Ministries if he/she wants to change the organizational structure of the Secretariat, even if this has financial implications. If the Speaker wants to make radical changes to the Secretariat, he/she can do it within a six-month time frame (PROGATI 2011: 16).

All officers and employees are responsible to the secretary who, in turn, answers to the Speaker. The secretary is supported by four additional secretaries, five joint secretaries, eighteen deputy secretaries, and several senior assistants and assistant secretaries, hierarchically organized for the due discharge of official responsibilities. The Secretariat, like other government ministries, is divided into wings; and those wings into branches and sections. There are, as such, seven wings in the Secretariat,[2] which are as follows:

1. Legislative Support (LS) Wing;
2. Committee Support (CS) Wing;

3. Inter Parliamentary Affairs, Security and Planning (IPASP) Wing;
4. Administrative Support (AS) Wing;
5. Human Resource (HR) Wing;
6. Finance and Public Relation (FPR) Wing;
7. Broadcasting and Information Technology (B&IT) Wing.[3]

Each wing has specific responsibilities as set out in the 'description of jobs' and approved by the Speaker. The LS Wing is the most diverse, comprised of seven functions: (a) reporting; (b) editing of debates; (c) printing; (d) government bills; (e) private bills; (f) legislative drafting; (g) public relations. The legislative drafting unit is fairly new and set up to assist the MPs with drafting private bills. It is staffed by lawyers on deputation from the law ministry. DFID has observed that the level of expertise in the legislation sections is low, although it is here that knowledge and experience are most called for (Watson and Williams 2000).

There are a number of specialized posts at deputy secretary level. These include director of editing of debates, director of public relations, director of library, director of reporting, and the sergeant at arms. As such, there are eighteen deputy secretaries and eleven directors in the Secretariat; and these specialized jobs do not generally transfer between posts. In addition, posts in the library, reporting section, and editor's section have been designated non-transferable. Other deputy secretaries appear to be transferred at will among the posts.

Other specialist posts include the deputy director of printing and publications, senior legislative draftsman, and law officer, all of which operate at senior assistant/assistant secretary level. In addition, there are further forty 'movable assistant secretaries', twenty-two of which support committees and some of which are designated committee officers. Each office appears to be a fiefdom, with a large number of frightened low-skilled junior staff attending to vague potential needs. For example, it appears that six staff are employed for every assistant secretary: two administrative officers, two typists, and two Members of Lower Subordinate staff (MLLS) (William and Watson 2000, Annex 6). Below the senior structure, it is unclear how staff are deployed or even the exact numbers employed. A simple calculation suggests that there are around 800 staff members below assistant secretary level. The functions likely to be performed by this huge group are office administration and support, security, cleaning, catering, and messenger services. How these groups of staff are supervised is unclear except in the case of security staff who are managed by the sergeant at arms (ibid.). Currently, there are around 1102 people employed in the Secretariat (see the organogram in Annex 2). In addition, another 130 staff are engaged on daily wages during parliamentary sessions. The officers and employees of the Secretariat are recruited in accordance with the Recruitment Rules made under the authority of the PSA 1994 (Parliament Secretariat Act 1994).

The Asia Foundation report observed that in order for MPs to be actively engaged in floor and committee work, they require considerably more support from the Secretariat that was not provided up to that point. Not only did they lack proper assistance in drafting their private members' bill, or various resolutions, motions or amendments, but also the range and level of information services they received was minimal at best. MPs were not even provided with basic services such as access to a pool of typists to help them with their official correspondence, let alone any sort of help handling queries from constituents (ibid.: 8). Lindley acknowledged that in practice no two parliaments in the world are identical; however, she put forward a long list of recommendations drawing on the best parliamentary practices around the globe.

In order to overcome the deplorable scarcity in services MPs were confronted with, the report suggested that at least four operational units be established, or expanded and strengthened, to provide the requisite legislative and informational support services. They were (a) legislative drafting, (b) library services, (c) research and documentation, and (d) member liaison (ibid.: 13). In addition, the report highlighted some priority areas for the Secretariat to improve parliamentary management. These included: (a) reorganization of the Secretariat; (b) creating highly professional staff; (c) revising job descriptions; (d) introducing performance standards in line with the new requirements of an independent and more highly professionalized parliament secretariat; (e) establishing a manpower development and training unit; (f) refurbishing the parliamentary library; (g) establishing a code of ethics for MPs; (h) providing research and documentation services to MPs; and (i) ensuring wider dissemination of parliamentary knowledge to the general (Lindley 1991). The following paragraphs will briefly discuss four basic operational units that, according to the Asia Foundation report, should be established and strengthened to improve MPs' involvement in parliamentary business.

Legislative Drafting

With the advent in the twentieth century of the modern welfare state, the functions of government have increased enormously with the consequent increase in the complexity of legislation such that most legislative bills now are initiated in government ministries. In Bangladesh, the Ministry of Law and Justice provides support for government bills. The bills initiated by non-ministers are called private members' bills and the Asian Foundation report recommended that for these bills an office of legislative advisory services be created with two or three assistant secretaries, or officers of equivalent rank, working under a deputy secretary. Staff engaged in provided this legislative support must be law graduates with a second degree in a relevant social science. They must have specialized training in legislative drafting and be capable of undertaking necessary legal research to assist MPs with proposed private members' bills, amendments, and resolutions. They would provide all assistance to members for developing draft proposals in the correct technical and legal format required for their introduction in the House. This section would assist MPs in presenting the policy implications of proposed legislation, or any such item which is likely to be on the agenda (Chowdhury 1997: 29).

Consequent to the recommendations of the Asia Foundation Report, Parliament made the provision of a legislative draftsman; usually a judicial officer on deputation. The Secretariat organogram shows that more than ten staff posts are dedicated to the legislative drafting section. However, 50% of these positions remain vacant. With some exceptions, the draftsmen are on deputation—as is the current director of the legislative drafting section. Surprisingly enough, a veterinary doctor is currently deputy secretary of LS Wing, and one frequent complaint made is that, in contrast to the Secretariat staff, deputed officials have no training in legislative drafting and little clue of what a private members bill is, let alone specific skills in making them technically sound for introduction in the House.

Library Services

Up until 2000, the Bangladesh Parliament did not make any provision for real legislative information services to MPs. The library that existed was essentially an archive of parliamentary documents and other historical and reference materials and there was no provision for research and documentation services in the library. In short, the library was a passive rather than an active center that had no sustainable outreach. The Asia Foundation expressed the need for its reorganization and expansion into a modern legislative information center (LIC) with research, documentation, and library units, headed by a full-time director (Lindley 1991). For such a transformation a legislative base was required, that is, the passage of an Act of Parliament designating the parliamentary library as a legal depository of documents and reports published by the government. In addition, the Asia Foundation recommended the creation of the post responsible for acquisitions and documentation for the collection and verification of library materials.

However, expanding library collections with relevant materials would not on its own remedy this shortcoming—steps would also need to be taken to improve the library's internal capacity and technical infrastructure by providing a comprehensive bibliographic database, accession lists, and an effective information retrieval system based on improved information communication technology (ICT) to facilitate literature searches. The maintenance of such a database would require specialized computer software such as that provided by the global tech giant UNISYS. Such a system was being utilized by the parliaments of Nepal, Sri Lanka, and Thailand. Developed by UNESCO, it was generally provided free of cost to parliamentary libraries in developing countries simply on the request of the parliamentary secretary to the Director General of UNESCO (Lindley 1991). The parliament library staff would, of course, require specialized training in order to use this or any other computerized bibliographic system (ibid.: 9–10).

Based on this recommendation, the parliamentary library in Bangladesh was refashioned as an LIC with a full-time director (again, a male official on deputation) as part of the reorganization scheme, although it has yet to reach the standard laid out in the report. The UNDP-funded SPD project later provided the Secretariat LIC with furniture, books, equipment, and a website. With the help of the project team's technical expertise, the LIC has now sorted and indexed its extensive holdings of around 100,000 items, including rare historical documents. Print materials have been bar-coded and online catalog facilities set up. Over 20,000 pages have been scanned and stored electronically. The LIC has a dedicated 'MP's reading room' equipped with computers with access to the internet and individual e-mail accounts—and a parliamentary website has also been established allowing Bangladeshi MPs to connect with the global parliamentary network. Despite all these works done, the LIC is still in a haphazard condition after the end of the projects because of very poor information management system of the parliament secretariat. In 2006, two assistant research officers were recruited by the PSC, although one of them subsequently left his job and joined the social welfare department of the government. Library materials like books, journals, and reference materials and other required information are not properly classified or annotated nor arranged in any systematic order, and the retrieval system is very weak without a bibliographic database. To date, there has not been a full implementation of the Asia Foundation's recommendation to convert the parliamentary library into a modern legislative center, although work is ongoing. One notable initiative is the USAID-funded PRODIP project to make further improvements to the parliamentary library in collaboration with BRAC University in Dhaka. BRAC University is contracted to establish an online archive of parliamentary debates that took place during the Eighth and Ninth Parliaments and install a server in the parliament library (USAID–PRODIP Project 2015).

Research and Documentation

An MP must be able to multi-task. He/she has to legislate, amend laws and the constitution, conduct oversight of the executive, scrutinize government spending, bridge the gap between parliament and constituents, engage and supervise work in his/her constituency, and receive and resolve complaints from constituents. While doing all this, every MP must attend regular parliamentary sessions and scheduled committee meetings, listen to the grievances of individual voters and redress their grievances as far as they can. Hence, every MP is confronted with a daunting challenge when they prepare for parliamentary business. They perform all these functions as representatives of the people and must ensure that the executive implements policies in accordance with the support of parliament. Just how satisfactorily they can perform these roles in the legislative process and monitor the implementation of policies and programs depends to a great extent on their access to authoritative and reliable information. For the successful execution of these functions, MPs need time and access to objective, non-partisan, and precise materials that present a "synthesis and analysis of the relevant facts necessary for them to intervene effectively on public policy issues addressed by a parliament" (www.IPU.org). The time needed to gather the necessary documents, facts, figures, and statistics to prepare statements in the House and in committees is extremely limited to MPs. If an MP has to spend hours, sometimes days, just to trace out facts, statistics, and quotations or historical references to prepare a House statement, they are unlikely to discharge the mandate bestowed on them effectively. An MP who is better fed with authoritative information for each distinctive type of work from the parliament research and documentation services can do his/her job more effectively. Research and documentation services are thus the bedrock of an effective parliament. In such a scenario, MPs can obtain independent, neutral, non-partisan, and balanced analyses of facts and figures from the dedicated parliamentary research and documentation office of the secretariat. It is the responsibility of the secretariat to prepare documents of varied ranges to enable members to carry on informed public debates and to effectively perform legislative and oversight work. From two weeks before the convening of a parliamentary session, the research section would switch its attention and efforts to preparing briefs for the MPs (Chowdhury 1997: 29).

A parliament's capacity to extend research services to MPs varies greatly from country to country. Parliaments in advanced democracies have established research services, developed over the course of several years, and can thus provide a satisfactory service. However, many parliaments in developing countries aspiring to establish or expand such a service struggle to move forward, often due to a lack of democratic continuity or basic infrastructure and resources. An independent research capacity helps strengthen parliament's autonomy as a premier organ in relation to the executive and other institutions that are part of a democratic system (www.ipu.org). Its capability in providing independent research can enable a real check on executive policy-making. Parliaments that receive comprehensive research support on legislation and oversight have succeeded in establishing supremacy over the executive and helped to consolidate their democracies. Figure 4.1 describes the key phases in establishing a research service in parliament.

A UNDP needs assessment conducted in 1997 made a strong case for establishing a full-fledged training and research institute called the Institute of Parliamentary Studies for institutional and operational capacity development of the Parliament/Secretariat. The proposed institute would be charged with providing a specialized legislative, research, and technical support service to MPs in order to augment their skills in parliamentary practice and legislative work. The training would take the form of a year-round program of skills enhancement for both MPs and Secretariat staff which would focus on ROP, parliamentary practices, techniques of parliamentary control, oversight of the executive, the budget, and the roles of the prime minister, Speaker of the House, Leader of the Opposition, and

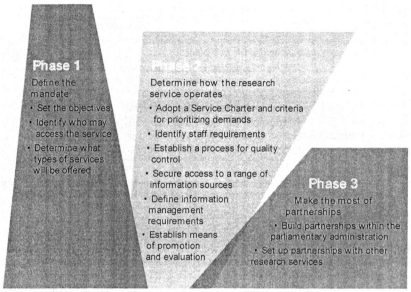

This document highlights the different considerations associated with these phases of planning.

Fig. 4.1 Establishing a parliamentary research service: key phases. (Guidelines for parliamentary research services, www.ipu.org)

the shadow cabinet. In addition, it would cover public policy issues including those related to gender equality, good governance, macroeconomic issues, and popular perceptions about MPs and Parliament (in the form of feedback from the public). The institute would undertake research programs on the basis of the carefully assessed needs of Parliament. Additionally, it would provide summary notes, policy analysis, press clippings, and research briefs on specific issues requested by MPs during sessions and committee chairs on a regular basis (Chaudhury 1997: 26–29).

The most crucial consideration was to recruit and appoint staff with the appropriate educational qualifications and experience to perform unbiased analytical work and be able to articulate their research findings orally and in writing at a level commensurate with international publication standards. To this effect, the Asia Foundation recommended that a dozen professional research analysts, two data entry operators, and a team of clerical support staff be assigned to the research and documentation office of the Secretariat (Lindley 1991: 11). At present, there are just two research officers servicing 350 MPs. Two assistant officers who had been recruited by the PSC have since departed and there is at present no documentation section in the parliamentary library. Over the last twenty-five years, a considerable amount of research has been carried out on the Bangladesh Parliament Secretariat by development partners and academics, including needs assessments, mid-term evaluation reports, final project evaluation reports, transfer of asset documents, books, and articles. However, none of these are traceable as official records in the parliamentary library. What the research section currently provides to members are paper clippings on current issues of national importance and remarks on bills to be considered at the upcoming session. However, the Secretariat does not provide relevant information on similar legislation existing in other countries as a point of reference for members.

Member Liaison

As representatives of the people, MPs must deal with innumerable problems raised by their constituents pertaining to the public services of the various ministries and government departments. To handle this daily rush of business, MPs had to spend a huge amount of time in the Secretariat after ministers. Much of this burden would be relieved if the parliamentarian had institutional support from a dedicated member liaison office of the Secretariat to communicate with their counterparts in the respective ministries and other government agencies. Thus, the fourth and final operational unit recommended by the Asia Foundation report was a member liaison office that would be engaged in public information sharing and determine for MPs the right person to contact to arrange appointments with colleagues in the ministries. Simply by locating the right person and fixing the appointment, the liaison office could save countless hours of time for both members and ministers to devote to more critical parliamentary and governmental business. Many of these matters constitute fairly routine bureaucratic business; since the state bureaucracy carries on government business they are in a position to know which ministry/government departments implement which policy and upon whose door to knock to get a problem solved. The Secretariat could easily facilitate this work. The Asia Foundation recommended a minimum of two to three staff be assigned to a dedicated member liaison office, set up under the joint secretary legislation and given the responsibility for interacting with ministers on MPs' behalf. The member liaison office would assist MPs on a 'time available basis' with typing their official correspondence (Lindley 1991: 12–13). However, at the time of writing the Secretariat has not taken any initiative to establish a member liaison office. Such an office remains an alien concept in the Bangladesh Parliament.

DFID Bangladesh Report, 2000

Nearly a decade after the Asia Foundation report, DFID Bangladesh (2000) formed a mission to make a thorough inquiry into the institutional capacity of Bangladesh Parliament. As the study progressed, a very gloomy picture emerged about the Secretariat as a basic support organization to MPs and standing committees in regard the legislation and oversight. The report, written by David Watson and Deborah Williams, described the organization of the Secretariat as chaotic and its staffing as unbalanced and haphazard. It identified a serious lack of managerial supervision and coordination, except in rare cases such as the sergeant at arms and possibly the library and editing sections. It observed serious levels of inexperience and inadequacy among staff at senior levels managing the administration of the Secretariat. These officials lacked parliamentary experience since most were on deputation from a government ministry and had little exposure to the business of the House. At more senior grades, some functions appear generously staffed while others, including the committee section, appeared to be inadequately staffed to undertake their work effectively (Watson and Williams 2000: 8). The DFID team found little or no concept of staff direction, teamwork, or supervision, and no evidence of setting performance standards or even job descriptions. Questions about supervision tended to bring only irritation (Watson and Williams 2000: 8–9).

After the passage of PSA 1994, it was anticipated that officials on deputation at the mid- and senior-level would gradually diminish as their careers moved on and that Secretariat staff would replace them. However, this did not happen. Even today, the Secretariat is reliant on deputed officials almost as much as it was before 1994. Despite there being sanctioned posts available at Class 1, adequate recruitment has not taken place. In addition, some committee officers/assistant secretaries recruited by the PSC have departed, frustrated with the lack of career progression opportunities. As a result, in recent years even desk-level functionaries, as well as senior decision-making posts, have been deputed from line ministries.

Indeed, this has become the rule, not the exception. However, the fact remains that however competent these deputed officials are in their ministerial posts, a position in the Secretariat holds less attraction since it offers little opportunity to advance political power or gain influence. Many of these officials, it seems, regarded their move to the Secretariat as a makeshift appointment and spent their time in the post looking for an opportunity to leave. The lack of knowledge and expertise in parliamentary affairs at the mid- and senior level in the Secretariat is a consequence of this ingrained reliance on ministerial officials on deputation from the executive branches. The DFID mission team recognized almost two decades ago that the Secretariat needed stability in senior management and expressed disappointment that there was little hope of it being led by suitably experienced staff (Watson and Williams 2000: 8). Against this backdrop, the authors of the report suggested a thorough organizational review of the Secretariat's provision of effective services to MPs and committee chairs. The organizational review of the Parliament Secretariat (2002), which formed one component of the SPD project, and the subsequent review conducted by a UNDP mission were established in response to these recommendations.

UNDP Organizational Review Report, 2002

In 2002 the UNDP Bangladesh branch engaged an organizational review mission to the Bangladesh Parliament to carry out an in-depth inquiry into the systemic and procedural shortcomings of the Secretariat as an organization. After extensive consultation with various stakeholders, the UNDP mission team made the following observation:[4]

> Parliament Secretariat being a traditional bureaucratic structure focused inward on rules and procedures, compartmentalized, structured on a class-based system and essentially frozen in time to a high command control organization with all of the authority for decision making being vested in the Speaker's Office and work being manually done (Buchanan et al. 2002: II).

Shortcomings of the Existing Secretariat

The UNDP mission team identified a number of shortcomings in the organizational structure of the Secretariat in general and deplorable conditions in its CS Wing in particular. In addition, they highlighted inadequacies in the ICT infrastructure for the proper dissemination of information to MPs for debate and legislation in the House and oversight functions of the committees through the LIC. The lack of function-based job descriptions for officers and employees of the Secretariat and the absence of effective delegation procedures which rendered timely and effective decision-making virtually impossible also created a situation where it was difficult to hold any individual employee to account for failing to produce results. The mission held the view that "Parliament secretariat finds it difficult to respond quickly to the needs of Members and cope with changing circumstances particularly emerging from the introduction of information technology" (Buchanan et al. 2002: II). After a thorough inquiry into the organizational structure and functional system, the mission team came up with thirty-three findings against ten core issues and put forward fifty-three recommendations. The core issues were identified as:

1. modernizing the organizational structure of the Secretariat;
2. centralization of decision-making;
3. assignment of work and management of organizational and individual performance;
4. recruitment and performance;
5. human resource legislation/rules/directives/policies/procedures and tools;
6. underrepresentation of women in the Secretariat's workforce;
7. management style, leadership accountability, and communication
8. management and financial planning process;
9. use and impact of technology;
10. office design, space allocation, and accessibility.

Of all thirty-three findings of the review, the overconcentration of both administrative and financial powers in the hands of the Speaker was considered to be calcifying the organization and making it less flexible to evolve with changing needs and priorities. The Speaker had ultimate authority for preparing, reviewing, and approving the budget, and played a dual role in approving all budgetary items at the formulation stage as well as being the cash disbursements officer for most items. Decision-making was top-down; tending to be compartmentalized and unsupportive of a holistic organizational approach. Management style was characterized by risk avoidance and the delegation of authority abysmal.

Human resources recruitment and management was based on class and rank, rather than the requirements of the job and the content and format of job descriptions was severely limited in identifying the skills, knowledge, and personal suitability required for performance and accountability. Top senior management posts in the Secretariat were filled on a contract basis or by deputation, resulting in barriers to career progression for existing Secretarial staff, and these appointments paid no attention to whether or not the candidate met the educational qualifications, skills, and aptitude required for effective performance in the post. In addition, there was no system installed for the online transmission of data and figures between the budget formulation and implementation units, the Secretariat, the recording unit, and the Office of the Comptroller and Auditor General (C&AG). The exact needs of MPs and Secretariat staff were not determined in a more detailed and systematic manner that can reflect their genuine needs (Buchanan et al. 2002: 4–9).

Main Recommendations of the Organizational Review Report

The mission team proposed fifty-three recommendations to address the ten crucial issues mentioned above. These recommendations were targeted toward creating an organization that is more flexible, with the capacity to focus outwards to respond to the needs of Parliament and MPs, that creates an independent and professional group of civil servants, allows for effective administration and managing of organizational resources (money, people, and technology) (Linda et al. 2002: iii). The recommendations emphasized issues such as the adoption of a modern organizational chart; reorganizing the CS Wing; decentralizing decision-making; developing an integrated planning process to set the priorities of the Secretariat; introducing merit-based human resource management and developing full job descriptions for all top-level and mid-level officers incorporating performance standards; using ICT-based management systems; nurturing an open and participative leadership style; rewarding good performance and holding poor performance to account (for all fifty-three recommendations, see Buchanan et al. 2002: iii–iv).

Implementation and Impact of Reform Measures

Based on the recommendations of the Asia Foundation, DFID, and UNDP studies, the Secretariat has published a new organizational chart in 2003—following the implementation of the Organizational Review Report, 2002—which clearly demonstrates its organizational structure and hierarchy of posts, as well as office and staff location, reporting channel, line management and staff relationship, interlinkages of the work units, and existing manpower in the Secretariat (See Annex 2). In order to increase speed in decision-making and service delivery, the administrative hierarchy has been reduced; the joint secretary and additional secretary levels have been levelled in the present organizational hierarchy as heads of each of the seven wings of the Secretariat. Unlike in the ministries, there are no divisions in the Secretariat. There is now the provision to hold monthly coordination meetings of wings, branches, and sections under the direction of the parliamentary secretary. This meeting monitors the progress of work, identifies problems, and sets priorities through open discussion.

With the view to removing systemic bottlenecks and establishing both the operational clarity and the 'institutional memory' of standing committees, such ministerial committees were reorganized into four clusters under the overall supervision of the joint/additional secretary of the committee support CS Wing: (a) finance and industry committees; (b) social sector committees; (c) agriculture & mineral resource committees; (d) regulatory ministries committees (Obaidullah 2011). This reorganization is discussed at length in Chap. 5. To enable the easy retrieval of committee decisions and proceedings of previous parliaments, the SPD project systematically streamlined, classified, and preserved all proceedings, and a long-standing backlog of C&AG Reports in the Public Accounts Committee was cleared by the project's special team of expert consultants.

Further reforms were made to speed up decision-making processes and ensure the quick disposal of files. For the first time, the Secretariat adopted a system of delegating authority in administrative and financial matters (to a limited extent) down to branch level. This would enable each branch and section to manage its own domain more effectively and respond to the needs of MPs more quickly. Job descriptions for all officers and employees, too, have been developed in order to hold post-holders to account for mandated tasks and gradually transform a traditional class-based bureaucracy into a functional and results-based one (Bangladesh Parliament Secretariat Order 2006).

Improving transparency was another key component of reform to the Secretariat. In order to make its operations more transparent, accessible, and responsive to the needs of MPs, the Secretariat is currently being brought into the government's e-governance scheme, which aims to improve information and service delivery and make government departments paperless. The scheme aims to create a comprehensive database in the Secretariat in several domains and will save time for MPs running pillar to post to receive bare minimum clerical services. A sophisticated information database in the parliamentary library will help MPs retrieve necessary information for legislation and debates in the House. It will also enable them to contact parliament electronically and submit notices without being physically present and monitor the status in ministries of the implementation of standing committee recommendations, provided the information is systematically stored and classified. The SPD project established a local area network (LAN) for electronic file sharing to speed up decision-making processes and increase transparency, and the e-governance scheme aims to electronically link MPs' offices or residence with Parliament. The Secretariat's digital fluency has been further enhanced in recent years with technical assistance from the USAID–PRODIP project (operational 2008–2014), which installed Wi-Fi connections, a new interactive website, and a digital display screen management system (USAID 2014 Bangladesh). It also installed a motorized projection screen at the entrance and closed-circuit television (CCTV) cameras in and around parliament building for strengthened security. The introduction of an human resource management (HRM) database to store personal records securely would modernize the Secretariat, while a financial management database would ensure transparent transactions within each branch and wing and enable more realistic and needs-based budgeting. E-governance would also minimize commonly-made allegations against the Bangladesh government for being overly centralized, sluggish, and unresponsive to the needs of the public (Obaidullah 2011).

A notable improvement in Secretariat services since 1994 has been the establishment of a 'budget help desk' in 2015 to better involve MPs in budget debates. The active and informed participation of MPs in budget discussions demands far-reaching support from budget analysis services and independent experts. Budget analysis offices provide non-partisan, objective analysis on the budget contents in relation to the prevailing economic situation of the country in order to facilitate parliamentary deliberations on the national budget (Anderson 2005; Bachrach 2008). The Secretariat made a modest start with around ten officers assigned to the help desk to assist MPs with budget analysis. Later, it was serviced by consultants from the Ministry of Finance, engaged by the USAID–PRODIP project.

An objective and exponential analysis of the organizational structure, legal provisions, and logistics for increasing its autonomy, power, and resources (www.IPU.org) it is obvious that parliament is better placed in 2018 compared to the situation prevailed in 1990. In that earlier era, Parliament itself and numerous members of the Bangladeshi development community conducted needs assessments and identified several problems. As we have seen, from about 2000 onwards several reform measures were implemented (Obaidullah 2011) and it is no exaggeration to say that many of the shortcomings identified by the Asia Foundation, DFID, and UNDP studies were addressed in the SPD project report. The question remains, however, is the Secretariat today in the position to provide efficient services to MPs and committees which it so evidently was not in the 1990s?

The studies mentioned anticipated that a modernized Secretariat with highly professionalized personnel, recruited on the basis of a revised human resource policy, should be capable of rendering efficient services to MPs and committees. After all, a reorganized CS Wing divided into four clusters would be instrumental to creating institutional memory in the committees, and the implementation of the suggested staffing pattern would facilitate better management and coordination of standing committees' oversight functions. The delegation of authority and introduction of an ICT Branch would enable the Secretariat to quicken the transaction of business. Delegating authority in financial and administrative matters down to deputy secretary level would free up the Speaker to give more time to concentrate on legislative issues (Buchanan et al. 2002: 218–220). The ICT Branch would expedite the decision-making process, and quickly communicate the C&AG financial information about the operating costs of wings, branches, and sections of the Secretariat. It would also disseminate parliamentary knowledge and coordinate the planning and monitoring of Secretariat business smoothly to produce organizational results.

In 2017, after more than two decades of reforms initiatives, the author interviewed a sample of MPs and committee chairs and asked whether they felt they received satisfactory services from the Secretariat in regard to legislation, debates, and oversight. Every respondent expressed their dissatisfaction with the Secretariat and indicated that it is still falling short of this goal.[5] One of the main reasons for Parliament's apparent inability to sustain operational efficiency in the secretariat is the failure to implement the core recommendation of the 1997 UNDP needs assessment report—the establishment of an independent Institute of Parliamentary Studies to enhance MPs' skills in parliamentary practice and legislative work and develop specialized legislative, research, and technical support services (Chowdhury 1997: 26). There are several reasons for this. The reformers of Bangladesh's Parliament remain outsiders to the situation they are trying to improve. They have no power, position, or status to influence those who can change things; or else they have no access to those with political influence, or they have no impact on the people who must be convinced. When the reformers propose worthwhile measures or intend to take action they soon discover how extremely conservative administrative systems are regardless of the recognized value of their suggestion (Caiden 1976: 142).

The USAID–PROGATI project made a comparative study in 2010 of Parliament's capacity in oversight and scored the Secretariat at 1.83 on a 0–4 scale against set criteria of sufficient skills and knowledge to support parliamentary oversight of the national budget (PROGATI 2010: 9). The study identified non-implementation of the PSA 1994 and Recruitment and Promotion Rules 2001 as chiefly responsible for the Secretariat's inefficiency. It also observed that as long as the Secretariat is managed by ministerial officials on deputation, MPs and committees cannot expect any improvement in services. Since MPs do not have personal staff, and services from the Secretariat remain minimal, they have little choice to long hours gathering information on government policies and administration and preparing speeches on floor statements and committee meetings themselves. Put bluntly, if democracy in Bangladesh is to be meaningful and a fact of national life, the Secretariat must afford all members of the Treasury and opposition benches, within reasonable boundaries, an opportunity to participate in the legislative and oversight duties of the House. One way to involve MPs in the legislative and oversight process effectively is by providing adequate information at their disposal via the Secretariat.

It is worth mentioning that the efficiency and effectiveness of any organization is dependent upon proper management of the system, sustaining the progress made, and keeping up with the demands of an ever changing world. Under increasing pressure from the donor community, the Bangladesh Parliament enacted the Bangladesh Institute of Parliamentary Studies (GOB 2001) BIPS Act 2001 to establish an institution in the guise of the Bureau of Parliamentary Studies and Training in India. The BIPS

Act is meant to institutionalize the project activities through the establishment of the BIPS as a full-fledged training and research institute of parliament.[6] The Bangladesh Parliament, however, remained indifferent to giving effect to the Act even after its notification in the official gazette for immediate establishment—it simply never considered institutional capacity-building and HRD to be of prime concern. The author's personal experience in the project management at UNDP and USAID Bangladesh suggests that the capacity development initiatives undertaken as part of the technical assistance programs discussed above ground to a halt of the end of the projects' lifespans. In fact, over the last two decades organization development and human capacity enhancement were sponsored by development partners through their respective projects. At the culmination of these projects, many of the facilities and tasks recommended had been accomplished—the library retrieval system and classification of committee proceedings for instance—but many were not or have since simply ceased to operate, for example the budget analysis services. So long as the SPD project was in operation, the proposed BIPS provided training and research support to MPs and Secretariat staff was a component part of it and performed all tasks vested in it by the BIPS Act 2001. However, with the exit of the SPD project in 2007 all activities carried out in the name of BIPS ceased to exist. The Asia Foundation and DFID very clearly pointed out that too much reliance on the deputed officials is the root cause of the inadequacies of the Secretariat particularly at the middle and senior management level. The UNDP organizational review report suggested diminishing this reliance on deputed officials in phases. However, at the cost of efficiency, the Secretariat still retains this practice today. Chapter 8 of this book will analyze the problem of capacity and HRD in the Bangladesh Parliament and Secretariat in more detail. We will also shed more light on this issue in Chap. 10, which looks at the present state of Parliament and democracy in Bangladesh, and seek to answer why the Secretariat has failed to improve efficiency even after a long series of reform initiatives by several development partners.

Notes

1. "Parliament shall have its own Secretariat. Parliament may, by law, regulate the recruitment and conditions of service of persons appointed to the secretariat of parliament. Until provision is made by Parliament the President, after consultation with the Speaker, make rules regulating the recruitment

and condition of service of persons appointed to the secretariat of parliament, and rules so made shall have effect subject to the provisions of any law" (Article 79).
2. Under the provision 6(2) of the Parliament Act 1994, the Parliament Secretariat Commission created the new B&IT wing. At present, the Secretariat comprises seven wings. See the Office Order of HR Wing, April 5, 2011.
3. A view about public service management in Bangladesh shared by the World Bank report, "Bangladesh—Government that Works: reforming the public sector" (1996), and further corroborated by TIB in their study at field level in 2007.
4. The UNDP mission team consulted the senior members of Parliament and the Secretariat, including the Speaker of the House, the Deputy Speaker, chief whips, government and opposition MPs, and top-rank officials in the Secretariat.
5. This conclusion is based on interviews with MPs and committee chairs in February and March 2017, as well as information gathered through a structured questionnaire.
6. Project activities included among others:

- Orientation program of new MPs after parliament elections
- Holding seminars for the members and standing committees
- Organizing training and refresher courses for the secretariat staff.

Project management thought that after the end of the project, BIPS would take over these programs that would help the Parliament to establish self-sustained capacity development programs.

References

Anderson, B., "The Value of a Nonpartisan, Independent, Objective Analytic Unit to the Legislative Role in the Budget Preparation", IMF, XVII Regional Seminar on Fiscal Policy. The Role of Parliament in the Fiscal Policy Formulation, January, 25, 2005, pp. 39–40

ATM Obaidullah (2011) "Reorganization of Standing Committees on Ministries of Bangladesh Parliament: A Quest for Increasing Operational & Institutional Efficiency", South Asian Survey, Vol. 18 (2)

Bachrach, E. (2008) Bangladesh Parliament Secretariat Budget Analysis and Monitoring Unit (BAMU) Needs Assessment and Recommendations Report, April, Dhaka

Bangladesh Parliament Secretariat Order (2004) Delegation of Authority to the Parliament Secretariat officials, Dhaka

Bangladesh Parliament Secretariat Order, September, 10, 2006
Buchanan, L. et al. (2002) Organizational Review of Parliament Secretariat, UNDP: Dhaka
Caiden, G. E. (1976), "Implementation—the Achilles Heel of Administrative Reform", in Leemans, A.F. (ed), Management of Change in Government, The Hague: Martinus Nijhoff
DFID: David Watson and Deborah Williams (2000) Support to Parliamentary Committees in Bangladesh, DFID Bangladesh. Dhaka
GOB (2001) Bangladesh Institute of Parliamentary Studies (BIPS) Act, Dhaka
GPRB, (Government of the People's Republic of Bangladesh). *The Constitution of the People's Republic of Bangladesh* (Dhaka, Ministry of Law, Justice and Parliamentary Affairs, 1998)
Parliament Secretariat Act 1994, Act N. 8, Bangladesh Gazette Extraordinary, May 18, 1994
PROGATI (2011) Promoting Accountability, Transparency and Integrity (PROGATI), An USAID financed and Development Alternative Inc (DAI) administered project
The Asia Foundation: Lindley, J. A. (1991) Needs Assessment of the Institutional Development : Needs of the Parliament of Bangladesh, Dhaka
UNDP: Chowdhury, N. (1997) Sangsad Unnayan Prokalpa (BGD/96/017, Implementation Plan of on Strengthening of the Parliament, Dhaka
UNDP: Buchanan et al. (2002) Organizational Review of Bangladesh Parliament Secretariat, Strengthening Parliamentary Democracy BGD/97/003, Mission Report, Dhaka
USAID (2008) Bangladesh: Promoting Governance, Accountability, Transparency and Integrity (PROGATI), Dhaka
USAID: Bangladesh (2014) Promoting Democratic Institutions and Practices (PRODIP program USAID Cooperative Agreement No. 388-A-0010-00092-00 Asia Foundation), Dhaka
World Bank (1996) Government That Works Reforming Public Sector, Dhaka

CHAPTER 5

Making Parliamentary Standing Committees Effective: Minimizing Systemic Constraints

Origin of Standing Committees[1]

In the previous chapter, we briefly discussed the remarkable disagreement among academics and policy analysts on the issue of Westminster parliament's influence on policy in comparison with the Congressional body in the presidential system. Several critics hold the view that "the U.S. Congress and the British Parliament serve as the emblematic examples of a strong Congress and weak parliament respectively" (Kreppel 2014 cited by Russell and Cowley 2015). Mezey (1979) considers the US Congress an example of an 'active' legislature; whereas most legislatures in parliamentary systems are merely 'reactive.' Even the British Parliament is no exception. In the 'Westminster' system, power is heavily concentrated in the executive and the legislature is submissive (Lijphart 2012). Such categorization helped establish the academic discipline of public policy. It viewed parliaments as relatively peripheral actors that approve executive policies largely formulated and negotiated elsewhere. However, this debate has gradually faded away with the growth of parliamentary committees, which extended the scope for parliament to be more engaged in the policy cycle.

The growth of standing committees on ministries in most Westminster parliaments is a relatively recent phenomenon. Committees originated in Britain and had been an influential part of parliamentary business in the nineteenth century, but their scope was increasingly limited in the twentieth century by the growing use of independent inquiries and royal commissions.

In a prolonged debate between backbenchers and the parliamentary leadership that lasted between 1965 and 1979, concerns were raised the balance between the executive and parliament was weighted too heavily toward the former. Backbench members had traditionally deferred to party leadership and followed party dictates. However, when they showed a tendency to defy the party line and vote independently of party allegiance if their advice was ignored (Ahmed 2007: 63), the party leadership was compelled to find alternative means to give them an opportunity to engage more in the parliamentary process. This situation paved the way for the creation of a new set of institutional arrangements to get backbenchers involved more actively and constructively in the policy cycle. One important way to do so was to set up a network of committees. On June 25, 1979, following the recommendation of a special Procedure Select Committee (established in 1976), the House of Commons agreed to establish a new system of departmental select committees to scrutinize the expenditure, administration, and policy of government departments. The introduction of the committee system settled the lengthy debate between the Procedure Select Committee and the Leader of the House by striking a balance between parliament and the executive and provide an alternative means of redressing backbenchers' grievances.[2] R.H. Crossman, who had been Leader of the House between 1966 and 1968, had set up six subject committees despite the disagreement of the Procedure Select Committee. The beginning of the 1970s thus marked a watershed in the history of British Parliament for the growth of new backbench assertiveness and activism. The House of Commons created twelve departmental select committees in March 1980. Each committee was assigned with the mandate of monitoring and scrutinizing the expenditure, administration, and policy of one or more government departments. Since then, their numbers have varied with changes in the organization of departments (as of 2017, there are nineteen). However, their jurisdiction in terms of powers, functions, and responsibilities has remained mostly unchanged (Ahmed 2007: 64). The establishment of the departmental select committee system led to changes in parliamentary structures and behavior and was successful in striking a balance between the executive and parliament. Today, they are virtually indispensable to the parliamentary business of the House of Commons. Indeed, Norton observes that "they have added a new dimension to the life of the House of Commons and it is difficult now to imagine life without them" (cited by Ahmed 2007: 64). Russell and Cowley demonstrate that due to committee work, British Parliament is far more influential than has been commonly perceived (Russell and Cowley 2015).

Parliamentary committees in the Indian subcontinent can be traced back to the Bengal Legislative Council Act 1861 though not with the scope of scrutinizing the policy and administration of the colonial government. The Constitution of Bangladesh in 1972 retained the provision under Article 76 for constituting the parliamentary committees. Notwithstanding constitutional sanction and provisions in the ROP, the First Parliament in Bangladesh elected in 1973 did not constitute any standing committees on ministry. However, they were introduced in 1980, one year after the election of the Second Parliament.

Imperatives of Parliamentary Committees

To put it simply, had parliamentary committees not been introduced, MPs would not be equal in their duties, opportunities, and responsibilities. Every MP in representing his/her constituency has an equal mandate and is expected to play a similar role in legislation, oversight, and representational function. As a representative, an MP must reflect the reality on the ground in their constituency and persuade the House to take measures that accord with the collective public will. For that matter, every member has a responsibility to pursue a substantive role in influencing policy decisions, scrutinizing the actions of the executive, departments, and agencies, when parliament is engaged in passing legislation, and overseeing the implementation of policy decisions. It is in the committees where members have ample opportunity to see that government decisions respond to the public will and do not infringe upon civil liberties. The members must "have an active voice in, as well as tangible share" of responsibility for parliament's day-to-day business of legislation and oversight (Obaidullah 2011: 318). However, the role of private members of the Treasury or opposition parties who do not occupy leadership positions and sit on the backbench is limited to not much more than an infrequent speaker on the floor in the House. Moreover, parliamentary time is scarce, and not always in session, so there is inadequate time for every member to discuss every matter in the House. Since the middle of the twentieth century, following World War II, with the advent of the concept of modern welfare state, the nature and activity of government business have undergone fundamental changes in volume and complexity with the changes in philosophy of the state and aspirations of the people. Parliament's regular sessions have become so loaded that it is unlikely to discuss highly complicated matters and thoroughly examine every nook and cranny of legislative bills and or executive business. It is in committees where MPs find the opportunity to scrutinize legislative bills and public spending and inquire into the performance of the government, thus holding the executive to account for programs and policy intentions (Rahman, T. 2008: 67–68). As has been pointed out, "The committee system is one of the parliament's most effective means of monitoring government and is sometimes referred to as the 'essence of the parliamentary system'" (Rush 2009). Committees are a microcosm of the whole House. To oversee or scrutinize the executive's activities is the raison d'être of committees in parliamentary democracies (Longley and Davidson 1998: 1–4 cited by Ahmed 2002). One US congressman has described parliamentary committees as "the eye, the hand and very often the brain of the House" (Quoted in Ahmed and Obaidullah 2007: 1).

Legislative Oversight under the Nigerian Presidential System · xml · Joseph "Yinka" Fashagba PhD. Pages: 439–459. Published online: 06 Nov 2009.

New MPs can gain diverse knowledge and expertise from their senior counterparts, which can help them specialize in different policy areas thus develop professionalism in the legislative and policy process (Emy 1978: 406 cited by Ahmed 2002). Committee engagement provides MPs with insight into the dynamics of government policy and program issues. A well-functioning and powerful committee system keeps MPs busy in the legislative and oversight process and equips them (Chowdhury 1997: 13; Rush 1983: 151 in Ahmed, N., ibid.) to participate in the governing process more effectively (Jogrest 1993: 126 in Ahmed, N., ibid.). "Committees allow legislatures to perform numerous functions that otherwise might not have been possible to be conducted at all" (Benda 1997: 17. in L. Longley A.... Agh 17–50, in Ahmed 2002: 29). Perhaps the most frequently-quoted statement on the committee system belongs to Woodrow Wilson who observed in 1885 that "Congress in its committee rooms is Congress at work" became the hallmark of scholarly understanding of US Congressional Committee in the century to follow than it was originally perceived back in 1885" (Quoted in Rahman, T. 2008: 68). The tremendous authority in the USA of the president and cabinet ministers in setting the legislative agenda is counterbalanced by congressional committees (the equivalent to parliamentary committees). The growth of the committee system across the world is the inevitable consequence of profound changes in the theory and practice of government in the late twentieth century. It has been globally acknowledged that committees now constitute the building blocks of parliament (or its equivalent) and act as the main center of legislative and oversight business by scrutinizing bills and policies and by suggesting improvements upon and overseeing the implementation of ministerial programs in both the parliamentary and presidential forms of governments (Longley and Davidson 1998: 2 in Obaidullah 2011: 319).

Legacy of Weakened Accountability

Westminster parliaments that cannot hold the executive to account on matters of policy and administration abnegate their reason for existence. Parliament can exert its authority and hold the executive to account when it is elected by popular vote and the government functions within the limits of constitutional boundaries. In authoritarian and quasi-democratic regimes, where parliament does exist it frequently cannot hold the executive to account. Bangladesh emerged from a long spell of colonial rule as part of British India that was negative in purpose and authoritarian in attitude. British rulers preferred to expand bureaucratic control mechanisms to representative institutions. They believed in the principle that if British authority over the Indian subcontinent was to be sustained it needed an elite bureaucracy (described by British Prime Minister Lloyd George as the 'steel frame of the whole structure') to man the top echelon of administration; civil and judicial services to supervise subordinate bodies, maintain close links with political authority at the center and provinces, and orchestrate them in such a fashion that they work like machine (Houghton 1913 cited by Ahmed 1981). People living in the area now occupied by modern Bangladesh experienced a degree of legislative activity under British rule with the passage of the Bengal Legislative Council Act 1861 and later the Government of India Acts of 1919 and 1935 (see Chap. 2). There also existed some committees, although they had little impact or importance in the context of the colonial government's complete control of the Bengal Legislative Council (Hussain 1991: 9). In reality, the laws passed were nothing more than the orders of the colonial government (Subramaniam cited by Rashiduzzaman 1965: 3). The concept of the rule of law is the core of the administration in Britain, yet they ruled British India more by discretion. More particularly, the wide-ranging discretion of the Governor-General or viceroy and governors of provinces at the center of the colonial administration reigned over any decision of the council of ministers and the legislatures of the provincial and central government of India. As representatives of the British crown, they were not accountable to the provincial and central legislatures respectively (Chowdhury 1968).

After the partition of India, it took Pakistan nine years to adopt its constitution. The executive branch dominated parliament in administering the state despite the fact the Westminster democratic model was accepted in principle as the form of government in the initial phase of independence. The Constitution of Pakistan of 1956 formally adopted the parliamentary form of government with the cabinet responsible to parliament for its actions and policies. However, M.A. Jinnah's decision to become Governor-General and exercise real executive power in the entire management of state affairs, unlike of a ceremonial head, cut clean through the roots of a parliamentary system of government. Much like the British viceroy, Jinnah preferred to exercise unfettered authority and deny accountability to parliament. This was to set the trend for deviant democracy and personal rule in Pakistan. The people of Bangladesh witnessed two dawns of independence. They fought a bloody war of liberation to establish a liberal democratic system but the failure of politicians who have ruled Bangladesh since to break from the British viceregal tradition constitutes one of the main stumbling blocks to developing an effective representative democracy (Hakim 2000: 24). Bangladesh spent two decades under civil and military autocratic rule masquerading as a democratic system. After Ershad's fall and the restoration of democracy in 1991, parliaments democratically elected under NCGs were expected to assert their legislative supremacy and hold the executive to account. However, think tanks and policy-makers quickly realized that parliamentary democracy could not be expected to deliver these objectives and implement the will of the people so long as it remained institutionally impotent and organizationally incapable.

In this context, the Bangladesh Parliament, along with various development partners, set about overhauling its organizational and institutional capacity in general and standing committees in particular. To clarify from the outset a key term, in this chapter 'institutional capacity' refers to: (a) rejuvenating standing committees by organizational readjustments of the CS Wing and committee structure for minimizing systemic pitfalls; (b) revising the rules of procedures governing oversight functions; (c) broadening the sphere of committee activity; (d) augmenting the skills of committee functionaries to facilitate vigilant oversight of the executive (Obaidullah 2011). This chapter shall: (a) identify the underlying causes of weak parliamentary oversight in the pre-restoration period (1972–1990); (b) focus on the findings and recommendations of the reorganization committees engaged at the behest of development partners in the post-restoration period (1991–2015); (c) assess the present status of implementation of the recommendations and state of parliamentary oversight; (d) suggest measures to make further headway in strengthening the oversight capacity of Bangladesh Parliament.

Constitutional and Legal Basis for Parliamentary Committees

Article 76 of the Constitution enshrines in law the provision for creating parliamentary committees. Bangladesh held its first parliamentary election in 1973 and framed its ROP in 1974 (Ahmed 1998). Since then, the ROP, parliamentary conventions, and the Speaker's rulings have laid the foundation and directives for constituting committees and determining their scope of work how they discharge their mandates (Hasanuzzaman 2007: 41 in Obaidullah 2011). Under Article 76, Parliament can constitute the following standing committees from among its members:

> (a) a public accounts committee; (b) committee of privileges; (c) such other standing committees as the rules of procedure of Parliament require (GOB, Article of the Constitution; see also Obaidullah 2011: 320). Furthermore, clause 76(2) accords standing committees with the mandate to:
> (a) examine draft bills and other legislative proposals;
> (b) review the enforcement of laws and propose measures for such enforcement;
> (c) in relation to any matter referred to it by Parliament as a matter of public importance, investigate or inquire into the activities or administration of a Ministry and require it to furnish, through an authorized representative, relevant information and to answer questions, orally or in writing (ibid.)

Despite the clear constitutional sanction and subsequent provision in the ROP framed in 1974, the First Parliament elected in 1973 did not set up any ministerial standing committee. The Second Parliament, elected in 1980, established thirty-six specific standing committees on different ministries by incorporating Rule 246 of the ROP (Obaidullah 2011). Subsequently, changes to some ministries and reorganization of others led to the amendment of the ROP in 1988 whereupon the list of specific standing committees introduced by the First Parliament was dropped. Rule 246 stated that Parliament shall appoint the standing committee on each ministry after the inauguration of each new Parliament as soon as possible. However, in some cases committees were appointed so late that ministerial accountability to Parliament became for that long period before appointment virtually non-existent.[3] This situation forced Parliament to amend Rule 246 in 2006 to incorporate a provision for appointing standing committees on each ministry within the third session of every new parliament (Rule 246 BJS; Obaidullah 2011).

On the basis of how committees are appointed, traditionally Parliament set up three types of committees: standing committees, select committees, and special committees. Standing committees exist so long as Parliament exists; they are not dissolved before the end of its tenure. Special and select committees are temporary bodies; they cease to exist when their job is completed. "Standing committees again are classified into number of categories, most important of which are Departmentally Related Parliamentary Committees (DPCs)—those that parallel different department/ministries. The other categories are scrutinizing committees, financial committees, and House committees" (Ahmed 2002: 131 cited by Obaidullah 2011). Broad groupings of the standing committees at Bangladesh Parliament are shown in the table below (Table 5.1).

The method of appointments, their composition, tenure, and mode of operations are laid down in the ROP. The ROP has been so designed that committees can work vigorously and effectively as organs of Parliament. A committee can act upon its policy and expediency and regulate its sittings and the modus operandi. Rule 2002 gives authority to a standing committee to "send for persons, papers and records. It can take evidence in normal fashion, or under oath. Procedures are laid down for examination of witnesses" (Rule 202 BJS). It is now the responsibility of Parliament to make committees real watchdogs (Siddiqi et al. 1994: 34–35 cited by Obaidullah 2011). Rules 203–213 administer how committee records and proceedings

Table 5.1 Standing committees at Bangladesh Parliament

Nature of committees	Number of committees (Parliament-wise)								
	First	Second	Third	Fourth	Fifth	Seventh	Eighth	Ninth	Tenth
Ministerial committees	–	36	–	35	35	35	35	39	39
Finance & audit committees	3	3	–	3	3	3	3	3	3
Other standing committees	8	8	4	8	8	8	8	8	8
Special/select committees	3	4	2	2	7	2	–	3	–
Total	14	51	6	48	53	48	48	53	50

Source: Adopted from Nizam Ahmed (2002) and the Bangladesh Parliament Secretariat

of committee meetings shall be maintained, evidence taken, witnesses examined, and reports prepared. Committees can publish their reports in full or in part. The report of a committee has to be considered confidential before it is submitted to Parliament (BJS Rule 210). The ROP makes the provision for taking evidence in camera. Of course, there are always demands for a public hearing from civil society organizations (CSOs). Very recently, under the auspices of the USAID–PRODIP Project (2008–2014), seven select standing committees of the Ninth Parliament managed to organize a good number of public hearings on a pilot basis. With the end of the project, this practice predictably ceased to exist (Obaidullah 2011; see also Final Evaluation Report of the USAID–PRODIP Project 2014).

Organization of Parliamentary Committees

Specific rules determine how many members shall constitute a standing committee. There are as many sets of rules as there are standing committees. Except for the Business Advisory Committee, the Public Accounts Committee, and the Library Committee, all standing committees comprise ten members. The Public Accounts Committee and Business Advisory Committee both have fifteen members and the Library Committee has the least number of members with eight. In the case of select or special committees, it is the discretion of the House to decide how many members shall comprise it. Parliament, as such, appoints standing committees in its first session by a motion made by the House (BJS Rule 188). No member can be appointed to a committee if said member has a personal or pecuniary interest likely to be a real cause of bias in the discharge of their business (Rules of Procedure 2007, Rule 188).

Until the Ninth Parliament was elected, traditionally chair positions of all standing committees including Public Accounts Committee were held by the ruling party. It was not by default of the opposition; rather, Parliament was reluctant to offer the positions. Since the Ninth Parliament, opposition members secured chair positions of standing committees on a pro rata basis. Parliamentary committees in advanced democracies are expected to carry out their business on a cross-party basis, yet in Bangladesh, it is frequently the case that ruling party members recourse to partisan interests. The chairperson of a committee is usually elected by the members of that committee unless designated by the House. If the chairperson ceases to be a member of the committee—whether due to becoming a minister, state minister, or deputy minister, or if he/she has any cause of personal bias—and remains absent from any sitting of the committee or is incapacitated to perform their duties owing to physical and mental infirmity, the committee is empowered to appoint another member to act as chairperson (Obaidullah 2011; Rule 191 (2).

INCREASED SCOPE AND REVISION OF THE RULES

Strengthening the parliamentary committee system received due attention as a concomitant feature of the fall of military autocracy and restoration of democracy in 1991. The democratically elected Fifth Parliament, the first in the new era, returned to the Westminster model as a result of the passage of the Twelfth Amendment. The Asia Foundation's needs assessment study of Parliament in 1991 (discussed in Chap. 4) observed that "in view of the shift made to parliamentary system the mandate of parliament has changed and for that matter the Rules of Procedure that relates to committees and oversight on the executive should appropriately be revised as soon as possible" (Lindley 1991: 8; Obaidullah 2011). The ROP, however, does not remain static; in fact, there is a need to update both rules and procedures of parliament at periodic intervals. One British parliamentarian underscored the raison d'être for regular updates to rules of procedure thusly:

> Parliament dies if it does not update its procedures. Procedures are muscles and sinew of parliament. If we do not exercise this muscle and keep it in good trim for contemporary challenge, then we shall have no real job to do. (Cited by Norton 1985: 163; see also Ahmed 2002: 73)

Against this backdrop, a subcommittee was formed in January 1997 with a definite mandate for making appropriate revisions on desired changes to the ROP, particularly relating to the committee system (Choudhury 1997: 14–15; Obaidullah 2011). The subcommittee identified the following shortcomings of the committee system as it was operating in Bangladesh at the time:

> Ministerial committees still could not be freed from the executive control while the respective minister held the chair of the committees; executive does not care about committee recommendations as committees have no authority to enforce their decisions; the public has no knowledge about committee proceedings; neither do they have any access to them; financial accounting is too slack to make any impact on the fidelity of the executive expenditure. (Obaidullah 2011: 323)

Fifth parliament constituted a three-member cross-party parliamentary team with L.K. Siddiqi as its chair which visited the British Parliament to see for themselves the oversight system of the British Parliament. They opined that that ROP as such in Bangladesh parliament were not fully consistent with our new parliamentary system and it needs amendment in order to make parliament more effective (Obaidullah 2011). The committee held that Standing Committees on Ministries (SCMs) 'should possess propitious role in regard to scrutinizing the policy and administration of the government 'to make itself driving force of parliament' (Siddiqi et al. 1994; Obaidullah 2011: 35). The committee recommended that the rules should be amended in commensuration with the spirit of the constitution and changed political mandate of government. For that matter certain rules like 202, 203 246, 247 and 248 should be revisited to strengthen the committee's role of scrutiny. (Obaidullah 2011: 324)

The subcommittee suggested that the success of institutional reform and realization of a parliament that delivers on its mandate would be unsuccessful unless the functions of committees and of the whole House were revised along with the associated rules that govern them (Chowdhury 1997: 6–17). It put forward several measures to make ministerial committees independent of the executive (Obaidullah 2011; Siddiqi et al. 1994: 35).

Since the restoration of democracy, significant changes have been made to the operational mode and scope of committee activity. The revision of the ROP in the Fifth Parliament in the spirit, if not the word, of the recommendations of the cross-party team in 1992 widened the scope of committee work to conduct oversight of the executive. They can now scrutinize and review the functions of ministries they parallel and investigate irregularities and complaints, making necessary recommendations. However, ministers holding the chair of standing committees in the Fifth Parliament did more to deter members from conducting objective and unbiased examinations of ministerial activities. This was addressed by the Seventh Parliament who stipulated that committee chairs should be held by MPs who are not concurrently government ministers (Rules of Procedure, 247 [2]). This amendment to the ROP represented a significant step toward committees functioning as genuine watchdogs. And, as mentioned earlier, this was followed in 2008 by an amendment that stipulated the formation of standing committees within the third session of every new parliament, which had a tremendous impact on improving parliamentary accountability. Thus, since 2008 standing committees have formed in the first session of the new parliament elect.

Secretarial Services to Parliamentary Committees

Committees can discharge their business effectively when they are efficiently supported by secretariat staff. In the British Parliament, each committee has four to five dedicated support staff. These staff members provide information, documentation, and analytical assistance to the committees in the scrutiny of legislative bills, ministerial operations, and investigations of any event. In order to facilitate committee business, the staff collects necessary data in regard to ministerial programs, their implementation status, the implementation of previous recommendations, quarterly expenditure reports of the ministry concerned, and key performance indicators to measure the success of executive programs. In addition, when the committee decides to investigate any complaint, it should prepare background papers. The staff should examine the volumes of papers the committee receives from interest groups, assimilate those opinions, and place them before the committee chair. The main service the committee can render is smooth and unobstructed communication with the ministry it shadows. The Procedure Select Committee in the UK had emphasized the need for staff support to committee members. The report noted "the House must recognize that unless members are provided with information services and staff support capable of relieving them of much of the routine and essential preparatory work, they will not be able to do their work properly whether under present arrangements or under any changed situation" (Obaidullah 2011: 325; also see Siddiqi et al. 1994). The skills and expertise of committee staff should be matched with the nature of the jobs the committee has to shoulder.

In the Bangladesh Parliament, so far as the ROP is concerned, the secretary of the Secretariat is the ex-officio secretary of all standing committees. In practice, however, he/she delegates this responsibility to officials working under his/her supervision. The normal practice is that this responsibility is carried out mostly by committee officers/assistant secretaries (heads of sections) and deputy secretaries (heads of branches) under the overall supervision of the joint/additional secretary who heads the CS Wing. In some cases, the joint/additional secretary also act as secretaries to the committees. The committee secretary acts as a channel of communication with committee chairs and ministry officials, monitors the production of committee proceedings on time and, if necessary, acts upon the quality of committee minutes before they go to the committee chairs for approval. He/she constitutes the institutional memory of the committee. Each committee chair has a private secretary, who is a 'privileged staff' (see Chap. 8), who provides personal assistance to the chairperson to discharge his/her mandate. In many Westminster systems, committee support staff are permanent. However, in Bangladesh Parliament, they are on rotation at the will of senior management, and with changes in regime normally comes changes in support staff personnel.

At present, parliamentary committees are organized under the CS Wing of the Secretariat, which is headed by a joint secretary. The wing is divided into four branches and fifteen sections. The deputy secretary usually acts as head of a branch, and a section is headed by a committee officer/assistant secretary. Secretarial support to the committee chair is provided by a group of officers—the committee officer/assistant secretary and staff from the reporting cell. In addition, an administrative officer, a stenotypist/office assistant, and an Member of the Lower Support Services (MLSS) all support the business of committee meetings. In some cases, the private secretary to the committee chairperson discharges the role of committee secretary. The functional support that committee chairs receive from the Secretariat is shown in the Fig. 5.1 below.

The UNDP Final Evaluation report of Strengthening Parliamentary Democracy project (SPD) by Sue Nelson in (2006), discussed in the previous chapter, held that in Bangladesh Parliament, the secretarial services available to committee chairs is conspicuously low due to haphazard staffing patterns and the low competency of employed staff. Again, too many standing committees and subcommittees were serviced by too few and often inexperienced staff.[4] At present, the Secretariat staffs twenty-two committee sections for servicing fifty standing committees, which includes thirty-nine ministerial committees. A committee section comprising only three staff has to provide direct support to up to three ministerial committees. The number of staff for recording committee proceedings is entirely inadequate considering the volume of work (Choudhury 1997: 23). Furthermore, there is a clear duplication of responsibility among staff engaged in committee work, which reduces the role of the committee officer to only convening meetings. Organizational pitfalls and the disarrayed staffing of the CS Wing thus constitute a serious hurdle to the effective oversight of parliament (Watson and Williams 2000). The UNDP organizational review that followed two years later painted a gloomy picture

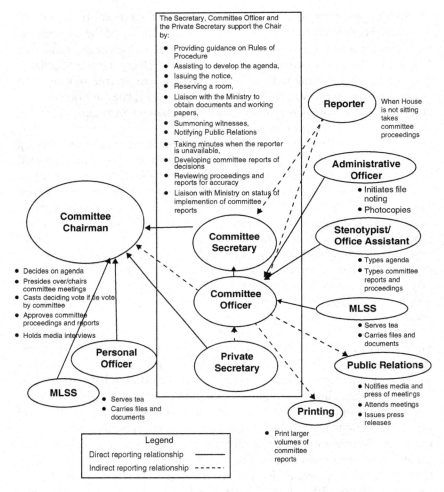

Fig. 5.1 Existing functional staff support provided by the Secretariat to committee chairs

of the secretarial services provided by the committee section. The report summarized the functions of what it called merely administrative assistance:

1. developing the agenda;
2. issuing the notice;
3. arranging for meeting rooms;

4. requesting working papers from the ministries and distributing them to committee members;
5. arranging for witnesses;
6. writing proceedings if a reporter is unavailable;
7. writing decisions of committee meetings;
8. distributing committee proceedings and minutes (Obaidullah 2011: 327).

Systemic Weaknesses in the Committee System

Parliament cannot keep effective oversight of the executive in a vacuum. It must refurbish parliamentary committees and establish an appropriate committee structure with adequate research and analytical services, a staffing pattern based on the rationale of the job, and personnel appropriately equipped with specific skills. Competencies need to be matched with objectives to ensure the effective delivery of outputs, and ultimately the strengthened accountability of the executive. In addition to increased organizational provisions, functionaries must have specialized knowledge of the ROP and understanding of the practices in other Westminster systems. They must have a clear vision of the mandate of the ministry and the committee they work on, the capacity to analyze data and prepare summary notes for the committee meetings, and knowledge of retrieving the precedents of preceding committees (Obaidullah 2011; Buchanan and Ahmed 2004: 10). From this perspective, it is not too much to say that without this the committee system in Bangladesh Parliament was ill-prepared to deliver efficient services.

The Asia Foundation and the UNDP diagnosed a myriad of systemic weaknesses underlying the ineffectiveness of committee operations in the 1990s. The UNDP study (Choudhury 1997) described the committee system at that time as 'mechanical functioning' and underscored the necessity of operationalizing it. The study held that institutional reforms of Parliament called for functional reforms of the committee system as a fundamental issue. A 'right man in the right place' philosophy has to be adhered to in assigning any person in the CS Wing, or its branches and sections. In British Parliament, there exists a separate committee to assess the suitability of all candidates to be inducted as members of standing committees. By contrast, in Bangladesh Parliament, it is the personal choice of the Leader of the House to decide who goes where. Neither the committee chair or members, nor its support staff, are appointed on the basis of any criteria around aptitude, competence, and experience. There is evidence that an appointment was made to the chair of the Public Accounts Committee business person-cum-newly elected MP with no understanding of the inner dynamics of executive business, public finance, and the expenditure management system.

The Secretariat's operational incapacity is further compounded by inadequate logistics, particularly poor library facilities, a lack of research and documentation services, poor performance standards, and a lack of quality committee proceedings. Parliamentary oversight is thus handicapped by innumerable institutional weaknesses: (a) non-existence of guidelines regarding conflicts of interest in MPs; (b) no provision for intercommittee consultations; (c) a dearth of knowledge of the ROP among committee support staff; (d) no uniform pattern of preparing committee proceedings; (e) no guidelines to administer committee–ministry relations; (f) no public access to committee proceedings (Obaidullah 2011).

Consequent to DFID's observations, the UNDP carried out a thorough inquiry of the organizational structure of the Secretariat as part of the SPD Project in 2002. This review took account of the organizational structure, staffing patterns, work procedures, decision-making processes, levels of delegation, and style of management in the Secretariat in general and committee structure in particular. Its findings were not positive. It concluded that the committee structure was in a haphazard state with committees disparately organized no proper coordination among committee functionaries. The system lacked institutional memory. Committee officers were constantly on rotation. For many, placements in the CS Wing would be akin to dumping their career. They considered it preferable to serve as private secretary to politically designated 'very important persons' (VIPs) than to be assigned to a committee: "At present in the tenth parliament, a good number of secretariat's own staff—assistant secretary/committee officers have been engaged with the VIPs as private secretary" (Obaidullah 2011). Despite the acute shortage revealed in most reports in the 1990s and early 2000s, a few well-trained committee officers have been permitted to leave to join VIPs as private secretaries. This only compound the already weak position of parliamentary oversight in Bangladesh.

To try to salvage the committee system from this wreckage, the 2002 UNDP mission recommended its total reorganization into a separate CS Wing under a joint secretary. For improved management and coordination, ministerial standing committees would need to be divided into clusters on the basis of the nature of work of the ministries it serves (Obaidullah 2011). The UNDP Organizational Review Committee recommended four clusters on the basis of broad groupings of functions. Accordingly, parliamentary standing committees were grouped into four clusters along the thematic lines of the work of the ministries (Linda Buchanan et al. 2002; see 'Implementation and Impact of Reform Measures' in Chap. 4). The clustering of committees would take into account the homogeneity of functions, appropriateness of staffing, and establish straightforward reporting relations in order to create the institutional memory of parliamentary committee system. Each cluster would be headed by the deputy secretary of the relevant branch, to be supported by the staff of the committee section, and would act as committee secretary of each committee under his/her cluster. The new system would develop the functional accountability of staff and improve their substantive knowledge of committee work and nourish high levels of professionalism throughout to ensure the effective discharge of committees' chartered functions. The Bangladesh Parliament Secretariat partially accepted the UNDP recommendations and introduced some changes in organizational management. The most important change was the adoption in 2002 of four clusters of standing committees on ministries.

Adoption of the Cluster System

Two years later, in 2004, another UNDP mission emphasized that if clustering was to work, certain changes would need to be made immediately. This included the formation of a core team of support staff to serve each committee chairperson, with specific job descriptions outlined in detail. The core team should comprise the committee secretary, the committee officer, and a public relations officer (Obaidullah 2011). Each member would be assigned distinct responsibilities and held accountable for their fulfillment, but would be strongly encouraged to interact as much as possible and work as a team to deliver results.

1. The team will constitute the institutional memory for the committee functioning and the same team members support different committee chairman over successive sessions of new parliaments.
2. Each team member would have a distinct set of responsibilities for which s/he is accountable while their effective functioning together as a team requires high levels of interaction (Obaidullah 2011: 335) (Fig. 5.2).

Under the proposed reorganization the committee secretary would provide administrative assistance to the chairperson, including organizing

124 A. T. M. OBAIDULLAH

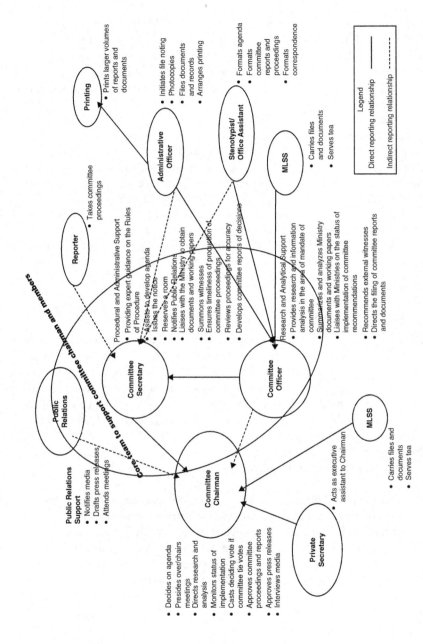

Fig. 5.2 Proposed functional support to committee chairmen

committee meetings and "issuing notice, arranging room, summoning witnesses, making arrangements for reporters, liaising with Public Relations office, liaising with concerned ministry official. In addition, s/he will assist in developing agenda and providing expert guidance on the Rules of Procedure" (Obaidullah 2011). A committee officer would be responsible for preparing a working paper and briefing notes, delivering subject-specific research and analytical services, liaising with ministry staff on the status of implementation of previous recommendations, preserving files, and recording committee proceedings, decisions, and reports. The public relations officer would be responsible for notifying the media of upcoming committee meetings, arranging press releases, and disseminating committee proceedings, decisions, and reports to relevant and interested parties. The existing job descriptions of committee staff overlapped with each other. Hence, the job descriptions of committee secretary, committee officer, and public relations officer would need to be revised to match the proposed reorganized committee structure and functions. It should be the responsibility of the joint secretary of the CS Wing to ensure that the functions of committee officials do not overlap and that the services they render to the committee are of the highest standard. He or she should also monitor the competency profile of key functionaries of the committee section, branch, and wings, note any deficiencies and remedy with training in partnership with the resource development office. This would also include evaluating the impact of training on staff performance so that standards can be continually improved and efficient services rendered to committees.

Modus Operandi of the Clusters

In the present organizational set-up of the Secretariat, the CS Wing falls under the jurisdiction of a joint secretary or, in some cases, an additional secretary. The joint secretary/additional secretary is responsible for providing overall supervision of the branches and sections that constitute the wing and strategic leadership for the efficient management of the committee system (Obaidullah 2011: 329; Bangladesh Parliament Secretariat Order, Job Description 2006). Since the CS Wing is now divided into four clusters, each cluster is put under the supervision of a deputy secretary to coordinate committee activities under his/her branch. The work of the CS Wing that takes place in the committee sections should be led by the committee officer. However, in the context of Bangladesh Parliament, the assistant secretary, or officer of equivalent rank, generally shoulders this responsibility. The committee officer/assistant secretary is supported by reporters to take notes and prepare committee minutes, and more junior clerical staff transcribe the minutes.

The recommendation of the UNDP 2002 review was that the deputy secretary of the branch not only be head of the cluster but also ex-officio secretary of all the committees under that cluster. This would help ensure effective management, operational convenience, and a full awareness on the deputy secretary's part of the reality of work going on within his/her cluster (Obaidullah 2011: 329). However, this recommendation has been totally flouted. In the present-day set-up, the twenty-one officers engaged in secretarial support to committees are neither deputy secretary of the respective clusters nor committee officers/assistant secretaries (ibid). Of the thirty-seven ministerial committees, only sixteen committees of four clusters are supported by the deputy secretary acting as committee secretary. In the case of the rest, officials from outside the CS Wing occupy that position, thus continuing the age-old practice in the Secretariat of engaging officials from outside to act as committee secretaries. This was initially considered an ad hoc arrangement due to the scarcity of the required committee staff. However, in accepting this practice, Parliament has been unable to standardize committee operations and constitute the institutional memory that the UNDP mission envisioned.

Under the present organizational layout, every committee has to conduct its business through at least five stages of approval:

1. committee chair;
2. cluster head;
3. committee officer;
4. reporting cell;
5. committee secretary (ibid.).

The underlying rationale for UNDP's recommendation to place the deputy secretary as ex-officio secretary of all committees under the relevant cluster was that it would enable him/her to be kept informed of the proceedings of each committee meeting. It was also recommended that the relevant minutes and other documentation could be stored in a single repository in the building that houses the Deputy Secretary Committee. This repository would thus constitute the institutional memory of the cluster he/she supervises—the raison d'être for introducing the clustering system to the CS Wing. However, the large number of committees in a cluster made the task difficult for the deputy secretary to act as ex-officio secretary of all committees under his/her jurisdiction. It is an issue of the span of control. The number of committees comprising each cluster varied from eight to fourteen. Fourteen committees were perhaps too many for one deputy secretary to maintain effective oversight. This might well be the reason why so many other bodies were drafted in to lighten the load. However, there are other ways the deputy secretary could have been unburdened, for instance by downsizing the scope of each cluster, without impairing the efficiency that was the purpose of creating clusters in the CS Wing in the first place. Below the supervisory level, the committee officer of each section should be the 'mainstay' of committee functioning. The committee officer is responsible for:

1. notifying the date and venue of the meeting;
2. preparing the meeting agenda and working paper, if any;
3. preparing the minutes of the meeting;
4. placing them before the deputy secretary of the cluster;
5. liaising with the committee secretary;
6. gaining the approval of the committee chair;
7. circulating the minutes among the chair, members, and concerned ministry officials (Bangladesh Parliament Secretariat Order, Job Description 2006).

Given these responsibilities, it is worth asking what substantive role remains for a committee secretary. Or, whether the committee officer really performs the above responsibilities? The current practice of cluster management by officers from all over the Secretariat creates room for a communication gap since the deputy secretary, as the cluster head, may know nothing about the decisions of a committee meeting under his/her cluster where the relevant committee secretary is from beyond the CS Wing. In such a scene of congested bureaucracy, normal reporting relationships break down. The question arises, where the committee secretary is not the deputy secretary for that cluster, who does the committee officer report to after each committee meeting? The prevailing practice is "where committee secretary is anybody other than DS of committee cluster, committee officer reports to the secretary instead of DS Committee cluster thus breaking vertical accountability chain and reporting relations between committee officer and DS cluster" (Obaidullah 2011: 332). Such a communication gap leaves the deputy secretary out of the loop on critical decisions being taken by committee chairs within his/her jurisdiction. Not only is the deputy secretary left in no-man's-land; such a situation creates barriers to building the institutional memory of the CS Wing and weakens Parliament's information retrieval system.

What is clear from all this is that the responsibilities of the committee secretary significantly overlap with that of committee officer, which has had the net effect of reducing the role of the latter in becoming a mainstay of committee functioning as the section head. If the reporting cell/reporter prepares the minutes of the meeting, and about 90% of cases they do, the role of committee officer is stripped down to simply convening committee meetings. The committee officer prepares the minutes only for subcommittee meetings. One of the main objectives behind clustering was to build the institutional provision for committee officers/assistant secretaries to master the bigger picture of the work of the committees to which they are assigned. Under the present practices that I have outlined here, however, this is unlikely to be built. The operational matrix below illustrates the weakness in the present cluster system in terms of staffing patterns (see Table 5.2).

Proposed Reorganization of Clusters

Against this backdrop, should Parliament wish to establish efficiency in the committee cluster system, its staff deployment needs to be rearranged to ensure improved clarity of business and better management of the clusters. Certain changes in the staffing and organizational structure of the clusters may help achieve these objectives.

Regrouping of Clusters

The composition of committees in each cluster is asymmetric; Cluster 2 (Social Sector Committees) is the biggest with fifteen committees, Clusters 3 (Agriculture & Mineral Resource Committees) and 4 (Regulatory Ministries Committees) comprise eleven each, and there are eight in Cluster 1 (Finance & Industry Committees). The managerial burden this places upon the deputy secretary of Cluster 2 to coordinate as ex-officio secretary of the committees could be relieved through an effective reorganization. If a particular cluster or clusters prove to be too large to function effectively, creating a span of control problem for the deputy secretary, they should be regrouped or reshuffled. For example, the SSC cluster may be divided into two groups—Cluster 2 and 2A—and placed under two separate deputy secretaries. In addition, clusters could be headed up by

Table 5.2 Organizational profile of the present cluster system of standing committees

Cluster 1 Finance & Industry Committees (F&IC) Under a Deputy Secretary (DS)	Com support staff	Com Scy	Cluster 2 Social Sector Committees (CCS) Under a Deputy Secretary	Com support staff	Com Scy	Cluster 3 Agriculture & Mineral Resource Committees (AMRC) Under a Deputy Secretary	Com support staff	Com Scy	Cluster 4 Regulatory Ministries Committees (RMC) Under a Deputy Secretary	Com support staff	Com Scy
Public Accounts Committee	Com sec 1 & Reporting Cell (RC)	DS of F&IC	LGRD & cooperatives	Com sec 10 & RC	Joint Secretary (JS) of CS Wing	Agriculture	Com sec 8 & RC	DS of AMRC	Establishment	Petition sec & RC	JS of HR Wing
Committee on Estimates	Com sec 2 & RC	DS of F&IC	Health & family welfare	Com sec 5 & RC	DS of SSC	Water resources	Com sec 9 & RC	DS of Finance	Defense	Com sec 13 & RC	JS of HR Wing
Public Undertakings Committee	Com sec 2 & RC	JS of CS Wing	Primary & mass education	Com sec 7 & RC	Director of reporting	Fisheries and livestock	Com sec 8 & RC	DS of AMRC	CHT Affairs	Com sec 13 & RC	Additional secretary of IPASP Wing
Standing Committee for Finance	Com sec 3 & RC	DS of HR	Education	Com sec 7 & RC	DS of RMC	Energy and natural resources	Com sec 9 & RC	DS of Admin	Home Affairs	Com sec 12 & RC	DS of RMC
Planning	Com sec 3 & RC	DS of F&IC	Social welfare	Com sec 5 & RC	DS of Finance	Environment and forest	Com sec 8 & RC	DS of Finance	Food	Com sec 7 & RC	DS of Legislative draftsman (LD)
Industry	Com sec 3 & RC	DS of F&IC	Labor & employment	Com sec 6 & RC	Director of Planning and Development	Communication	Com sec 10 & RC	DS of Admin 2	Land	Com sec 12 & RC	Director of Planning and Development
Jute	Com sec 3 & RC	DS of F&IC	Women & children affairs	Com sec 6 & RC	DS of SSC	Posts and telecommunications	Com sec 11 & RC	Director Debates	Shipping	Com sec 12 & RC	DS of AMRC

(*continued*)

Table 5.2 (continued)

Cluster 1 Finance & Industry Committees (F&IC) Under a Deputy Secretary (DS)	Com support staff	Com Scy	Cluster 2 Social Sector Committees (CCS) Under a Deputy Secretary	Com support staff	Com Scy	Cluster 3 Agriculture & Mineral Resource Committees (AMRC) Under a Deputy Secretary	Com support staff	Com Scy	Cluster 4 Regulatory Ministries Committees (RMC) Under a Deputy Secretary	Com support staff	Com Scy
Textiles	Com sec 3 & RC	DS of F&IC	Youth & sports	Com sec 3 & RC	Sen legislation draftsman	Shipping	Com sec 12 & RC	DS of AMRC	Law, Justice & Parliamentary Affairs	Com sec 14 & RC	DS of AMRC
			Religious affairs	Com sec 4 & RC	DS of SSC	Civil aviation	Com sec 11 & RC	JS of CS Wing	Foreign Affairs	Com sec 14 & RC	DS of LS
			Cultural affairs	Com sec 5 & RC	DS of Finance	Science & technology	Com sec 9 & RC	DS of AMRC	Commerce	Com sec 15 & RC	JS of CS Wing
			Freedom fighters affairs	Com sec 6 & RC	DS of SSC	LGRD	Com sec 10 & RC	JS of CS Wing	Information	Com sec 15 & RC	DS of RMC
			Disaster management & relief	Com sec 7 & RC	Director of Planning and Development						
			Overseas employment	Com sec 7 & RC	DS SSC						
			Science & technology	Com sec 9 & RC	DS AMRC						
			Housing & public works	Com sec 6 & RC	JS of CS Wing & RC						

Source: Obaidullah 2011, Table 1, pp. 31–32

officers at deputy secretary or the equivalent level from Parliament's own staff. Moreover, heads of wing should be careful that committee secretaries do not rotate too frequently, which is often the case where a deputy secretary on deputation from a ministry is posted as committee secretary but departs very soon after. A competent and trained officer is unlikely to be replaced right away. This problem could also be minimized by reassigning some of the committees among other clusters where they fit in thematically. This will help establish a balance of work among the four clusters. For example, food and land committees might be reassigned to the AMRC cluster, the Commerce Ministry Committee to the F&IC cluster, and the Information Ministry Committee to SSC as they seem to be more thematically related to the core business of these clusters (Obaidullah 2011).

Reducing the Number of Standing Committees

Unlike other Westminster parliaments, the Bangladesh Parliament has too many standing committees. One of the reasons why is that each ministry has its own ministerial standing committee, in addition to eleven other standing committees that include the Business Advisory Committee, House Committee, Rules of Procedure Committee, and so forth (Obaidullah 2011). Parliament's thirty-nine ministerial committees could be reduced because, so far as exercising governmental oversight is concerned, their mandates overlap with other critically important committees such as the Public Accounts Committee, the Estimates Committee (EC), and the Government Assurance Committee. The Asia Foundation report observed in 1991 that to a large extent they duplicate each other. Given the complexities of today's world today, the issues and problems that parliament has to deal with are interdisciplinary and sectoral by nature. As a matter of fact, there is hardly any problem the country faces that can be said to fall exclusively into the domain of a single ministry. Therefore:

> Maintaining separate ministerial committees for the purpose of facilitating the formulation and review of public policy are counterproductive. It only tends to fracture rather than comprehensively focus parliament's attention on the multifaceted aspects of major public issues. (Lindley 1991; Obaidullah 2011: 338)

Having considered this situation, the SPD project, operational between 1997 and 2007, recommended abridging the number of standing committees to half their present volume (UNDP; Obaidullah 2011).

Developing Resources to Support Clusters

Committees can function as effectively as they are manned. Since committees perform scrutinizing functions of policy/legislation and programs of the executive, they call for specialized skills and methods to discharge this watchdog function. In order for committees to render efficient services, the Secretariat must take measures to ensure a constant supply of well-equipped and competent staff for maintaining the effectiveness of committees. But under the present HRM policy, the Secretariat is under constant threat of facing a crisis in trained committee functionaries. This risk can be tackled by creating a pool of human resources alongside existing committee staff.

Such a pool should comprise four or five deputy secretaries, up to twenty-five committee officers/assistant secretaries, and a few officers of equivalent rank to deputy secretary considered capable of serving committees as secretaries. Pool members should undergo comprehensive and uniform training program focused on committee functioning, techniques of oversight, and skills augmentation. They could act as fillers to avoid the vacuum caused by the departure of deputed officials or retirement of key functionaries. This training program should cover, in addition to skill development, knowledge acquisition on the mandate of each committee, management of committee system, modality of committee functions, and liaison with government ministries. It should also cover the day-to-day operation of committees which includes inter alia:

1. preparing committee meeting agenda and working papers;
2. preparing summaries of relevant documents/briefing papers;
3. standardized and uniform format for preparing committee proceedings;
4. writing reports;
5. keeping records;
6. training of committee officers/assistant secretaries on the mandate of the cluster they serve (Obaidullah 2011; Buchanan and Ahmed 2004).

Once the Secretariat has undertaken structural reorganization and staff development measures, it should emphasize the provision of research and documentation services for committee officers/chairs. As we discussed in the previous chapter, a full-fledged research wing or BIPS is yet to be established and this seriously hinders the services provided to committee chairs by the CS Wing and LIC. Unless committee chairs are provided with adequate research support in regards to the vision and mission of the respective ministry, as well as its annual work plan, budget allocation for the fiscal year, development projects, allocation of Annual Development Program (ADP), and key performance indicators for monitoring budget implementation, it will not be possible for them to carry out effective oversight of ministerial programs (Obaidullah 2015).

Between 2002 and 2004, the USAID–PRODIP project sponsored some research support to the nine Standing Committees on Ministries (SCMs) as a pilot program. The PRODIP project team conducted a research needs assessment of SCMs in consultation with six chairpersons and two ministers to ascertain what kind of facilities they lack and what they need most urgently for carrying out effective oversight of ministry business. During the two years of the project's tenure, it supported these committees with research documents. It was anticipated that after the end of PRODIP, Parliament would provide this research service on a regular basis. However, this has not been the case.

The PRODIP project team organized meetings with chairmen and members of thirteen key committees in 2012 in Dhaka in order to sharing experience and work out a strategy for making committee functions more effective. In this regard, a 'Manual on Public Hearing' was also published by the project in the same year. Though the ROP does not provide the opportunity for holding public hearings on legislation or committee functions, the project persuaded the MPs and committee chairs to adopt them. The provision of public hearings and site visits established improved linkages between Parliament and CSOs, the media, and citizens at large that eventually helped MPs to gain a better understanding of citizens' perceptions and priorities about legislation and how to keep the executive on its feet. On the basis of divergent views received from a cross-section of people, MPs can reflect these issues in the House during debates and in standing committee meetings. The PRODIP project conducted twenty-seven public hearings of seven SCMs in 2013–2014. The project focused on those activities that it reckoned most essential for bringing changes in the way institutions operate and perform its functions effectively in respect of legislation, oversight, citizen outreach, and representation which are likely to be sustained by Parliament beyond the life of the project (USAID–PRODIP Asia Foundation, 2015: 3).

PRODIP intended to create and leave behind a more informed and skilled secretariat staff for increasing parliament's role in policy-making, legislation, and fiscal oversight in particular. The manuals, reports, training materials, and templates that the project produced would be archived in the parliament library for future use so that new comers in the secretariat service get the opportunity of consulting, learning and developing skills of their own (PRODIP program USAID Cooperative Agreement No. 388-A-0010-00092-00 Asia Foundation, 2014: 3).

The introduction of improved processes and procedures, particularly in the conduct of committee business—for example, preparing annual committee work plans commensurate with budget and the creation of committee briefings—has met with a great degree of success in PRODIP's target of nine committees and is likely to become standard operating procedure. Public hearings of committees have become a popular and successful tool for reviewing upcoming legislation or considering policy options. These practices had been well-received by committee chairs of the Ninth Parliament, who advocated amendments in the ROP to permit more hearings and open committee meetings (PRODIP program USAID Cooperative Agreement No. 388-A-0010-00092-00 Asia Foundation 2014: 3).

Concluding Observations

Parliament's decision to only partially accept committee reorganization plans developed by domestic and international partners and to continue legacy practices in staffing the CS Wing have totally marred the objectives of creating a more effective parliamentary committee system in Bangladesh. As a matter of fact, two decades of reorganization efforts have not made any substantive impact on the systemic capacity of parliamentary committees to provide effective oversight of executive power. Reforms aimed at systemic change need strong political backing and active support from the upper echelons of the state bureaucracy (Khosla 1970). In this regard, the crucial issue is how Parliament perceives the importance of oversight functions. The less the oversight the more it is preferred to the executive. However, if Parliament fails to exercise rigorous oversight of the executive its raison d'être for existence is lost. In the context of Bangladesh, several questions emerge about the intentions of Parliament itself. Does it really want to assert its supremacy over the executive? Does it take institutional and systemic reforms to increase the oversight capacity of its committees seriously? Has it put the right man or woman on the right committee? Does it care about the skill and efficiency of committee support staff? Do committee chairs ask committee officers for research services from the CS Wing? These questions all deserve further in-depth academic inquiry. Parliament could have enhanced its institutional capacity had it been committed to adopting the recommendations offered by international parliamentary experts to from the old tradition-bound organization to a modern results-oriented organization (Schick 2002: 7). The list of opportunities missed by Parliament is considerable. Had it committed to developing specialized staff with knowledge and techniques of oversight on committees (what the UNDP mission called a 'core team of support'), nourished a specialized parliamentary cadre based on merit with adequate opportunity for career progression, provided regular opportunities for skills and professional training, decreased its reliance on deputed staff, adopted a modern HRM policy to ensure a rolling supply of competent personnel, and build a provision of research, documentation, and analytical services in the Secretariat to support (Butcher 2004) committees work, then the Bangladesh Parliament might have made a big stride in realizing that key component of a functioning, modern democracy—a system of parliamentary committees that conduct robust and effective oversight of executive power.

Note

The nine SCMs are: Agriculture, Education, Health, Local Government, Power Energy and Mineral Resources, Finance, Communication and Women and Children Affairs as pilot program (USAID–PRODIP Asia Foundation 2014: 3).

Notes

1. This chapter draws heavily on the author's paper, "Standing Committees on Ministries in the Bangladesh Parliament: Need for Reorganization." *South Asian Survey*, Vol. 18. No. 2 September, 2011, pp. 317–342.
2. The proposal for the constitution of DSCs on government-wide scale first came from the 'Study of Parliament Group' to strike a balance between the executive and the parliament. The group in their report argued that they would strengthen accountability system of the parliament over the executive. There was a feeling that the executive prospered at the cost of the parliament. The Procedure Committee did not agree to the submission of the study group on the ground that they would detract the attention of the members from the House to the committees. Consequent to this diversion somebody would emerge with a new influence. However, eventually backbenchers' denial to obey the dictates of the party leadership persuaded them to find some alternative institutional means to open up opportunities for the backbenchers to take part in the parliamentary policy process. This kind of realization thus paved the path for the creation of the network of DSCs in the House of Commons.

3. For example, committees to the Eight Parliament were appointed eighteen months after inauguration.
4. At the time DFID prepared its report in 2000, there were forty-eight committees and 100 subcommittees.

REFERENCES

Ahmed, E. (1981) Development Administration, Centre for Administrative Studies, Dhaka University, Dhaka

Ahmed, N. (1998) "Reforming the Parliament in Bangladesh: Structure, Constraints and Political Dilemmas, Frank Cass Journal: Commonwealth and Comparative Politics, Vol. 36, No. 1

Ahmed, N. (2002) The Bangladesh Parliament, Ashgate: Anthony Rowe Limited, Chippenham, Wiltshire London

Ahmed, N. (2007) Departmental Select Committee in the British House of Commons in Ahmed, N. and Obaidullah, A. T. M. (eds) The Working of Parliamentary Committees in Westminster System, University Press Limited, Dhaka

Benda, S. R. (1997) 'Committees in Legislatures: A Division of Labour': Longley and Agh (eds.) The Changing role of Parliamentary Committees, Research Committee of Legislative Specialists, International Political Association, Appleton, 17–50 cited in Ahmed 2002: 59

BJS, Secretariat Order (2006), Job Description, The Bangladesh Parliament Secretariat, Dhaka

Buchanan, L. et al. (2002) Organizational Review of Parliament Secretariat, UNDP: Dhaka

Buchanan, L., & Nizam Ahmed (2004) Report on Parliamentary Committees, 2004, BDG/97/003 UNDP, Dhaka

Butcher, D. (2004) The UNDP Mission Report, UNDP, Dhaka

Chowdhry, M. A. (1968) Government and Politics in Pakistan, Puthighar LTD, Dhaka

Chowdhury, N. (1997) Implementation Plan on Strengthening of the Parliament, UNDP, Dhaka

DFID: David Watson and Deborah Williams (2000) Support to Parliamentary Committees in Bangladesh, DFID Bangladesh, Dhaka

Emy, H. (1978) The Politics of Australian Democracy, Macmillan, Melbourne

Hakim, A. (2000) The Changing Forms of Government in Bangladesh: The Transition to Parlia,mentary system in 1991, in Perspective, Bangladesh Institute of Parliamentary Studies, Dhaka

Hasanuzzaman, A. M. (2007) 'Role of Parliamentary committees in Bangladesh' in Ahmed, N. and Obaidullah, A. T. M. (eds) The Working of Parliamentary Committees in Westminster Systems: Lesson for Bangladesh, University Press Limited, Dhaka

Hollis Christopher (1950, 64) Can Parliament Survive? London: World Affairs Book Club

Houghton, B. (1913) Bureaucratic Government: A Study in Indian Polity, Natesan & Co

Hussain, S. A. (1991) Politics and Society in Bengal – 1921–36: A Legislative Perspective, Dhaka: Bengla

Jogrest, M. (1993) Reform in the House of Commons, The University Press of Kentucky, Lexington

Khosla, J. N. (1970) "Administrative Reform in India: Perspective and Lessons" in Lee, H. B. and Samonte, A. G. (eds) Administrative Reforms in Asia, Manila, Philippines: Eastern Regional Organization for Public Administration

Kreppel, Amie (2014) "Typologies and Classifications." in Shane Martin, Thomas Saalfeld, and Kaare Strom (eds) The Oxford Handbook of Legislative Studies. Oxford: Oxford University Press

Lijphart, A. (2012) Patterns of Democracy Yale University Press

Lindley, J. A. (1991) An Assessment of the Institutional Development Needs of the Parliament of Bangladesh, Asia Foundation

Longley, L. and Davidson, R. H. (eds) (1998) The New Roles of Parliamentary Committee, Frank Cass, London, p. 2

Meg Russell and Phillip Cowley (2015) The policy power of the Westminster parliament: The "parliamentary state" and the empirical evidence. https://constitution-unit.com/2015/11/26/the-policy-power-of-the-westminster-parliament-the-empirical-evidence/

Mezey, M. (1979, 26) Comparative Legislatures, Duke University Press, Durham, NC

Norton, P. (1985) "Recent Structural and Procedural Changes in the House of Commons in P. Norton (ed) Parliament in the 1980s, Basil Black well, London.

Norton, P. (1994) 'Legislative Power of Parliament ' in C Flinterman, A Heringa and L. Waddington (eds) The Evolving Role of Parliaments in Europe, METRO, Nemos Verglag.

Obaidullah, A. T. M. (2011) "Reorganization of Standing Committees on Ministries of Bangladesh Parliament: A Quest for Increasing Operational & Institutional Efficiency", South Asian Survey, Vol. 18, No. 2

Obaidullah, A. T. M. (2015) Strengthening Budget Process and Oversight Capacity of the House of Representatives (HOR) of Somaliland Parliament. UNDP Constitutional and Parliamentary Support Project, Mission Report, Hargeisa, Somaliland

Obaidullah, A. T. M. (2017) "Civil Service Reforms and Development of Professionalism: A Case Study of Bangladesh" in Basu & Rahman (eds) Governance in South Asia, Rutledge UK South Asia edition London

PRODIP Evaluation Report (2015) The Asia Foundation, Dhaka

Quoted in Nizam Ahmed & ATM Obaidullah (ed) The Working of Parliamentary Committees in Westminster Systems UPL Dhaka 2007, p. 1

Rahman, T. (2008) Parliamentary Control and Government Accountability in South Asia, Routledge, London

Rashiduzzaman, M. (1965) Central Legislature in British India: 1921–1947, Mullick Brothers, Dhaka, p. 4

Rules of Procedure. Parliament of the Peoples' Republic of Bangladesh (as modified up to 11th January 2007 (Reprinted : December, 2013)

Rush, M. (1983) Parliamentary Committees and Parliamentary Government: The British and Canadian Parliament

Rush, M. (2009) The Working of Parliamentary Committee in Westminster System: Lesson for Bangladesh. A book Review in Legislative Studies, Vol. 15, pp. 547–52

Schick, A. (2002) Can National Legislature Regain an Effective Voice in Budget Policy?, OECD Journal on Budgeting

Siddiqi, L. K. et al. (1994) Making Parliament Effective: A British Experience. This is an unpublished study tour report by the Bangladesh Parliament Members, Dhaka

Soliman, Magdy M. and Kendra P. Collins (Project BGD/97/003) "Strengthening Parliamentary Democracy", Advisory Opinion on the Reform of the Rules of Procedure, BIPS, Dhaka

The Asia Foundation Report (2014) Promoting Democratic Institutions and Practices (PRODIP) program USAID Cooperative Agreement No. 388-A-0010-00092-00 Asia Foundation), Dhaka (This project was administered by the Asia Foundation, Bangladesh)

The Asia Foundation (2015) Tim M. eisburger, Strengthening Democracy in Bangladesh (The Asia Foundation) asiafoundation.org/resources/pdfs/OccasionalPaperNo11FINAL.pdf

UNDP, Linda, B. et al. (2002) Organizational Review of Bangladesh Parliament Secretariat, UNDP, Dhaka

UNDP Sue Nelson (2006) The Final Evaluation Report of the Strengthening Parliamentary Democracy Project, BGD/00/97 UNDP, Dhaka

USAID PRODIP (2011) Promoting Democratic Institutions and Practices (PRODIP program USAID Cooperative Agreement No. 388-A-0010-00092-00 Asia Foundation), Dhaka

USAID-PRODIP Project (2014) USAID: Bangladesh (2014) Promoting Democratic Institutions and Practices (PRODIP program USAID Cooperative Agreement No. 388-A-0010-00092-00 Asia Foundation), Dhaka (This project was administered by the Asia Foundation, Bangladesh. This is why sometime it is referred to as Asia Foundation Report

CHAPTER 6

Parliamentary Oversight: A Conceptual Framework

Why Parliamentary Oversight

The cardinal feature of a modern democratic system is its accountability to the public who vote it into state power. All state actors remain vertically accountable to citizens for their policies and programs through periodic elections. They are also subject to constant oversight through horizontal accountability mechanisms such as the judiciary, the media, and CSOs. MPs are potential agents of both vertical and horizontal accountability (Johnston 2009). In Chap. 2 we discussed that superiority of the parliamentary form of government, if there is any, over the presidential government, lies in parliament's capacity to hold the executive to account for their actions and policies. The constitution of every country in principle confers the parliament with the authority, responsibility, and means to hold the executive to account for its actions on behalf of the public. Parliament holds the government to account for ensuring that government policy and administration are both efficient and reflective of the will and diverse needs of the public.

The philosophical support for parliamentary oversight in a democratic country rests on the constitutional system of checks and balances among the three organs of the state: the legislature, executive, and judiciary. Rockman argues for "legislative monitoring" of the executive on the grounds of ensuring the triumph of representative government by lines of accountability running through the organ that embodies popular sovereignty. Legislative oversight of the executive is desirable because it provides

© The Author(s) 2019
A. T. M. Obaidullah, *Institutionalization of the Parliament in Bangladesh*, https://doi.org/10.1007/978-981-10-5317-7_6

the opportunity to hold it to account and a means to evaluate its performance (Aberbach 1982: 390). By exercising a legislative oversight function, parliaments strike a balance of power between the two organs and assert its role as the defender of people's interests (http://www.agora-parl.org/resources/aoe/oversight). If parliament fails to hold the executive to account in a parliamentary democracy, that parliament is of no use, however democratically elected it is.

An ineffective accountability system can cause widespread corruption, abuse of power, human rights violations, and maladministration—all of which are frequent charges made by the public against governments in developing countries. All these complaints are subject to review by parliament on the floor of the House and in standing committees.[1] It is due to the ineffectiveness of parliamentary oversight that a popularly elected government may turn into an unaccountable elected autocracy, simply an elected government, not a "constitutional government."[2] The influential political philosopher Thomas Paine observed in 1791 that a popularly elected government can claim to be constitutional when its administration is wisely pursued and power is exercised in the interest of the people and maintenance of individual liberty (available at https://en.wikipedia.org/wiki/Rights_of_Man).

The discussion of accountability revolves around four queries: who, why, whom, and how. Namely, (a) who is held accountable; (b) for what are they held accountable; (c) to whom are they accountable; (d) how is accountability to be enforced (see Griffith 2005a). In the context of parliamentary government, the answers to these queries are: (a) the individual minister and the collective cabinet; (b) the abuse or excessive use of power, misappropriation of the public purse, and so forth; (c) parliament; (d) through various different oversight mechanisms and individual and collective methods. There are at least five types of committee in parliament established to hold the executive to account. These are: (a) legislative review committees which scrutinize government and other bills; (b) public accounts committees which monitor and ensure public spending achieves value for money (*ex post*); (c) estimate committees which examine the reasonableness of appropriations of government departments and agencies before public money is appropriated (*ex ante*); (d) ministerial committees which scrutinize policy and administration; (e) specialized oversight committees which investigate complaints (https://www.parliament.nsw.gov.au/researchpapers/Pages/parliament-and-accountability-the-role-of-parlia.aspx). Each committee has its own mandate. The objectives of all committees considered together ensure that legislatures do not infringe upon individual rights, public money is not misused, government policy and administration does not go off track, and the integrity of government functions in terms of policy, administration, and public expenditure remains efficient and cost-effective (Griffith 2005a, b; https://www.parliament.nsw.gov.au/researchpapers/Pages/parliament-and-accountability-the-role-of-parlia.aspx).

Ideally, in Westminster democracies, every aspect of the executive function is under the purview of parliamentary oversight to ensure the executive's compliance with legislative intent. Even the defense sector is no longer a forbidden area for parliament. As has been pointed out, "Governance can only stand to gain from the growing prominence and scope of parliamentary oversight" (Yamamoto, H. http://www.ipu.org/PDF/publications/oversight08-e.pdf). Parliamentary oversight is geared to reducing corruption, ensuring value for money, and guarding against maladministration, that is, dishonesty, waste, misuse of power, arbitrary and unresponsive administration (Rockman 1984: 414–15). Robust monitoring of parliament is one of the basic indicators of good governance.

Parliamentary oversight has manifold objectives:

1. ensuring transparency and openness of executive functions;
2. monitoring policies and execution of government activities;
3. ensuring the proper implementation of government policies to achieve desired impact;
4. reducing waste in public spending; ensure economy, efficiency, and effectiveness of public expenditure;
5. protecting the human rights of citizens;
6. upholding the rule of law;
7. minimizing abuses of power, arbitrary behavior, and illegal actions of the government (Yamamoto 2008; Griffith 2005a, b; Parliamentary Function of Oversight http://www.agora-parl.org/resources/aoe/oversight).

Parliamentary oversight not only aims to identify and publicize the failures and lapses of the executive in the management of public programs; oversight can also pay off for those members who engage in it in getting re-elected, securing uplift (backbench to front bench), and setting programs in a desired way (Ahmed 2008). Oversight can be both adversarial and supportive. For example, parliaments not only conduct investigations, hold public hearings, ask for reports from the executive and commission studies to gauge the reaction to complaints, criticisms, or abuses surrounding the operation and management of an executive program; they also help bolster a program (Ahmed 2008).

Types of Parliamentary Oversight

Accountability is often intermingled with responsibility. But they are not the same thing. For the political scientist Matthew Flinders, responsibility and accountability connote different aspects of political wrongdoing. Responsibility involves guilt and may be subject to blame for failure and loss, whereas accountability involves obligations to account for. The distinction between them is 'providing an answer' in the former and 'liability' in the latter (Flinders 2001). Accountability may be of varied types. Based on the specific objectives parliament pursues, accountability can be political accountability, legislative accountability, administrative accountability, financial accountability, legal accountability, and so forth (Griffith 2005a, b; www.parliament.nsw.gov.au/).

Political accountability refers to elected officials' responsiveness to their constituents (Romzek 2000). It constitutes the core of responsible government and bedrock of constitutionalism as formulated by A.V. Dicey in the nineteenth century (Griffith 2005a, b). It is the accountability of the elected government to the public and to legislative bodies (en.wikipedia.org/wiki/Accountability#Political). Legislative accountability can be *ex ante* or *ex post*. Legislatures must determine prior to implementation whether or not legislation passed gives the executive too much power or jeopardizes citizens' civil liberties (*ex ante*). The essence of a constitutional government is to recognize the existence of any law that in effect exercises the arbitrary will of the executive. Just as parliament carries it out its *ex-ante* responsibilities, so must it monitor the effect and impact of laws already passed (*ex post*). It exercises its oversight through various accountability tools such as parliamentary questions, various committees, the ombudsman, the C&AG, and so on. An overbearing executive and even drastic laws can be rendered tolerable by enforcing parliamentary accountability (Griffith 2005a, b). Financial accountability is parliament's power of purse control over the national budget. Through the financial accountability system, parliament can inquire into the source of public money, the intent of allocation, and verify the result of intended public expenditure. This section of the chapter is focused on political accountability. Parliament can exercise political accountability on the executive by monitoring the legislative process and implementation of laws and their execution and overseeing public expenditure of the government, which is mainly carried out by the civil service.

Civil servants are in theory non-partisan officials who are not directly accountable to parliament. Of course, civil servants come under parliamentary accountability when individual MPs inquire into activity or policy of a particular ministry from the floor of the House or in ministerial committee meetings. In addition, ministerial expenditure comes under the scrutiny of the public accounts committee and other watchdog institutions such as the C&AG, the ombudsman, and the Independent Commission Against Corruption (ICAC). These institutional arrangements are designed to safeguard the financial probity of the government and check against maladministration. Griffith (2005a, b) held that "guards are placed against inefficiency, maladministration and corruption" (Griffith 2005a, b; https://www.parliament.nsw.gov.au/.../parliament...accountability...role.../Parliament%). The development of administrative law has made the decisions and actions of public servants more exposed to parliamentary and judicial review. Government under rule of law demands proper legal limits on the exercise of power. Powers must first be justified by parliament, and must be granted by parliament within definable limits so that a standard is imposed on the administration which commands itself to the public conscience (Wade 1971). The essence of democratic governance is that every individual and every appropriate authority is accountable to the public for their actions. Table 6.1 depicts the different values and behavioral expectations emphasized by the various accountability relationships.

Table 6.1 Accountability, value emphasis, and behavioral expectations

Accountability	Value emphasis	Behavioral expectations
Hierarchical	Efficiency	Obedience to organizational directives
Legal (legislative and judicial)	Rule of law	Complaisance with external mandates
Professional	Expertise	Deference to individual judgment and expertise
Political	Responsiveness	Responsiveness to key external stakeholders

Source: Romzek (2000) cited in Rahman (2008: 11) value and behavioral expectations of different accountability types

Oversight Tools and Form of Government

In all Westminster democracies, parliament exercises some kind of accountability on the executive. However, not all parliaments use the same accountability tools; they vary according to the form of government and the economic/development status of a country. Parliaments usually have an array of tools at their disposal to maintain oversight of the executive. Irrespective of the form of government, parliaments commonly use certain tools such as committee hearings, hearings in the plenary session of parliament, inquiry committees, parliamentary questions, interpellations, the ombudsman, auditors general, and public accounts committees. In all parliaments, these oversight tools are divided into two categories on the basis of when parliaments use them (Pelizzo and Stapenhurst 2004). When parliaments exercise oversight prior to the enactment of legislation or implementation of actions, these are "instruments categorized as ex-ante oversight." As such, examples of *ex-ante* oversight tools would include committee and plenary parliamentary hearings and requests for documents and persons (Pelizzo and Stapenhurst 2004). Of course, committee hearings may also be used as means of *ex-post* oversight. Instruments in the *ex-post* category enable the legislature to conduct oversight after the enactment of government policy to check whether it is properly implemented in the light of the legislative intent. These include questions, interpellations, and the creation of committees of inquiry (Pelizzo and Stapenhurst 2004). The second dimension pertains to where tools are established, that is, inside or outside of parliament. Parliaments use both internal and external oversight tools. The ombudsman and C&AG are examples of external oversight tools (Pelizzo and Stapenhurst 2004).

In 2004, the IPU and World Bank Institute conducted a survey of 180 parliaments including the European Parliament with regard to 'executive–legislative relations.' The survey inquired into several issues including: (a) whether the government in that country must report to parliament; (b) how parliament in these countries exercise oversight; (c) if MPs could question government officials; (d) whether parliaments allocate adequate time and space for questions; (e) whether interpellations were predicted beforehand; (f) whether the country has an institution of ombudsman (Pelizzo and Stapenhurst 2004). The research was carried out with two fundamental objectives. First, to ascertain if parliaments have potentials for effective oversight and which institutional arrangements they have adopted to strengthen oversight. Second, whether the tools of oversight are independent variables, or dependent variables like the form of government, economic status of the country, per capita income, or level of democracy in the country as measured by the Gastil Index (Pelizzo and Stapenhurst 2004).

The data revealed that there is considerable variation in the use of oversight tools in different countries. It found that 95% of parliaments use inquiry committees and committee hearings as the most frequently used oversight tools of parliamentary control. By contrast, interpellations and the ombudsman are substantially less common—about 75% and 73% respectively (Pelizzo and Stapenhurst 2004). The main common theme was that all parliaments use more than one tool, though they vary from country to country. Of those parliaments that furnished complete information, 12% used four tools, 14% five tools, almost 33% six tools, and 40% seven tools (Pelizzo and Stapenhurst 2004).

The magnitude and intensity of oversight vary from country to country and depends largely on the form of government and political culture of the country. Not necessarily the number of tools but rather their functional effectiveness is to a great extent influenced by the type of government, per capita income level, and levels of democracy (Pelizzo and Stapenhurst 2004: 14–18). In general, countries with parliamentary forms of government use a higher number of oversight tools than those with presidential governments. However, those countries that enjoy higher income levels and stronger protections of civil liberties tend to use a greater number of oversight tools with higher degrees of success. Despite a general trend of increasing use of oversight tools, the study found that the use of inquiry committees, interpellations, and an ombudsman office remain outside the normal pattern.

The study found that interpellations are used mostly in high-income countries, are less common in low-income countries, and least common in middle-income countries. By contrast, inquiry committees and ombudsman offices are most common in middle-income countries, less common in high-income countries, and least common in low-income countries (Pelizzo and Stapenhurst 2004: 15).

Survey data revealed that Westminster models use more oversight tools in general than presidential and semi-presidential systems and tools such as committee hearings, hearings in plenary sessions, questions, and interpellations in particular (Table 6.2). This, however, should lead us to conclude parliaments in Westminster democracies are more effective in terms of

Table 6.2 Number of oversight tools by form of government

Number of oversight tools						
Form of government	4	5	6	7	Total	Mean
Presidential	2	2	7	2	13	5.69
Semi-presidential	3	3	3	5	14	5.71
Parliamentary	1	2	6	11	20	6.35
Total	6	7	16	18	47	

Source: Pelizzo and Stapenhurst (2004) and Tools for Legislative Oversight an Empirical Investigation (2004: 12)

Table 6.3 Number of oversight tools by level of democracy

Number of oversight tools						
Level of democracy	4	5	6	7	Total	Mean
Democracy	1	2	9	15	27	6.41
Quasi-democracy	2	3	6	3	14	5.71
Non-democracy	3	2	3	x	8	5.71
Total	6	7	18	18	49	

Source: Pelizzo and Stapenhurst (2004) and Tools for Legislative Oversight an Empirical Investigation (2004: 18)

oversight—"only that they have more oversight tools at their disposal" (Pelizzo and Stapenhurst 2004: 15).

Pelizzo and Stapenhurst investigated whether the level of democracy in a country has any bearing on the number of oversight tools being used by its parliament. They found that there is a "clear, and strong linear relationship between the level of democracy and the number of oversight tools." They found that non-democracies have an average of 0 5.71 tools, whereas democracies have an average of 6.41. Their findings are presented in Table 6.3 below.

The study also unearthed a relationship between the use inquiry committees, interpellations, and the ombudsman offices and the income level of a country. In general, interpellations are used mostly in high-income countries. They are not so frequently used in low-income countries, and least of all in middle-income countries (see Table 6.4). Eighty-one percent of high-income countries use them compared to 77% of low-income and 70% in middle-income countries. Finally, the use of inquiry committees

Table 6.4 Use of interpellations by income level

Do the countries in these income level use interpellations?

Income level	No	Yes	Total	% yes
Low	5	17	22	77.3
Middle	8	18	26	69.2
High	3	13	16	81.3
Total	16	48	64	

Source: Pelizzo and Staphenhurst (2004)

and ombudsman offices operate mostly "in middle-income countries, less common in high-income countries and least common in low-income countries" (Pelizzo and Stapenhurst 2004: 16).

Bangladesh Parliament and Oversight Tools

The tools and mechanisms that parliaments use are outlined in the rules of procedures or standing orders from which they derive their constitutional authority. How effectively a parliament can exercise its oversight prerogative depends to a great extent upon the scope and authority of those rules they use for the government to behave. The broader the rules are in scope and unambiguous in intent, the greater the opportunity for the parliament to institutionalize its position as an oversight institution and establish its powers and independence within the political system (Parliamentary Functions of Oversight http://www.agora-parl.org/resources/aoe/oversight).

As was discussed in Chap. 5, Article 76 of the Bangladesh Constitution retains the provision for establishing parliamentary standing committees to hold the executive to account for their policies and actions. In addition, the ROP made elaborate provisions for an array of both individual and collective mechanisms to enforce government accountability. Despite all these constitutional and procedural arrangements, the Bangladesh Parliament is allegedly weak in carrying out effective oversight. The previous chapter traced out the organizational pitfalls and systemic bottlenecks of SCMs that have hindered Parliament's oversight function. The rest of this chapter presents the types of tools that Bangladesh Parliament uses under the framework of the Constitution and the ROP.

Constitutional and Procedural Sanctions

Article 65 entrusts all legislative authority to Parliament. The Constitution also mandates by Article 55(3) that the cabinet shall be collectively responsible to Parliament. Article 76 empowers parliament to appoint as many standing committees as it deems necessary to conduct its oversight functions effectively. The ROP enshrines a number of devices to make the government answerable and accountable for its actions. These rules can be grouped into individual and collective techniques. The section below discusses these in more detail.

Individual Oversight Methods

Rules 41–71 of the ROP prescribe various individual oversight methods to hold the government accountable to Parliament. These include questions, adjournment motions, motions for half-hour discussion, motions for discussion on matters of public importance for short duration and call attention motions (BJS 2007: 15–24). Of these methods, questions and call attention motions are common in almost all parliamentary sittings. In fact, the first hour of every sitting, unless otherwise directed by the Speaker, is earmarked for members to ask questions on matters of public importance (Rule 41). In addition, the introduction in early 1997 of Prime Minister's Question Time (PMQT) once a week (Wednesday), part of several major reforms in parliamentary procedures carried out by the Seventh Parliament, has added an extra flavor of oversight in parliamentary sittings.

The first thirty minutes of every Wednesday are open to backbench members of the Treasury and opposition to grill the prime minister on matters of policy and performance. During this period, the prime minister addresses a wide range of questions of which she has been previously notified. But she must also respond to supplementary questions raised from the floor of the House of which no previous notice is given. This mechanism has brought the chief executive under direct parliamentary accountability. In addition, Rule 60 provides MPs an opportunity to discuss in more detail questions of public importance deemed not to have been answered sufficiently in the previous sitting. It is intended to clarify matters. Rules 61–67 create provisions for a motion of adjournment of the business of the House for the purpose of discussing matters of recent and urgent public importance. Rules 68–71 provide MPs the opportunity to discuss matters of urgent public importance under various captions such as short duration and call attention in which ministers may make a brief statement. MPs can also move private members' resolutions in demand for government action and/or support. In addition to these regular means of scrutinizing government business on the floor of the House, MPs are given the opportunity to scrutinize the president's speeches and the finance minister's presentation of the national budget. The individual techniques the MPs use are shown in Table 6.5.

Table 6.5 summarize the scope and limitations of individual oversight methods employed by Bangladeshi parliamentarians. These techniques can be applied with prior notice given to the secretary of the Bangladesh Parliament Secretariat. Questions and call attention motions can be moved in every sitting day (except the day the budget is presented). Half-hour discussions and discussions for short duration can be held only twice a week. A motion for short duration discussion requires the signature of five other MPs and consent of the Leader of the House. Each procedure requires the Speaker's admissibility before it is moved. Each must meet certain other conditions; in particular, they have to satisfy admissibility criteria before being accepted. This conditional acceptability is necessary to ensure the maximum use of Parliament's valuable time. The extent to which these techniques can secure the accountability of the executive depends on the readiness and capability of MPs to make maximum use of them (Ahmed and Ahmed 1996; Ahmed 2002).

Enforceability of Individual Methods

In recent years, more questions have been answered in Parliament compared to previous parliaments. But whether questions can secure the answerability of the executive depends to a great extent on intention and quality of the questions. If they glorify the executive in the House rather than grilling it, the number of questions is of no consequence. If they do not involve the policy and performance of the executive and critical issues that affect public life, they merely ask for information that serves no benefit to the public (Aminuzzaman 1996: 17). In the last two decades, not a single adjournment motion has been accepted (Rahman 2008: 49) and the number of short duration discussions negligible. The main reason underlying the refusal of adjournment motions may be to keep the government's image intact and protect ministers from public criticism; as one commentator has said, "the governments do not want to expose weakness to the public" (Ahmed 2002: 117). Thus, individual methods of

Table 6.5 Summary of individual oversight methods practiced in Bangladesh Parliament

Oversight method	Frequency	Duration required for notice	Consultation with Leader of the House	Admissibility criteria	Other MPs' support	Maximum limits to accept
Questions	Every sitting day except the day budget is presented	Clear fifteen days	N/A	Rules 53–55	Not required	One oral and three written questions for MPs
Short-notice questions	Every sitting day except the day budget is presented	Up to five days	N/A Ministers need to agree to reply	Rule 59	Not required	No limit
Half-hour discussion	Only two sitting days in a week	Clear three days	N/A	Rule 60	Not required	Two notices only in a week
Adjournment motion	Any sitting day except the day budget is presented	Two hours before commencement of sittings	N/A	Rule 63	Support of twenty-five MPs required, if objection raised	Maximum two hours on the day determined by the Speaker
Short-duration discussion	Two sitting days in a week	Clear two days	Required	Rules 68–69(1)	Five MPs' signature	One hour for selected day
Calling attention to matters of urgent public importance	Any sitting day	Two hours before commencement of sittings	N/A	Rule 71	Not required	Three notices. Fifteen MPs read only their notices within thirty minutes

Source: Rules of Procedure of Bangladesh Parliament (BJS 2007: 15–24; Akhtar 2012)

parliamentary oversight have been virtually ineffective in ensuring the accountability and transparency of the Bangladeshi government.

The oversight tools Parliament uses to hold the executive accountable substantially vary with the research findings of Pelizzo and Staphenhurst (2004). The study suggests that middle-income countries predominantly use inquiry committees, investigations, and ombudsman offices. Bangladesh uses too many oversight tools in relation to its level of democracy and its economic status. Most tools fall into the individual category. It is not surprising that interpellations are used in Bangladesh Parliament; this seems to corroborate the study's findings on middle-income countries. But the abovementioned tools commonly used in other middle-income countries are non-existent in Bangladesh.

COLLECTIVE OVERSIGHT METHODS

The limitations of individual oversight tools are compensated by collective methods of committee oversight. With the emergence of parliamentary committees in Bangladesh, Parliament's capacity to hold the executive to account gained extra momentum. Given the time limitations imposed on the House during session, committees have been an appropriate forum for going deeper into a particular matter, examining it in greater detail, and exploring possible remedies (Ahmed 2006: 24). For example, since they can access files, retrieve records, and call witnesses, committees tend to fare better than other oversight methods in probing into the operations of the government. Committees can conduct inquiries into complaints and follow up on pending matters. Committees perform so many functions that would have been impossible for parliament to perform otherwise (Benda 1997: 17). Besides scrutinizing legislative bills and ministerial programs, committees act as training grounds for inexperienced MPs to develop specialized policy knowledge and expertise in the specific area of government business the committee work on (Emy 1978: 406 in Ahmed, N., ibid.). Committee activity arouses a sense of professionalism and expertise required for the legislative phase of the policy-making process (Obaidullah 2011). Committee deliberations throughout the year provide a means for MPs to keep busy and feel useful (Rush 1983: 151 in Ahmed., N., ibid). Committee work leaves room for MPs to more actively participate in the governing process with experienced members (Jogrest 1993: 126 in Ahmed, N., ibid.).

As we have discussed, Article 76 obligates Parliament to set up the Public Accounts Committee and a Privileges Committee and confers it with the authority to formulate its own ROP and constitute thereby as many committees it deems fit (GOB 2007: 30–31). The ROP is the other major source of institutional arrangement to keep the committee system in motion. The ROP contains rules for the composition of each committee and determines the mode of appointment, its term of office, functions, and procedures for conducting business (BJS 2007: 61–74). Parliamentary committees in Bangladesh thus enjoy constitutional authority and status and have extensive powers to exercise.[3] As per the ROP, a committee can regulate its sittings, conduct its business the way it wants and may appoint as many subcommittees as it considers necessary. Each subcommittee enjoys the authority and privileges of its parent main committee. Committee members enjoy immunity for their activities in committees. Committees meet in private and can call for any person to give evidence in person before its members. It is in committees where public officials explain the policy intentions of the government, give hearings, and account for their performance when asked to do so. Committees can inquire, investigate, and review any matter on its own or on the basis of public complaints. Effective parliamentary committees not only strengthen the accountability mechanism but can also constitute the difference between an effective and ineffective parliament. The effectiveness of committees empowers the parliamentarians themselves (Obaidullah 2011). With these collective methods in place notwithstanding, their enforceability and effectiveness in Bangladesh have been limited, as was discussed in the previous chapter.

Barriers to Effective Accountability

There are a number of major obstacles and risks that can prevent executive accountability in a modern democracy. These are:

1. Party dominance of Parliament: real debates take place in within the party resulting in a decreased quality of debate in the House.
2. Executive dominance of Parliament: members are committed to, and serve the interests of, the executive.
3. Lack of time given to opposition backbench members and increased parliamentary time for government business.

4. The tendency of opposition parties to become obsessed with backbiting rather than dialogue.
5. The media focusing more on opinion than analysis which can mean government is easily able to manipulate and control it through reward and punishment.
6. Dominance of personal interest over parliamentary interest.
7. Anachronistic rules, parliamentary practices, and procedures that fail to cope with changes in the scope of government activity (Australasian Parliamentary Review 2008)

In the context of Bangladesh parliament, despite prolong reform attempts to strengthen parliamentary oversight, significant improvement is not noticed because of its legacy of dominant executive over the whole machinery of the government. The head of the government is head of the party, leader of the House, and also head of the parliamentary nomination board during parliamentary elections. Over concentration of powers in person tends to transform the parliament a subservient to the executive. Parliament, instead of making the executive accountable, very often endorses what the prime minister/leader of the house desires. Moreover, Article 70 of the constitution exacerbates the weakness of the parliament and venom of the party domination. In any critical situations, prime minister's decision is panacea to overcome them. Members of parliament merely carry out party decisions, and the source of party decisions is the same person. On the other hand, the main opposition is engaged in opposing the treasury bench for the sake of opposition and boycotting the parliament session on any issue leaving the executive and treasury bench opportunity to decide the things in way they deem fit. Given this situation, parliamentary oversight has been more a routine business than holding the executive to account for their policies and actions.

Notes

1. The ROP of Bangladesh Parliament states that "the functions of the committee shall be to examine any bill or other matters referred to it parliament, to review the works relating to a ministry which falls within its jurisdiction, to enquire into any activity or irregularity and serious complaint in respect of the ministry and examine, if it deems fit, any such other matters as may fall within its jurisdiction and to make recommendations" (BJS Rule 248). This chapter is more focused on fiscal and budgetary oversight than legislative and administrative oversight.

2. For the conceptual difference between 'government by constitution' and 'constitutional government' see Andrews (1968).
3. For details, see Rules of Procedure of Bangladesh Parliament, pp. 61–65.

References

Akhtar, R. (2012) Parliamentary Oversight: A Study of the Parliamentary Standing Committee on the Ministry of Women and Children Affairs, An unpublished MPA Dissertation to civil Service College, Dhaka, pp. 56–58

Aberach, J. D. (1982) 'Congressional Oversight' in D. Kozac and Macartney (eds) Congress and Public Policy, The Dorsey Press, Illinois, pp. 389–402

Ahmed, N. and Ahmed, A. (1996) "The Quest for Accountability: Parliament and Public Administration in Bangladesh" Asian Journal of Public Administration, Vol. 18, No. 1, pp. 70–95

Ahmed, N. (2008) "Parliamentary Oversight: Process and Practice". An unpublished note provided to the Asia Foundation administered project PROGATI, 2008–12, Dhaka

Ahmed, N. (2006) Limits of Parliamentary Control, Dhaka: University Press Limited

Ahmed, N. (2002) The Parliament of Bangladesh, Ashgate, Grower House, England

Aminuzzaman (1996: 17) Rahman, M. (2008: 49) 'Accountability and Promotion of Ethics and Standards of Behavior of the Public Bureaucracy in Bangladesh', Asian Review of Public Administration, Vol. 8, No. 1, pp. 13–27

Andrews, William G. (1968) Constitution and Constitutionalism, Third Edition, Princeton: D. Van Nostrand

Australasian Parliamentary Review (2008) "Executive Accountability to Parliament—Reality or Rhetoric?*", Australasian Parliamentary Review, Vol. 23, No. 2, pp. 157–165

Benda, S. R. (1997) 'Committees in Legislatures: A Division of Labour' in L. (Longley and Agh (eds)) The Changing role of Parliamentary Committees, Research Committee of Legislative Specialists, International Political Association, Appleton, pp. 17–50

Emy, H. (1978) The Politics of Australian Democracy, Macmillan, Melbourne

Gareth Griffith (2005a) http://www.aspg.org.au/journal/2006autumn_21_1/1-1%20Griffith.doc

Gareth Griffith (2005b) Parliament and Accountability: The Role of Parliamentary Oversight Committees Briefing Paper No. 12/05, https://www.parliament.nsw.gov.au/.../parliament...accountability...role.../Parliament%; https://www.parliament.nsw.gov.au/researchpapers/Pages/parliament-and-accountability-the-role-of-parlia.aspx

GOB (2007) Rules of Procedure of the Bangladesh Parliament

Jogrest, M. (1993) Reform in the House of Commons, The University Press of Kentucky, Lexington

M. Flinders, The Politics of Accountability in the Modern State, Ashgate 2001, p. 12

Nail Johnston Financial Oversight: A Handbook for Parliamentarians (2009) http://gopacnetwork.org/Docs/Oversight_handbook_EN.pdf

Nizam Ahmed. "Development and working of parliaments in South Asia", Asian Journal of Political Science, 6/2001

Obaidullah, A. T. M. (2011) "Reorganization of Standing Committees on Ministries of Bangladesh Parliament: A Quest for Increasing Operational & Institutional Efficiency", South Asian Survey, Vol. 18, No. 2

Parliamentary Function of Oversight. http://www.agora-parl.org/resources/aoe/oversight

Pelizzo, Ricardo and Stapenhurst, Fredetick C. (2004) Tools of Legislative Oversight: An Empirical Investigation, Policy Research Working Paper 3388, World Bank, 2004, Washington D.C. World Bank. http://openknowledge.worldbank.org/handle/10986/14143 *License: CC By 3.0IGO*

Peter Loney Executive Accountability to Parliament—Reality or Rhetoric?' www.aspg.org.au/journal/.../III-3-LONEY%20REVN%20Exec%20Accountability.do

Rahman, T. (2008) Parliamentary Control and Government Accountability in South Asia, Routledge, London

Rockman. http://www.agora-parl.org/resources/aoe/oversight

Rockman 1984: 'Legislative-Executive Relations and Legislative Oversight' Legislative Studies Quarterly, Vol. 9, No. 3, pp. 387–440

Romzek, B. S. (2000) 'Dynamics of Public Sector Accountability in an Era of Reform', International Review of Administrative Sciences, Vol. 66, No. 1, pp. 21–44

Rules of Procedure of Bangladesh Parliament (BJS 2007: 15-2)

Rush, M. (1983) 'Parliamentary Committees and Parliamentary Government: The British and Canadian Experiences' Journal of Commonwealth and Comparative politics, Vol. 26

Tools for Legislative Oversight an Empirical Investigation (2004) World Bank Policy Research Working Paper 3388, pp. 1–22, September

Yamamoto, H. (2008: 9) Yamamoto, H. (2008) Tools for Parliamentary Oversight: A comparative Study of 88 Parliaments, Geneva

Yamamoto, H. Tools for parliamentary Oversight A comparative study of 88 national parliaments. http://www.ipu.org/PDF/publications/oversight08-e.pdf

Wade, H. W. R. (1971) Administrative Law, Oxford: Clarendon Press

CHAPTER 7

Comparative Budget Process in Westminster Parliaments: A Lesson for Effective Fiscal Oversight

BUDGET AS AN INSTRUMENT OF FISCAL POLICY

The national budget is one of the most important policy documents that a government produces every year. No other piece of legislation requires the same time, expertise, and involvement of so many government ministers and resources in the process of preparation and enactment. The budget portrays a country's prevailing socioeconomic conditions and the policies and resources required to address them in a fiscal year. It is not only crowded columns of dreary dead numbers but also an embodiment of government's fiscal and monetary policies with the aim to achieve growth and stability, control inflation, expand employment and alleviate poverty. The budget defines, "in the most concrete terms, the direction of national policy, the plan of action and the cost implications of government programmes and projects during the fiscal year and identifies the resources required to implement them" (Wehner 2003). Without it, even the best policy of the government will get thwarted in practice. National budgets guide the crucial functions of development and progress of a country. The budget allocates national resources to various priority sectors. The distribution of wealth and income aims to reduce inequalities in society; stabilize the economy; achieve growth rates; reduce fiscal deficits; stabilize prices, and so on. In short, the national budget is the major policy instrument to achieve the macroeconomic targets (Anura Priyadharshana Yapa 2003; IPU 2002). It is a huge trade-off among different government policies (Chowdhury 2006).

The enactment of the finance bill, called the budget, is one of the most important functions of the parliament yet paradoxically the majority of the budget-making process—from planning, formulating, and designing programs, identifying priorities, allocating resources to priority sectors, and implementing the budget—are primarily functions of the executive. Not only that, the executive is also responsible for reporting back to parliament on the implementation scenario of the budget regularly or at least once at the end of a year.

In the process of budget formulation, adoption, and execution, parliament must ensure that the fiscal policy it authorizes is well conceived and sound in perspective; that is to say, where the government gets its revenue from, where it spends it, whether it matches the needs of the population with scarce resources, whether the resources are spent with financial fidelity, and programs are implemented with economy and efficiency. Legislatures in both developed and developing countries are now convinced that their role in the budget process should be strengthened. The budgets they authorize should be treated as a benchmark for measuring government's performance and accountability against the targets set to be achieved in a fiscal year (IPU 2002). And the mounting challenge for parliament is to make sure that it can keep constant watch on every aspect of the budget process including the raising of revenue and spending of the allocations and its impact on the economy (East 2003a: 33). The information provided during formulation stage is crucial if a legislature is to play a real role in the total budget-making process, that is, planning, formulation, and adoption.

Budget Process in Parliaments in the Developed World

So far as constitutional spirit is concerned, parliaments in all countries play a key role in the budget process. But there is a great divergence in the budget process and actual potential for parliaments to play an involved role. The actual role of parliaments varies significantly even within the Westminster system of developed countries like the UK, New Zealand, Canada, and so on. Some parliaments are very seriously involved and some very minimally so. As a matter of fact, no two budget processes are identical. The adoption of the central budget is a highly formalized, complex, labor intensive, and time consuming process (Staskiewicz 2002). It does not just involve the presentation of government proposals of income and expenditure of a fiscal year for the consideration and approval of parliament. It has its planning, drafting, adopting, implementing, and evaluation stages. This is called the budget cycle or budget process, in which both the executive and parliament have their respective roles. Usually, in all countries, the national budget passes through various permutations and combinations. These are:

1. planning, formulating, and drafting of the budget;
2. legislative stages of the budget;
3. implementation of the budget;
4. evaluation and audit of the budget—the value for money stage (Wehner 2003: 27).

The diagram in Fig. 7.1 illustrates the budget process which shows two clear sets of activities. The executive functions are typically controlled by the ministry of finance. These set of activities are "internal audits, managerial reporting and debt management." These activities are shown within the circle above (Stapenhurst 2003). These sets of activities relate to financial management issues internal to the systems of government. In this area, parliaments rarely have scope to be directly involved (Stapenhurst 2003: 40). There is also other parts of the budget process external to this circle.

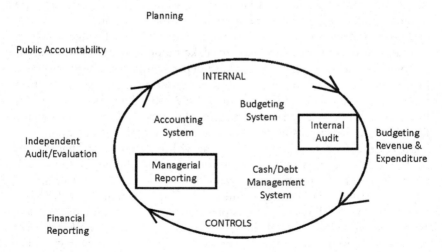

Fig. 7.1 Budget cycle in parliaments in the developed world

These are the authorization of the budget, overseeing implementation of budget spending by parliament, and independent audit of public spending by the supreme audit institutions and scrutinizing of the audit reports by the public accounts committee (Stapenhurst 2003: 40). It is in this area of financial accountability that parliaments can play a major role in the budget process. Thus, parliament can be effective in the external management of the budget, rather than in the area internal to government control systems (ibid.). Only a few developed parliaments in the West have the opportunity to provide input during the drafting stage of the budget. In these countries, economic think tank organizations, concerned CSOs dealing with economic policy analysis, and parliamentary committees discuss budget issues with different stakeholder groups and try to build a greater public consensus around the budget. On the basis of involvement in the budget process, parliaments across the world are categorized as:

1. budget making parliament (US Congress);
2. budget influencing parliament (Nordic parliaments);
3. budget approving parliament (Westminster type Parliaments).

The first is the "budget writing" approach. Like most parliaments, US Congress does not approve or adopt consolidated executive budget proposals. It is the Congress which can literally write the budget. Perhaps the largest number of parliaments fall into the second type of approach, the budget influencing parliament, in which parliament can influence the executive budget proposal after it is presented by the finance minister. Budget influencing parliaments often make modest changes like, realigning priorities, giving incentives to those departments doing well in spending and vice versa for the opposite—they can bring significant impact on the margin of the budget (Stapenhurst 2003: 40). The third category of budget approach is designated as budget approving parliament, essentially found in the Westminster tradition of parliamentary government that approves the executive budget proposal without significant changes. In these countries, if parliament withholds its assent to the budget presented by the finance minister, its disapproval would mean that "executive do not enjoy support of the majority members of the parliament" and therefore the government will resign. This is perceived as a "no confidence motion against the government" (Wehner 2003: 27–28). Most of Westminster parliaments adopt the budget proposed by the executive with marginal changes only and thus fall in the second category. The Nordic countries, most of continental Europe, Germany, France, Italy, and Latin American countries like Mexico, Nicaragua, Honduras, Panama, and Costa Rica belong to this group (Wehner 2003: 27–28). This section of the chapter will shed light on the budget process of developed parliamentary practices based on the Westminster tradition with the objective of present undergoing reforms in the budget process of developed parliaments. This study also envisions gathering policy inputs for Bangladesh Parliament to undertake changes in the budget process to match with other Westminster practices.

Why Parliament Should Be Involved in the Budget Process

In a democracy, sovereign power belongs to the people and parliament, as their representative body, is the custodian of the public purse. The executive can neither levy taxes nor incur any expenditure without the approval of parliament. Financial bills passed by parliament are not challengeable in the courts. As a matter of fact, parliament's control over the public purse justifies its claim to be sovereign. The parliament plays an essential role as the link between the taxpayer and the units of government that spend the money. As the guardian of the public purse, parliaments have the right to oversee the budget process in its totality. Joachim Wehner mentions several reasons for parliament to be involved in the budget process. First, the constitutional mandate for legislative approval of the budget. Second, parliament can ensure that the budget reflects the priorities of the nation as it represents the broader range of views in society. Third, parliament's involvement provides a system of "checks and balances and transparency of government." Fourth, participation can build consensus on difficult trade-offs. Fifth, parliament contributes to improve budget policy by the participation of a cross-section of the people of the country (http://www.ipu.org/splz-e/srilanka03.pdf; Wehner 2003: 27).

If parliament is to play its constitutional mandate in a true sense, it is expected to oversee the whole process of preparing the national budget (*ex-ante* oversight) and oversee its execution after its adoption (*ex-post* oversight). That is, parliament has a responsibility to exercise oversight before the money is appropriated (*ex-ante* control) and monitor public spending after it has been approved by the House and spent by public agencies (*ex-post* control). By exerting such influence over public finance, which is at the core of government accountability, parliament can oblige the government to remain within the bounds of legitimate authority. Without it, there would be no reason at all for the executive government to take parliament seriously (Emy 1975 in Ahmed 2002). The national budget should be a benchmark against which the government can be held to account and its performance evaluated (Anura Priyadharshana Yapa 2003: 26–28). When the legislature fails to meet this obligation, a lengthy budget process turns into "a total waste of time." And the challenge that parliaments face is to make sure that it has continuous oversight of the budget process in order to effectively keep track of all the revenue and spending issues (East, P. 2003a :33).

The Move Toward Budget Openness

Parliaments in the Westminster system are denigrated as being the least involved in the budget process; they only rarely do more than approve the executive proposal. Even in the UK, the budget process was shrouded in secrecy a decade ago. Nobody used to talk about the budget prior to the day of its presentation, and there was a lot of speculation and rumor prevailed in the weeks leading to its announcement. This situation has changed in the UK since Kenneth Clarke and Gordon Brown were Chancellors of the Exchequer (1993–1997 and 1997–2007 respectively) and continues to change in many Westminster parliaments. Today, substantial information is presented on the fiscal framework before the budget is tabled and often more parliamentary debates take place with greater transparency. Best practice in the budget process for the presidential system is to be found in the US Congress and parliamentary system in New Zealand.

The International Budget Project from the Center on Budget and Policy Priorities, a non-partisan, non-profit research organization based in Washington set up to support CSOs around the world, conducted a research in 2008 amongst eighty-five countries on the openness of eight key budget documents to the public and prepared an 'Open Budget Index.' The Open Budget Index assesses countries on the basis of how far information is made available to the public; it evaluates what type and what extent of information the government disseminates to the public in a country's budget documents. A country's position within a performance category was determined by averaging the response to ninety-one questions on the extent and depth of information disseminated about the following eight key budget documents:

1. Pre-Budget Statement;
2. Executive's Budget Proposal;
3. Citizens Budget;
4. Enacted Budget;
5. In-Year Reports;
6. Mid-Year Report;
7. Year-End Report;
8. Audit Report (Open budget Index 2008; www.openbudgetindex.org).

The research demonstrates that in respect of the openness of budget documents to the public, UK remains top with 88% openness, followed by South Africa (87%), France (87%), New Zealand (86%), and USA (82%). Bangladesh stands near the middle of the scale with 42% while India has managed to ensure 60% openness (Open Budget Index 2008; www.openbudgetindex.org). In the table below, Bangladesh's position is compared with neighboring countries. The active and informed participation of MPs in the budget process requires far-reaching information during the formulation and implementation stages of the budget process. If legislatures are to play a substantive role, they need to be well-served by an independent source of budget information. Table 7.1 presents budget transparency in South Asian countries. The level of parliaments' participation in the budget process depends to a great extent on the extent of the availability of a number of things such as:

Table 7.1   Budget transparency in South Asian countries

Document	\multicolumn{3}{c}{*Publication Status*}		
	Bangladesh	*India*	*Sri Lanka*
Pre-budget	Not published	Not published	Published
Executive's budget proposal	Published	Published	Published
Enacted budget	Published	Published	Published
Citizens budget	Not published	Published	Published
In-year budget	Not published	Published	Published
Mid-year budget	Not published	Published	Published
Year-end report	Not published	Published	Published
Audit report	Produced not published	Published	Published

Source: International Budget Partnership http://www.parliament.gov.za/content/3.1%20Parliamentary%20Fiscal%20Oversight-Camparative%20Cases.pdf

1. information on the budget proposal at the planning and formulation stage;
2. monthly/quarterly implementation status report from spending entities;
3. timely audit reports of the public expenditure from independent audit body like C&AG (Krachic and Wehner 2004)

Budget Process in British Parliament

A basic principle of the UK Constitution is that the Crown makes proposals about expenditure and taxation and the House of Commons examines and grants them.[1] This can be traced back to December 16, 1689, when the Bill of Rights was presented to William III and Mary II to become joint sovereigns of England. The Bill of Rights placed restrictions on the powers of the monarch and enshrined the rights of the Parliament, "including the requirement for regular parliaments, free elections and freedom of speech in Parliament." It laid the foundation that Parliament has to approve all new taxes and government must be accountable to the House for the way money is spent. Thus, the UK budget process is fixed to consist of the following stages.

1. Government requests;
2. Commons approves;
3. Lords consent (a formality as the House of Lords has no financial power to overturn Commons' approval);
4. National Audit Office/Parliament evaluates.

Pre-budget Discussion

The Procedure Committee (Commons) in 1998–99 described Parliament's control over public finance as "feeble" and the House's power over expenditure is close to a "constitutional myth" (Sixth Report of the Select Committee on Procedure, Procedure for Debate on Government Expenditure Plan, HC 295 of 19998-99, Para 1). Approval is always given to government proposals. However, British Chancellors Kenneth Clarke and Gordon Brown (who later became prime minister) changed this practice to some extent. Gordon Brown's decision to publish his budget proposals during November in a "pre-budget report" marked a departure from tradition (Gordon Brown, Commons Hansards, 25 November 1997, col. 773). On the other hand, the retrospective scrutiny and audit of expenditure decisions is seen as an area in which the British Parliament has made progress in recent years with both quantitative and qualitative improvements in financial scrutiny over a wide range of public policy. As such, the budget process in the UK undergoes the following stages.

The pre-budget report starts the budget process in November, six months before the fiscal year begins. It is a recent initiative, commenced in 1997, to report the government's assessment of the economy to MPs. The Chancellor of the Exchequer appraises MPs of the state of the economy in the 'Autumn Budget.' Through this statement, the government presents a mini-budget with certain proposals on budgetary policy to discuss with MPs. The pre-budget discussion provides MPs with the opportunity to have an informed debate in Parliament on the detailed choices of the government (http://eurocrisislaw.eui.eu/country/uk/topic/budgetary-process-changes/). The Treasury Committee, however, believed that the debates could be more meaningful if Parliament was given at least four weeks' notice by the Treasury of the date of the report. The government has pledged to announce the date of the report (and the actual budget) at the earliest convenient opportunity (House of Commons Treasury Committee 2007). The Treasury Committee undertakes an inquiry into the pre-budget report and takes evidence from the Chancellor of the Exchequer and other officials and experts. A Hansard Society report (Brazier and Ram 2006) recommended that, in addition to the work already carried out by the Treasury Committee, other parliamentary committees should feed their recommendations back to government after receiving evidence of the government's plans and analyzing their impact on the economy. And, for that matter, parliamentary committees should make greater use of the time between the pre-budget report and the presentation of the main budget.

Budget Process in the House of Commons

A Supply and Appropriations Bill is passed. The new tax proposal in the budget comes immediately into effect by a single motion taken after the budget speech by the Chancellor in pursuance of the Provisional Collection of Taxes Act 1968. This system is called 'vote on accounts.' It allows the House of Commons to allocate money to the government up to a certain limit until the Supply and Appropriation (Main Estimates) Bill is passed, setting a new limit and making adjustments if the government has already overspent. Votes on account are not debated.

The Chancellor makes a 'Budget Statement' to the House of Commons on a Wednesday in March, ahead of the beginning of the fiscal year on April 1. In the budget presentation, the Chancellor sets out plans as to how the money authorized by the House will be spent in the coming fiscal year. The budget statement contains all the revenue legislations for the year. General debates on the budget take place in the Commons for four days and one day in the House of Lords. Before the Finance Bill is enacted, resolutions are passed for imposing a new tax, renewing an annual tax, increasing or widening the burden of an existing tax, or for other provisions that need to be in operation within ten sitting days. Financial resolutions announced in the budget take permanent legal effect through the passage of the Finance Bill. Three or four weeks after budget day, a one-day second reading debate considers the principles of the Finance Bill, that is, in much the same way as other second reading debates take place for other legislation. The committee-level scrutiny of the Finance Bill takes place in the Public Bill Committee (a committee set up by the House of Commons to examine the details of a particular bill) and on the floor of the House depending on the nature of the subject to be debated. Non-controversial measures go the Public Bill Committee. The Public Bill Committee, comprised of opposition MPs, choose the clauses to be debated on the floor (normally the most controversial clauses). The Public Bill Committee's report on the Finance Bill goes to the House and a third reading takes place on the same day. The nature and complexity of the Finance Bill constitute a big challenge to effective scrutiny, yet Blackburn and Kennon argue that the debates during general discussion are the best argued and most effective of any devices held in the House (2003: 353). There is a day to debate the estimates of each department for the coming year and the Finance Bill goes to the House of Lords for a second reading in July and is passed without a vote and further debate on the same day. Finally, the Supply and Appropriations Bill is introduced which is passed without debate and committee stage proceedings authorizing the government to spend the amount as determined in the main estimates http://eurocrisislaw.eui.eu/country/uk/topic/budgetary-process-changes.

The budget process, as such, is highly transparent in the UK. But that does not in itself guarantee the right policy judgments nor the careful scrutiny of budget decisions (http://blogs.lse.ac.uk/politicsandpolicy/budgeting-in-the-uk-is-highly-transparent-but-that-does-not-mean-that-budget-decisions-are-carefully-s). The principal shortcoming of the British Parliament in respect of financial scrutiny is the absence of a specialized budget or appropriations committee. The public expenditure scrutiny that departmental select committees carry out under their jurisdiction vary greatly in respect of quality and process by international standards and "remains patchy at best" (Wehner 2003). On the contrary, Sweden and Germany have powerful finance and budget committees that review the total spending of budget allocations and how they are allocated across sectors. There is a risk of getting a set of executive decisions passed in parliament which were made in a high-pressure and error prone environment without using a rigorous process that irons out mistakes. This vacuum is particularly noticeable at non-incremental times when budget cuts have to be carefully prioritized (http://blogs.lse.ac.uk/politicsandpolicy/budgeting-in-the-uk-is-highly-transparent-but-that-does-not-mean-that-budget-decisions-are-carefully-s).

Budget Process in New Zealand Parliament

In New Zealand, the budget is prepared by the Treasury on behalf of the finance minister. The finance minister makes the budget statement in Parliament between June 1 and July 1. The finance minister proposes economic and fiscal measures for the upcoming year given the international economic perspective and present state of New Zealand's economy (en. Wikipedia.org). Documents generally released on the budget day are:

1. Appropriation (Estimates) Bill;
2. budget executive summary;
3. budget speech and fiscal strategy reports;
4. budget economic and fiscal update;
5. estimates of appropriations for the government of New Zealand;
6. information supporting the estimates of appropriations;
7. statement of intent press statements (en.M.Wikipedia.org).

Budget-making in New Zealand is not the sole responsibility of the finance minister. It is the outcome of a long drawn-out process in which all ministers play a major role. Ministers collectively decide on the budget strategy and spending priorities. Before commencement of the fiscal year, government departments provide necessary information to help ministers prepare the estimates. Departmental chief executives prepare the guide for budget submission of each ministry on the basis of priorities identified by ministers. Vote minister/ministers delegate the responsibility of preparing baselines appropriations of each ministry for submission on the basis of the priorities identified by individual minster/ministers as part of the government's overall budget package. Then ministers concerned develop, fine tune, and negotiate with the finance minister to set packages for their vote areas (See www.treasury.govt.nz/budget/process). The budget process allows the government to:

1. set its financial objectives in respect of revenue, expenditure, debt repayment and investment;
2. maintain effective fiscal control and plan for the coming year and beyond;
3. allocate available resources, consistent with government's strategic objectives and priorities;
4. seek authority from parliament for spending (www.treasury.govt.nz/budget/process).

In most Westminster systems, parliaments play a budget-adoptive role and do not undertake serious parliamentary scrutiny. Parliamentary members, in general, do not have the opportunity to know the content of the budget until it is presented in the House by the finance minister, nor do have adequate time to scrutinize the entirety of it during general discussions. In New Zealand, the budget process is slightly deviant to standard Westminster practice: Fig. 7.2 outlines the executive–parliament relations in the budget process in New Zealand.

Executive/Strategic Phase The executive has the responsibility to fix development and budget strategy, prepare baseline submissions, review budget initiatives, take cabinet decisions on the budget, and, finally, present it to the Parliament. The executive phase sets out strategic priorities, targets for spending, revenue, projected fiscal surplus, and public debt intentions. The strategic phase generally occurs from June to December (Budget Process_ALL/Budget PROCESS–Treasury-New Zealand.htm). These decisions are reflected in the government's budget policy statement (BPS) which requires being tabled in Parliament by no later than March 31 (see www.treasury.govt.nz/budget/process).

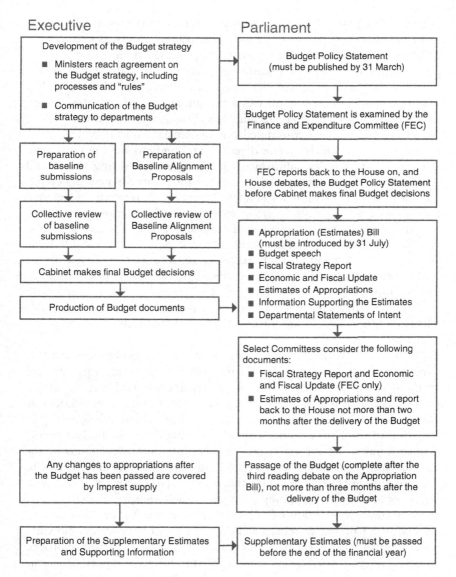

Fig. 7.2 Key phases of the New Zealand budget. (Source: http://www.treasury.govt.nz/budget/process)

Initiative/Decision Phase The initiative/decision phase generally occurs from January to April. In this phase, all spending proposals or votes are collated and coordinated as a budget package for the budget minister (the prime minister, the finance minister and the two associate finance ministers) for submission to the cabinet for consideration and final decision. The Treasury makes an assessment of all the initiatives and prepares recommendations on which initiatives ministers should support. Vote ministers' submissions are usually considered on two separate tracks: budget baseline submissions, which update departmental budgets for the next three years with any technical adjustments required under existing policy; and budget initiative submissions, which detail proposals for new policy initiatives (www.treasury.govt.nz/budget/process). A number of external panels and groups like the Social Investment Panel, the Investment Panel, and the Business Growth Agenda Leadership Group also consider and examine budget initiatives File: Budget Process_ALL/Budget PROCESS–Treasury-New Zealand.htm. On receiving approval of the cabinet on the budget package, the Treasury prepares all the necessary documents for presentation on budget day, the budget is presented to the House, and undergoes several stages for adoption in sequential order. The documents which are presented include 'Estimates of Appropriations.'

Parliamentary Phases It is in the final phase of the budget process that Parliament's approval is required for the government's budget package (all spending for the year ahead). The role of parliament is not limited to adopting the budget as it is prepared by the executive. On the contrary, its role is extended to deliberations on the budget policy statement before its presentation to the House. Following the presentation of the budget by the finance minister, all the estimates for each vote automatically go to the Finance and Expenditure Committee. This committee is entrusted with the responsibility to examine the estimates for each vote by the appropriate select committee. The spending proposal of each ministry that constitutes votes is the responsibility of the respective minister. The Finance and Expenditure Committee retains some votes for its own consideration and refers most to other select committees to examine on the basis of appropriateness. The select committees consider the fiscal strategy report, economic and fiscal reports, and estimates. The budget document is communicated to the party caucus as well as to media journalists in a 'lockup' shortly after reading the document in the House (Ahmed 2006: 53).

Select committees report back to the House within two months after budget day after examining each vote. The committees often ask the responsible minister to give evidence and justify spending proposals. The ministers concerned justify their votes in assistance with officials from their department (https://www.parliament.nz/en/get-involved/features/detailed-examination-of-the-budget/). Select committees register their observations on the main issues they have considered and put forward recommendations on whether the House should accept or change the appropriations contained in the votes. After the select committee reports are presented in the House, there is open debate among MPs on the spending proposals contained in each vote—this debate is known as the 'Estimates Debate' (www.parliament.nz/en/get-involved/features/detailed-examination-of-the-budget). Finally, the budget is passed after no more than three months of deliberations on the Appropriation Bill.

Implementation Phase During the course of budget implementation if additional appropriations are needed, Parliament authorizes spending before the end of the financial year through a (Supplementary Estimates) Bill. Parliament is authorized to provide additional spending for the period by the Supply Act.

BUDGET PROCESS IN CANADIAN PARLIAMENT

The Canadian government presents a federal budget in February or March every year before the start of the fiscal year. It presents planned government spending, expected government revenue, and forecast economic conditions for the upcoming year. All provincial budgets are released after the federal budget since provincial finances are dependent upon money from the federal government (http://en.wikipedia.org/wiki/Canadian_federal_budget).

The Budget and National Priorities

Each year, all departments of the federal government submit their 'the Main Estimates' to the Treasury Board Secretariat with planned expenditure of each department clearly stating what objectives and priorities of the current ruling government are targeted and what programs the money will be spent on. A clear linkage is shown between proposed expenses and the policy objectives of the government. The Treasury Board Secretariat compiles an initial proposed budget combining these proposed departmental budgets. The cabinet and the Office of the Prime Minister adjust the budget, taking into account a series of economic, social, and political factors such as key regions and lobby groups that might impact on the re-election of the government. Following the budget, Parliament passes an Appropriation Act to allow individual departments to spend a quarter of their annual budget (the fiscal year in Canada runs from April 1 to March 31). This authority to approve of certain portion of the budget enables Parliament to spend more time in examining the Main Estimates documents. Parliament appropriates 'Full Supply' in June.

The Expenditure Management System

"The Expenditure Management System" (EMS) constitutes the bedrock of the Canadian budget process. It sets the outline or the framework for budgeting, identifies the timetable, resources to be allocated, and set out the key roles of various actors like the legislature and executive on the one hand, and the public participation and accountability for results requirements on the other. Figures 7.3 and 7.4 illustrate the EMS and roles of the key players in the budget process. The key steps and main actors in the Canadian budget cycle are discussed below:

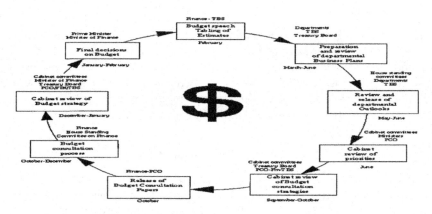

Fig. 7.3 Expenditure management systems

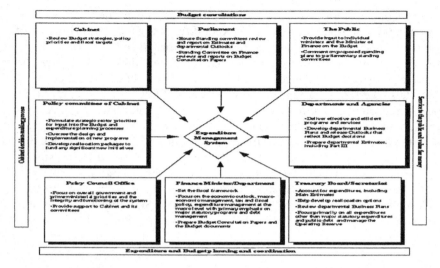

Fig. 7.4 Roles of the expenditure management system

Step 1: Budget preparation (June to September)

In Canada, the fiscal year commences on April 1 each year. The federal budget process begins in June each year and concludes by March 31. The cabinet and Cabinet Policy Committees consider the fundamentals of the upcoming budget in June. At this stage, the cabinet prepares a report on the general priorities of the government considering the public issues and concerns on the basis of the economic and political perspectives of the country. It formally sets out a plan to guide officials in central agencies and departments for the preparation of the budget. Central agencies like the Privy Council Office, the Department of Finance, and the Treasury Board Secretariat, in cooperation with government departments, integrate the advice from the Cabinet Policy Committees. The parliamentary committees develop strategies and options for the finance minister to consider as part of the budget consultation process.

Step 2: Budget consultation (September to December)

The Department of Finance, with the assistance of central agencies and other government departments, prepares the budget consultation papers on the basis of macroeconomic analyses, the country's fiscal position, and potential revenue and expenditure targets. The Minister of Finance releases the budget strategy in October in the form of a "mini-budget" and starts consultations with the Standing Committee on Finance, provincial finance minister, the general public, and other stakeholders (Federal Budget Process _ The Wildlife Society CAN.htm). Drawing on the results of the consultation process, that is, the recommendations of the Cabinet Policy Committees, the Standing Committee on Finance, and the proposal for reduction and reallocation options that the president of the Treasury Board has put forward, the Minister of Finance develops the budget strategy. The role of the Standing Committee on Finance is to advise and recommend changes in the budget. Compliance with the recommendations of the Standing Committee is not mandatory (Canada Federal Budget Process _ The Wildlife Society CAN.htm).

Step 3: Cabinet review of budget strategy

The strategy includes revenue targets, new spending initiatives, and reductions of allocations. The prime minister and finance minister make the final decision. The Treasury Board Secretariat finalizes the Main Estimates and the Department of Finance finalizes the budget documents. Thus, the budget is divided into two parts:

1. The budget speech: presents a general overview of the government's financial scenario and includes three parts:
   (a) details of the revenue budget;
   (b) general overview of spending;
   (c) overall financial state for the year.

2. The tabling of the Estimates presents spending plans for individual federal departments and includes three parts:
   (a) general overview of spending as reflected in the budget speech;
   (b) Main Estimates, a detailed requirement by individual federal departments and agencies for program delivery;
   (c) department expenditure plans (http://www.parlcent.org/en/wp-content/uploads/2011/04/articles_and_papers/Canadian_Budget_Process_EN.pdf).

Followed by the tabling of Estimates, the Minister of Finance delivers the budget speech in February, which sets out the detailed allocations of resources to departments and programs by the president of the Treasury Board.

Step 4: Budget review and approval

The deliberations on the budget commence following the presentation of the budget by the finance minister. The House of Commons under the standing order of parliament tables the Estimates no later than March 1. As a matter of practice, the Estimates are referred to the Commons standing committees. The committees call upon all concerned—ministers, senior officials, other interested parties—to appear before them. The committees examine the individual spending plans and for that matter hold necessary documents. The documents are "the budget, the government expenditure plan, the Estimates and Report on Plans and priorities for the department, and the departmental performance Reports tabled in Parliament the previous Fall" (http://www.parlcent.org/en/wp-content/uploads/2011/04/articles_and_papers/Canadian_Budget_Process_EN.pdf). The standing committee reports back to the House of Commons by May 31.

Figure 7.3 below clearly demonstrates the relations chain throughout the year and roles of different actors in the EMS (http://www.parlcent.org/en/wp-content/uploads/2011/04/articles_and_papers/Canadian_Budget_Process_EN.pdf).

If the process goes as planned, Parliament supports the government's federal budget through a vote of confidence and passes an 'Interim Supply' Appropriations Act that allows individual departments and agencies to spend a quarter of their annual budget by April 1, the start of the new fiscal year (http://www.parlcent.org/en/wp-content/uploads/2011/04/articles_and_papers/Canadian_Budget_Process_EN.pdf).

BUDGET PROCESS IN BANGLADESH

Constitutional Legal Framework

The Constitution of Bangladesh provides the basic legal framework for government budgeting. Article 82 unequivocally vests Parliament with this authority. The main articles that outline the requirements of the budgetary procedures include:

1. Article 83 says that "No tax shall be levied or collected except by or under the authority of an Act of Parliament."
2. Article 87 relates to the laying before Parliament of statement of receipts and expenditure for a financial year in the form of an Annual Financial Statement.
3. Article 88 indicates charged (e.g. non-voted) items of expenditure on Consolidated Fund.
4. Article 89 indicates that other items of expenditure are submitted to Parliament in the form of demands for grant and may be voted upon.
5. Article 90 provides for the Bill for Appropriation out of Consolidated Fund to meet requirements.
6. Article 91 provides for supplementary budget requirements for the current year (GPRB 1998: 32–35).
7. 92 (1) makes provision for any grant in advance in respect of the estimated expenditure pending the completion of the procedure prescribed in Article 89 and 90 in relation to that expenditure (GOB, Constitution of the People's Republic of Bangladesh).

Additionally, Rules 233 and 246 of the ROP stipulate parliamentary oversight over the draft. However, in that context in Bangladesh, budget preparation and its placement in Parliament is an executive business responsibility and its approval a parliamentary one.

Executive Phase of the Budget

Budget Structure

The budget in Bangladesh has generally two parts: revenue and development. These are often referred to as the revenue budget and the development budget. The former is concerned with the maintenance of normal priorities and essential services of the government and the latter is involved in development activities. The revenue budget presents current or day-to-day non-development expenditure, which may be classified according to their economic orientation into several categories such as pay and allowances, goods and services, payment of interest, subsidies and current transfers, block allocations, procurement of assets and public works, and deduction. Non-developmental expenditures are divided into two groups: non-developmental revenue expenditure and non-developmental capital expenditure. Development expenditure is used to implement projects included in ADP; these are also needed to finance non-ADP programs such as the Food for Work Programme (FWP).

Under the traditional/incremental budgeting system which prevailed in Bangladesh until very recently, the executive government was vested with the responsibility for planning public expenditure. The Finance Division of the Ministry of Finance has the overall responsibility for the preparation of the budget that outlines, amongst others, the government's proposal for raising and spending public money for a certain period of time, usually a year. The Budget Wing and the Development Wing of the Ministry of Finance are respectively charged with preparing the revenue budget and the development budget. The Development Wing, however, has to prepare the estimates of development outlay in close collaboration with the Planning Commission. The Planning Commission plays a dominant role in making the development budget (Ahmed 2006). Table 7.2 describes the budget process in a fiscal year.

Different actors and agencies, both within and outside the government, are involved in the budget preparation process. The outside actors' involvement, however, mostly remains confined to the financing of the budget; not to its making. Within the government, three organizations—the National Bureau of Revenue (NBR), the External Resources Division (ERD), and Planning Commission—play a crucial role. The NBR is mainly concerned with mobilizing resources from internal sources, while the ERD negotiates with bilateral and multilateral donors, seeking foreign aid and assistance mostly to finance development projects included in the ADP. The way these agencies behave largely influences the budgetary process, especially in respect of financing it. One thing that is noticeable is that a part of development expenditure often remains unspent, while the revenue expenditure invariably exceeds the amount voted by Parliament, thereby necessitating the introduction of supplementary budgets every year almost as a routine matter. Rarely can one find any deviation from this established practice.

Of late, Bangladesh has dispensed with incremental budgeting and shifted to what is known as a medium term budgetary framework (MTBF), as is demonstrated in Table 7.2. One of the reasons for preferring incrementalism was the fact that it at least helped most of the

Table 7.2 Budget calendar

Sl.	Particulars	Last date
1	Printing of departmental estimates	July 31
2	Printing and distribution of budget (estimating officer's forms and controlling officer's forms	August 31
3	Preparation, printing, and supply of budget form to the accounts officer concerned	September 30
4	Submission of estimates by estimating officers	October 10
5	Receipt of estimates in the Accounts office and the Ministry of Finance from controlling officers with 3 months actual	October 31
6	Receipt of consolidated estimates in the Ministry of Finance with three month's actual from the accounts officer	November 25
7	Completion of examination of budget estimates in the Ministry of Finance	January 20
8	Receipt of schedule of new expenditure in the Ministry of Finance	January 22
9	Receipt of six month's actual from the accounting officer	February 15
10	Completion of review of estimates on the basis of six month's actual in the Ministry of Finance	February 28
11	Preparation and dispatch of first edition of the budget and the schedule of new expenditure	March 1
12	Receipt back of the first edition of budget from press and dispatch to ministries/divisions	March 10
13	Forecast of foreign assistance for development program	March 14
14	Completion of discussion on estimates with administrative ministries/divisions	March 28
15	Receipt of final annual development program from the Ministry of Planning	March 28
16	Preparation and printing of budget documents	May

Source: Ahmed (2006: 58)

actors engaged in competition or conflict to be "satisfied," if not "maximized" (Simon 1957). It generally guards against radical departures from policy and reinforces the status quo. There is, however, no 'one best way' of reconciling the conflicting interests of different departments in the allocation of resources. The responsibility for deciding how much to give to different contenders rests with the Ministry of Finance. Essentially, the allocation is based on the previous year's budget with special attention given to a narrow range increases or decreases. Incrementalism, however, tended characterize more the revenue budget than the development budget. As Wildavsky observes, "The men who make the budget are concerned with relatively small increments to an existing base. Their attention is focused on a small number of items over which the budgetary battle is fought" (Wildavsky 1964: 15). One of the important drawbacks of incremental budgeting is that it was more concerned with financial inputs than with what those inputs were designed to achieve; and that it ignored outputs, performance, and the attainment of policy objectives and their relationship to costs (Dean 1989: 2).

The New Trend in Bangladesh Budgeting

The introduction in 2004 of the MTBF based on a broad macroeconomic framework is a marked departure from a traditional, centrally-driven planning, and budgeting system in Bangladesh. The MTBF was supported by the National Strategy for Accelerated Poverty Reduction (NSAPR) and ensured by the government's fiscal and public policies. Though it is a long-term process, it is already yielding positive results and is "putting in place a system of resource management which has shifted decisions to the line ministries and agencies" (GoB, MOF 2008). The MTBF now covers thirty nine ministries and accounts for 100% of total program spending.

1. a macroeconomic and fiscal framework that provides realistic estimates of the resources that will be available to the budget over the next three years;
2. an analysis of key strategies and choices that should inform the allocation of budgetary resources;
3. ministry/division-level budget strategy frameworks that link the strategic objectives of a ministry to the identification of budget priorities and allocation of available resources;
4. resource ceilings and expenditure plans that require ministries/divisions to allocate their budgets between policy programs against realistic medium-term spending plans;
5. Strengthened budget implementation procedures that ensure the timely and efficient implementation of ministry/division budgets (GPRB, Government of the People's Republic of Bangladesh, *The Constitution of the People's Republic of Bangladesh*, Dhaka, Ministry of Law, Justice and Parliamentary Affairs 1998).

The MTBF is a multi-year approach to budgeting that provides a medium-term framework for government receipts and expenditures. It links the spending plans of government to its policy objectives and requires a credible estimate of resources available for expenditure (PROGATI/BAMU: note No. 2, 2012, Medium Term Budget Framework, USAID-PROGATI). It requires decision-makers to balance what is affordable against the policy priorities of the country. It is opposed to the traditional budget approach which is incremental, that is based on percentage added to the previous year's allocation. The budgetary approach under MTBF is depicted in the diagram below. It mainly focuses on: (a) projects; (b) dual budgets; (c) making line ministries more accountable; (d) a more integrated budget structure (MOF) (PROGATI/BAMU: note No. 2, 2012, Medium Term Budget Framework, USAID-PROGATI).

The Finance Division of the Ministry of Finance, through its 'Circular 1,' presents in a consolidated way the details of preparations of the budget framework for MTBF. It spells out the objectives of the MTBF "to improve the efficiency and effectiveness of public expenditures and ensures the attainment of the goals set out in the NSAPR". The same circular spells out a preparation process that is divided into three phases: (a) strategic phase; (b) estimating phase; (d) budget approval. The three phases are further divided into several subphases (MOF) (PROGATI/BAMU:

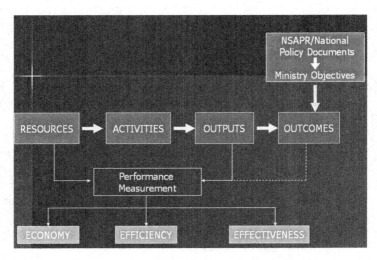

Fig. 7.5 Medium-term strategic objectives and key activities. (Source: GOB, Ministry of Finance, Budget Circular I, 2009 cited in PROGATI/BAMU: note No. 2, 2012, Medium Term Budget Framework, USAID-PROGATI)

note No. 2, 2012, Medium Term Budget Framework, USAID-PROGATI). Strategic objectives are an important part of MTBF. The table below shows the linkages among strategic objectives, activities, and concerned department/agencies. The design of the process needs the framer of projects to justify each and every project listed by each agency. This will definitely discourage unnecessary projects in the budget (Fig. 7.5).

Procedures of Budgeting under MTBF

The procedures for the preparation of the budget under the MTBF take the following stages into consideration:

1. developing/updating the Medium Term Macroeconomic Framework;
2. developing/updating the Ministry Budget Framework;
3. reviewing the budgetary framework of the line ministries/divisions;
4. finalizing and approving the ministry-wise/division-wise indicative expenditure ceiling and revenue target;
5. preparing and issuing the budget circular;
6. preparing the estimates by the line ministries/divisions;
7. reviewing and finalizing the estimates/projections prepared by the line ministries/divisions (MOF).

Figure 7.6 demonstrates the broader MTBF in relation to macroeconomic national policies/NSAPR and annual budget process and depicts the roles of different actors across government in the entire budget process. Figure 7.6 clearly suggests that the budget process is no longer the activity of the Ministry of Finance alone; it now spreads over a whole gamut of government machinery and is accomplished through an interactive and reciprocal process.

The MTBF facilitates a more integrated and unified approach to budget planning. The MTBF has introduced a single resource ceiling covering both development and non-development expenditures. This has enabled ministry/division budget submissions to address the appropriate distribution of resources between recurrent and project spending. The framework includes an estimated budget for the ensuing fiscal year and projections for the following two. Thus, the coming annual budget represents the first year of the MTBF. Each year, the MTBF process involves the rolling forward of the

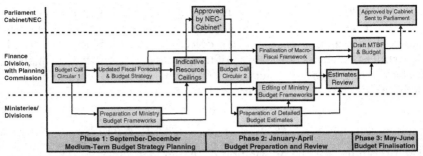

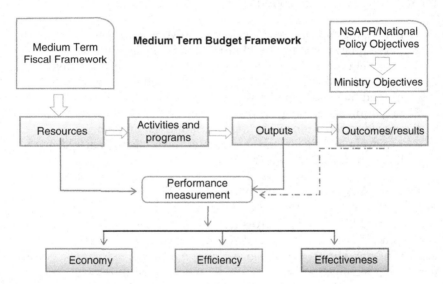

Fig. 7.6 MTBF and annual budget preparation. Integration of budgeting under MTBF. (Source: PROGATI/BAMU: note No. 2, 2012, Medium Term Budget Framework, USAID-PROGATI)

previous estimate by one year and the addition of a new out year. It ensures an improved budget documentation that is contributing to a more transparent and informed budget debate. An MTBF document is published together with the Annual Budget Documents and contains: (a) the medium-term macroeconomic and fiscal projection on which the budget has been placed; (b) the government's key spending priorities to support the implementation of its policies; (c) the medium-term strategies and spending plans of individual ministries/divisions.

Every ministry has to set targets and key performance indicators (KPIs) for its budgeted programs under 'Budget Call Circular I' and eventually the performance of each ministry is measured against these. The KPIs for each ministry are set in line with other sectoral and national goals and indicators previously set in the Millennium Development Goals (MDGs) and the Poverty Reduction Strategy Paper (PRSP). The budget entities are held to account for accomplishing the strategic goals and objectives, and the efficiency of public spending is measured against the KPIs.

Parliamentary Phase of the Budget Process

The Parliament of Bangladesh, in general, does not have significant role in the planning of public expenditure which remains the responsibility of the executive government. It is only after the budget is presented in the House that members have formal scope to deliberate over the proposals embodied in it. The presentation of the budget in Parliament follows a six-step process (Rules of procedure 111–127 and 96):

1. Presentation of the Budget (Rule 111);
2. General discussion on the Budget (Rule 115);
3. Discussion and Vote on Demands for Grants and Appropriations (Rule 116 & 122);
4. Appropriation Bill (Rule 126);
5. Finance Bill (Rule 127);
6. Presidential Assent Rule 96.

Parliament's role in the budget process may be viewed from *ex-ante* and *ex-post* perspectives. The ROP in principle retains provision for both *ex-ante* and *ex-post* parliamentary oversight. The Estimate Committee is best-placed to exercise some form of *ex-ante* control. Its main task would be to examine the estimates of expenditure and to suggest economies in spending, improvements in organization, and the form in which estimates are to be presented in the House. Parliament retains a provision to form an Estimate Committee in the ROP (BJS Rule 235). However, the Estimate Committee is allegedly an inactive standing committee in Bangladesh Parliament. Parliament only comes to know about the budget when it is presented by the finance minister to the whole House. General discussion and voting on the budget at different stages theoretically provides MPs one of the most important means of *ex-ante* control. The ROP prohibits referral of the budget to any parliamentary committee for scrutiny thus depriving the members the opportunity to go into budget contents in more depth before general discussion in the House begins.

In step two of the parliamentary phase general discussion on the budget takes place after it has been presented by the finance minister. The degree of MPs' involvement in the budget process depends on the level of information that legislatures avail. Legislatures require reliable, unbiased information to be able to hold informed debate on the contents of the budget in the general discussion. The type of information that MPs need most are an unbiased analysis of the macroeconomic situation, proposed taxation policy, its impact on the livelihoods of the poor, employment opportunities for young people and income generation for marginal communities, and for that matter provisions of explanatory notes, historical data, and comparative study, and so forth. As we have discussed in previous chapters, the Secretariat has little or no capability to provide research services to furnish MPs with this type of information. Without it, it is difficult for them to hold meaningful informed debates on the budget and influence the government to fix their priorities. MPs' opportunities to participate in the general discussion and influence the budget is limited too by a lack of time; 350 MPs get only twenty to twenty-four working days to discuss and give suggestions. There is no pre-budget discussion in Parliament or any standing committee. Time constraints are compounded by the presentation of a revised or supplementary budget at year-end, along with the proposed budget, yielding no chance to question or change the course of revisions, and further reducing the time available for deliberations of the proposed budget. Even during the passage of the supplementary budget, law-makers neither properly examine the rationale for the additional use of money nor have the opportunity to determine whether the money allocated in the previous year was properly and effectively spent (USAID-PROGATI 2011: 19). Regardless of the little time they have, MPs in Bangladesh do not seem to focus on scrutinizing policy, policy priorities, policy implications, nor make any suggestions for alternatives. Their discussions in the House suggest that they do not prepare their speeches on the issues contained in the budget proposals in advance. Rather, they use the time instead to make political statements and attack political rivals. In the name of a general discussion on budget, Bangladeshi law-makers spend more time praising their party leader and abusing the main opposition (USAID – PROGATI 2011). In addition, the restriction implied in Article 70 of the Constitution further strangulates backbencher voices, assuring budget approval without serious criticism (Bachrach 2008). Akbar Ali Khan (2008) describes this process as "rubber stamping" in order to give legitimacy to the budget prepared by the executive through certain legislative stages.

Financial Accountability System: A Triangular Relationship

Financial accountability is the core of any parliament's oversight of the executive. Since the executive cannot raise revenue without the approval of parliament it cannot proceed without proving that money allocated to it was spent for the purpose for which they were authorized. For exercising this financial accountability in the context of Bangladesh, there is a set of finance committees that include the Estimate committee, the Public Undertakings Committee, and the Public Accounts Committee. Of these three committees, the Public Accounts Committee is most engaged in *ex-post* accountability.

The Public Accounts Committee has the mandate to examine public accounts, financial statements, and the operations and audit findings of the C&AG. Collectively, this is known as the legislative audit of public finance. Independent auditors carry out two types of audits. First, a compliance audit which determines whether public expenditure has complied with regulations and legislative intent. Second, an audit to determine if expenditure incurred produced value for money, that is, it achieved its intended outcome within the agreed budget. Parliament retains the right to authorize, oversee, and supervise the public purse, which fosters transparency and accountability of government expenditure (East 2003a, b: 37). Parliament makes it an obligation for the supreme audit institution to audit the public accounts of the government and report back to the Public Accounts Committee. In Bangladesh, this function is performed by the C&AG who, along with other watchdogs, examine the government's expenditure and reports back. Thus, financial accountability in Bangladesh is formed in the relationship between three interrelated institutional organs—the executive, the C&AG, and Parliament. Parliament authorizes the budget, the executive spends it, and the C&AG verifies it; after which Parliament, via the Public Accounts Committee, reviews the audit reports

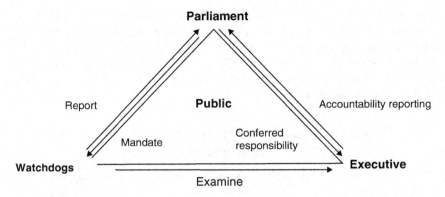

Fig. 7.7 Triangular system of financial accountability

delivered by the C&AG. As is evident, the effectiveness of financial accountability in Bangladesh then depends on how these three institutions honestly and efficiently perform their constitutional responsibilities. Stapenhurst (2003) calls it a "triangular system." If one edge of the triangle, one body within this relationship, does not work, financial accountability will fail. The health of the national economy depends on the proper use of national resources and for that matter watchdog bodies must keep watchful eyes to safeguard purse misuse and waste (Blais and Schenkelaars 2010: 1). The financial accountability system can be described as triangular institutional relationship bound by obligation and through Parliament accountable to the public (East 2003b: 37). This triangular relation is shown in Fig. 7.7.

Stapenhurst (2003: 47; www.ipu.org/PDF/publications/colombo_en.pdf) has pointed out that if the legislative recommendations based on the audit findings are forwarded to the executive and reflected in the future budgets, this could facilitate continuous improvements in government budgeting and the financial accountability system (Stapenhurst et al. 2005: 3). For both Parliament and civil society to provide greater input into the budget process, the budget content and its estimates must be both informative and understandable. Government must report to Parliament on time and provide a fair representation of the facts; the C&AG must provide useful and precise reports to the Public Accounts Committee and parliamentary oversight should be open and encourage public participation to make a difference (Stapenhurst 2003: 48).

Ex-post Oversight of the National Budget

As we discussed earlier, Bangladesh Parliament has little opportunity to exercise any form of *ex-ante* oversight of the budget. We should, however, evaluate in closer detail its exercise of *ex-post* oversight. Although *ex-post* oversight is usually considered the responsibility of the Public Accounts Committee at the end of the fiscal year, we should broaden to SCMs since they have the opportunity to scrutinize ministerial budget allocations before they go to the Public Accounts Committee as C&AG's audit reports. Each SCM has the opportunity in its monthly routine committee meeting to review how efficiently the ministerial budget is being used for implementing sanctioned programs. The unfortunate reality is, however, that SCMs in Bangladesh cannot do this effectively because the information they need is not provided to them. In many developing countries like Bangladesh, information on budget implementation is weak. Only recently has the Ministry of Finance begun to post monthly and quarterly fiscal reports on its website and provide parliamentarians and committees the chance to keep track of public spending and the status of budget implementation. Moreover, MPs in Bangladesh have to be trained effectively to make use of this information.

The main responsibility of *ex-post* parliamentary oversight is thus placed with the Public Accounts Committee. This committee derives its mandate from Article 76 of the Constitution and Rule 233 of the ROP. The Public Accounts Committee predates the establishment of other oversight committees. The scope of *ex-post* scrutiny of expenditure by such a committee exists in almost all parliaments, with some notable exceptions, for instance in New Zealand. Its responsibility in all cases assess how money granted by Parliament is spent and whether it is used most efficiently to achieve its intended purpose. In order to do this, it must scrutinize the appropriation accounts of government and examine the reports of the C&AG that include an annual audit report, issue-based reports, a special audit report, and a performance audit report.

After budget implementation, the C&AG in Bangladesh audits the government's accounts and delivers its audit findings to Parliament (as prescribed by Article 127). The Constitution makes it obligatory that all public accounts of the Republic and of all government agencies be audited and reported on by the C&AG. In order to carry out audits the audit office shall have access to 'all records, books, vouchers, documents, cash, stamps, securities, stores or other government property in the possession of any person in the service of the Republic (Article 128 of the Bangladesh Constitution). In most countries, the legislative audit is followed by the consideration of the audit findings. The auditors carry out both compliance audit and performance audit, that is to say, whether money spent has produced the intended results – the 'value for money.'

A legislative auditor audits government accounts, financial statements, and the operations of the spending units. Much of what the Public Accounts Committee has to do is decided for it by the C&AG. Through finance audit and compliance audit, the C&AG ensures financial accountability and transparency of the public sector, and through performance audit ensures the administrative accountability and transparency (Azad 2007: 38). The C&AG's office conducts strict audits of every expenditure, big or small. The constitutional mandate of the C&AG is to see that the executive has adopted all rules and regulations of financial propriety in the process of spending public funds.

The C&AG reports explain the extent to which expenditure voted by Parliament has been incurred as per prescribed rules, regulations, and laws and also the extent to which it has been incurred with faithfulness, wisdom, and economy. These reports provide the basis of the Public Accounts Committee's work. The Public Accounts Committee cannot examine any account which has not yet been audit by the Office of the C&AG. It carry out its job unless government spending units have used public money with due regard to financial discipline and the purpose voted for by Parliament. But it will struggle too if the C&AG's report are not user-friendly and clear.

The Public Accounts Committee checks a number of things. Arguably the most important is to ensure money has been spent legally and for the purpose for which parliament authorized it. It is now generally observed that a significant portion of government resources is wasted. In any case, if money has been spent in excess of the amount granted by the House for that purpose, the Public Accounts Committee must examine that carefully on a case-by-case basis. In terms of the degree of excess expenditure, the Public Accounts Committee may make recommendations as it deems fit (ROP 123 (2) (4)). With regard to financial oversight, the role of the Public Accounts Committee is exact in content and narrow in scope, whereas the Estimate Committee must define for itself the issues which it considers important and requiring a broad view of the kind that it seeks to address (Johnson 1966).

The main purpose of a performance audit is to examine an organization's programs, activities, functions or management systems, and procedures to assess whether the organization has spent money with economy, efficiency, and effectiveness in the utilization of its resources and produced value for money. The C&AG does not raise any questions about the merits of government policy during the performance audit; rather it provides fact-based and analytical information of how well the policy and program have been implemented. If the organization could not achieve expected goals, the performance audit will try to identify what the causes are behind this and how in the future the organization can achieve its goals (Office of the Comptroller and Auditor General. Government Auditing Standards, Dhaka).

As we have seen, financial accountability is anchored in triangular relations among Parliament, the executive, and the Office of the C&AG. Vigilance in, and symbiotic relations between, these three constitutional organs can construct a safeguard against the abuse of administrative/financial excesses. Unfortunately, this is extremely weak in Bangladesh, if not totally ineffective. The flow chart below presents the framework of financial oversight among the three constitutional bodies of the government of Bangladesh (Fig. 7.8).

Considering the mandate and huge responsibility assigned to the Public Accounts Committee, it neither has the adequate manpower nor logistics and infrastructure facilities. In many developing countries, public accounts committees rely on the expert services of the C&AG. At present, only one officer from the C&AG's office acts on deputation in the Public Accounts Committee, and they are severely handicapped by the lack of support services from Secretariat.

It is a common allegation in Bangladesh Parliament that the Public Accounts Committee fails to deliver its audit reports on time. This is true; the committee reviews and disposes only about 5% of C&AG reports in a year. Since independence, the C&AG has submitted 799 reports of which at the end of 2004 the Public Accounts Committee had delivered only 166. There are several reasons underlying this deplorable situation; a key one is that the Committee consistently forms late, often several months after the formation of Parliament, appropriate members are not engaged as its members and chairperson. Table 7.3 below shows the trend of delayed formation.

Until the Fifth Parliament in 1991, the Public Accounts Committee only rarely held meetings and produced reports.[2] It suffers from lack of the experienced staff, necessary electronic equipment, expert assistance, and research facilities. Many members, specially newcomers to the committee, find it difficult to grasp the technicalities of audit reports. Again,

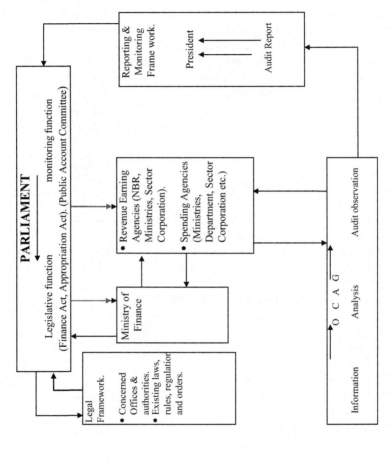

Fig. 7.8 Frameworks of accountability and transparency. (Source: Md. Shahidul Islam (2010) BRAC University Dhaka)

Table 7.3 Timelines of Parliament sitting and Public Accounts Committee formation

Parliament	Date Parliament convened	Date Public Accounts Committee formed	Delay in Committee formation
Fifth Parliament	April 5, 1991	June 8, 1991	3 months 3 days
Seventh Parliament	July 14, 1996	November 20, 1996	4 months 6 days
Eighth Parliament	October 28, 2001	May 15, 2003	18 months 17 days
Ninth Parliament	January 25, 2009	February 18, 2008	23 days
Tenth Parliament	January 29, 2014	April 1, 2014	4 months 16 days

Source: Parliament Secretariat

there is no institutional mechanism to follow-up the recommendations of the committee, nor any legal obligation for ministries or public agencies to comply. The decisions of the committee are effective only if the ministries and government agencies voluntarily obey (Azad 2007: 64–69). The chart below presents how ministries respond to the audit objections of the Public Accounts Committee. In order to improve relations between the Committee and GAG officials, a manual on the operational relationship among them was prepared under the auspices of the UNDP/SPD project (Chowdhury 2006), which was not accepted by Parliament.

The reasons underlying the underperformance of the Public Accounts Committee are manifold. They include: lack of government interest in accountability, lack of government responsiveness, uninformed committee members, closed hearings, lack of follow-up, and lack of feedback (Mitchell O'Brien, Legislative Audit, Public Accounts Committee and PBOS? (https://www.oecd.org/gov/budgeting/49788465.pdf Parliamentary Strengthening Program World Bank Institute Email: mobrien@worldbank.org) Mitchell O'Brien, Governance Specialist, Team Lead.

As we saw in the previous chapter, committee activity in general is somewhat too affected by parochial party politics; and this includes the Public Accounts Committee. Many members often fail to overcome partisan sentiment and derail a collective approach. In Westminster parliaments in which public accounts committees are reasonably effective in overseeing public expenditure, their composition is markedly different. For example,

Table 7.4 Composition and output of Public Accounts Committees

Country	Committee composition		Chair	Reports produced
	Government	*Opposition*		
Bangladesh	13	2	Treasury	1
India	14	8	Opposition	10
Canada	9	8	Opposition	10–20

Source: Public Accounts Committees, Bangladesh National Parliament http://www.pac-bd.org.bd/aboutpac.aspx

in the UK, Canada, and India, the committee is chaired by an opposition party member and the balance in membership ratio between government and opposition parties is nearly equal. Table 7.4 illustrates the disparity in committee composition between Bangladesh and two other Westminster parliaments, India and Canada.

In addition, the lack of professionalism among auditors to conduct effective audits and produce quality reports for users are due to the dual function of the C&AG: auditing and accounting (Rahman 2008: 122–d124). The structural and systematic weakness of auditing and reporting, absence of any set pattern to guide committee–ministry relations, absence of an integrated performance management and planning mechanism, and lack of public access to committees have all counteracted the Public Accounts Committee's effectiveness (Ahmed and Obaidullah 2007: 56).

From the Fifth Parliament onward, the Public Accounts Committee has been more effective than before. In that Parliament, the committee surpassed its predecessors in almost every respect although it continued to mainly discuss age-old audit objections. The Public Accounts Committee in the Seventh Parliament took the initiative to discuss recent audit objections along with the old ones. Besides, the committee took some other very important policy decisions to ensure government accountability. The Public Accounts Committee in the Eight Parliament, though formed eighteen months after the first sitting of parliament, disposed of audit objections involving larger amounts of money than its predecessors and even formed a tripartite forum to discuss long-pending old audit objections. It also suggested some policy decisions of far-reaching impact in controlling government behavior. The Public Accounts Committee in Seventh Parliament discussed audit objections and settled 25 million Bangladeshi taka in cash and kind, while the committee in the Eight

Parliament settled audit objections of 132.5 million taka. This committee resolved more than five times as many financial objections than its predecessor in the Seventh Parliament. In that Parliament's tenth session on March 31, 2004, the committee discussed and settled audit objections dating back to 1971–1972 and 1989–1990 in a tripartite forum composed of C&AG representatives, ministry representative, and an audit organization which was set up to expedite the disposal of the huge backlog of undiscussed and unresolved audit objections. The C&AG's office was instructed to produce before the committee the findings of tripartite meeting every two months (Islam 2005).

Despite this evident progress, the general conclusion that emerges is that the Public Accounts Committee in Bangladesh remains deficient in respect of exercising oversight on government spending. It has, in different parliaments, failed to be a good watchdog; and its various individual techniques of accountability have exerted little influence over the ways the Bangladeshi government has planned and spent public money. It has been consistently toothless in reigning in the unbridled exercise of arbitrary power by the executive. What is needed, as such, are measures to make the existing mechanisms of committee control more effective (Islam 2010 http://dspace.bracu.ac.bd/xmlui/bitstream/handle/10361/2089/Public%20Accounts%20Committee.pdf?sequence=1&isAllowed=y).

The USAID–PROGATI project conducted a baseline perception survey on Bangladesh Parliament's oversight capacity of the national budget and public expenditure management in January 2010. The survey team comprised several veteran MPs, former MPs, civil servants, academics, and CSO members. The research measured the perceptions of Parliament against the following variables:

1. the extent of the authority of Parliament in conducting oversight on the budget and public expenditure;
2. Parliament members' participation in the budget formulation and implementation process;
3. the effectiveness of the standing committees in oversight functions;
4. Parliament's use of media organizations and CSOs in overseeing government spending and policy;
5. MPs' use of oversight tools to serve their constituents (USAID–PROGATI 2011: 6).

Table 7.5 Parliament's ability to use its authority and resources

Sl.	Objective	Score Jan 2010	Score Dec 2010
1	The Parliament is independent in conducting oversight of the national budget and public expenditure	2.04	1.83
2	Parliament plays an active role in the annual budget process	1.44	2.01
3	Standing committees of Parliament carry out oversight on public expenditure	1.42	1.56
4	Members of Parliament make use of external resources to fulfill their oversight responsibilities	1.65	1.14
5	Members of Parliament perceive oversight responsibilities as important to serving the needs of their constituents	1.72	1.58

Source: USAID–PROGATI 2011: 6

The baseline survey was conducted in January 2010. In the December of the same year, the survey team conducted a follow-up exercise on the same issues and revealed a decline in the average score: 1.58 against 1.72 in the baseline survey on a 0–4 scale (Table 7.5).

Improving Bangladesh Parliament's Fiscal Oversight Capacity

Parliament faces several challenges in strengthening its role in fiscal oversight. Despite the institutional provisions of Public Estimates and Public Accounts Committees, and the legal provisions in place requiring it, Parliament's involvement in the budgetary process in general and fiscal oversight in particular has been and continues to be very marginal. Both these committees are crucial to fiscal oversight elsewhere in the world, but Bangladesh lags behind. Members of these committees are not properly oriented to the techniques of financial management and fiscal oversight, nor are supporting staff fiscal experts with deep understanding of budgetary issues or with the skillset to analyze complex budget documents (Policy Dialogue on Legislative Development, Brussels 2002, see in www.undp.org/governance/eventsite/policy). Against this backdrop, Parliament must look to introducing institutional and procedural changes in the budgeting system. This section proposes a series of measures worth considering.

STRENGTHENING THE PUBLIC ACCOUNTS COMMITTEE

Given the fact that the public accounts committees in many emerging democracies are weak and unable to cope with the heavy volume of tasks, David McGee has suggested an ideal form of public accounts committee efficient and effective in its operations. McGee argues that parliaments should regard the public accounts committee as its pre-eminent committee. The committee should be relatively small and composed of fair-minded and respected senior parliamentarians with an opposition party member as chair. This chimes with the UNDP's recommendation in 1997 to appoint an opposition MP as chairman (UNDP 1997. Kendra Collins and S. Magdi). The committee should prepare an annual work plan in advance and prepare an agenda for each meeting, which should be held frequently. It should be adequately resourced and all members and staff clear about their role and responsibilities. Hearings should be open to the public and a full verbatim transcript and summary minutes made promptly available to the public. "The Auditor's report is automatically referred to the committee and the Auditor meets with committee to go over the highlights of the report" (McGee 2002). In addition to the issues raised by the auditor, the committee should occasionally investigate other matters. Witnesses should be senior public servants (the accounting officer) accompanied by officials who understand every nook and cranny of the issues under examination. The committee in all its deliberations should accept the auditor as an expert advisor. Finally, parliament should hold an annual debate on the work of the committee (McGee 2002).

McGee (2002) identifies three main principles for public accounts committees to render more effective services. The principles are:

1. Parliaments pay special attention to increase their functional ability by deploying adequate resources, trained staff with access to relevant expertise.
2. Legal provisions confer the public accounts committee to act Independently of any legal and political constraints that could inhibit them to objectively and neutrally.
3. Provisions for unobstructed flow of information and ideas to be up-to-date with important developments, changing standards, and best practices as they emerge globally (McGee 2002).

Pre-requisites for Effective Budget Debates

Allen and Tommasi (2001) and Carlos Santiso (2004) observe that parliament's effectiveness in the budget process is contingent on four sets of variables:

1. whether empowerment of parliament is legal to engage in budgeting;
2. whether parliament has resources and technical support services to provide fiscal analysis;
3. whether government has the mindset to be accountable and exhibit necessary political will;
4. whether the governance situation is conducive.

The degree of MPs' involvement in the budget process depends on the information available to them. Legislatures require reliable, unbiased information to be able to participate in a constructive manner in formulating the budget and carefully monitoring its implementation. Thus, parliaments must be able to access information on the budget proposal, implementation plans, and internal and independent audit findings.

The active and informed participation of MPs then requires far-reaching support from the budget analysis office. In advanced democracies, where MPs can effectively contribute and a well-resourced parliament extends reliable expert services on the macroeconomic situation of the country, policies adopted in the budget, their likely impact, and comparative data for analysis. On the contrary, parliaments that do not provide these research services often struggle to engage in budget debates (Wehner 2003: 28–29). The value that an independent budget analysis office can provide are: simplifying the budget, promoting transparency and accountability, improving the budget process, serving majority and minority members on an equal footing, and providing rapid responses to members' requests (Anderson 2005: 39–40).

Members should be provided with non-partisan and authentic analytical services on macroeconomic and macro-fiscal analysis (David 2004). Briefings should be available on the assumptions on which the budget is prepared, the basis of revenue projection, implications of taxation policy on the overall economy, and a linkage between the budgetary allocation and government's strategic objectives, policies and priorities reflected in the NSAPR and other policy documents of the government. The PROGATI initiative extended this service to Bangladeshi MPs through establishing a Budget Analysis & Monitoring Unit (BAMU) in Parliament during lifetime of the project.

More Time for Deliberations Usually, the budget is tabled so late that hardly any meaningful discussion is possible; altogether two to three weeks, which is tiny compared to other Westminster parliaments (Ahmed 2006: 78). Bachrach suggests an early submission of the budget, no later than May 1 and revising the ROP based on the experiences of other Westminster-derived parliamentary practices discussed above, in particular Rule 111(3) that prohibits budget referral to the committees. Further, a minimum of two weeks should be given to committees for detailed scrutiny before general discussion commences in the House (along the lines of the Indian Parliament). After the end of the committee review period, the Estimate Committee should receive and compile standing committee submissions, along with its own, and report the recommendations to the floor, as in the mid-year budget review; and as soon as feasible, amendment to Article 70 be made (Bachrach 2008: 12). More time for increased deliberations on the budget can be created in two ways. First, early presentation of the budget in the House; second, in the event that the Ministry of Finance is unable to prepare the budget by this deadline, parliament may approve estimated expenditure for a part of the fiscal year two to three months before the end of the fiscal year under Article 92(a) and give adequate time to legislators to consider the budget (Khan 2008: 26–27).

Rejuvenated Role of SCMs Parliamentary committees should have an opportunity to review and discuss budget proposals before they are finalized and tabled in the House and review periodically the implementation of the budget (www.cpd-bangladesh.org Bangladesh Vision 2021, 2007: 10). The SCMs cannot only probe into the estimates and expenditure plans before adoption of the budget, they can also closely monitor implementation of each and every program planned in the approved budget. As matter of fact, this commitment of SCM work can ensure that programs are well-directed and produce quality outputs to achieve the strategic objectives of each ministry for which budgetary allocations are made. SCMs can regularly follow on fiscal monthly and quarterly reports, fiscal and macroeconomic updates, and the implementation status of the budget. There are three types of information that should be referred to the appropriate committees for detailed scrutiny:

1. The overall report on the implementation of the current-year budget for first six months should go to the Public Accounts Committee with the advice from the C&AG.
2. Reports on budget implementation by ministry/function and program, and projected allocations for the coming year, should be referred to the appropriate SCM for each to examine and then report findings and recommendations for its portion of the budget to the relevant finance committees.
3. One of the finance committees, probably the Estimate Committee, reviews the aggregate estimates for next year's budget, receives and compiles the SCM reports, and reports its recommendations for full consideration by Parliament (Bachrach 2008).

Strengthening Financial Committee Control on Public Expenditure

The Parliament of Bangladesh has set up most of the paraphernalia used by many established Westminster parliaments to exercise control over public expenditure. This includes setting up committees such as the Public Accounts Committee, the Public Undertaking Committee, and the Estimate Committee, which are designated as finance committees in addition to a large number of SCMs. However, the main problem identifying the way to make them more effective. To strengthen the parliamentary budget process requires a reorganization of finance committees that includes:

1. Creating a budget committee to perform the functions described above and be the focal point for BAMU analyses and strengthening Parliament's role in the budget process generally.
2. Giving the Public Accounts Committee more support to enable it to better perform its current functions.
3. Considering setting up separate committee to deal with tax and revenue legislation and policy, a vital aspect of the budget and influence on the economy which appears to get little scrutiny under the current structure (Bachrach 2008).

Institute Pre-budget Sessions The pre-budget report contains the government's assessment of the medium-term economic impact of policies and instruments included in the budget. It sets out the government's tax and spending plans, including public investments, in the context of its overall approach to social, economic, and environmental objectives. A pre-budget report also includes updated forecasts for the economy and projections for public finances. Parliaments in the UK and Canada have adopted pre-budget consultations in recent years (www.hm-treasury.gov.uk/media/D/1/PBR03completerep[1].pdf). Their success gives Bangladeshi parliamentarians food for thought in introducing something similar.

Involving Civil Society in the Preparation of Budget CSOs can provide their input in the budget particularly in regard to the composition of spending, quality of service delivery, and the implementation and monitoring of the budget when institutional mechanisms are in place (http:/prebudgettreasury.gov.uk/prebudget2008). The Bangladesh Vision states that by 2021 the budget should be prepared through a comprehensive consultative process, reaching out to the grassroots, and that all public spending should be made fully transparent and linked to the specific outcomes which are spelt out in the budget (www.cpdbangladesh.org Bangladesh Vision 2021, 2007: 10).

Access to Documents As we have noted, Bangladesh Parliament has suffered a chronic lack of important document provision in guiding oversight. Problems underlying the dearth of information stem from the non-cooperation of government ministries. It is alleged that often many ministry staff procrastinate with furnishing necessary information even after repeated requests. Information, when furnished, is often incomplete despite the caution expressed various committee chairs that ministries must be serious about it. However, no significant improvement has been noted in this regard (Ahmed 2006: 135) (Fig. 7.9). Measures need to be put in place to remedy this shortcoming.

Provision of Mid-Year Budget Review Under this provision, government would be required to submit by a fixed date, for example March 1, the following materials for parliamentary consideration:

1. a detailed report on the implementation of the current year's budget for the first six months, by ministry/function and program;

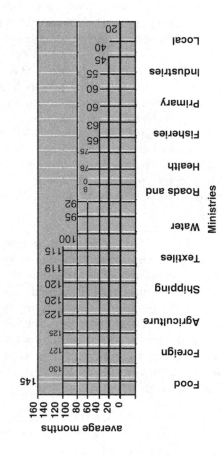

Fig. 7.9 Delays in ministry response to audit objections. (Sources: Rahman (2008) and 1st report of PAC in 8th parliament)

2. its initial projections for the coming year's budget, including aggregate expenditure, revenue and development budget estimates, and projected allocations by ministry and program;
3. draft of revised/supplemental budget (Bachrach 2008: 12).

Local Participation In an opinion survey conducted in May 1997 on the role of MPs in the budget process an overwhelming proportion (85%) of MPs reported that there was actually no participation of local representatives in budget-making. However, they cautioned that given the existing mechanism of budget-making the role of local representatives would be extremely limited (IDPAA, PROSHIKA, and Shamunnay 2002: 101). It was also pointed out that local government would need to determine the local development requirements while national parliament determine national demands. Under the current budget mechanism, the budget-making authority collects information on local demands and requirements only through administrative channels (ibid.). Thus, at the end of the day, the budget is prepared by officials who are not representatives of the people, nor answerable to MPs. In order to ensure local level participation in the budget process, MPs thus recommended that:

1. an outline of the budget be published six months to a year before formal presentation in Parliament;
2. opinions of MPs be taken in good time the budget is finalized so that necessary changes determined by local demands and priorities can be made;
3. MPs meet with pressure groups, interest groups, specialist groups, and so forth, in their local constituencies to identify local issues and ensure they are fed into a budget that is people-oriented as a result and addresses local concerns as well as national interests (ibid.).

Promote Transparency, Strict Oversight, and Public Disclosure

There should be requirements for the executive to provide more information to Parliament on a regular basis. Moreover, a greater amount of information should, where appropriate to do so, be made public. Measures to accomplish this would include:

1. A greater frequency of reports to Parliament on budget implementation. A six-month report for mid-year budget review would be ideal, but Parliament should receive reports on budget implementation at least quarterly, preferably monthly.
2. Requiring ministries to submit written responses to recommendations from committees or from Parliament, either indicating compliance or providing a detailed explanation for rejection.
3. Removing government minister from membership on the standing committees.
4. Directing that committee meetings be open to Parliament, unless committee votes affirmatively for closure, and making committee reports available to the public, including responses from ministries to committee recommendations.
5. Making reports by the C&AG, and ministry responses to them, available to the public. Reports issued by BAMU should also be made public (ibid. 14).

The government's current propensity to make changes to the budget without coming to Parliament for legislative authorization, which clearly infringes on Parliament's constitutional rights, needs also to be addressed and remedied.

Lessons for Bangladesh

The discussions in this chapter leave very clear lessons for policy-makers and parliamentarians in Bangladesh. The key one is that budgets are no longer secret documents in modern Westminster parliaments. Rather, a substantial amount of information is presented on the fiscal framework ahead of the tabling of the budget which provides MPs the opportunity to play a key role in shaping informed parliamentary debate and increases the transparency of government policy (Krafchic and Wehner 2004: 4). Government budgeting in the British Parliament, once shrouded in mystery, is now 88% open, surpassing even the US Congress' record on transparency in budget-making. And in the presidential system, the legislature is at liberty to make changes to the budget proposed by government. The rejection of a budget does not necessarily cause the president to resign and the government to fall. The structure of parliamentary democracy does to an extent constrain parliamentary participation in budget-making, particularly if one compares it with the presidential system. But reform in the

UK and New Zealand successfully created room for parliaments there to be meaningfully engaged in the budget process. The need for formal amendment on the budget proposal after tabling is likely to diminish if parliament's views are effectively taken into consideration during the drafting or consultation process in line with the MTBP (Krafchic and Wehner 2004: 4).

The introduction a few years ago in Bangladesh of the MTBF signifies a critical step toward open participatory budgeting. The new system of budgetary allocations for multiple years, opening up opportunities for Parliament to receive projected budget information two years in advance and take forward their inputs and insights in the budget, was unthinkable in the past. Furthermore, a law passed in 2009 states that the government should prepare a progress report of budget implementation on a quarterly basis. In the last few years, the Bangladeshi finance minister presented mid-term budget review reports to the House, although this is not yet institutionalized in the budget process or calendar. While these are all welcome developments, it remains the case that MP involvement in the budget process is still limited by time, restrictions on referrals to committees, and a lacuna in budget analysis services from the Secretariat. Bangladesh now needs to follow India, New Zealand, and others, and adopt the referral of budget to SCMs. Doing so will be a huge stride for parliamentary participation in budget-making and open up opportunities to ensure both *ex-ante* and *ex-post* fiscal oversight, thus stepping closer to Parliament's constitutional mandate as guardian of the public purse.

Notes

1. The UK does not have a codified or written constitution as such, but rather is formed of Acts of Parliament, court judgments, and conventions.
2. Between 1973 and 2006, the Public Accounts Committee published only thirteen reports. During the same period, the equivalent committee in the UK and Canada published on average ten to twenty reports each year and in India, more than ten each year (See Woodly B, Saghal B and Stapenhurst F (eds) Scrutinizing Public expenditure: Role of Public accounts Committee, pp. 12–18. In Bangladesh, there were only four and five reports in total published in the tenures of the Fifth and Seventh Parliaments respectively (Ahmed 2000: 9).

References

Ahmed, N. (2000) Parliament and Public Spending in Bangladesh: Limits of Control. Bangladesh Institute of Parliamentary Studies, Dhaka

Ahmed, N (2002) The Bangladesh Parliament, Ashgate: Anthony Rowe Limited, Chippenham, Wiltshire London

Ahmed, N. (2006) Limits of Parliamentary Control: Public Spending in Bangladesh, UPL, Dhaka

Ahmed, N. and Obaidullah, ATM. (2007) (eds.) The Working of Parliamentary Committees in Westminster System, University Press Limited, Dhaka

Allen, Richard and Daniel Tommasi (eds) (2001) Managing Public Expenditure: A Reference Book for Transition Countries, OECD, Paris

Anderson, B. "The Value of a Nonpartisan, Independent, Objective Analytic Unit to the Legislative Role in the Budget Preparation", IMF, XVII Regional Seminar on Fiscal Policy. The Role of Parliament in the Fiscal Policy Formulation, January, 25, 2005, pp. 39–40

Anura Priyadharshana Yapa, "Parliament and the budgetary process from a Gender Perspective", Regional Seminar (Colombo, 2003), pp. 26–28 (IPU: 2002 http://www.ipu.org/splz-e/manila02/report-e.pdf)

Azad, A.K (2007) Towards Good Governance in Public Sector of Bangladesh: The Role of Public Accounts Committee and Office of the Auditor and Comptroller General, Dissertation for the Masters of Economics, Graduate School of Economics, Faculty of Economics, Yamaguchi University, Yamaguchi, Japan

Bachrach, E. Bangladesh Parliament Secretariat Budget Analysis and Monitoring Unit (BAMU) Needs Assessment and Recommendations Report, April, 2008

Bangladesh Parliament: Rules of Procedure See Rules 246 and 247

Blackburn, R. & Kennon, A. (2003) Parliament Functions, Practice and Procedures, Thomson, Sweet & Maxwell

Brazier & Ram, V. (2006) The Fiscal Maze: Parliament, Government and Public Money, Hansard Society, London

Budget Process New Zealand Government The Treasury. http://www.treasury.govt.nz/budget/process

Canadian federal budget. http://en.wikipedia.org/wiki/Canadian_federal_budget

Carlos Santiso (2004) Legislatures and Budget Oversight in Latin America: Strengthening Public Finance Accountability in Emerging Economies, OECD Journal on Budgeting, Vol. 4, No. 2 © OECD 2004

Chowdhury, R. R. (2006) Riazur Rahman Chowdhury, Manual on Public Accounts Committee, PAC and Comptroller and Auditor- General (C&AG) Operational Relationship, UNDP, Dhaka

Daniel Blais and Fred Schenkelaars (2010) Institutional Risk Assessment Best Practices Compendium (anti-Corruption and Integrity Auditing (A private Publication)

David McGee (2002) Scrutinizing Public Expenditures: Assessing the Performance of Public Accounts Committees. https://openknowledge.worldbank.org/handle/10986/8244 World Bank. http://openknowledge.worldbank.or/handle/10986/8244 *License 2.0IGO*

Dean, P. Government Budgeting in Developing Countries (London, Routledge, 1989)

East, P. (2003a) "The Budget: Purpose, Composition and Terminology", Regional Seminar on the National Budget, Regional Seminar on the National Budget, (www.ipu.org/conf-e/104.pdf. Colombo, 2003)

East, P. (2003b) "The Respective Roles of Government and Parliamentary Process", Regional Seminar 26-28, (Colombo, 2003 https://www.iom.int/jahia/webdav/shared/.../colombo/colombo_report_2003.pd)

Emy, H. (1975) The Politics of Australian Democracy, Macmillan, Melbourne.

GOB: Constitution of the Peoples Republic of Bangladesh

House of Commons Treasury Committee (2007) "The 2006 Pre-Budget Report: Government Response to the Committee's Second Report of Session 2006–2007". HC 423, p. 14

Islam, S. M. (2005) Public Accounts Committee: *Its Role in Bangladesh:* A Dissertation by BU ID NO. 07272005 MA in Governance & Development Course. BRAC University, Dhaka

Islam, Shahidul (2010) Public Accounts Committee: Its Role in Bangladesh. A Dissertation for the Degree of M. A. in Governance and Development, Institute of Governance Studies BRAC University, Dhaka

Johnson, N. (1966) Parliament and Administration: The Estimates committee 1945–65, George Allen and Urwin, London

Khan A. A. (2008) People's Participarion in Budgetary Process: In Search of Some Policy Reforms, Unnayan Shamunnay, 2008, p. 25

Krafchic, W. and Wehner, J. (2004) Legislatures and Budget Oversight, Presented at the open forum held in Kazakhstan, Revenue Watch in Almaty (April 8, 2004)

Mitchell O'Brien, Legislative Audit, Public Accounts Committee and PBOS? (https://www.oecd.org/gov/budgeting/49788465.pdf

MOF (2008). Stands for Ministry of Finance, Government of the Peoples Republic of Bangladesh (GPRB)

Open budget index 2008. www.openbudgetindex.org

Pre-Budget Report (2003) Presented to Parliament by the Chancellor of the Exchequer by Command of Her Majesty. www.hm-treasury.gov.uk/media/D/1/PBR03completerep[1].pdf

Parliament and the budgetary process, including from a gender perspective

Policy Dialogue on Legislative Development, Brussels, 2002, PP2022 see in www.undp.org/governance/eventsite/policy

Rahman, T. (2008) Parliamentary Control and Government Accountability in South Asia, Routledge, London

Regional seminar for ASEAN+3 Parliaments Manila (Philippines) 23-July 2002. http://www.ipu.org/splz-e/manila02/report-e.pdf

Santiso, C. "Legislative and Budget Oversight in Latin America: Strengthening Public Financial Accountability in Latin America", OECD Jo

Shamunnay (2002) The Budget Making Process, A Study Commissioned by IDPAA, PROSHIKA and conducted by, UNIversity Press Limited

Simon, H. Administrative Behaviour (New York, 1957).

Stapenhurst, R. (2003) "Accountability and Transparency in the Budgetary Process: Parliamentary Oversight of the Budget: Reading, Analyzing and Questioning Parliamentary Tools and Mechanism", Regional Seminar, Colombo. www.ipu.org/PDF/publications/colombo_en.pdf

Stapenhurst, Rick, Sahgal, Vinod, Woodley, William, and Pelizzo Ricardo (2005) "Scrutinizing Public Expenditure: Assessing the Performance of Public Accounts Committee" WB Policy Research Working Paper, 3613. WO Washington D.C. World Bank. http://openknowledge.worldbank.or/handle/10986/8244 *License 2.0IGO*

Staskiewicz, W. (2002) Budget Analysis for Parliaments: The Case of Poland, Bureau of Research, Chancellery of the Sejm Warsaw, Polland) 68th IFLA Council and General Conference August 18-24, 2002 https://www.oecd.org/gov/budgeting/43411793.pdf

The Constitution of the People's Republic of Bangladesh (Dhaka, Ministry of Law, Justice and Parliamentary Affairs, 1998

The Ministry of Finance (2008) Budget Call Circular. GOB

UNDP: Chowdhury, N. (1997) Sangsad Unnayan Prokalpa (BGD/96/ 017, Implementation Plan of on Strengthening of the Parliament, Dhaka

UNDP: David Butcher (2004) Mission Report, November, Dhaka

USAID (2011) Bangladesh: Promoting Governance, Accountability and Transparency (PROGATI) Assessing Parliament Capacity to Conduct Public Expenditure Oversight, DAI/Asia Foundation: Dhaka

Wehner, J. (2003) General Introduction to the Budgetary Process, Reviewing the Variety of National Approaches, Regional Seminar on the National Budge, (www.ipu.org/PDF/publications/colombo_en.pdfGColombo, 2003)

Wieslaw Staskiewicz (2002) Budget Analysis for Parliaments: The Case of Poland, Bureau of Research, Chancellery of the Sejm Warsaw, Polland) 68th IFLA Council and General Conference August 18–24, 2002. https://www.oecd.org/gov/budgeting/43411793.pdf

Wildavasky (1964) An Incrementalist View of Budget outcomes. https://books.google.com/books?isbn=1416577629

IPU (2002) http://www.ipu.org/splz-e/manila02/report-e.pdf

Constitutional Mandate Office of the Comptroller and Auditor General. www.cagbd.org

CHAPTER 8

Human Resource Development in Parliament Secretariat: An Overlooked Agenda

CONCEPTUAL DEFINITION OF HRM AND HRD

HRM refers to the art of managing all aspects of personnel employed in an organization. It encompasses the whole process of organization management: recruitment, selection, induction, training, compensation, performance appraisal, employee development, and so on. It is geared to creating an efficient organization by providing an enabling environment for employees to fully and freely utilize their skills to the best of their potential in order to achieve the organization's intended output. HRM is focused on policies and systems that manage people within organizations. In doing so, it operates consistent with the broader rules and regulations of the government. To look at HRM more specifically, it is a process consisting of four functions—acquisition, development, motivation, and maintenance of human resources. The duties of the HRM department are to plan and coordinate the organization's use of employee talent (Nadler 1984).

HRD involves employee training, employee development, succession planning, talent management, and so forth (http://www.citehr.com/184771-difference-between-hrm-hrd.html). It is a framework that focuses on developing the personal skills, knowledge, and abilities of staff to achieve organizational aims and objectives. It is a the component of HRM that focuses on the augmentation of employees' skills. Organizations need manage changing expectations and that necessarily requires increased capacity of the staff to do that. Every organization needs specific types of knowledge and skills that cannot simply be made readily available through recruitment. Moreover, hiring new employees is a time consuming and costly process. That is why most organizations employ a HRD strategy to scale up the efficiency profile of personnel to shoulder new responsibility and be equipped to progress within the organization. HRD is engaged in developing a superior workforce for the organization in general and individual employees to help achieve that organization's overall objectives and meet customer service needs (https://www.linkedin.com/pulse/difference-between-hrd-hrm-shahir-ahmed). With this in mind, the HRM department will continually identify strengths and weaknesses of different employees and devise training programs to compensate deficiencies. In short, "HRM deals with all aspects of human resource functions and HRD is a sub section of HRM concerned with skill enhancement of the staff" (http://www.differencebetween.net/business/difference-between-hrm-and-hrd).

No administration can be better than the men and women who administer it. Workforce management as a responsibility of the organization itself is relatively new concept and practice, and evolves with the transformation of a state from underdeveloped to developed. HRM is concerned with how to attract, retain, and manage the people who make up the organization (Bogardus 2004: 2). HRD provides a professional roadmap for employees and identifies competencies required to discharge assigned functions efficiently and open up opportunities for career progression. The Association for Talent Development (ATD) has sponsored several HRD-related competency studies over the last four decades (Konan 2010) http://www.academia.edu/26623482/Models_for_Human_Resource_Development_Practice_Contributions_from_the_American_Society_for_Training). The first empirically sponsored study by the ASTD was conducted by Pinto and Walker in 1978. Pinto and Walker (1978) examined the training and development roles of organizations guided by a sound HRD policy to bring about optimism in the attitudes and abilities of those who operate the organization and carry out its functions. It found that those organizations that are able to acquire, develop, and stimulate the employees are both efficient and effective.

McLagan (1989) defined HRD as those functions of an organization geared to increasing competencies that are essential for the present and future of the employees (McLagan 1989). HRD departments must put the right person in the right place according to their knowledge, experience, and skills. This is true regardless of the type of organization—public, autonomous, or private. It is important to determine both current and future organizational requirements for the uninterrupted provision of competent manpower to meet the ever changing situation of the contemporary world and to attain the long-term objectives of the organization. McLagan (1989) identified organization development and career development as key components of HRD. Consequently, he defined HRD as "the integrated use of training and development, organization development and career development to improve individual, group and organizational effectiveness" (McLagan 1989: 7). McLagan's (1989) model presents HRD as a wheel, in which its relationship with HRM is illustrated, and his this theory has had an continues to have a profound impact on HRD practice. Areas of professional expertise are identified as specialized areas that build and rely on the application of foundational competencies http://www.academia.edu/26623482/Models_for_Human_Resource_Development_Practice_Contributions_from_the_American_Society_for_Training).

HRD is a framework for the expansion of human capital within an organization (McLean et al. 2004). At the organizational level, the HRD department, in view of the organization's perspective planning, prepares staff through organized learning over a period, divided into phases for short- and long-term objectives. Extensive orientation training helps employees assimilate and align with the organizational vision, mission, and culture. Mid-level employees receive professional development training that includes functional objectivity, performance management, managerial skills, employee relations, and so on. Employees who demonstrate high potential are given training on planning, leadership, and strategic management to prepare them for future roles as change-makers (Nadler 1984; Obaidullah 2016). HRD thus constitutes a subsystem within the organizational system for continual improvement and growth of individual employees and the wider organization through institutional training and education that aim to equip staff with the skills to address increasing demands and accomplish the organization's long-term objectives (McLean et al. 2004). There has been little agreement as to the underlying definition and primary theories that form the basis for the field. Nadler argues HRD is a series of organized processes, "with a specific learning objective" (Nadler 1984).

Scope of Human Resource Development

There can be no universal attributes applicable to human resource development for all types of organizations. However, of late, some kind of consensus seems to have emerged among HRM specialists. The model developed by the ASTD provides a focus on the scope of HRM. It identifies nine human resource areas:

1. training and development;
2. organization and development;
3. organization/job design;
4. human resource planning;
5. selection and staffing;
6. personnel research and information systems;
7. compensation/benefits;
8. employee assistance;
9. union/labor relations (Association for Talent Development, ATD, 1983 in DeCenzo and Stephen (2002: 7).

Each of these nine areas has been imagined as a spoke in McLagan's wheel. Each area has an impact on human resource outputs, performance standards, efficiency, and preparedness for change. The objective of this chapter is not to study any particular model; rather, we will focus on a few general aspects of HRD in relation to HRM in the Bangladesh Parliament Secretariat.

HRM and HRD in the Secretariat

An HRD approach is contingent upon organizational mandate and the types of services and outputs it produces. In general, specific types of skills are required for specific types of organization. Public-sector organizations are more concerned with making and executing policy and providing services to the public than they are, say, manufacturing and marketing products. The parliament secretariat is a premier political organization engaged in providing support services to MPs in making laws and maintaining oversight of executive power. Such an organization inevitably comprises employees who differ from employees in other public-sector organizations in terms of job orientation, skills, knowledge, and aptitude to work with the highest level representatives of the people. However, like other public-sector organizations, the Secretariat in Bangladesh must follow the normal process of recruitment procedure as set out in the 'Recruitment Policy' (1981) of the Bangladesh Civil Service (BCS) that is administered by the PSC. To translate the mandate of

Parliament, Article 79 of the Constitution empowers it to constitute its own secretariat and enact laws to administer its activities. To give legal effect to this, Parliament enacted the PSA 1994 which accorded the Bangladesh Parliament Secretariat an autonomous status, independent of executive control in regard to its HRM. Later, the Recruitment and Promotion Rules 2001 were framed to translate the vision enshrined in PSA 1994.

Legal Foundation of Parliament Secretariat's HRD Policy

Chapter 4 discussed the organization, and reorganization, of the Secretariat, as well as features of the PSA 1994. At the risk of repetition, it is worth simply mentioning that under this Act, the Secretariat enjoys complete independence to determine its manpower—including increasing or diminishing posts as it sees fit and undertaking internal reform and reorganizations as necessary. The Parliament Secretariat Commission, headed by the Speaker of the House along with key personnel from both government and the opposition, has authority to decide on the annual budget for the Secretariat. As such, the service conditions of officers and employees of the Secretariat are administered by the Recruitment Rules 2001 framed by the Speaker in consultation with Secretariat Commission under authority of Article 21 of the PSA 1994.[1]

Recruitment Policy and Staffing

Unless a recruitment policy is soundly conceived it is unlikely to build a first-rate staff. The selection process is the cornerstone of any large organization. There are two methods of recruiting members to the BCS. First is the direct recruitment by the PSC on the basis of open competition. The second is the indirect method based on promotion. The recruitment policy of the Secretariat, however, is guided by the PSA 1994. The Act specifically states that officers and employees of the Secretariat shall be recruited in such manner as may be prescribed by rules set out (Article 10(1) PSA 1994).

In order for the Secretariat to recruit sufficiently qualified individuals, the previous Recruitment Rules of 1982 made elaborate provisions that included direct recruitment by PSC. The indirect method comprises recruitment or contracting by internal promotion, deputation from the line ministries, and absorption from other organizations. Article 10 (2) of the PSA states that Parliament and "employees performing services in the Parliament Secretariat, excepting officers and employees obliged to perform services in the said Secretariat, immediately before the commencement of this Act shall, on the commencement of this Act, be deemed to be officers and employees of the said Secretariat" (Secretariat Act, No.8 (10(1) 1994.

The PSA 1994 made the provision that direct recruitment to Class 1 and 2 shall be made through the PSC. Accordingly, one assistant director (Research), one assistant director (Public Relations), one accounts officer, five assistant secretaries, seven committee officers, two system analysts, and one computer engineer were recruited by the PSC to the Secretariat at Class 1 in 1996. It was thus that the Secretariat, as an autonomous body in Bangladesh, begun its journey to building a permanent cadre of parliamentary officials. It was expected that these officers would be promoted over time to the higher rank positions of senior assistant secretary, deputy secretary, joint secretary, additional secretary, and secretary, and until then the Secretariat would be staffed by officials on deputation from line ministries or by contractual appointment of retired officers. This was a kind of interim arrangement which followed a pattern set in India, Pakistan, Sri Lanka, and even the British House of Commons.

It is usual practice that VIPs in Parliament and the Secretariat—the Speaker, Deputy Speaker, chief whip, whips, and prime minister's adviser for parliamentary affairs—are entitlement to engage an assistant private secretary and a few other staff of their personal choice, usually known as personal or 'privileged staff,' for their administrative assistance. They are considered political appointees and remain in office so long as the VIPs hold their office. But in 2000, twenty-two such officials were absorbed to different positions of the Secretariat's regular service in posts such as deputy secretary, assistant secretary, assistant director (of Public Relations), committee officer, legislative draftsman, computer programmer, librarian, and so on. In the case of these appointments, conditions enshrined in the Recruitment Rules (such as age limit and educational qualifications) were disregarded. The appointments did not go through any selection board. Since then, direct recruitment to the Secretariat was suspended up until 2014 with a one or two sporadic exceptions. With the direct recruitment and departure of officials (through retirement, voluntary redundancy, or death), the Secretariat's strength in manpower has stagnated and been eroded. In 2006, the Secretariat had sixty-nine parliamentary staff. By 2011, this number had reduced to fifty-three, including absorbed political appointees. To prevent further erosion, the Secretariat recruited twenty-four Class 1 officers between 2013 and 2014 into several positions including two assistant research officers. However, within a year, some of the new recruits had left their jobs.

At present, 1105 staff members are employed by the Secretariat (see the organizational chart in Annex 2). There are 123 sanctioned posts for Class 1 services, eighteen of which remain vacant. The bulk of employees belong to Class 3 and 4. Among the existing 105 Class 1 officials on the job, the majority are on deputation from line ministries of the government. Table 8.1 depicts the current staff profile of the Secretariat.

Table 8.1 reveals that the majority of Class 1 posts (i.e. the decision-making positions) in the Secretariat, from the secretary down to deputy secretary, are officials on deputation from different ministries. According to the Recruitment Rules of 1982, recruitment by promotion was the prime criteria for filling Secretariat positions. For example, the Rules set various quotas for each senior position to be filled by promoted Secretariat staff: joint secretary (75%), director (25%), deputy secretary (100%), and assistant secretary (75%). Where there exists a dearth of suitable candidates from within the Secretariat, recruitment may be made by deputation. Quotas exist too for direct appointments made by the PSC: assistant director (66%) and assistant secretary (25%). There is also provision for direct recruitment through the PSC for certain positions like committee officer, deputy director of training, legislative draftsman, research officer/assistant research officers, and so forth (for full details, see the Recruitment Rules

Table 8.1 Profile of Class 1 staff in parliament secretariat

Nature of staff profile	*Number*
Direct recruit & recruitment by promotion from Class 2	42
On deputation	52
Absorbed from other organizations	11
Positions vacant	18
Total	123

Source: Parliament Secretariat (2011)

Table 8.2 Nature of appointment in the Secretariat

Name of position	Number of posts	Nature of appointment		
		By direct recruitment promotion	By promotion	By deputation
Secretary	1	x	x	1
Additional secretary	4	x	x	4
Joint secretary	5	x	x	5
Deputy secretary	18	x	x	18
Senior assistant secretary	10		4	6
Assistant secretary	19		2	9

Source: Bangladesh Parliament Secretariat, February 2017
Eight position of assistant secretary remain vacant

of Parliament Secretariat 1982 and 2001). However, contrary to this rule, assistant and senior assistant secretary positions are frequently also drawn from ministries on deputation. The Recruitment Rules provides that 100% of deputy secretary posts be filled by promotion from within the Secretariat; but, to date, none have been filled in this way. This is why the former chief whip of Parliament and present Deputy Speaker and a former BNP MP holds that the PSA 1994 is yet to be implemented.[2] Makeshift arrangements have become a permanent system of recruitment.

Positions at director and assistant secretary level remain vacant, with seemingly no plan to fill them by either direct recruitment or internal promotion. Table 8.2 illustrations current recruitment patterns. The apparent unwillingness to recruit to these positions, which are critical roles in delivering support to MPs, has and continues to cause serious impediment to the formation of a permanent professional cadre of parliamentary officials.

In 2000, DFID presented a very grim picture of the hollowness in middle and senior management level at the Secretariat (Watson and Williams 2000). Committees are manned by inexperienced, inefficient, and inadequate staff. Subsequently, the UNDP review in 2002 pointed out that keeping 21% of regularly approved posts vacant, recruiting by deputation from ministry and contracting staff at lower and senior level who do not meet specific post requirements like academic background, knowledge, and personal skills constituted a big hurdle to the formation of an efficient professional cadre of parliament officials (Linda Buchanan et al. 2002: 30–31).

The UNDP mission put forward certain recommendations to counteract this gloomy situation that included setting out the career paths of different streams of work in the Secretariat with clear details of specific knowledge, skills, and experience; developing a new recruitment/appointment policy on the basis of merit and requirement of the post; and, as a matter of policy, using deputation only in exceptional circumstances (ibid.). The mission strongly recommended the development of comprehensive and coherent human resource policies, procedures, practices, and tools to support the effective management of human resources to better support the needs of Parliament. Reference was made to implementing a system delegation of authority and developing policies for gender equality, discipline, training, and human resources (Buchanan et al.: 33).

Unfortunately, the reality is that Parliament has not made any progress in building its own professional cadre, nor minimize reliance on deputed officials. Rather, the situation has worsened further since 2006. The questions we must now ask is: what are the reasons underlying this entrenched staffing pattern? Why are Secretariat staff ill-equipped to provide support to MPs and committees efficiently? Are they not ready to assume the greater responsibilities of more senior positions? How much importance does Parliament accord to enhance the capacity of its Secretariat? What kind of training programs exist to push career development? The remainder of this chapter attempts to address these queries.

Staff Development and Training in the BCS

The purpose of training is to increase the knowledge and skill of individuals in order to equip them with greater capacity in their field of work to cope with ever changing situations and increasing demands of the day, and minimize the shortage of trained personnel (UN Handbook 1961, in Hoque 1970: 50). It is a form of applied education closely related to the skillset required by the job. From this point of view, there is no uniform training program applicable to all types of public-sector organizations, though there is provision for the Foundation Training Course (FTC) for all cadre and non-cadre officials in the BCS. The entrants, cadre or non-cadre, should be furnished with good understanding of the nature and functions of the organization and its mandate they are called upon to fulfill.

After the FTC, specialist training institutes under each ministry deliver subsequent training. The UN Handbook emphasizes that training must always be job-oriented. The main emphasis should be on improvement in the performance of duties, and for that matter, methods of instruction should be designed to give participants the opportunities to practice improved work methods. Training focused on knowledge-building, managerial skills, and attitudinal changes should not be treated as a one-time event for civil servants, but rather a continuous personal development spanning their career. It should be a *recyclage*, the French term denoting continuous of change, renewal of skill and knowledge. The UN Handbook underscores that training needs to be organized as any other administrative undertaking. And for that, this means training the trainers and ensuring a constant supply of knowledgeable and good administrators in training programs (Hoque 1970: 49–54).

Bangladesh has a fairly elaborate public service training system for BCS cadres as far as the formal training apparatuses are concerned. This includes the Bangladesh Public Administration Training Center (BPATC), the apex training institution for civil servants which emerged in 1984, BPATC regional training centers bases at BCS divisional HQs, and a variety of other cadre-based specialized training institutes managed by government ministries and departments. Twenty-five different institutions deliver training for Class 1 officers, inclusive of BCS administration cadre officers. These training institutions provide specialist training, specific to the ministry or department, as well as training in general administration, and are closely linked to individual cadres (World Bank 1998: 29). Since Secretariat staff do not belong to any of the BCS cadres, the above-mentioned training do not apply to them except for the FTC. The FTC is the basic training course on public service management and development. As per the BCS Recruitment Rules of 1981, the FTC is compulsory for all new entrants to the BCS. The contents and methods of this course are so designed that the participants can enhance basic knowledge of various theories, concepts, and issues on administration and development in general and of rules, regulations, process, and procedures in public service delivery in particular. The course aims at building personality, stimulating creativity, and instilling leadership qualities into trainee officers (Foundation Training Courses, BPATC: Brochure P 61FTC.pdf). Strengthening Public Administration Training in Bangladesh (World Bank 1998) however found that:

> Around 50% of all officers have not attended the Foundation Training Course (FTC), although they know it is pre-condition for promotion to the mid-level; officers acknowledged the training needs and lack skills in many areas that are fundamental. (World Bank 1998)

Officers in the Secretariat did not receive systematic institutional training before the commencement of the SPD project in 1997. Training in Bangladesh has received very low priority in the career development of individual civil servants, the BCS' promotion policy, or as incentive for cadres or non-cadre officials. In regard to the total management of training—the pedigree and profile of trainers, the design of curriculums, the selection of methods—is alleged to be reinforcing the status quo, rather than changing it. In this training is anathema to the cherished reform process, rather than a facilitator and partner in the change management process.[3]

Training for Secretariat Staff

The Secretariat is unlike any other public-sector organization in regard to its purpose, organization, and composition, the nature of jobs, norms, and rules of the game. It is engaged in the unique functions of making laws and exercising oversight on the executive branch of the government. Unlike any ministry or department of the government, the Secretariat is an autonomous body and managed by a variety of officials with diverse character, experience, and academic background. After joining to Secretariat, an official may be assigned to any section—for example, legislation, committee, reporting, public relations, establishment, protocol, and so forth—under respective wings and branches to carry out the specific responsibilities for the post and mandate of that area. However, like government ministries and department, the Secretariat does not have its own training institute in which new entrants may gain the skills they require or existing staff the knowledge they need to progress their career. Training is universally seen as the sine qua non of capacity development programs. And yet, the Secretariat has hardly acknowledged this fact. The initial batch of officers recruited by the Secretariat in 1994 did not receive even the FTC or equivalent until SPD took the initiative to train them in 2000.

Likewise, MPs come from all walks of life with varying educational qualifications and professional backgrounds. It is too much to expect newly elected members to excel immediately in the craft of legislation, oversight, and governance. The earliest on in their career they can equip themselves with knowledge of parliamentary practices and procedures through institutional means or more informally from their veteran counterparts the better. But even now there is no formal institutional arrangement for MPs in this regard.

It is worth mentioning that the PSA 1994 retains a provision for training Secretariat officials and employees. Two deputy directors on deputation, designated as 'training specialists' were appointed to a 'training cell' that was established in 1998. It was simply a small unit and it was too much to expect that it could shoulder the massive responsibilities of delivering training and refresher courses for all categories of officials in the Secretariat, organize study tours and orientation programs for new MPs, and hold seminars and roundtables on parliamentary practices and procedures—all things which could be accomplished with a full-fledged parliamentary training and research institute. As such, after the launch of the SPD project, the training cell ceased to exist.

In view of the growing role of Bangladesh Parliament following the restoration of parliamentary democracy in 1991, the SPD project identified the importance of establishing a similar type of training and research institute to the Indian Bureau of Parliamentary Studies and Research. The conceived body, the BIPS, was intended to be such an institute delivering comprehensive training and providing research support to MPs and parliamentary staff. With rapid socioeconomic transformation and development of information technology, Parliament had to perform increasingly complicated functions. The need for mutual cooperation and exchange of experiences among parliaments and parliamentarians across the world became the demand of the day. This resulted in increasing parliamentary reforms globally. Against this backdrop, the SPD project proposed the BIPS to help answer this call.

The issue of the BIPS also cropped up in connection with discussion at the time on developing a parliamentary culture. It was conceived that the BIPS would arrange orientation programs for new members and MPs nominated for overseas study tours prior to their departure, as well as organize seminars and debriefing upon their return. The BIPS in whatever format would arrange training on procedure and parliamentary practices, techniques of parliamentary control of the executive, the budget process, and the key roles in the House. It would also arrange debates among MPs and CSOs on issues of national importance and facilitate discussion on public policy issues including those related to good governance, gender equality, macroeconomic analysis of the country, and so on (UNDP 1997: 28–29).

To put into place this proposal, Parliament introduced the Bangladesh Institute of Parliamentary Studies (BIPS) Act in 2001. The management and administration of the institute was vested in the executive committee and in a managing board. The qualifications, experience, and service conditions of the directors would be determined by the Recruitment and Promotion Rules 2001.

The Act envisioned a knowledge-based Parliament and well-equipped Secretariat to cope with the demand of MPs in twenty-first century. As such, the BIPS would provide orientation to new MPs, support legislation and oversight, publish issue-based research documents, and exchange experience with the Commonwealth Parliamentary Association and other countries where the parliamentary system is well established. It would deliver training the Secretariat staff to increase their awareness, efficiency, and effectiveness, publish newsletters and journals on matters relating to parliamentary affairs, and confer certificates and diplomas to graduates of the institute training programs (see activities of BIPS Act 2001). It would act as a center of excellence for all parliamentary training. Such an institution with the same kind of same vision and missions exists in Canada, India, and Australia.

After the BIPS Act was passed, an announcement was made in the official gazette and the institute came into effect immediately as a component of the SPD project. It was planned that Parliament would gradually take on management of the BIPs after the end of the SPD project. The project carried out all the programs incorporated in the BIPS Act until its end on December 31, 2007. The project's final evaluation report revealed that several interviewed MPs mistakenly referred to SPD itself as the BIPS without realizing there was a difference (Sue Nelson 2006). The project assessed the institute's needs, prepared an organizational chart, determined staff strength, and the financial cost involved in its management. An additional secretary from the Secretariat was placed as interim rector to keep things moving after the end of the project. However, Parliament showed no interest in taking over the BIPs and once the SPD project team left Bangladesh, it ceased to exist, despite the Act remaining in force.

Donor-Funded Staff Development Programs

Initially under the auspices of UNDP project BGD/1997 and later USDAID and World Bank, a series of massive capacity development programs for Bangladeshi MPs and Secretariat staff were launched and ran for more than a decade in different areas of parliamentary procedure, practices, law-making, oversight, budgeting, and parliamentary management. The activities that the project embarked on included orientation programs, seminars and workshops for new MPs and committee chairs, and research support. Simultaneously, a training program for Secretariat support staff was launched as enshrined in the BIPS Act. All these activities were undertaken under the BIPS component of the SPD project. The section below describes in more detail some of these staff development initiatives run by development partners and foreign donors.

Orientation of MPs One area of interest expressed by all members during the needs assessments of Parliament since 1991 was the arrangement for appropriate orientation programs to acquaint members with parliamentary procedures and practices to broaden their understanding of the systemic intricacies of parliamentary government and gain comparative knowledge of other Westminster systems to familiarize them with their rights and responsibilities as parliamentarians. This is, in fact, standard practice in most well-established parliaments of the world. The SPF project thus introduced such an orientation program, the scope and content of which was very wide. It covered elementary knowledge of the parliamentary system as enshrined in the Constitution and aspects of legislation, oversight, budget process, and rules governing these core functions of Parliament. New MPs were grouped into three batches and taken through phases by leading personalities in parliamentary affairs that included veteran members of parliament, constitutional experts, senior judges, legal practitioners, and academics. After orientation in the core functions, periodic seminars and workshop were organized on different issues of national importance. Prior to the commencement of the SPD project, this program was commissioned under the aegis of the Speaker's office on a limited scale.

The SPD final evaluation report in 2006 described the orientation sessions as one of the most valuable of activities undertaken. The low level of knowledge of Bangladeshi MPs on their role and the proper functioning of parliament, especially among new MPs, is a major constraint to Parliament developing its appropriate role in a democratic society. This situation is aggravated by increasing numbers of business persons who pursue elected office as an economic investment. The evaluation team also held that ensuring all MPs a solid foundation on their role and responsibilities in a parliamentary democracy, along with procedural aspects of Parliament, is an essential area for future project activities (Nelson 2006: 12). After the end of the SPD project and in absence of the BIPS, an orientation program for new members of the Ninth Parliament was carried out in assistance with National Democratic Institute and International Republican Institute. In this respect, the final evaluation report of the PRODIP project stated that sustaining institution is more important than paying for organizing events/programs (PRODIP Evaluation Report 2014).

Seminars and Workshop for MPs

The SPD project organized a series of workshops and seminars with MPs and committee chairs to find out ways and means for an increased role for MPs in legislation, oversight of the executive, involvement in the budget process, improving women empowerment, and establishing a poverty reduction strategy, to mention a few. About forty-five parliamentarians undertook study tours to other parliaments with donor support. Several MPs attended a week-long orientation program in the Canadian Parliamentary Center to widen their horizons on developed parliamentary practices. This trip left a visible impression among participants about the potential power of the committee system for oversight (Nelson: 12). These tours provided useful comparative experiences, such as the one committee chairs had when visiting the Congressional Budget Office of US Congress. The MPs and committee chairs were exposed to British Parliament and US Congress to see for themselves developed parliamentary practices and replicate them in Bangladesh parliament to the extent possible.

The SPD project included research provision too, arranging the commission and publication of ten monographs by national experts that included veteran MPs, academia, senior judges, legal practitioners, and CSOs covering a wider area of parliamentary development and governance in Bangladesh.[4] All were published in the name of BIPS. In addition, while the project was live it published a quarterly newsletter. In order to facilitate research for MPs and Secretariat staff, the parliamentary library was renovated as an LIC in line with the Asia Foundation recommendations.

Training Programs

The training curriculum designed for Secretariat officials as part of the project was divided into three categories: foundation training, legal advance training, and specialized training. Training curricula was formulated following a thorough needs assessment of staff. Moreover, workshop and skill augmentation training took place at regular intervals throughout the project period.

Foundation training was intended to instill elementary knowledge of the Constitution of Bangladesh, forms and organs of government, the ROP, the legislative process, parliamentary committees, the budget process, and so forth—the fundamentals required to understand the nature of Bangladesh Parliament, its mandate, and its interfaces with other organs of government. Advanced legal training aimed at infusing deeper knowledge about the legal fabrics of government and society and important Acts that underpin how government administers the state, institutionalizes democracy, ensures good governance, the rights of citizens—the fundamentals that members of a supreme law-making body should know. In addition, specialized training was imparted to committee support staff and committee secretaries in view of the special nature of their job. They were trained in preparing agendas, writing minutes/reports, and record management (Buchanan and Nizam 2005).

It deserves mention that more than 500 officials of the Secretariat, ranging from Class 1 to Class 3, have been trained under the umbrella of the SPD-administered BIPS. Abreast of parliamentary procedure, comprehensive training on ICT by a tech business and English language and communication training by British Council experts were regular programs of the project. Both were mainstays of the project, with over half of Secretariat staff receiving computer training. This training, coupled with the computers donated by the SPD project, has enabled Parliament to shift from a manual typewriter system to a computerized word-processing system, triggering a cultural and institutional change in attitudes and practices. The project also provided specialist training and fellowships abroad for twenty committee staff (Nelson 2006: 7). Moreover, journalists who cover Parliament during session were provided training with a view to improving their capacity to report on parliamentary business in an objective and non-partisan manner to make constituents aware of what their representatives are doing. In addition, some officials have been trained overseas, for instance at the Royal Institute of Public Administration in the UK and International Law Institute in the USA, in parliamentary administration, performance and rewards and management, legislative drafting, problem solving, and financial management. Table 8.3 demonstrates the quantum of expenditure for training provided under the auspices of the SPD project.

Specially focused training programs were designed for committee secretaries and committee officers to upgrade their competency profile on the basis

Table 8.3 Heads of expenditure for secretariat training

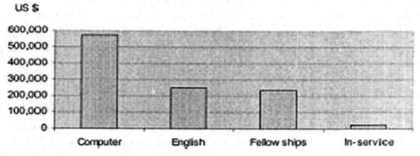

Source: Final Evaluation Report of SPD Project, 2006

of the needs assessment report of committee advisers, (Obaidullah 2011). In view of the prevailing anomalies in the sphere of committee proceedings and committee report writing, the report suggested standardization of writing committee proceedings and reports following a uniform format for all parliamentary committees. The report resulted in a series of programs that included orientation of committee chairmen and members and training of all committee officials and council officers of ministries (Buchanan and Nizam 2005). As the CS Wing had no functioning information storage and management system, the report suggested establishing an information database and easy retrieval system to provide a quicker service to committee chairs in future (Obaidullah 2011). The hitherto prevailing haphazard committee record management system was modernized by streamlining reports chronologically (from First to Eight Parliament while the SDP project was running). Records pertaining to the implementation status of committee recommendations were systematically preserved for future use in the CS Wing under the supervision of its joint secretary. MPs (until the end of the Eighth Parliament in late 2008) admitted that committees were becoming client-responsive and capable of providing services with relative ease now than before (Obaidullah 2011). Of course, after the end of SPD project, the Secretariat did not continue the systematic record-keeping of committee proceedings. In Chap. 10 we will see how MPs now rate the committees.

An assessment of impact study of the training conducted during the SPD project showed a varying range of success at different stages in terms of end results. However, it concluded the training made a satisfactory impression on officials in the context of their day-to-day work. The majority of participants in the foundation and advance legal training have rated them as having almost fully achieved their objective (75–100%). The impact study revealed that further training should be focused on those areas where specific individuals need specific skills development and included such areas as motivating subordinates, preparing minutes, setting objectives, and so on (Katrin 2004). Most of the SPD project's expenditure (20%) were directed towards the Secretariat, which is where the final evaluation team subsequently found most institutional impact. Table 8.3 shows the different heads amount of expenditure.

A survey of participant revealed largely positive impressions, though a group of participants held that it did not result in as much productivity as expected (Nelson 2006: 19) since the opportunities to put new skills into practice and reflect productively on the new knowledge gathered at home and abroad have been very limited (PRODIP Evaluation Report 2015). Buy-in from beneficiaries is essential if donor initiatives are to make any institutional impact. Moreover, there appears to have been no attempt by Parliament to set up any scheme that allows these participants to continue to upgrade these skills over a longer period of time. Measures need to be taken to ensure the sustainability and productivity of training, including strengthening the secretariat training unit, reviving the idea of the BIPS, and finding innovative and cost-effective ways to provide in-service professional training to both MPs and Secretariat staff (Nelson 2006: 19).

The training unit in the Secretariat exits on paper, but it is not functional. There is no office within parliament to take over and institutionalize the SPD training programs (Nelson 2006: 13). This is an issue that requires immediate attention. As the project neared its end in December 2006, and it became increasingly apparent that no progress was being made to establish the envisioned training institute, the project team reverted to refurbishing the existing but inactive training cell.

The project team planned to refurbish the defunct training cell as a "second line of defense." To this end, the UNDP provided logistics on the basis of need assessments (Hossain 2006) of the training cell and organized 'training of the trainers' programs to create a resource pool so that the Secretariat could continue necessary interim training programs until the BIPS is instituted. To date, however, Parliament has not made use of these resources. This has been the sorry fate of the much-need BIPs.

Promotion

The civil service is a career. It is intended to be a life-long vocation for able and competent persons with opportunities for growth, development, and promotion to higher ranks. The objective of an efficient civil service cannot be attained unless it has in place a proper and just system of promotion. The authors of the Trevelyan–Northcote Report, which catalyzed the development of the UK civil service in 1854, realized that the problem of civil service was not merely to determine what the best method was of providing it with a supply of good workers, but of making the most of them after they had been admitted. Not only should efficient and able people be retained, but persons of outstanding capacity should be discovered early and given opportunities of finding their way to positions of higher and greater responsibility while still young, fresh, energetic, and vigorous. Again, promotion is important not only for efficiency but also for morale and motivation in the service. A fair system of promotion is necessary to make this possible and also to supply enough experienced manpower to fill the higher posts of services (Hoque 1970: 46 and 296). Promotion is considered to be a very crucial area of HRD. Generally, it is given as recognition of a person's past performance and future promise.

It goes without saying that promotion is not a right. It has to be earned through one's performance. Performance needs to be judged impartially on objective criteria. Promotion to a higher grade in the civil service should always be based upon objective evidence that the person is prepared to assume a job of higher responsibility and of greater difficulty. The system should be of a kind that will command the respect and confidence of the service as a whole. To that end, the system of promotion must be thoroughly impartial and free from prejudice, nepotism, favoritism, and caprice as human ingenuity can make it (Obaidullah 2017). Again, it must be dynamic to discover the more enterprising and able. At the same time, it has to be equitable. An effective system of promotion thus has to achieve three important goals, namely, (a) to select the best people for higher positions, (b) to satisfy those to whom it is applied that it is free and just, and (c) to have creative influence on the whole staff structure.

How should the promotion system should be administered? What should be the criteria for promotion? Should it depend on seniority alone? Or merit/performance alone? Should both these factors be combined? These issues revolve around the promotion system in any organization in any country. In Bangladesh, promotion cannot be obtained on the grounds of seniority alone, but other things being equal, it becomes the determining principle. Furthermore, performance is assessed on the cumulative strength of an annual confidential report. However, the World Bank report in 1996 observed that the principle of seniority-cum-merit is only rarely followed (WB, Government Works 1996). The UNDP organizational review mission suggested in 2002 the development of a new promotion policy in the Bangladesh Secretariat that included a combination of criteria such as minimum years of service experience, written tests and interview, service record, and assessment conducted by an objective body to allow people to move upward through the hierarchy. Annual performance records used to assess the quality of employees is essentially one-way traffic. The mission stressed the need for two-way communications between the administrator and the employee with respect to performance issues, training needs, and career progression (Buchanan et al. 2002: 31).

The World Bank report mentions that promotion policy has become one of the most contentious civil service issues and a major cause of friction between cadres and services. "The promotion system is alleged to be politicized and that it offers unequal opportunities among cadres to move up the higher echelons of government" (WB, Government That Works 1996: 131). The present situation is no better than it was a decade ago. As a matter of fact, with a change in regime, a set of large-scale promotions to different positions within the civil services inevitably takes place and, equally inevitably, what follows is allegations that the civil service rules, seniority, and merit are ignored in favor of political allegiance (Obaidullah 2001). This is a common complaint about promotion for officials who belong to different cadres. As officials of the Secretariat do not belong to any cadre of the BCS, their system of promotion is different; administered under different Rules and enforced by different authorities.

Indifference to Promotion Rules

The Parliament Secretariat Recruitment Rules 2001 retains wide opportunity for career progression for all staff serving in the Secretariat. It sets out detailed provisions for promotion to all positions in Class 1—from the secretary down to a Class 3 position from Class 3–4. Rules clearly specify the conditions of service, such as required academic qualifications and experience, as well as recruitment methods. This section gives a brief picture of the promotion scenario in the Secretariat.

According to the Rules, Class 1 officials recruited by the PSC are eligible for promotion like other BCS cadres serving in government ministries and departments. The Rules state that if anybody in the position of assistant secretary/committee officer/assistant director is recruited into the Secretariat through the PSC, he/she is eligible for promotion to the next higher rank after completing three years' service. To be eligible for promotion to deputy secretary and joint secretary, candidates must have completed ten and fifteen years of total service respectively, provided that he/she has undergone the due promotion process set out in the Rules and is found suitable by the departmental promotion committee. Any official that completes twenty years of service in a Class 1 position is eligible to be considered for promotion to additional secretary, and two years' service in that position can make him/her eligible to be secretary of the Secretariat (See Recruitment Rules 2001 for detail qualification and procedure). The Rules also suggest that 100% of deputy secretary positions be filled by promotion from among senior assistant secretaries or equivalent posts in the Secretariat. Moreover, 75% of joint secretary posts be filled by promotion from among existing deputy secretaries and 25% from among the existing directors. The Secretariat, as such, has five additional secretaries, six joint secretaries, and eighteen deputy secretaries. But since the enactment of the PSA 1994 and commencement of the Recruitment Rules 2001, nobody has been promoted to deputy secretary or joint secretary/additional secretary. Only two officials to date have been promoted to director who have completed more than twenty years of service. Only one director has completed more than five years of service in the same position and technically met the criteria to be eligible for promotion to joint secretary. But as such all joint secretaries are drawn from the line ministries.

The promotion process is both very slow and damaging to the potential of many to serve effectively while they are energetic and capable to serve. When the positions of deputy and senior assistant secretary level remain vacant, secretariat management prefer to fill such positions by deputation, not by promotion from among eligible officials of the Secretariat. This is a glaring disregard of existing promotion rules. Currently, the Secretariat has seven senior committee officers, only two of which qualify for promotion to deputy secretary level. There are three senior assistant secretaries, directly recruited by the PSC, each of whom served fourteen years and eight months in Class 1 service. However, two of them have three years of experience as senior assistant secretary and are considered to be eligible for promotion to deputy secretary. The other officials, at senior assistant secretaries/

senior committee officer level have completed more than ten years in Class 1 service; but did not get promotion when it was due as per recruitment rules and thus making them ineligible for promotion to deputy secretary. This sluggish promotion system makes parliament staff de-motivated and indifferent to work.

The library and research sections are now both headed by a director, an official of equivalent rank to deputy secretary, who is a deputed official. The current deputy director of the Parliament Library has completed more than sixteen years in Class 1 service (five years in the deputy director position) and is thus eligible for promotion. However, they were not considered. There is a myriad of other cases of officials working in different sections who have completed fifteen to eighteen years of Class 1 service without a sniff of promotion. This career stagnation understandably causes a great deal of simmering frustration. It is no exaggeration to say if the recruitment rules were followed and officials were promoted when they became eligible, many of the most senior positions in the Secretariat would now be staffed by Parliament's own cadre of professional staff. This certainly would have minimized the reliance on deputed officials which has hampered the efficiency of the Secretariat over the last few decades.

Motivation and Employee Morale

Motivation is in many ways the key to the success of the HRD process. It has a direct bearing on performance in the workplace. For a leader to be effective they must understand how performance relates to environment, ability, and motivation. The extent to which subordinates accept a superior as a leader depends heavily on that person's ability to stimulate motivation (Henderson and Soujanen 1975: 25). As institutions become larger and bureaucratized, requiring greater and careful planning of all the steps in the operational process, it is evident that nothing is more important than motivation (Dimock and Dimock 1964: 238). Staff may feel motivated by material and also non-material incentives. At certain stages, employees accord more importance upon recognition for their work than anything else. In developed countries, employees are recognized not only by promotion but by reward non-material incentives such as, for example, end-of-year awards or expressions of especial appreciation of their sincerity and commitment to performance. This kind of non-material motivation is not commonplace in Bangladesh, particularly in public-sector organizations. Promotion is the only recognition of work that employees receive and expect. And if it is discriminatory and not based on transparent criteria, employees inevitably feel de-motivated to work and acquire new skills.

As we noted above, the promotion of officials in the Secretariat is irregular. It has been mentioned already that in 2000, several officials were absorbed in the regular cadre of parliamentary professional services who were political appointees and considered the privileged staff of VIPs in Parliament. Later, their recruitment in the service was considered irregular since it did not comply with the normal process of recruitment set out in the 2001 Rules. After their induction into the regular service, senior management made a provision to consider their previous service for promotion and approved a 'seniority principle' for the promotion of absorbed officials via a gazette notification in July 2001. This seniority principle helped absorbed officials supersede those officials who were regularly recruited before them through the PSC. This understandably caused resentment among the regular staff. The Secretariat Officers' Welfare Association lodged a writ petition in the High Court Division (HCD) of the Supreme Court in 2001 (Petition No.4714/2001) against this recruitment by absorption and seniority principle for promotion, which the HCD declared unlawful, and hence void, in a judgment passed on March 3, 2006. The Appellate Division, however, stayed the operation of the HCD judgment on an appeal by those appointees. The case still remains unresolved today. As a result of the long-pending decision in the highest court of the country, several officials recruited through the PSC have left the parliamentary services out of frustration.

Whether the Supreme Court determines the appointment of absorbed officials to be legal or not, however, these officials have experienced fluctuating fortunes over the years with the changes of power structure in Parliament. Between 2001 to 2006, they were treated as underdogs, deprived of some opportunities to train overseas on the grounds that they were undergoing legal proceedings in the High Court. The officials who were recruited by the PSC and became eligible for promotion between 2001 and 2006 were not considered for promotion since they might have been considered *sub judice* as the dispute in the Supreme Court wrangled on. After the election of a new parliament in 2008, fortune smiled upon absorbed officials, who received promotion despite the pending court ruling. This situation has created deep-seated discontentment and frustration among those regular officials who have been deprived of their promotion due to ongoing disputes in court. Their frustration is compounded as, frozen out, they fall behind junior officials in the regular parliamentary services.

Final Observations

We have seen in this chapter that the Secretariat has passed laws and adopted several policies intended to make it independent, resourceful, and self-sustained. To address issues around recruitment, a new HR Wing was created in the Secretariat in 2004.

However, HRD has not proceeded along the lines expected after the enactment of the Acts and framing of the recruitment and promotion rules to make a transition from subordination to independence/empowerment. If Parliament had realized and capitalized on the benefits of the changes made in the post-restoration period, the Secretariat could stand on its own in respect of its staffing, training, and research provision to render wider support to MPs in legislation and oversight. But this has not taken place. The main reasons underlying this setback is the indifference of Parliament's senior management to HRD in general, and unwillingness to establish a full-fledged research and training institution in particular, as a permanent solution to these existing problems. The SPD final evaluation team observed in 2006 that "the failure to establish an institute of parliamentary studies is a significant setback to the establishment of institutionalized and sustainable training and research capacities" (Nelson 2006: 12). Three successive regimes since the BIPS Act was passed did not take the initiative to establish BIPS as an organ of the Secretariat.

In addition, Parliament failed to develop a professional cadre of parliamentary staff as provided for by the Act and envisioned by the Rules. The gloomy picture presented by DFID and UNDP in the early 1990s and 2000s regarding staffing patterns and the concern expressed for the excessive reliance on deputed officials persists today. Of course, very recent steps have been taken by the Secretariat to reorganize its structure and create a new B&IT Wing under the authority of PSA 1994. Moreover, several posts have been created at director, deputy secretary, senior/assistant secretary, senior committee/committee officer, and senior system analyst levels (see Bangladesh Parliament Secretariat Order, HR Wing, April 5, 2011). A number of officials have been promoted to deputy director following the creation of new posts, mostly in the Public Relations office, the beneficiaries of which have been mainly absorbed officials. However, this change did not result in the career progression of regular

Secretariat officials inasmuch as satisfy a handful of officials who were considered to be politically privileged staff.

A considerable stumbling block in Bangladesh's journey to creating a modern and efficient professional parliamentary cadre is the Secretariat's indifference to recruiting fresh assistant secretaries, committee officers, and research officers through the PSC and promoting them in due time after a program of rigorous needs-based training at home and abroad on parliamentary practice and procedure. In fact, between 1996 and 2014, the Secretariat nearly shut the door completely to new entrants, preferring to fill vacancies with officials on deputation. Its spurning of the 2001 Recruitment Rules and refusal to promote its own officials to senior decision-making posts sparked an adverse chain effect on the experience and efficiency of both senior and middle management.

The reason underlying the Secretariat's indifference to fresh recruitment and promotion is party-political. In principle, it follows the merit criteria in recruitment and seniority-cum-merit in promotion. Yet, some kind of patronage system has continued to be in operation throughout, irrespective of regime change. The basis of inducting officials on deputation is their political allegiance to the regime. And parliamentary senior management has more trust in the deputationists than it does its own regular officials. With every change of government, responsible leadership positions in the Secretariat go to deputed ministry officials or by contract to whomever the top brass considers to share their political ideology and belief. This has caused a barrier in the development of institutional memory. The SPD final report observes that there is a nucleus of trained staff, especially in the CS Wing. However, the impact of training is limited without specialized cadres at the higher level of Parliament. For instance, the SPD project trained six staff to run the computer center. Of the six, only two remain there today. Three have left Parliament completely and the other is working in the law section. Most Secretariat staff are civil servants on rotation or deputation within Parliament. "These officers have little interest in developing career in parliament and valuable institutional memory is lost as the project trained staff move on" (Nelson 2006: 7).

The strong words contained within the Secretariat Recruitment Rules ring hollow. HRD has been ignored where it could, if implemented effectively, have provided the Secretariat with a strengthened backbone of professional staff able to deliver effective support to Parliament, its members, and its committees. Instead, recruitment has been politicized, with ideology and cronyism taking precedence over skill and expertise. Until Parliament's top tier decides to eschew parochialism and minimize its reliance on ministry officials, an effective Secretariat in Bangladesh remains a distant dream.

Notes

1. Framing of rules:
   1. The Speaker may, on consultation with the Parliament Secretariat Commission, by notification in the official Gazette, make rules for carrying out the purpose of this Act.
   2. In particular and without prejudice to the generality of the foregoing power rules shall be made in respect of all or any of the following matters:-
      (a) arrangements for the development of, and the proceedings of, the Parliament Secretariat;
      (b) distribution of duties among the officers and employees;
      (c) maintenance of records and papers;
      (d) conduct of the library;
      (e) preparation of gratuity, journey bills and their signature and counter-signature;
      (f) security of the Parliament Secretariat (http://www.commonlii.org/bd/legis/num_act/psa1994228/_)
      (g) all matters concerning the residences of the Members of the Parliament;
      (h) preparation of bills relating to remunerations, allowances and other privileges of the Members of the Parliament and discharge of the relevant duties connected with all those bills.
2. The author interviewed several key personnel on the subject of the Secretariat's continued inadequacy even after prolonged training and capacity development initiatives in the post-restoration period. All respondents argued that the present staffing of the Secretariat is the root cause of its inefficiency; had the PSA 1994 been implemented in full the Secretariat would have been manned by its own permanent and efficient staff from day one.
3. For deficiencies of Training System in Bangladesh See GOB: Towards Better Government 1993, UNDP: Raga Makharita, Mission report 1999 and ATM Obaidullah, "Image and Weakness of Bangladesh civil Service: an Overview" Administrative Change, January–December, 2001: 50.

4. Monographs were prepared by senior MPs, academics, and think thank organizations, and published by the SPD-administered BIPS. The ten monographs include: *Parliamentary Rules and Practices* (in Bangla), Ahmed. N. *Parliament and Public Spending in Bangladesh: Limits of Control,* Hakim., A. *The Changing Forms of Government in Bangladesh: The Transition to Parliamentary Democracy,* Obaidullah. ATM. *Democracy and Good Governance in Bangladesh: The Role of Ombudsman,* Rahman, N. *The Independence of the Speaker: The Westminster Model and the Australian Experiment,* Ali Ashraf MP, *Ethical Standard of Parliamentarians,* Bhuiyan. R. *Women, Democracy and Parliament,* Khan, M.M. *Relations between the Executive and Legislature.*

References

Bangladesh Institute of Parliamentary Studies (2001) BJS Dhaka
BJS (1982) Recruitment and Promotion Rules of the Bangladesh Parliament Secretariat, Dhaka
BJS (2001) Recruitment and Promotion Rules of the Bangladesh Parliament Secretariat, Dhaka
Bogardus, A. N. (2004) Human Resource Basic, San Francisco, London
Brochure of 61st Foundation Training Course, Bangladesh Public Administration Training Center: 4 48_Brochure
Buchanan, L. and Ahmed Nizam (2005) Final Report: Competency Skills Workshop for Committee Secretaries and Committee Officers (Dhaka, SPD/UNDP, Dhaka
David Watson and Deborah Williams (2000) Support to Parliamentary Committees in Bangladesh, DFID Bangladesh
DeCenzo, D. and R. Stephen (2002: 7) Personnel: Human Resource Management, Wiley John Wiley & Sons
Dimock, M. E. and G. O. Dimock (1964) Public Administration, Oxford & IBH Publishing Company, New Delhi
For Deficiencies of Training System in Bangladesh See GOB: Towards Better Government, 1993, UNDP: Raga Makharita, Mission report 1999 and ATM Obaidullah (2001) "Image and Weakness of Bangladesh civil Service: An Overview" Administrative Change, January–December
BJS. For details see Recruitment Rules of Bangladesh Parliament Secretariat (1982 and 2001)
Henderson, R. I. and W. W. Soujanen (1975) Operating Manager, Prentice Hall of India, New Delhi
Hoque, A. N. Shamsul (1970) Administrative Reforms in Pakistan, NIPA, Dhaka
http://www.academia.edu/26623482/Models_for_Human_Resource_Development_Practice_Contributions_from_the_American_Society_for_

Training). (McLagan, 1989) (McLagan 1989: 7). (McLagan's (1989) http://www.academia.edu/26623482/Models_for_Human_Resource_Development_Practice_Contributions_from_the_American_Society_for_Training); http://www.citehr.com/184771-difference-between-hrm-hrd.html; https://www.linkedin.com/pulse/difference-between-hrd-hrm-shahir-ahmed

Katrin, L. (2004) Impact Assessment: Training for Bangladesh Parliament Secretariat (imparted under Strengthening Parliamentary Democracy Project, BGD/97003, UNDP, Dhaka

Konan, A. (2010) The HRD competencies as perceived by the human resource development professionals in banks in Cote D'Ivoire. Unpublished doctoral dissertation, College of Graduate and Professional Studies, Indiana State University, Terre Haute, Indiana (available at Models for Human Resource Development Practice: Contributions from the American Society for Training and Development (ASTD). http://www.academia.edu/26623482/Models_for_Human_Resource_Development_Practice_Contributions_from_the_American_Society_for_Training

Buchanan, Linda et al. (2002) Organizational Review of Bangladesh Parliament Secretariat, Dhaka

Lindley, J. A. (1991) An assessment of the Institutional Development: Needs of the Parliament of Bangladesh, Asia Foundation, Dhaka

McLagan, P. A. (1989) Models for HRD practice. American Society for Training and Development, Alexandra, VA: ASTD Press (available at Models for Human Resource Development Practice: Contributions from the American Society for Training and Development (ASTD)). http://www.academia.edu/26623482/Models_for_Human_Resource_Development_Practice_Contributions_from_the_American_Society_for_Training

McLean, G. N., Osman-Gani, A. M., and Cho, E. (eds) (2004) "Human Resource Development as National Policy", Advances in Developing Human Resources, Vol. 6, No. 3 https://books.google.com/books?isbn=1605093343

Nadler, L. (ed) (1984) The Handbook of Human resources Development, John Wiley and Sons, New York. https://www.amazon.com/Handbook-Resource-Development...Nadler/dp/0471892343

Nelson, S. (2006) Final Evaluation Report of the Strengthening Parliamentary Democracy Project, BGD/97/003, UNDP, Dhaka

Obaidullah, A. T. M. (2001) "Bangladesh Civil Service: Its Image and Weakness", Administrative Change, Vol. 29

Obaidullah, A. T. M. (2006) "Reorganization of Bangladesh Parliament Secretariat: A Move Towards NPM", presented in international conference on administrative reforms in South and South East Asia, June 28–29, at Bangladesh Public Administration Training Center, Savar, Dhaka, 2006

Obaidullah A. T. M. (2011), "Reorganization of Standing Committees on Ministries of Bangladesh Parliament: A Quest for Increasing Operational & Institutional Efficiency", South Asian Survey, Vol. 18 (2)

Obaidullah, A. T. M. (2017) "Civil Service Reforms and Development of Professionalism" in Studies in South Asian Governance (eds) Rumki Basu and M. Shamsur Rahman, Routledge, London

Parliament Secretariat Act, No.8 (10(1)) 1994, BJS, Dhaka

Petition No.4714/2001

Pinto, P. R. & Walker, J. W. (1978) A Study of Professional Training and Development Roles and Competencies, Madison, WI: American Society for Training and Development

PRODIP Evaluation Report (2015) Promoting Democratic Institutions and Practices The Asia Foundation, Dhaka

Trevelyan North-Northcote Report on Civil Service Reform (1854) http://www.publications.parliament.uk/pa/cm201314/cmselect/cmpubadm/74/7405.htm

UNDP and Chowdhury, N. (1997) Implementation Plan on Strengthening of the Parliament, Dhaka

UNDP and Hossain, S. (2006) BIPS Needs Assessment Report, UNDP/SPD, Dhaka

United Nations (1966) Handbook of Civil Service Laws and Practice, New York, United Nations Department of Economics and Social Affairs, Public Administration Branch

USAID: Bangladesh (2014) Promoting Democratic Institutions and Practices (PRODIP program USAID Cooperative Agreement No. 388-A-0010-00092-00 Asia Foundation), Dhaka

World Bank (1996) Reforming Public Sector Government That Works Reforming Pubic Sector, Dhaka

World Bank (1998) Strengthening Public Administration Training in Bangladesh, Dhaka

CHAPTER 9

Gender Mainstreaming in Parliament

CONCEPT OF GENDER

Since the beginning of human civilization, gender inequality has existed in society. This inequality is not natural. There are no differences in intellect and capabilities between men and women. Rather, each society for its own convenience has created distinct roles for men and women. This has come to be neatly summarized by the term 'gender issues.' In simple terms, gender connotes the division of labor and role assignment for men and women, boys and girls that a particular society considers appropriate under prevailing social norms and practices. The realization of gender inequality as a barrier to sustained sociopolitical and economic development has come to the forefront in development communities from since the last quarter of the twentieth century. Despite a plenitude of reforms and initiatives to minimize gender inequality over the last four decades, it continues to prevail in most of what we would call advanced societies in the Western world.

Sex is frequently confused with gender. However, the biological difference between men and women has nothing to do with gender. The terms "male" and "female" indicate difference in biological sex; while "masculine" and "feminine" are indicative of gender categories. The differences between "male" and "female" is biological and gender are not given. Rather, they are socially constructed and "depend on traditions, beliefs, religion, literacy, socio-cultural values and economic variables that determine the role and place of men and women in society" (www.IPU. Wehner

2004a, b: 56). Differentiating between men and women from a gender perspective in modern democracies is contrary to international law and human rights.

Gender is an overarching concept that relates to a set of cross-cutting sociocultural variables such as race, class, age, and ethnic group. Gender construction is based on the sociocultural background of a society that determines what is expected and valued in woman/man and girl/boy in a specific context (http://www.un.org/womenwatch/osagi/pdf/factsheet2.pdf). Gender roles change over time and are learned through socialization processes. Gender systems are institutionalized through the traditions and norms a society bears, education systems it establishes, political ideology it believes in, economic systems it considers suitable, culture heritage it practices, and customs and legislations that govern it. A gender approach does not focus on individual men and women; it focuses on the societal system which determines gendered roles and responsibilities, access to and control over resources, and decision-making. Gender, as such, is interchangeable with 'women' as it is frequently misconstrued. It refers to both men and women and the relations between them in a given society.

A gender approach promotes a society which can engage men and women equally in all types of activities. However, research on gender perspectives in recent years has tended to lay the focus directly on men. The reasons underlying increased this are manifold. First, men are considered the main allies to gender equality. Second, until men change their attitudes and behavior in areas such as reproductive rights and health, gender equality is unlikely to progress. Third, in many contexts the gender systems in place are negative for both sexes—creating unrealistic demands to behave in narrowly defined ways. The increased focus on men will have significant impact on future strategies for working with gender perspectives in development. And a considerable amount of research is taking place on male identities and masculinity by both women and men.

Gender Equality

Gender equality is established when a society ensures equal rights and opportunities for men and women across all sectors, including economic activities, and extends opportunities to women to participate in decision-making positions. Such a society favors and values equally the behaviors, aspirations, and needs of women as it does men (http://www.genderequality.ie/en/GE/Pages/whatisGE). Again, gender equality can be established when the diverse needs, rights, and opportunities of both men and women are not dependent on biological identity. Gender equality is a human rights issue and a precondition for, and indicator of, sustainable people-centered development (http://www.un.org/womenwatch/osagi/pdf/factsheet2.pdf). It is more often than not women and girls who are discriminated against in health, education, and income generating activities with negative repercussions on their freedom. The UN Gender Inequality Index measures gender inequality on these criteria. Similarly, Social Watch's Gender Equality Index focuses on the gap between women and men in education, the economy, and political empowerment (http://www.genderequality.ie/en/GE/Pages/whatisGE).

The World Economic Forum introduced the Global Gender Gap Index in 2006 to capture the magnitude and scope of gender-based disparities and measure national gender gaps on economic, political, education, and health criteria. This Index "looks at economic participation and opportunity deviation; educational attainment deviation; health and survival deviation and political empowerment deviation" (http://www.genderequality.ie/en/GE/Pages/whatisGE).

The UN prefers the term 'gender equality' to gender equality. The Beijing conference in 1995 arrived at a consensus that the term 'equality' would be preferred to any other. The concept of gender equality involves an element of social interpretation of justice based on tradition, religion, or culture that constitutes a hindrance to women's advancement and can be detrimental to reducing the gender gap. The essence of gender equality is that the rights, responsibilities, and opportunities of individuals are not dependent on sex identity—whether one is born male or female. The promotion of gender equality does not mean women and men will become the same (Concepts Underlying Gender Mainstreaming (http://www.un.org/womenwatch/osagi/pdf/factsheet2.pdf).

Gender equality between women and men has both a quantitative and a qualitative aspect. The quantitative aspect refers to the representation of women: increasing balance and parity in elected bodies, public services, and facilities in the workplace. The qualitative aspect refers to achieving equitable influence in decision-making and establishing development priorities for women and men. In a sociopolitical context, men and women have different roles and responsibilities because of their differing priorities and needs, yet equality envisions giving equal weight to both men and women in planning and decision-making. There is a dual rationale for promoting gender equality. First, human rights law and social justice require that women and men have equal rights, opportunities, and responsibilities. Second, sustainable people-centered development requires greater equality between women and men. Women and men have different perceptions, interests, needs, and priorities, and all should be taken into consideration in the planning and decision-making process, not only as a matter of social justice but also as necessary pre-condition for enriching development processes (Important Concepts Underlying Gender Mainstreaming (http://www.un.org/womenwatch/osagi/pdf/factsheet2.pdf).

Throughout history, and even today, women have suffered gender inequality. Men and boys enjoy civil and political rights and access to key resources such as education, land, credit and decision-making power, while women and girls lag behind in most societies. Globally, women are more resource-poor, illiterate, and more likely to be affected by health conditions such as HIV/AIDS compared to men. On a worldwide scale, less than 5% of women own land, occupy fewer government positions, and have an average of just over 15% of seats in parliaments (http://www.ipu.org/wmn-e/world.htm).[1] This inequality and poorer access to resources squeezes women's capability to influence decisions in personal domestic issues at home and in communities and at the national level as well (http://www.ipu.org/wmn-e/world.htm).

Gender equality is not simply a women's issue; rather, it is a human rights issue that concerns the equal rights, responsibilities, and opportunities for men, women, boys, and girls. Gender equality presumes that the interests, needs, and priorities of both women and men are diverse and should be taken into consideration prior to any planned action. Mainstreaming gender, therefore, does not mean increasing women's participation and adding a 'woman's component' or even a 'gender equality component' into an existing set of activities. It means making full use of the experience, knowledge, and interests of women and men to formulate any policy on a development agenda. Gender mainstreaming may call for changes in goals, objectives, and strategic management so that both women and men are in a position to influence, participate in, and benefit from development processes. Mainstreaming gender is thus focused upon transforming unequal social and institutional structures into equal and just structures for both men and women.

Experts have developed ways and means to measure gender relations and assess progress toward equality. One such measure is adopted by the Task Force on Gender Equality and the MDGs, co-chaired by the World Bank and UNDP and established by the Inter-agency Network on Women and Gender Equality in 2003. The Task Force views the level of gender equality between women and men from three different perspectives:

1. gender equality in relation to capabilities;
2. gender equality in relation to access to resources and opportunity;
3. gender equality in relation to the security domain.

The three domains are symbiotically related to enhance women's capability to shape and influence decisions that affects their life at the household, community, national, and global levels (www.IPU. Wehner 2004a, b, See Box 35, p. 33; www.ipu.org/PDF/publications/budget_en.pdf). In all countries, irrespective of development status, gender roles and relationships are determined by society and transmitted through cultural traditions, beliefs, and norms that undergo change slowly over time. Gender identities, their relationships, and varying roles generate different needs and concerns in society. National governments and international organizations collect data on different aspects of gender roles and relations. For example, "the Inter Parliamentary Union (IPU) collects data on women's participation in parliaments worldwide and the United Nations Development Program (UNDP) publishes annual data on women and men's capabilities" (www.ipu.org/wmn-e/world.htm).

GENDER MAINSTREAMING

The Fourth World Conference on Women held in Beijing in September 1995 reached a consensus that gender mainstreaming is a worldwide strategy and intergovernmental agenda to promote gender equality through the Platform for Action at the United Nations (http://www.un.org/womenwatch/osagi/intergovernmentalmandates.htm). Gender mainstreaming goes beyond creating separate women's projects within work programs, or adding women's components within existing plan of actions/ or allocating special grant for women (http://www.un.org/womenwatch/osagi/pdf/undppaper.PDF). It means consideration of gender perspectives as part and parcel for all planned activities throughout the program. Central to the gender perspectives is that men and women have equal access to resources and participation in the decision-making process, policy development, research, advocacy, and in the implementation and monitoring of all development programs. The UN General Assembly held a special session to follow up on the Beijing Conference in June 2000 which reinvigorated the mandate for gender mainstreaming considerably. The UN did not thrust gender mainstreaming upon governments. Rather, member states reached a consensus in intergovernmental discussions in the mid-1990s to adopt mainstreaming gender as an important global strategy for promoting gender equality. The mainstreaming strategy did not discard targeted activities to support women. Since gender equality has not been attained and mainstreaming processes are not well developed activities, specifically targeting women's priorities and needs would continue through, legislation, policy development, research, and separate projects/programs.

Sometimes women-specific initiatives are intended to reduce existing disparities and to serve as a catalyst for promoting gender equality and creating an empowering space for woman; an incubator for ideas and strategies. It is crucial to bear in mind that empowering women and mainstreaming gender are mutually complimentary strategies, not in competition or mutually exclusive. "The two strategies are complementary in a very real sense as gender mainstreaming must be carried out in a manner which is empowering for women" http://www.un.org/womenwatch/osagi/pdf/undppaper.PDF. In July 1997, the United Nations Economic and Social Council (ECOSOC) defined the concept of gender mainstreaming as follows:

> Mainstreaming a gender perspective is the process of assessing the implications for women and men of any planned action ... at all levels. It is a strategy for making the concerns and experiences of women as an integral part of the design, implementation ... of policies and programs ... The ultimate goal of mainstreaming is to achieve gender equality (http://www.un.org/womenwatch/osagi/intergovernmentalmandates.htm)

GENDER RESPONSIVENESS AND GENDER SENSITIVENESS

Gender responsiveness is an approach that organizes and operationalizes organizations in such a way that they take into account and respond to the needs and interests of both men and women alike (IPU 2008). A gender-sensitive organization is based on the principle of gender equality where organizationally both men and women enjoy equal position and equal right to participate in the decision-making process without discrimination.

How gender equality can be achieved by setting of priorities and strategic, well-targeted interventions is directed by a gender equality policy

(IPU 2008). Gender responsiveness is defined by Bloom and Covington as "creating an environment ... that reflects an understanding of the realities of women's lives and addresses the issues of the participants." (cited by NIC 2001: 75). Being gender responsive means creating an environment through site selection, staff selection, program development, content, and material that reflects an understanding of the lives of women and girls and responds to their strengths and challenges (Covington and Bloom, http://www.stephaniecovington.com/assets/files/assessment/GRAssessmentToolNonCj.pdf). To what extent a program is gender responsive can be assessed by a tool which program administrators, program evaluators, and agency monitors can use to evaluate the gender responsiveness of programs for women and girls and obtain feedback for improving the quality of a program's services (http://www.stephaniecovington.com/assets/files/assessment/GRAssessmentToolNonCj.pdf).

Importance of Gender Equality in Parliaments

Since parliament is the apex representative institution comprising the people in all their diversity (IPU 2006)—men, women, ethnic groups, and social classes—gender equality in parliament is crucial. A parliament cannot claim to be democratic and legitimate unless it is constituted with the support of all segments of the society it claims to represent. The IPU believes that should a country claim to be democratic it needs first to ensure that both men and women participate in administering state affairs in a balanced way. When the role of women is undermined in the management of public affairs the overall institutional legitimacy suffers as a result (http://iknowpolitics.org/en/discuss/e-discussions/parliamentary-oversight-gender-equality).

The parliament of a country should as far as possible be an inclusive institution with diverse representations and range of different perspectives. However, most parliaments in the world do not equally represent men and women. Article 4 of its 1997 Universal Declaration of Democracy states that: the objectives of democracy is likely to be achieved in favorable conditions when men and women work in partnership in the conduct of the affairs of society and when both can enrich from their differences and diverse qualities (www.Quotaproject.org/CS/CS_Europe-Jabre05. Kareen Jabre, "Strengthening Women's Participation in the Inter-Parliamentary Union").

Men and women have separate needs and interests in society; when women members constitute so small a portion of parliament that it cannot take full account of the diverse needs of a major segment of the population, parliament itself loses its representational ability and institutional efficacy in general. In this situation, parliament's core institutional functions degenerate and it loses public trust http://iknowpolitics.org/en/discuss/e-discussions/parliamentary-oversight-gender-equality). The Commonwealth Ministers Responsible for Women's Affairs met in Fiji in 2004 and held the view that parliamentarians are strategically placed to provide leadership in advancing gender issues in the political decision-making process. This resulted in finalizing the new Commonwealth Gender Plan of Action, 2005–2015. Of the diverse functions of parliamentarians now they are expected to push forward gender equality issues as central to their business because:

1. parliament presents both men and women;
2. laws impact differently on men and women;
3. gender equality is a global objective;
4. parliament plays a crucial role in enforcing the international conventions;
5. gender rights are human rights;
6. budgets and other national policies differently impact on the lives of men and women;
7. parliamentarians reflect the needs and demands of their constituents—all men and women, specially marginalized groups (Strengthening Capacity of People's Elected Bodies in Vietnam, ONA–UNDP Project Vie/02/007, Gender Mainstreaming in Parliaments: International Best Practices, October 2005, P.5)[1]0.11

Parliaments are key stakeholders in the promotion and achievement of gender equality. The international community holds the view that promoting gender balance in parliament is essential for increasing legislative capacity, performance, and legitimacy. The effectiveness of legislative oversight should be assessed on the basis of impact on both men and women (Kinyondo et al. 2015). The more equitable representation of women in parliament the more it is likely to reflect the wide spectrum of views of society in its enactments and enforcements. The larger the presence of women in parliament the greater is the benefit for the nation. Parliaments with greater gender balance are more representative, are more responsive, are more effective in overseeing the executive and enjoy higher levels of trust (http://iknowpolitics.org/en/discuss/e-discussions/parliamentary-oversight-gender-equality). If we correlate the data on the levels of trust in parliament made available by the Afrobarometer we find that trust in legislatures increases as women's diverse interests are taken into account (Women in Parliament: www.parl.gc.ca/content/lop/researchpublications/prb0562-e.htm). This correlation is demonstrated in Fig. 9.1.

However, women, who constitute 50% of the population, have much lower representation in most parliaments of the world (Helena Hofbaurer Balmori, BRIDGE-Gender Budget Package Report, www.Bridge.ids.ca.u). Against this backdrop, the international community has taken a number of resolutions and adopted a number of commitments to get the issue of underrepresentation of women raised in parliaments. For example, equal participation of women and men in public life constitutes the crux of the Convention on the Elimination of all Discrimination Against

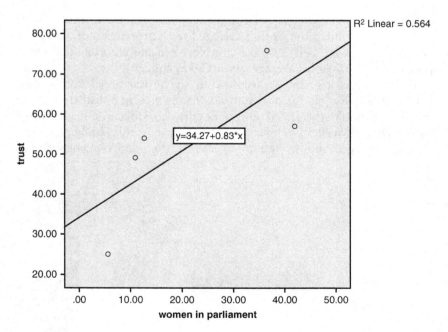

Fig. 9.1 Representation of women and level of trust. (Source: Women in Parliament: www.parl.gc.ca/content/lop/researchpublications/prb0562-e.htm)

Women (CEDAW) convention of 1979. As a matter of fact, the CEDAW convention has brought governments across the world under commitments to attain the advancement of women since 1985 as signatories to the convention. Bangladesh is one such signatory. Since the situation did not progress despite the commitments made a decade previous, the Beijing Platform for Action 1995 identified twelve areas for action of which 'reducing inequality between men and women in positions of state power and decision-making was a prime one' (Women in Parliament: www.parl.gc.ca/content/lop/researchpublications/prb0562-e.htm).[1] All these initiatives, however, failed to turn the tide and move societies toward greater gender equality. The UN MDGs and Target 3.A in particular emphasized the need for increasing the number of seats in national parliaments reserved to women to 30% across UN member states by 2015. The UN target and actual seats held by women in national parliament is shown in Fig. 9.2 below.

However, the current proportion of women members in national parliaments stands at around 20%. There are parliaments where women representation is far below 10% or completely non-existent. In this respect, the Pacific region has the world's average lowest proportion of women in parliament, just 3.5% (if Australia and New Zealand are excluded) compared to the 20% global average (www.Crikey.com.au).

Parliament is a country's window to the international community. Parliaments reflecting a gender imbalance thus present a distorted image of their country (http://iknowpolitics.org/en/discuss/e-discussions/parliamentary-oversight-gender-equality). Against this backdrop, this chapter makes a modest attempt to analyze the gender mainstreaming

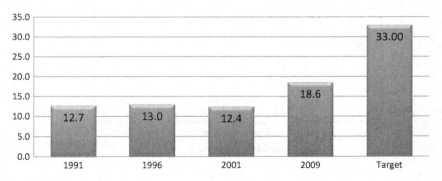

Fig. 9.2 Proportion of seats held by women in national parliament (%)

perspective of Bangladesh Parliament from its organization, composition, and functional standpoints. The chapter has been prepared based on secondary sources of data and issues have been analyzed in the light of those parliaments in the Commonwealth and elsewhere where affirmative measures have been adopted to mainstream gender in parliaments and achieved a certain degree of success. It asks to what extent Bangladesh Parliament is gender responsive in its organization, representation, legislation, oversight, and budgeting functions.

Barriers to Gender Mainstreaming in Parliaments

Representation matters because it shapes policy. It is through democratic representation in parliament that women can make their voices heard to the nation. The role of men and women constantly changes in society and new policies being formulated to facilitate the changes. If women members in parliament do not increase in number they risk lagging behind their male counterparts in crafting policies and legislation concerning these changes. Like other human rights, gender equality is a Human Right too and they need more seats in parliament (http://www.huffingtonpost.co.uk/frances-scott/gender-equality_b_7540358.html). Yet, hardly is there any country in the world today where men and women strike an equally weighted balance in national parliament. On the contrary, parliaments in most parts of the world have been criticized for promoting a culture of patriarchy restricting women's participation and perpetuating gender inequality. Bangladesh Parliament is no exception.

Internationally, women's low representation in parliaments constitutes a focus. It is true that the international community came on a consensus and demonstrated willingness to increase women's representation. Article 7 of the CEDAW convention reiterated the need for increasing the number of women's representatives in the political life of member countries. But a number of factors have made it very difficult for women to run and be elected to parliaments.

By May 2010, only twenty-four countries worldwide had achieved the MDG target of 30%. Nordic countries, due to long-standing initiatives, have been successful in increasing women's participation in politics. African countries made commendable strides in increasing women's representation in their national parliaments by reforming electoral law and political party practices. This remarkable progress was achieved not by gradual organic improvement but by a radical reconceptualization of the electoral and parliamentary practices in a way that recognized the importance of establishing equality between men and women (Women in Parliament: www.parl.gc.ca/content/lop/researchpublications/prb0562-e.htm). Table 9.1 below demonstrates the proportion of women's representation in world parliaments.

There are number of steps that individuals must go through to get elected. First, they need to make up their mind to run in the national elections; second, they need to be selected to run by their political parties; third, they need to be voted by their constituents (Women in Parliament: www.parl.gc.ca/content/lop/researchpublications/prb0562-e.htm). A number of barriers obstruct the path to parliament for women who decide to run; particularly societal phenomena and behavioral attitudes which are unlikely to be remedied by legal and institutional reform. For example, women are weaker compared to men in family because their low income and often non-involvement in income generating activities. Moreover, they receive disproportionate share of household income and bear the burden greater family responsibilities than men. In addition, social norms give women an understanding that politics is an unsuitable or undesirable vocation for them (Canada's Royal Commission on Electoral Reform and Party Financing. Lortie Commission 1991). In this situation, the political parties can take a leading role in advancing women's increased representation in parliament. They can be a catalyst for increasing nominations and persuading and supporting women to contest elections. The reality, however, particularly in Asian democracies, is that political parties do not often lend this support to women.[1] (Women in Parliament: www.parl.gc.ca/content/lop/researchpublications/prb0562-e.htm).

Table 9.1 Proportion of women in world parliaments

Region	Single or Lower House	Upper House or Senate	Both Houses combined
Nordic countries	40%	–	40%
Americas	20.6	21.6%	27.7%
Europe OSCE (including Nordic)	19.2%	16.9%	18.8%
Europe OSCE (excluding Nordic)	17.3%	16.9%	17.2%
Sub-Saharan Africa	17%	17.6%	17.1%
Asia	16.4%	17.6%	16.5%
Pacific	12.1%	27.4%	14.1%
Arab States	8.2%	6.0%	7.7$

Source: http://www.ipu.orgwmn-e/world.htm
OSCE: Objective Structured Clinical Examination

Gender and Bangladesh Parliament

Constitutional Commitments

The Bangladesh Constitution retains an elaborate provision for fundamental rights of its citizens, male and female. Article 26(2) states that the state shall not make any law inconsistent with any provision of fundamental rights enshrined in the Constitution, and any law so made shall, to the extent of inconsistency be void. Article 11 states that Bangladesh "shall be a democracy in which fundamental human rights and freedoms and respect for dignity and worth of human person shall be guaranteed" (Article 11 of the Bangladesh Constitution). The Constitution is the supreme law of the land and retains provisions for gender mainstreaming from all walks of life. Article 10 states unequivocally that the state shall take steps to ensure the participation of women in all spheres of national life. The state shall not discriminate against any citizen on the grounds of sex or place of birth and Clause 2 of the same provision makes it clear that women shall have equal rights with men in all spheres of the state and of public life (Article 28). There shall be equality of opportunity for all citizens in respect of employment or office in the service of the Republic (ibid., Article 29); and all citizens are equal before law and are entitled to equal protection of law (ibid., Article 27). So, let us analyze how far these constitutional guarantees of gender mainstreaming are realized by Parliament in its composition, representation, procedures, and functions.

Gender Makeup of Ninth Parliament

Parliament is constitutionally vested as the legislative power in Bangladesh. In Accordance with the original Constitution in 1972, the House comprised 300 members elected in accordance with law from single territorial constituencies by direct election (Article 65). Clause (3) exclusively reserved fifty seats for women members elected by the House on the basis of proportional representation through single transferable vote, "provided that nothing in this clause shall be deemed to prevent a woman from being elected to any of the seats provided for in clause (2) of this article" (Article 65).

Following the Fifteenth Amendment in 2011, Parliament grew to 350 members of whom only nineteen women were directly elected, dashing any hopes of equal representation. Moreover, there has been a chronic

Table 9.2 Gender makeup of the Ninth Parliament

Positions	Total	Male	Female
Member of parliament	350	281	69 (19 directly elected and 50 indirectly by the House)
Speaker	1	1	0
Deputy Speaker	1	1	0
Standing committees	49		
Chairperson of SCM	38	36	2
Chairperson of other parliamentary committees	11	11	0
Chief whips	2	2	0
Whips	6	5	1

Source: Parliament Secretariat. The two women chairpersons were in the Women & Children Affairs Ministry (MCWA) and the Primary & Mass Education Ministry. Of the sixty-nine women MPs in the Ninth Parliament, nineteen were directly elected and fifty elected by the House

lack of women in the top tier of the House. Until the Tenth Parliament formed in 2014, no woman was elected Speaker or Deputy Speaker. In the Ninth Parliament formed at the end of 2008, the two chief whip positions—one from the Treasury, the other from the opposition bench—were held by men. Just one whip was a woman (out of six). In addition, of the forty-nine standing committees just two were chaired by women members. Table 9.2 below presents the gender makeup of the Ninth Parliament.

The experience of more gender balanced legislatures demonstrates that with the increase of women membership so the sensitivity of male MPs to women's concerns increases. Men can easily act for women when there are more women around (Joni Lovenduski, Speakers Conference 2012). In this respect, parliament has a crucial responsibility to spearhead the social reforms to make our society more gender equal and fit for the twenty-first century (http://www.huffingtonpost.co.uk/frances-scott/gender-equality_b_7540358.html). It is expected that MPs will welcome change and decide upon actions to bring about a better balance of women and men at Westminster-derived parliaments (http://www.huffingtonpost.co.uk/frances-scott/gender-equality_b_7540358.html). For the increased participation of women, parliaments have to adopt a culture of gender equality (Grey 2001).

Table 9.3 Women members in Bangladesh Parliament from 1973 to 2012

Year of election	% of women candidates	Won in direct seats and by-elections	Total elected women	Reserved seats	Total women members	% of women in parliament (total seats)
1973	0.3	0	0	15	15	4.8 (315)
1979	0.9	0 + 2	2	30	32	9.69 (330)
1986	1.3	5 + 2	7	30	37	11.21 (330)
1988	0.7	4	4	0	4	1.33 (300)
1991	1.5	8 + 1	9	30	39	11.81 (330)
1996	1.36	13+2	15	30	45	13.03 (330)
2001	1.79	6	6	45	51	17.85 (345)
2009	–	19	19	50	69	20 (350)

Source: Bangladesh Parliament Secretariat, BJS; Parliamentary Oversight: A Study of the Parliamentary Standing Committee on the Ministry of Women and Children Affairs, An unpublished MPA Dissertation to civil Service College, Dhaka, (2012: 56–58)

In an effort to achieve gender equality, parliaments need to foster a culture of equality between men and women. Women's membership of Bangladesh Parliament increased during the four decades since independence in 1972 but did not reach the target set by the UN MDGs by 2015. At the time of writing, women members in Parliament constitute 20% of total seats compared to 4.8% in the First Parliament of 1973. Table 9.3 demonstrates the steady increase in numbers of women MPs in Parliament since 1973.

This steady increase in the number of MPs (excepting 1988), though a good sign, must be backed up by increased women's participation in politics beyond seat membership. There is also needs to be an integration of a gender equality perspective into the day-to-day function of Parliament, and an adherence to the international commitments related to gender equality (Women's Environment and Development Organization (2005) 50/50 by 2005 Getting the Balance Right in National Parliaments: Fact Sheet 4. www.Wedo.org). 'Women members are ornaments of the House' is perhaps not too quaint a saying in the context of the Bangladesh Parliament. Gender mainstreaming calls for ensuring equal rights, equal access to information and resources, equal participation in the decision-making process, office environment, and the opportunity to exert equal influence in the activities of Parliament. To bring about this change in terms of parliamentary functions, change in the attitude of established male leadership toward women in all parliamentary affairs is of utmost importance. The organizational structure discussed above suggests that against these parameters Bangladesh Parliament is not currently well placed.

Tackling Underrepresentation

In any given society, men or women may be underrepresented in parliaments. To counteract underrepresentation, and this issues it produces, requires especially gender-focused activities and affirmative action wherever women or men are marginalized or disadvantaged. It is frequently the case that women, men and women together, or only men are targeted to strengthen their standing in parliaments to enable them to reflect their voices and diverse needs in the public forum and benefit equally from development efforts. These interventions are adopted as temporary measures to combat the direct and indirect consequences of perennial discriminations existing in society (www.un.org/womenwatch/daw/csw/gms).

Countries such as Sweden, Norway, Denmark, Finland, and the Netherlands, which have achieved 30% or more women's representation in parliaments, adopted three common strategies. The strategies include setting quotas, proportional representation or party list, and using campaign subsidies (Women's Environment and Development Organization (2005) 50/50 by 2005 getting the Balance Right in National Parliaments: Fact Sheet 4. www.Wedo.org). Gender mainstreaming in Bangladesh Parliament should be analyzed against these parameters. The electoral systems of these countries are based on proportional representation and a party quota legal system. In these systems, a list is furnished to the electorate for a number of seats relative to the share of the national vote.

In the context of parliamentary elections, Bangladesh has adopted none of these measures. In Bangladesh, as such, there is no electoral law that mandates political parties to set quotas for women representatives, nor practices to nominate at least 30% women candidates from each party. Moreover, elections have become more and more costly and campaigning an uphill task requiring huge finance and propaganda machinery. Women candidates lag behind their male counterparts vis-à-vis financial backing. In this respect, neither political parties nor the Bangladesh Election Commission seem to be as supportive to women candidates as to their male counterparts. The gender imbalance in Parliament is thus perpetuated and women candidates only rarely wish to run against a male candidate (or even other women candidates) in direct election.

Resourcing Parliament

Gender inequality in Parliament can be counteracted by streamlining its organizational setup, making it a more socially inclusive workplace and increasing its physical and infrastructural resources to enable parliamentarians to perform their roles the best they can (ONA–UNDP Project Vie/02/007, Gender Mainstreaming in Parliaments: International Best Practices, October 2005, p. 9). Projects and programs supporting parliamentary development should focus on and address gender equality issues from two divergent but complementary points of view. First, the current needs of women parliamentarians, Secretariat staff, and the parliamentary committees who are working on gender equality/women's rights issues must be prioritized. These kinds of incentives on the part of parliamentary authorities can help transform the hitherto gender-biased institution into a gender-sensitive one and ensure balanced participation in all parliamentary business to mainstream gender throughout its work so as to deliver on gender equality goals (http://iknowpolitics.org/en/discuss/e-discussions/parliamentary-oversight-gender-equality).

Parliament can be resourced by modernizing physical infrastructural facilities—renovating and expanding its organizational structure, increasing logistical support, increasing provision of intangible resources like access to knowledge and information, adopting new modernized policies, and upgrading parliamentary rules which can facilitate the active participation of men and women parliamentarians. Changes in leave provisions, childcare facilities, separate restrooms for women and men can better support the work of parliamentarians (ibid.). In some countries, organizational resources have been tailored to meet the practical needs of men and women, for example, providing a space for women parliamentarians to breastfeed or a crèche for children (ibid.). Provisions have to be made so that men and women parliamentarians have equal access to information and resources for making decisions or participating in debates (ibid.). In light of these experiences, Bangladesh Parliament should replicate provision of extra space for mothers and crèches for children, rescheduling committee meetings, leave arrangements, and so forth, to meet the practical strategic needs of women in their reproductive role.

Gender Consideration in Rules and Procedures

Every parliament has its permanent written rules framed under the authority of its constitution or other legal basis for regulating the business of its House. Some parliaments have elaborate procedures; others have relatively few rules. The nature and character of parliament is greatly determined by its rules and procedures. Rules regulate the behavior of parliamentarians—their power, privileges, duties, discipline, and status. Parliamentary procedure is based on the principles of allowing the majority to make decisions effectively and efficiently, while ensuring fairness toward the minority and giving each member or delegate the right to voice an opinion. The House makes decisions by voting to reflect the will of the assembly. Though each parliament frames its own rules, there is marked similarity noted with others. One common practice is to adopt a standard reference book on parliamentary procedure and modify it as and when necessary through the procedure prescribed in its set of rules (https://en.wikipedia.org/wiki/Parliamentary_procedure).

A basic feature characterizing the parliamentary form of government is that any matter under consideration is resolved by free deliberations on multiple options. To ensure orderly debates, parliaments in most counties maintain an elaborate system of the rules of procedure, outlining various devices such as questions, discussions, debates, motions, and so on (see Chap. 6 on how these devices relate to oversight). In some parliaments, such devices are known as standing orders. Rules of procedure are meant to ensure that all members, men and women, are treated alike in respect of participating in the proceedings of the House or in the determination of a question before the House (http://www.asgp.co/sites/default/files/documents//TIPFBHJGTBSEYLYCYBBCQNOMAFIRPB.pdf). However, in Commonwealth and other countries, men have dominated politics and the parliamentary domain. Top leadership positions in parliament were reserved for men and, accordingly, procedures were established on this premise. In many ways, this was a historical inheritance—countries emerging after years of colonial rule established their legislatures borrowing from the parliamentary rules of predecessors and, therefore, "perhaps unwittingly, tended to continue the same traditions, which left women out of political decision making structures." Another reason may be the fact that many parliaments wrote their rules when matters relating to women's rights were not openly discussed. As a result, many rules and practices make the work of women MPs more difficult. Even the wording of some rules of procedure do not make women MPs feel welcome. "The use of gender neutral language is a case in point" (http://www.asgp.co/sites/default/files/documents//TIPFBHJGTBSEYLYCYBB CQNOMAFIRPB.pdf).

Gender-blind terminology in parliamentary rules creates a sense of discrimination between women and men parliamentarians. For example, the designations may be changed to 'Chair' or 'Chairperson' from the usual 'Chairman' (Unit 3: Women in Parliament). Gender blindness can be a form of unintentional gender bias. Hence, some parliaments are also reviewing the masculine language used in their rules and procedures to make it gender responsive (ibid.: 8). Bangladesh Parliament has not initiated this kind of reform. Much of the ROP is steeped in masculine language, for example:

Rule 93	The member in-charge may at any stage of a bill move for leave to withdraw the bill introduced by him, and if such leave is granted, no further motion shall be made with reference to the bill.
Rule 103 (1)	The full name and address of every signatory of a petition shall be set out therein and shall be authenticated by his signature, and if illiterate by his thump impression.

Gender Consideration in Legislation

Parliament is empowered to enact laws subject to the provisions of the constitution and that do not contradict fundamental rights enshrined in it. Since gender is a human rights issue, parliament should ensure that no legislation in the process of enactment or enforcement makes a differential negative impact on establishing equality between men and women (ONA–UNDP Project Vie/02/007, Gender Mainstreaming in Parliaments: International Best Practices, October 2005, p. 13).

It is very important for legislators to bear in mind that laws do not impact men and women similarly in the same manner and to the same extent. For instance, poverty affects both sexes but the different role assignment of men and women in a particular society means that it manifests and is experienced differently. Traditionally, the roles society allocates to women reduce their opportunity, security, and capacity for empowerment compared to men (Kareen Jabre, (IDEA)/CEE Network for Gender Issues Conference). It is the responsibility of legislators to emphasize that laws enacted must ensure men and women have the same rights as human beings. To ensure the same rights for both sexes may require necessary legislative reform to protect women's rights and equal access to justice.

Bringing a gender perspective into the legislation raises several issues. Do existing laws protect the interests of men and women equally? How are existing laws enforced to uphold the rights of men and women. Gender report in parliament needs a review of the total legislative process—how legislative bills are worded at the drafting stage (e.g. from a gendered viewpoint?), how women's concerns are debated/considered in the scrutiny process, and how to ensure assessment tools measure the impact of policies and laws on both sexes.

> Existing laws in overseas parliaments which have contributed to gender equality include, Australia's Sex Discrimination Act 1984, Laos' new law on trafficking in persons, Denmark's Gender Equality act 2002 and the United Kingdom's Gender Recognition bill 2003 (ONA–UNDP Project Vie/02/007, Gender Mainstreaming in Parliaments: International Best Practices, October 2005, pp. 13–14)

Canadian parliament has constituted a committee to consider and report the legislative impact in regard to gender equality issues. In Canada, the rules are so used to set a parliamentary agenda that reflects women's concerns. This highlights parliament's recognition of the fact that the life experiences of both sexes are different and saves issues that might otherwise be buried into otherwise gender-blind debates. Merely increasing women's representation in parliament does not necessarily guarantee equal rights of women in all walks of life. It has to be ensured that legislations following implementation accord equitable benefit as far as possible for both sexes (www.cpahq.org/uploadstore/docs/gendersensitizingcwparliaments.pdf). Approximately 70% of legislatures across the world do not have gender policies or gender strategies, nor have formulated any guidelines for gender transformation. Many legislatures that do, have a gender policy that is not detailed enough to give precise and real guidance. The reality is that many such policies treat 'both men and women in the same manner while their realities are very different' (Final Project Report Presented by GETNET, Kailash Bhana, April 2008).

The United Nations Population Fund (UNFPA) ran the Strengthening Parliament's Capacity in Integrating Population Issues in Development (SPCPD) project in 2012–2016 in Bangladesh Parliament in order to incorporate population development and gender issues into legislation and national policies. Under this program, the Bangladesh Association of Parliamentarians on Population and Development (UNFPA, BAPPD 2012) was constituted in 2014 with nineteen members with the Speaker of the House as the chair. To date, this project has organized several activities with the support of the Secretariat such as policy dialogues, seminars, workshops, and advocacy programs on population control, maternal health, maternal mortality, gender equality, and campaigns against drug abuse/addiction.

Parliament consequently introduced several new laws: Acid Prevention Act 2002, Prevention of Oppression against Women and Children Act 2003, Family Oppression (Prevention and Protection) Act 2012, and so on. These Acts concern more the protection of women against violence and oppression than establishing equal rights or empowering them in relation to male dominance in Bangladeshi society. The Local Government (Union Parishad) Act 2009 and the Fifteenth Amendment in 2011 increased the number of reserved seats for women in Parliament to fifty. This change, again, can be considered affirmative action addressing existing disparities rather than promoting gender equality.

Reviewing the gender aspect to any legislation is an alien concept in Bangladesh Parliament. Throughout the law-making process—ministry drafts bill, bill is vetted by the Law Ministry, bill is endorsed by the cabinet, presented to the House, scrutinized by committees, and approved by Parliament—there is little or no consideration, let alone special attention, of the gender sensitivity of the bill or how it will impact upon women once implemented. In addition, there is no separate committee assigned to review the state of women empowerment or assess the extent of the national implementation of international commitments/agreements where Bangladesh is a signatory. Neither is there any committee looking at whether existing laws are responsive to gender equality or if new national legislation is required to give effect to international commitments. SCMs have the scope to do but to date do not seem to have done so.

Gender Legislation Review

The Case of Sudan

At the regional level, Sudan established five State Standing Committees on Empowerment of Women In five states with the support of the UNDP. The Sudan Legislative Assembly has several types of regular and permanent committees both at national and state levels. The State Standing Committees on Empowerment of Women constitute part of a larger set of committees. These committees are mandated to review existing laws and analyze the present situation of women in the state in regard to their quality of life and human rights. They make new legislative proposals to improve existing legislation and to ameliorate the overall living quality of women in the region and monitor the implementation of relevant legal developments in the region. The Committees also have a mandate to suggest necessary amendments to existing national legislation in line with the provisions of international agreements which have been signed (yet constant violations of women's rights are evidence that they have not been adhered to). The UNDP supported the capacity development of the members of these Standing Committees so that they can discharge their role in the areas of human rights, gender budgeting, planning, and oversight of the implementation of national legislation and international commitments. In addition, the UNDP supported these committees to design the Women Empowerment Strategy for 2012–2016 in each state of Eastern Sudan and two states of Darfur. As an outcome of long-term UNDP engagements, the State Standing Committees are now capable of proposing revisions to the national legislation for protecting women against violence in the region as violence against women remains the greatest problem in Sudan. The perpetual violence has left women in Sudan severely damaged in terms of their physical, psychological, and sexual well-being. Sex and gender-based violence continues unabated and in some regions has increased. Against this deteriorating situation, the UNDP has provided additional assistance in the form of rule-of-law activities. Given the financial constraints and other national issues like political instability and insecurity, along

> with developmental works, the Legislative Assembly of Sudan might not consider the issue of violence against women as a high priority. However, "the consideration of legislation to criminalize violence against women is very important and UNDP will continue to provide support to the Committee on this matter" (Parliamentary Oversight of Gender Equality http://iknowpolitics.org/en/discuss/e-discussions/parliamentary-oversight-gender-equality).

Parliamentary Oversight of Gender Issues

Gender mainstreaming in parliaments is essentially accomplished in the oversight process. Every piece of legislation requires examination of purpose and benefit—what and who it targets and how it will impact lives. In a democracy it is the parliament's obligation to ensure gender equality is achieved in all spheres of life since it represents all segments of the population (http://iknowpolitics.org/en/discuss/e-discussions/parliamentary-oversight-gender-equality). "As democracy is supposed to transform gender inequalities, the parliamentary oversight role on gender equality is a key aspect of modern parliaments and a fundamental contribution for the achievement of sustainable democratic processes and practices." It is equally important that women MPs have the same opportunities to engage in oversight as their male colleagues. There is, unfortunately, very little systematically collected data to investigate this area. More information is needed to ascertain how frequently, and from what positions of leadership (e.g. committee chairs, ministers), women and men MPs engage in oversight activities.

Parliamentary gender oversight in this context refers to the review and scrutiny of legislative bills and public policy to examine their gender sensitivity, implications on women, and enforcement of international commitments. The effectiveness with which legislatures perform their oversight of gender issues depends on the oversight tools and indicators at their disposal.

Pelizzo reported that the effectiveness with which legislatures perform the oversight function, measured on the basis of their ability to constrain the power of the executive branch, was directly related to the presence of women in parliaments. Parliaments with a greater gender balance are

Table 9.4 Standing committees of Ninth Parliament

SL No.	Name of committee	Number of committee members Male	Number of committee members Female	Total members	Committee chairperson
1.	Business advisory committee	12	3	15	Male
2.	Committee on private members bills and resolutions	9	1	10	Male
3.	Committee on petitions	10	0	10	Male
4.	Standing committee on public accounts	14	1	15	Male
5.	Committee on estimates	9	1	10	Male
6.	Committee on public undertakings	9	1	10	Male
7.	Standing committee on privileges	7	3	10	Male
8.	Committee on government assurances	7	1	8	Male
9.	House committee	11	1	12	Male
10.	Library committee	6	4	10	Male
11.	Standing committee on rules of procedure	10	2	12	Male

Source: Bangladesh Parliament Secretariat (BJS)

more effective watchdogs. In this respect the oversight committee composition of Bangladesh Parliament may be cited as a reference of prevailing gender inequality. Table 9.4 presents the scenario of Bangladesh parliamentary committees in regard to gender representation in composition and chair positions.

In addition, there are 39 standing committees on ministries of which only two committees are chaired by women MPs meaning that out of 50 parliamentary standing committees 48 are chaired by male MPs. The ratio is 48:2 favoring men. Men also dominate committee membership, with most standing at a 10:1 ratio. Only six committees have 30% or more women members. Only in the Committee for the MCWA do women members outstrip men (8:10). These ratios fall well short of the MDG targets. The composition of the MWCA is stark evidence that parliament management sees gender issues more as a 'women's issue' than as part of a wider key program to mainstream gender in Parliament. This is a critical mistake—gender mainstreaming is more than the 'insertion' of 'women's issues' in legislation and oversight functions. Rather, gender mainstreaming is the reorganization of parliamentary review processes to ensure that no policy, no piece of legislation, no parliamentary motion discriminates against women or men, girls or boys. It includes the following measures:

1. Parliamentary leadership has to accept the need for gender equality and take necessary steps to achieve this. There needs to be some buy-in from those in charge.
2. Some kind of institutional mechanisms have to be devised that will make gendered oversight easier. Mechanisms may include a women's caucus, a dedicated gender equality committee, a human rights committee, and so on. All these committees will keep their eyes on whether new policy and legislation is made from a gender perspective.
3. Effective parameters and indicators such as checklists of questions need to be developed for staff and MPs to ensure policies and legislation are gender sensitive.
4. Provision should be made for gender-sensitive training for all MPs. Training will focus on gender dynamics of specific parliamentary oversight practices, such as responding to questions or chairing committees. This kind of training should be incorporated in the induction programs for new MPs immediately after election (iknowpolitics.org/en/discuss/e-discussions/parliamentary-oversight-gender-equality).

All members and parliamentary staff must undertake gender-sensitive training. For new MPs and staff it should be an indispensable part of their induction program as well as part of an ongoing professional development course for all MPs. Training can be used to highlight the gender dynamics of specific parliamentary oversight practices, such as responding to questions without notice or chairing committees. The oversight tools and indicators should necessarily be gender sensitive. Table 9.5, prepared in the light of the IPU's 2007 report, provides examples of how each 'tool' can be gender sensitized (http://iknowpolitics.org/en/discuss/e-discussions/parliamentary-oversight-gender-equality)

Based on the experience of Latin America and Caribbean countries, the UNDP has worked out tools for gender mainstreaming in parliaments. The proposed tools comprise a series of strategic steps or stations geared to bring equality in legislation as the arrival point. The parliaments intending

Table 9.5 Oversight tool

Oversight tool (based on the IPU 2007 report)	Gender sensitizing the tool
Parliament asks the government for information	Questions on all policy areas—including security, defence, economy—are always asked by both men and women MPs Questions are always asked about the beneficiaries of all government policies and the economic and social consequences for any potentially marginalized groups
Parliament asks the government for public clarification of policy	Parliament always questions the process by which policies are developed; determines whether the data on which the policy is based is sex-disaggregated; and uncovers whether there was sufficient consultation of women in the design of the policy
Parliament obtains information from sources outside the government	Parliament systematically communicates with women's organizations or gender-based CSOs, think tanks and academic institutions, and interested individuals and experts—either through committee hearings, or by inviting submissions or accepting petitions
Parliament expresses its views to the government and the public	Recommendations always aim to eliminate unequal gender power relations and gender-based discrimination Parliament should be an environment where a gender lens is encouraged—rather than stigmatized—in the course of debate Parliament should be entitled to debate government responses to international and regional commitments on gender equality, including CEDAW, UNSC 1325, and its successor resolutions

Source: IPU's 2007 report and Parliamentary Oversight of Gender Equality http://iknowpolitics.org/en/discuss/e-discussions/parliamentary-oversight-gender-equality

to get into this process will undertake self-diagnosis, that is to say, identify where gender mainstreaming is thwarted—is it in the design, planning, and implementation of legislation or parliament's lack of capacity? Effective parliamentary oversight of gender equality thus depends on a group of factors. It needs courage and endurance on the part of those taking it forward.

The first step in exercising parliamentary oversight of gender issues is being aware of the implications of new laws and enforcement of international commitments. The most significant convention addressing gender equality is CEDAW 1979. The international conventions which member countries are signatories to bring their government under obligation to ensure that women and girls enjoy the same civil, political, economic, social, and cultural rights as men and boys (CEDAW and its Operational Protocol: Handbook for Parliamentarians (2003) UNDP). Other notable international conventions that have direct bearing on gender equality include the Beijing Platform for Action 1995 and the MDGs 2000. The Beijing Platform for Action includes twelve focus areas:

1. women and poverty;
2. education and training of women;
3. women and health;
4. violence against women;
5. women and armed conflict;
6. women and the economy;
7. women in power and decision-making;
8. institutional mechanism for the advancement of women;
9. human rights of women;
10. women and the media/women and ICT;
11. women and the environment;
12. the girl and child (www.engagenz.co.nz/.../2014_12-Critical-Areas-of-Concern_Beijing-Platform-for-Ac...).

It is the responsibility of the national parliament to oversee whether the respective government implements the international conventions it is committed to. If necessary, the government of member countries would take measures to enact new laws conducive to uphold the rights of both women and men. Some countries have established a commission on gender equality, an ombudsman for gender equality, or machinery whose primary role is to monitor gender equality in laws and operations of government (http://www.coe.int/en/web/genderequality/gender-equality-commission). In the context of Bangladesh, gender mainstreaming is a donor-induced concept, a misnomer—very often it is equated with women's participation issues and activities basically confined to subnational-level organizations like the Union Parishads and Villages. At the national level, the main policy actors are seldom bothered about it. Only rarely a few MPs—both men and women—have knowledge about gender mainstreaming, what the international conventions are, what Bangladesh is a signatory to, what extent those conventions have been implemented, and what deters implementation. MPs and committee chairs have no training to analyze the gender sensitivity of a legal draft and anticipate its likely impact on both men and women. With these handicaps, committee oversight of legislation and its enforcement and impact analysis are crying in the wilderness.

It is wrong to assume that the MWCA, and the committee it parallels, alone are entrusted with the responsibility of gender mainstreaming and monitoring implementation of gender-related programs. This committee, like other SCMs, deals with routine issues like: scrutinizing legislative bills relating to the ministry, and other executive/bureaucratic functions coming under the jurisdiction of the MWCA. But gender mainstreaming is a government commitment and the fulfillment of the objectives of international commitments is not the responsibility of a single ministry. As a matter of fact, fourteen sectoral ministries have policies and program for the welfare of women and development. As the executive and legislative leads, the MWCA and its committee advise the government to take specific initiatives for women's advancement (NCBP, Advancement of Women in Bangladesh: Gaps and Challenges, Bangladesh NGO Report Beijing + 10, 2005, Dhaka). However, to be successful, gender mainstreaming programs call for sustained measures across all sectors, and this is only possible with the full support of all ministries of the government and Parliament (http://www.ipu.org/splz-e/srilanka03.pdf).

All SCMs have a mandate, inherent in their work, to consider how the projects and policies impact on men and women. Gender mainstreaming calls for coordinated efforts of a joint parliamentary committee meeting of concerned ministries to holistically address gender issues and set out new policies, to enact new laws if necessary and to implement them efficiently. It is not the responsibility of a single the ministry and one standing committee.

A study of the oversight capability of the Standing Committee for MWCA in 2012 holds the view that SCMs are not well resourced to provide expertise and research services necessary for effective oversight. The chairperson and members of the Committee for MWCA were of the opinion that though ministerial programs are subject to the scrutiny of SCMs, MWCA committee is not fully aware of the status of implementation of international conventions like CEDAW, Beijing Plus, and the UN MDGs. Members acknowledged that the committee is more engaged in overseeing projects concerning infrastructure development, employment creation for women, and measures against oppression than mainstreaming gender (Aktar 2012: 56–58).[1]

Gender Responsive National Budget

The national budget in Bangladesh is traditionally a gender-neutral fiscal legislation; but there is increasing realization by the government that budgetary policies have a differential impact on men and women. From 2005 onwards there has been a move in Bangladesh toward gendered budgeting, that is, ensuring that local and national budgets meet the needs of both men and women. It is Parliament's responsibility within its mandate to accommodate women's concerns in the budget, scrutinize and evaluate budget proposals before its approval, assessing whether it matches government's commitment to ensuring gender equality and measures adopted to implement its gender mainstreaming programs/initiatives (ASEAN+3 Parliaments Manila (2002); Anders B. Johnson, Secretary General, Parliament and the Budgetary Process, Including from a Gender Perspective, Regional (www.ipu.org/PDF/publications/colombo_en.pdf Seminar for Parliaments of South West Asia, 26–28, Colombo, 2003). The need for making the national budgets gender responsive has been reiterated in the following events:

1. Monterrey Consensus on Financing for Development (2002);
2. Doha Declaration on Financing for Development (2008);
3. Third International Conference on Financing for Development in Addis Ababa (2015) reaffirmed the commitment of governments to address gender-responsive public management. (Paramita Majumdar 2017)

Gender responsive budgeting does not mean simply increasing budgetary allocations for women; rather, ensuring that resources allocated in the budget are so utilized to make a positive impact upon the quality of life of men and women alike.

> Gender responsive budgeting (GRB) allows parliaments to analyze government revenue and expenditure from a gender perspective .... Carefully designed targets and indicators will maximize the impact of (limited) resources, and are more likely to deliver sustainable results. (http://www.ipu.org/splz-e/srilanka03.pdf)

Gender responsive budgeting disaggregates when the government's entire budget takes account of society's underpinning gender relations, roles and opportunities to access and control resources. Gender analysis of the budget aims at ensuring equal or equitable benefits for men and women in society (Kailash Bhana 2008: 21). Australia started gender-specific budget analysis in 1984 by committing government agencies to evaluating the impact of budgets on women and girls. The Australian Women's Budget expenditure is analyzed against three main criteria:

1. women-specific targeted expenditure;
2. equal employment opportunity expenditure for women;
3. mainstream expenditures: the bulk of remaining expenditures not covered by first two categories (Budlender 1999).[2]

Other countries have followed. The Philippines, Australia, South Africa, Sri Lanka, Barbados, Namibia, Tanzania, Botswana, and Mozambique all use gender analysis in the planning, implementation, and evaluation of their national budgets (ONA–UNDP Project Vie/02/007, 2005, pp. 14–1). Gender analysis needs baseline data. Once parliamentarians are provided with accurate baseline data, they can analyze the different needs of men and women and evaluate impacts that budget allocations have on men and women (Kailash Bhana 2008: 21).

Recent Trends in Bangladesh Budgeting

In recent years, the national budget in Bangladesh has leaned slightly toward gender-responsive budgeting in implementing the vision and strategic objectives of the PRSP. The PRSP in one of its strategic goals envisioning a society where men and women will have equal opportunities and will enjoy all fundamental rights on an equal basis. To achieve this vision, the mission is to ensure women's advancement and rights in activities of all sectors of the economy. The PRSP adopted strategies to integrate gender concerns into all national policies/programs/projects of ministries and agencies; allocation and expenditure of funds in favor of benefiting women; and integration of poverty and gender impact assessment criteria under Section 3 of the Business Competitive Index (BCI) of MTBF (Unlocking the Potential: National Strategy for Accelerated Poverty Reduction, General Economic Division, Planning Commission, GOB, 2005). The vision of the PRSP is now translated under the recently introduced MTBF, which differs from traditional incremental budgeting system. Gender budgeting, though it is known as a concept to legislatures, is not used as an approach in the budget cycle (GETNET, Kailash Bhana 2008: 5). Comparing rhetoric and reality demonstrates an enormous gap in budget-making under MTBF. In reality, the main agencies such as the Finance Division, the Budget Wing, and the Development Wing of the Ministry of Finance, which are respectively charged with preparing the revenue budget and preparing the estimates of the development budget outlay in close collaboration with the Planning Commission, do not work on accurate baseline sex-disaggregated data from various sectors at no stage of the budget-making process (www.ipu.org/PDF/publications/colombo_en.pd, Wehner 2003: 30).

Gender Equality in the Staffing of the Secretariat

During the Ninth Parliament, up to 2014, the Secretariat has 1102 sanctioned posts of officers and staff. Currently, 638 posts are filled (Class 1–4); their class-wise disaggregated data is presented in Table 9.6.

The composition of the Secretariat in respect of gender equality is no better than it is in the House (see Table 9.2). Despite constitutional protection, quota reservation in the Civil Service Recruitment Rules for increasing women's representation in the BCS, and provision of creating new posts in the Secretariat made by the Parliament Secretariat Commission, the situation has not yet improved. The SPD project suggested integrating gender equality considerations into a new Secretariat HRD policy and implementing a recruitment target of 10% for Class 1 and 15% for 2, 3, and 4, as set out in the BCS recruitment policy in 1981. Unfortunately, this recommendation did not appear to make any impression on the Secretariat management (See Parliament Secretariat Act 1994).

Table 9.6 Gender-based staff profile of the Bangladesh Secretariat (Class 1–4)

Class	Number of staff (as of)		Total	% of women
	Male (Jan 31, 2012)	Female (Jan 31, 2012)		
Class-1	82	19	101	19
Class-2	62	19	81	23
Class-3	329	47	376	13
Class-4	165	31	196	16
Total (1, 2, 3, and 4)	638	116	754	15

Source: Bangladesh Parliament Secretariat (BJS)

The Way Forward

Although some progress in respect of representation in national parliaments has been made in some countries, the potential of women MPs to engage in and contribute to decision-making as public leaders has not been realized. The political leadership of any country has to establish it as a matter national policy that gender equality and the effective participation of women are important for sustainable development. And for that matter, measures to be taken to prioritize programs to promote gender equality and women's empowerment in all spheres of society, including the removal of barriers to their full and equal participation in decision-making and management at all levels.

Those countries signed up to the international conventions have to accelerate the implementation of the commitment they made in words and spirit through targeted action. Institutional reforms must be carried out for the adoption of innovative and specialist approaches to enhance the competence and capacity of women and to create an enabling environment where they can contribute. For accelerating gender equality, collection and analysis of sex-disaggregated data for all policy and programs, gender-sensitive indicators in program design and for evaluation are of critical importance in order to measure the success of the programs. Capacity development programs should be developed to help women MPs to develop skills in parliamentary debates and advocacy on gender mainstreaming, international gender equality commitments, and strategies that can be of use. In this venture, the assistance of international organizations, such as the UN, the IPU, and other international financial institutions, regional banks and major groups, and also the private sector, can extend their support in designing gender-responsive programs. MPs should receive training as to how international commitments on gender equality can be integrated into legal enactments and how it can be monitored during implementation of the programs.

Commonwealth ministers responsible for women's affairs recognized in 2004 that the 30% target of women in decision-making in the political, public, and private sectors by 2015 was too ambitious; having hovered around 12–13% for long periods. Some parliaments in the Caribbean do not even have any women members (Kareen Jabre 2004). Hence, something radical would need to happen for that target to be met. One possible method that countries have applied to incorporate more women into positions of leadership is the quota system, through which political parties reserve a number of their safe and winnable constituencies for women candidates.

To ensure political participation, eighty-one countries adopted some form of affirmative action, such as reserving seats in parliament, by the end of 2004. Uganda, for example, made constitutional reform measures that each district has at least one woman MP and one-third of local political positions be reserved for women (Jabre 2004). The IPU does not, of course, consider quotas as the substitute for enhancing women's participation in politics. However, quotas may be accepted as temporary special measures and only means of a way forward when faced with deadlock and change could not be otherwise possible (Jabre 2004).

The Commonwealth Plan of Action for Gender Equality (2005–2015) focuses on four critical areas: gender, democracy, peace, and conflict; gender, human rights, and law; gender, poverty eradication, and economic empowerment; gender and HIV/AIDS (Unit 3: Women in Parliament). The Commonwealth Women Parliamentarians Group has initiated training and development programs for women candidates in countries and regions (ibid.). Recommendations have been made in certain countries for all parties to have women's caucuses to look after the interests of women. The Uganda Women Parliamentary Association is a good example of women working together on gender issues.

In order to promote women's participation in politics and bolster their contribution to parliament, the IPU has developed numerous activities such as conducting surveys and producing research reports on a regular basis on women in parliament. It also monitors the percentile increase of women in national parliaments and publishes a monthly status report; facilitates contact between women parliamentarians and encourages them to share their experiences; and organizes technical assistance projects in specific countries (Unit 3: Women in Parliament).

BARRIERS TO IMPLEMENTATION OF GENDER MAINSTREAMING PROGRAMS

Implementing gender mainstreaming programs and evaluating their effectiveness in reality is far more difficult than adopting it in principle. The CEDAW convention was signed by UN member states who agreed in principle to eliminate all forms of discrimination against women and acknowledge their responsibility to implement the convention. And yet, its implementation scenario in many of these member states is very bleak. Twenty years after the CEDAW convention was signed, when UN members met in Beijing in 1994 to establish principles for advancing gender equality, discrimination against women remained stark around the world even if there had been a numerically modest increase in the numbers of women MPs in some parliaments (Women in Parliaments 20 Years in Review). As had been noted, "genuine progress were few and far between" (https://freedomhouse.org/sites/default/files/FH_FITW_Report_2016.pdf).

Simply enacting gender-sensitive reform does not ensure gender equality if it is not properly implemented and evaluated. Many parliaments seem to be indifferent to ensuring well-intended legislation translates into real results. Commitment has not been translated into action. The officials and agencies responsible for this failure in implementation escape accountability by limited information sharing and lack of transparency, and "regrettably—by the politics of parliamentary agenda setting." To compound this, parliamentarians were not in a position to assess the reality on the ground because they lack the time, resources, technical support, and training. The gender equality issue often fails to catch the same attention as budgeting, energy, or defense (http://iknowpolitics.org/en/discuss/e-discussions/parliamentary-oversight-gender-equality). The UNDP, World Bank, and International Labour Organization have reviewed gender mainstreaming policy and found that the gender component of projects frequently does not have adequate budget, sufficient analytical skills, and effective supervision of implementation. But the most striking lack, and thing required most, is in political will (www.en.Wikipedia).

Gender mainstreaming requires diverse initiatives across the government and this is often missing where budget is lacking (GETNET, Kailash Bhana, April, 2008: 5). With a few exceptions, most parliaments where committees have been established to work on gender equality and women's empowerment have not received the due attention they deserved. Rather, gender equality issues have been diluted with other priority areas like youth, older persons, disability, and children (GETNET, Kailash Bhana, April, 2008: 4).

Conclusion

The preceding discussions reveal that gender mainstreaming in Bangladesh Parliament remains a distant reality. From the experience of those countries where parliaments have achieved certain degrees of gender equality, it is obvious that Bangladesh Parliament needs to make a major shift in policy areas such as electoral reform that would include fixing party quotas, financial support from the Bangladesh Election Commission for the campaigns of women candidates, revision of rules and procedures to ensure equal participation of men and women members in parliamentary standing committees, gender-sensitive training, and the provision of logistical changes to establish more working environments friendly to gender equality. Parliament should build on analytical skills and provide research support to the members reviewing legislative bills from a gender perspective, track the progress of international conventions on gender issues, and integrate gender variables into all policies as well monitor/evaluate them from a gender perspective (Lombardo 2005) 12(3): 412–432 cited by en.wikipedia.org/wiki/gender_mainstreaming). Gender mainstreaming is a long process and requires diverse initiatives and close attention from across the board. It must be institutionalized from within through concrete steps, mechanisms, and processes in all aspects of the parliament (Charlesworth (2005) HARV. HUM RTS.JI in en.wikipedia.org/wiki/gender_Mainstreaming).

Notes

1. See Parliamentary Oversight: A Study of the Parliamentary Standing Committee on the Ministry of Women and Children Affairs, An unpublished MPA Dissertation to civil Service College, Dhaka, (2012: 56–58).
2. Budlender D. (1999) 'South African Women's Budgets Initiatives' paper presented for the women and political Participation in twenty-first Century Challenges, 1999, Cited in Helena Hofbaurer Palmori, BRIDGE-Gender Budget Package Report, www.Gender–budgets.org/index, p. 25.

References

ONA–UNDP Project Vie/02/007, Gender Mainstreaming in Parliaments: International Best Practices, October 2005

BJS: Bangladesh Parliament Secretariat Act 1994

Budlender, D. 'South African Women's Budgets Initiatives' paper presented for the women and political Participation in 21st Century Challenges Workshop, 1999, New Delhi, Cited in Helena Hofbaurer Balmori, BRIDGE-Gender Budget Package Report, p. 25. www.Gender–budgets.org/index

CEDAW and Its Operational Protocol: Handbook for Parliamentarians (2003) UNDP

Charlesworth, H. (2005) 'Not Waving but Drowning: Gender Mainstreaming and Human Rights in the United Nations' 18 HARV.HUM RTS.JI in en.wikipedia.org/wiki/gender_Mainstreaming

Concepts Underlying Gender Mainstreaming. http://www.un.org/womenwatch/osagi/pdf/factsheet2.pdf

Covington and Bloom. Gender Responsive Program Assessment. http://www.stephaniecovington.com/assets/files/assessment/GRAssessmentToolNonCj.pdf

Democracy and Electoral Assistance (IDEA)/CEE Network for Gender Issues Conference

Foreword by Anders B. Johnson, Secretary General, Parliament and the Budgetary Process, Including from a Gender Perspective, Regional Seminar for Parliaments of South West Asia, 26–28, Colombo, 2003

Gender Mainstreaming in Parliaments: International Best Practices, October 2005, Parliamentary Oversight of Gender Equality http://iknowpolitics.org/en/discuss/e-discussions/parliamentary-oversight-gender-equality, http://iknowpolitics.org/en/knowledge-library/report-white-paper/ipu-report-gender-sensitive-parliaments-%E2%80%93-global-review-good

Global Gender Gap Index

GPRB The Constitution of the Peoples Republic of Bangladesh

Grey, S. (2001) Women and Parliamentary politics Does Size Matter? Critical Mass and Women MPs in the New Zealand House of Representatives. Paper for the 51st Political Studies Association Conference 10–12 April 2001, Manchester, United Kingdom

Helena Hofbaurer Balmori, BRIDGE-Gender Budget Package Report. www.Gender-budgets.org/index http://iknowpolitics.org/en/discuss/e-discussions; http://www.genderequality.ie/en/GE/Pages/whatisGE; (http://www.un.org/womenwatch/osagi/pdf/factsheet2.pdf); http://www.ipu.org/wmn-e/world.htm

Joni Lovenduski (2012) Feminizing British Politics, // online library. willey.com

Kareen Jabre, (2004) Strengthening Women's Participation in the Inter-Parliamentary Union. A paper presented at the international Institute for Democracy and Electoral Assistance (IDEA)/CEE Network for Gender Issues Conference.

Kinyondo et al. (2015) a "Functionalist Theory of Oversight", Nigerian Journal of Legislative Affairs", // works.bepress.com

IPU (2008) Equality in Politics: A Survey on Women and Men in Parliaments http://www.ipu.org/pdf/publications/gsp11-e.pdf

Wehner, Joachim, Parliament, the Budget and Gender, IPU, UNDP, WBI and UNIFEM, 2004a, Parliament, the Budget and Gender—Inter-Parliamentary Union. www.ipu.org/PDF/publications/budget_en.pd

Buchanan, Linda et al., (2002) Organizational Review of Bangladesh Parliament Secretariat, UNDP

Lortie Commission (1991) Royal Commission on Electoral Reform and Party Financing, Canada

Lombardo, E. (2005) "Integrating or Setting Agenda? Gender Mainstreaming in European Constitution Making Process", Social Politics, Vol. 12, No. 3, pp. 412–32, cited in en.wikipedia.org/wiki/gender_mainstreaming

NCBP, Advancement of Women in Bangladesh: Gaps and Challenges, Bangladesh NGO Report

Parliament and the budgetary process, Including from a gender perspective parliamentary-oversight-gender-equality

Majumdar, Paramita (2017) Gender Responsive Budgeting : Tool for Gender Mainstreaming The Colombo Plan Gender Affairs Programme 4th May 2017, Negombo, Sri Lanka

Regional seminar for ASEAN+3 Parliaments Manila (Philippines) 23–25 July 2002. http://www.ipu.org/splz-e/manila02/report-e.pdf

Rehana Akhtar, Parliamentary Oversight: A Study of the Parliamentary Standing Committee on the Ministry of Women and Children Affairs, An unpublished MPA Dissertation to civil Service College, Dhaka

Right in National Parliaments: Fact Sheet 4. www.Wedo.org

Social Watch gender equality index. http://www.socialwatch.org/taxonomy/term/527

Strengthening Capacity of People's Elected Bodies in Vietnam, ONA–UNDP Project Vie/02/007, Gender Mainstreaming in Parliaments: International Best Practices, October 2005

Strengthening Capacity of People's Elected Bodies in Vietnam, ONA–UNDP Project Vie/02/007

The United Nations Gender Inequality Index

Towards Mainstreaming Gender in the Legislative Sector, Final Project Report presented by GETNET, Kailash Bhana, April, 2008 http://www.sals.gov.za/research/gender.pdf

UNFPA (2012) Strengthening Parliament's Capacity in Integrating Population Issues in Development (SPCPD project in 2012–16)

United Nations Security Council (UNSC) Operational Effectiveness and UN resolution 1325

Unit 3: Women in Parliament. http://siteresources.worldbank.org/PSGLP/Resources/commonwealthunit3.pdf

Unlocking the Potential: National Strategy for Accelelarated Poverty Reduction, General Economic Division, Planning Commission, GOB, 2005

Wehner, J. (2003) "The Budget: Purpose, composition and Terminology", Regional Seminar, Colombo www.ipu.org/PDF/publications/colombo_en.pd

Wikipedia. wikipedia.org/wiki/gender_mainstreaming

Women in National Parliaments. http://www.ipu.org/wmn-e/world.htm

Women in Parliament. www.parl.gc.ca/content/lop/researchpublications/prb0562-e.htm

Women in Parliaments 20 Years in Review. http://www.ipu.org/pdf/publications/WIP20Y-en.pdf, www.Crikey.com.au

Women's Environment and Development Organization (2005) 50/50 by 2005 Getting the Balance

Jabre, Kareen "Strengthening Women's Participation in the Inter-Parliamentary Union" A paper presented at the international Institute for www.Quotaproject.org/CS/CS_Europe-Jabre05; www.cpahq.org/uploadstore/docs/gendersensitizingcwparliaments.pdf; www.un.org/womenwatch/daw/csw/gms

Yamamoto, H. (2007) Tools for Parliamentary Oversight: A Comparative Study of 88 Parliaments, Geneva

Wehner, J. (2004b) Parliament, Budget and Gender www.ipu.org/PDF/publications/budget_en.pdf

http://www.coe.int/en/web/genderequality/gender-equality-commission

www.engagenz.co.nz/.../2014_12-Critical-Areas-of-Concern_Beijing-Platform-for-Ac

CHAPTER 10

Paradox of Reforms: A Reflection on Present State of Democracy and Parliament

INSTITUTIONALIZATION OF PARLIAMENT

The people of Bangladesh have seen two dawns of independence and passed through the second and third waves of democracy,[1] having fought a liberation war against Pakistan to establish a liberal parliamentary democracy. Formally speaking at least, Bangladesh has been a democracy since 1972. The Constitution ensures that the Republic shall be a democracy in which fundamental human rights, freedoms, and respect for human dignity and worth of human persons is guaranteed (Article 11 of the Bangladesh Constitution). However, the reality is a little different. After forty-five years of independence, a democracy with guarantees of fundamental rights and civil liberties remains an unattainable dream for the people of Bangladesh. Flawed parliamentary elections under party government—stuffed ballot boxes, intimidated opposition candidates, manipulated election results—are the legacy of civil and military rulers. Elklit (1994) and Elklit and Renolds (2000) argues that a flawed electoral system is often a central factor behind the failure of democratization in many new democracies in the so-called third world. Bangladesh's struggle for democracy which began with the liberation war in 1971 is still underway. But it is essentially limited to organizing free, fair, and contested national elections and to establishing a parliament which bears the confidence of the public—the first step to establish any democracy. Bangladesh fell into the pit of flawed elections in 1973 and has remained there since, except for the period of NCG elections. The Fourteenth Amendment in

© The Author(s) 2019
A. T. M. Obaidullah, *Institutionalization of the Parliament in Bangladesh*, https://doi.org/10.1007/978-981-10-5317-7_10

2006 was a cynical attempt to politicize the NCG system in favor of the sitting government. It led not to a reform of the system but its scrapping with the Fifteenth Amendment in 2011, an act which ultimately jeopardizes the democracy that has been very hard-earned. In this chapter, we shall assess the present state of democracy in Bangladesh and the extent to which Parliament has been effective in the shift from authoritarianism to democratic consolidation. Democratic consolidation should be measured against certain benchmarks. These include the nature of parliamentary elections, the quality of legislation and oversight, the enforcement of the rule of law, the extent to which civil liberties are safeguarded, and role Parliament plays in checking and restraining unfettered executive power.

In the first two decades parliamentary elections were heavily rigged, suffered legitimacy crises, and Parliament had to operate under civil and military dictatorships which prevented it from being institutionalized. It was subservient to the executive irrespective of regime type, remaining ever prepared to rubber-stamp the chief executive's desire. Prior to 1991 the ineffectiveness of Parliament was attributed to a lack of continuity of constitutional rule, frequent dissolutions of the House, and a chronic lack of authority, resources, and logistics. Frequent dissolution jeopardized the growth of a stable pattern of rules and procedures or sound methods of conflict resolution. It caused discontinuity in membership and placed Parliament at a disadvantage to executive and bureaucratic power. These excuses hold no ground today. Since 1991 parliamentary elections were fair and credible and highly contested and constitutional rule is in place, at least formally. Longer stability provided Parliament with the opportunity to gain experience, generate precedents, customs, and take ownership of rules and best practices. Post-restoration parliaments had the opportunity to be distinct political organizations and develop their own way of doing their works and thus become institutionalized (Loewnberg and Patterson; Ahmed 2002: 241).

After deposing military dictatorship and restoring parliamentary democracy, the main thrust was to enhance the legislative and oversight capacity of Parliament and institutionalize it to shoulder the onerous responsibility of a functioning modern Westminster democracy. The more Parliament is institutionalized the greater the potential to succeed. The task of the institutionalization of parliament, according to Copeland and Patterson (1995), 'is a process of establishing and maintaining organizational structures and linking the organization to its environment', is extremely difficult (cited in Ahmed 2011: 62). Patterson and Copeland identify four main attributes of institutionalization: autonomy, formality, uniformity, and complexity. Institutionalization of parliament calls for its autonomy and independence of the control of other organizations, that is, it is not dominated by other external institutions, such as the bureaucracy, the military, or pressure groups (Patterson and Copeland 1994: 4 cited in Ahmed 2011). Patterson has also referred to two other dimensions of institutionalization: coherence and adaptability. Institutionalization of parliament is a continuum. As Rose observes, 'It takes time, a decade or more to demonstrate a regime's commitment to rule of law and to changing control of government in response to changes in the electoral behavior' (cited in Norton and Olson, p. 231, in Ahmed 2002: 241). Parliamentary institutionalization is the culmination of a three-stage process, with transition and consolidation preceding it (ibid.).

Since 1991 rigorous attempts have been made to institutionalize Bangladesh Parliament for more than two decades. Significant institutional and organizational reforms were carried out to make it resourceful, autonomous, and independent in respect of legislation and oversight of the executive. Simultaneous organizational reforms were carried out in the Secretariat and committee structures with extra emphasis placed on increasing human capacity and logistics support to give effect to new institutional reforms. The anachronistic ROP of the presidential era has been revised to allow backbench MPs to be involved in legislation and oversight in the House and its committees. Parliamentary standing committees' scope of work was widened enough to exercise legislative, administrative, and fiscal oversight throughout the year. Committees are left with room for scrutinizing bills on their intent and consequence on citizens and probe ministerial programs to determine the efficiency, economy, and effectiveness of government operations. And in the process of implementation to examine whether ministries are liable for any irregularity, waste, abuse of money, violation of civil liberties and constitutional rights, or bad governance. Moving deeper, they can also investigate whether or not the money is being properly used and the projects are being implemented efficiently (PROGATI 2011: 19).

Given this welter of reforms, it is no exaggeration to say that the Bangladesh Parliament today has greater independence, better capacity in its organization, manpower, rules and resources to consolidate its position and contribute to democratic transition. Yet, paradoxically, rather than contributing to the consolidation of the nascent democratic process, Parliament has in fact actually declined. Its ability to undertake its mandatory functions of law-making and oversight, as the discussions in this book have demonstrated, still appears to be extremely limited in the second decade of the twenty-first century.

Between 1991 and 2008, Bangladesh held four successive parliamentary elections under the supervision of an NCG that were fair, free, and highly contested. Two major political parties alternated in wielding state power. According to Samuel Huntington, if a nascent democracy can pass two successive electoral turnover tests it can make a transition from authoritarianism to democracy. After the first turnover, the new administration often reverts to authoritarian rule, trampling on democratic institutions and undermining rule of law. Therefore, the nation must undergo a second turnover. Only after passing turnover test two can it move to the next stage, a stable democracy (Riaz 2015: 6). The experience of Bangladesh appears to defy this theory. It has passed four turnover tests and power has changed hands peacefully, yet the country failed has failed to institutionalize Parliament and make the shift to a consolidated democracy.

This section closely examines the unique political milieu in which post-restoration parliaments in Bangladesh had to operate. Establishing democracy and institutionalizing parliament in reality is far more difficult than adopting it in principle. If the ground is unprepared democracy remains a formal apparatus rather than a reality (McIver 1948, 1950). From 1991 parliaments were popularly elected and legitimate in a democratic sense but were unable to grow as an institution and never functioned as an effective forum of informed deliberation regardless of which party was in power. In fact, all elected parliaments in Bangladesh have been overshadowed by the prime minister—who often happened to be the head of government, Leader of the House, chair of the party, and chair of the parliamentary board during elections. The prime minister—Sheikh Mujib, Khaleda Zia, Sheikh Hasina, or the sundry others who held this position in name or de facto since independence—has been consistently the ultimate source of all decisions in the House and in the cabinet. Other MPs have only ever worked in the prime minister's shadow.

In no parliament has the opposition played a constructive role in making objective criticisms to keep the executive on track; rather they have considered it their prime duty to unseat the government as soon as possible. The culture of parliament boycott has reigned and opposition parties have generally preferred extra-parliamentary practices, such as taking to street demonstrations, to protest government repression and parliamentary impediment or the alleged manipulation of frontbench seat shares, rather than engage in constructive dialogue in the House. Their absence from the House, however, left ruling parties to enjoy unfettered power without checks and balances.[2] Even where opposition parties have remained in the House, the Leader of the Opposition has frequently remained absent. The opposition, though expected to form a shadow cabinet to offer alternative policy suggestions, was rarely seen working in Parliament irrespective of which party was in power. On the other hand, the treasury bench consistently failed to show any spirit of compromise, consensus, or accommodation to retaining the opposition in the House. Hence, Parliament, though a body possessing legal authority and a degrees of logistical support, trained personnel, and institutional capacity, consisted of MPs who did not make use of them.

Apparently post-restoration parliaments made some improvements in the legislative process. Bills were duly sent to appropriate standing committees for scrutiny, yet generally as a matter of compliance. No marked improvement in the quality of legislations was noticed. Despite elaborate provisions for three stages of reading, adequate deliberations on bills never take place. The practice has been reduced to a mere formality. The government has an inherent tendency to rush bills through with unnecessary haste, especially those with partisan overtones. This trend was noticeable more in the Fifth Parliament led by the BNP than in its successors. The ROP empowers SCMs to thoroughly scrutinize bills and other resolutions. However, the time spent at the committee stage of a bill was always too short—three days including its return to the House. Th main reasons for this is probably that governments wanted to get legislation passed in the House without too many questions and even less objections or criticism in the committees (Ahmed 1997: 77). For example, on the last working day of nineteenth session of the Ninth Parliament four bills were passed in a sitting day which was vehemently opposed by an independent member, Fazlul Azim. Azim made the charge that the normal stages of passing a bill were being skipped and thus grossly violating the ROP (see Parliament proceeding of 20 November 2013, Statement of Mohammad Fazlul Azim, Nowakhali 6). Ahmed (1997) observes that an analysis of parliamentary proceedings leaves no room for doubt that the role of Parliament remains mostly limited to validating the desire of the executive in the actual sense (Ahmed 1997: 76–77). In this author's own interviews, some of the ruling party MPs interviewed felt that the current practice of law-making in Parliament is an improvement upon the past in respect to debate and scrutiny. However, a marked difference was noted among respondents in regard to their opinions on the time allowed for committees to scrutinize bills.[3]

Studying the nature of legislation enacted by popularly elected parliaments in Bangladesh, several political analysts hold that there is no fundamental distinction between the pre- and post-restoration parliaments. All civilian regimes, before and after autocratic rule, have passed repressive laws. For example, the Special Power Act and Law and Order Disruption Offence (Speedy Trial) Act abused the criminal codes, established powerful law enforcement agencies such as the JRB and the Rapid Action Battalion (RAB) with little or no accountability and indemnified human rights violations. Table 10.1 below presents the nature of legislative measures in pre- and post-restoration regimes.

In terms of parliamentary oversight, the committees formed since restoration seem to be no less effective than those before, particularly concerning their capacity to make the government behave. They have been accused of failing in their duty to hold the government to account and contribute positively to the legislative process. The main complaints have

Table 10.1 Legislative measures limiting human rights adopted under elected civilian governments in the pre- and post-democratic period

Regime leader	Ruling party	Tenure	Legislative measures	Year of promulgation
Sheikh Mujib	AL	1972–1975	Second Amendment allowing the state of emergency suspension of fundamental rights	Sep 22, 1973
			Special Power Act	Feb 9, 1974
Khaleda Zia	BNP	1991–1996	Suppression of Terrorist Offences Act	Nov 6, 1992 (lapsed 1994)
Sheikh Hasina	AL	1996–2001	Public Safety Act (Special Provision)	Feb 15, 2000 (repealed 2002)
Khaleda Zia	BNP	2001–2006	Law and Order Disruption Offence (Speedy Trial) Act	9 April, 2002 (initially passed for two years)
Sheikh Hasina	AL		Law and Order Disruption Offence (Speedy Trial) Act	Parliament extended the law up to 2019
Sheikh Hasina	AL	2008–2013	Fifteenth Amendment	

Source: Riaz (2015: 30)

been outlined as: (a) gross irregularity in holding meetings; (b) improper application of the ROP; (c) indifference to the way the ministries function; (d) uncritical endorsement of departmental positions; (e) spending more time on the irregularities of the previous regime; (f) failure to vent public grievances by discussing vital issues of socioeconomic and political importance; (g) acceding to the pressure of senior government officials; (h) unwillingness to accommodate the opposition's viewpoints; (i) allowing the partisan approach and party-political position of members to prevail in committee decision-making. It has also been alleged that many committees merely echoed ministerial explanations and played a sycophantic role (Hasanuzzaman 2007: 53).

Committee oversight has been constrained by systemic bottlenecks in the CS Wing, inappropriate staffing of the committees, scarcity of research and documentation support, and inadequate time allowed for scrutinizing ministerial programs and analyzing necessary papers. Some MPs interviewed, of course, held that within these institutional arrangements the purpose of parliamentary oversight was achieved.[4] All respondents agreed that the allegation often made against poor parliamentary oversight is not unfounded and held that within present limitations it was unlikely for committees to deliver the outputs and outcomes constituents expect.[5] The current ruling party's Deputy Speaker was of the opinion that parliament's oversight capacity is rendered ineffective due to the indifference of the executive ministries to implement the recommendations of committees. There is no obligation of ministries to comply with committee recommendations under the present ROP. He suggested incorporating in the ROP that can facilitate the implementation of the committee recommendations.[6] Hence, the reforms carried out since the restoration of parliamentary system have proved to be insufficient in developing legislative viscosity, increasing committee surveillance, and institutionalizing the wider Parliament at large.

In respect to constitutional amendments, whenever any party/alliance secured a supermajority in the House it opted for amendments that served their own political interests without considering the consequence. Except for a few amendments, such as the Twelfth and Thirteenth, constitutional amendments were made in the interests of the regime in power. There is no evidence during any regime that the legislative intention of the executive, either in the form of a normal bill or constitutional amendment bill, encountered any resistance from Parliament. Just in the last few years, the passage of the Fifteenth Amendment, which scrapped the NCG system amid loud opposition from political parties, lawyers, academia, and CSOs, is a glaring example of how the ruling party/alliance in Bangladesh uses its supermajority in Parliament in disregard of public opinion or the consequence of its actions on democratic development. Hence, there is no plausible grounds to argue that democratically elected parliaments behaved differently from the parliaments which suffered legitimacy crises in the pre-democratic period.

Now, the question is why all the parliaments behaved more or less in the same fashion and failed to resist the arbitrary desires of the executive. Is it due to Parliament's lack of authority and power to do that? So far as the legitimate basis is concerned, parliaments in the post-restoration period have been vested with the authority outlined in the Constitution and in the ROP to carry out such oversight. However, they failed to use that authority. This was not to do with a lack of resources. It was to do with a lack of will. Parliament throughout remained despondent to assert its legislative supremacy despite the legal provisions to do so.

The issue of Parliaments' weakness may be addressed from several standpoints. First, Bangladesh still bears the legacy of the British viceregal tradition of an executive that is unwilling to be held accountable to parliament. Parliament, as such, cannot exert its authority over the executive due to the presence of an anti-defection clause in the Constitution. Any MP who chooses to play a critical role and risk upsetting the prime minister/Leader of the House may face grave consequences. Bangladeshi MPs very often find they cannot speak their mind in a way they think appropriate. Article 70 strangulates dissenting voices. The PROGATI assessment team observed in 2011 that "the lawmakers are not fully independent to discharge their duties; because of the stringent constitutional provision, political parties' undemocratic charters, authoritarian attitudes of top leadership, adversarial political culture constitute big hurdles to perform their parliamentary duties independently." The desire of the chief executive thus prevails under any circumstance on any issue; any disagreement may amount to floor-crossing under Article 70 of the Constitution. This kind of strangulating situation has made Parliament subservient and powerless to assert its supremacy. A.B.M. Kairul Haque, while a judge in the Supreme Court, observed in a verdict in 2006 that Article 70 made MPs "prisoners" of the party (PROGATI 2011: 11; Riaz 2017).[7] Existing constitutional provisions like Article 70(a) restricts the rights of MPs to such an extent that they have no other option than to approve whatever measures their party leadership propose. In the present situation, the executive directly controls Parliament since the prime minister, who heads the cabinet, is also Leader of the House and chief of the ruling party in it. "The current constitutional provisions and prevailing political culture in fact makes the premier a parliamentary dictator" (PROGATI 2011: 11). The prime minister is not only first among the equals; he/she is much more than that. It was assumed that resourcing Parliament and increasing its power would be greatly instrumental for members and committees to assert their constitutional authority over the executive as per its mandate in a parliamentary democracy. However, due to provisions such as these, MPs remain gagged and Parliaments as docile as it was before 1991.

The weakened state of Parliament may also be viewed from the perspective of staffing of the Secretariat (as was discussed in Chap. 8). Even after the series of multifarious training programs held at home and abroad under the auspices of the donor community, most MPs interviewed complained about Secretariat's continuing inefficiency. One veteran AL MP, who previously held positions of opposition chief whip and chief whip of Parliament, maintained that the Secretariat is still not independent. After the passage of the PSA 1994, it should have been resourced by neutral, non-partisan professional staff developed in-house.[8] Instead, the Secretariat continues to be serviced in large part by deputed ministry officials who are not only unaware of parliamentary procedure but largely indifferent to it. In some cases, these officials are hand-dropped into technical positions that require specialist skills they do not possess. In one case, a veterinary doctor was put in charge of legislative matters as deputy secretary and found it impossible, despite all sincerity, to furnish MPs with support on legislation.[9] The current Deputy Speaker held that the inefficiency of the Secretariat is rooted mainly in the failure to efficiently implement the PSA in full.[10]

A selection of the Secretariat officials recruited by the PSC in the mid-1990s were asked why MPs still complain about the inefficiency of the Secretariat even after the provision of so much training and support over the last two decades. The collective reply of these officials was 'secretariat management knows the cause well; but they don't want the remedy.' Their pessimistic view was that the Secretariat was placed in the hands of novices in parliamentary business. Management does not want its own officials assuming decision-making responsibilities and prefer deputed officials because, in the view of the interviewees, they would be more amenable to their dictates. One interviewee, from the Secretariat's own cadre, expressed irritation that parliamentary management never intended to build an institutionalized Secretariat; the consolidation of their political power prevails over everything else.[11]

HRD in Parliament has always been subject to the caprice of the regime and hence its development is reduced to a 'zero sum game.' As a matter of fact, both the AL and the BNP, when in power, have ensured allegiant civil servants have been deputed to serve in senior and middle parliamentary management. The deputed officials are initially limited in discharging their duties due to their lack of training and experience. By the time they've begin to learn the ropes, they get transferred to another ministry or department and leave the Secretariat. Their departure makes room for another novice to replace them, and on the cycle goes. As a result, Parliament has been consistently managed officials who are inexperienced in parliamentary business. This constitutes one of the most important constraints to building a well-trained and resourceful workforce at the Secretariat. The UNDP organizational review report in 2002 suggested that: "Over the next five years, the deputized secretariat staff should be phased out to a target of not more than 10% of the staff undertaking the core functions". However, fourteen years after the UNDP report was published, the situation in the Secretariat remains as it was in 2002, if not worse. The scarcity of efficient staff in the Secretariat thus has been a perennial problem (PROGATI 2011: 12).

Because of the constant rotation of staff, the impact of the training is not significantly reflected in functional efficiency compared to the volume of the resources invested. The UNDP-financed SPD project spent 20% of its budget (US$1.07 million) on training Secretariat staff. The subsequent UN project, USAID-funded PROGATI and PRODIP projects, and a World Bank project means that a huge amount of resources have been spent on human capacity development of the Secretariat in last fifteen years. It is questionable as to whether these projects have gained value for money. The model of a professional parliamentary service with its own career structure is now widely accepted, in parliamentary and presidential systems alike (www.ipu.org). However, Bangladesh Parliament does not seem motivated to do the same.

Democratic Consolidation

Democratic consolidation does not necessarily depend on the number of successful electoral turnovers (Huntington 1991). In Asia and Africa, many countries have long-standing experiences with regular elections yet have failed to establish democracy on a firm footing. Party politics, flawed electoral processes, restricted civil liberties, politicized civil administrations, use of muscle and black money, and dynastic rule thwarted successful transitions to a stable democracy (Jahan 2008). Nascent democracies in East European and Central Asian countries have experienced similar patterns of rigged elections, restricted civil liberties, and unaccountable executives. In South Asia, India and Sri Lanka have succeeded in institutionalizing rudimentary electoral democracies. Nepal, Pakistan, and Bangladesh have oscillated between autocratic and democratic rule (Haynes 2001). Successful democratization requires a political milieu where all major political actors indisputably decide there is no alternative for changing government but to adopt a democratic process (Mainwaring et al. 1992: 3). Democratic consolidation is the total institutionalization of democratic practices; it completes only when citizens and political actors alike accept democratic practices as the only way to resolve conflict (Bratton and van de Walle 1997: 235).

Countries once ruled under stable authoritarian governments seldom make smooth transitions to consolidated democracies. There are a number of necessary conditions for making the transition from authoritarianism to sustained democratic consolidation: first, open political competition without confrontation; second, agreed-upon rules of the game; third, stable democratic institutions; fourth, a constitutionally guaranteed range of political and civil rights upheld by enforcement and rule of law (ibid.). In transitional democracies a number of factors retard democratic progress including: excessive executive domination and unwillingness to be accountable to parliament, patron-client relationship in political systems, very high levels of state corruption, weak rule of law, and massive use of discretion. In addition, serious ethnic, cultural, and/or religious divisions, widespread poverty, and an international climate unpropitious to democracy act as barriers to democratic development (Haynes 2001). A political system to be regarded as a fully democratic polity requires a prolonged process of democratic institution-building developed through trial and error—reversals, as well as advances (White 1998: 46). Once consolidation is established, this does not in itself guarantee its sustenance unless all political and non-political actors are committed to maintain it; otherwise democracy will unravel (ibid.).

After deposing authoritarianism democratic consolidation can take place when, first, political actors' behavior appears decisively to shift towards democratic patterns; second, when pro-democracy political actors have open access to the political system; third, when political decision-making takes place according to legitimately coded procedures; fourth, when the mass of ordinary people, political leaders, and activists perceive that no other form of government is better than the democratic system; finally, when leaders of all political parties agree to subordinate their strategies and divisions to the common goal of not facilitating a return to authoritarianism (Haynes 2001: 11–12). There is a consensus that democracy consolidates and sustains in a new kind of political environment that creates novel challenges for both civil society and political actors. The challenge takes two forms: first, democratic competition among power contenders has to be institutionalized, and second a balance of interests must be struck among those groups previously united in opposition. In order to cope with this new challenge a new commitment among these groups is of utmost necessity to bring a transition from authoritarianism (Haynes 2001: 12).

Why Democratization Has Failed in Bangladesh

Making a successful transition to a consolidated democracy is more difficult than deposing authoritarian government. Many countries have discovered that after attaining a triumphant victory over autocratic regimes through prolonged mass movement, new elected governments trample over democratic values and norms and followed the trail of previous regimes "rather than break away from the old mold and chart a new democratic path" (Jahan 2015: 31). Bangladesh is such a case. Nascent democracies have not only the responsibility of addressing foundational challenges of holding elections in a free and fair environment on regular intervals but also paying due attention to the challenges of transforming electoral democracy into substantive democracy by establishing the rule of law, guaranteeing the civil liberties of citizens, ensuring horizontal and vertical accountability, and being responsive to the public's needs and demands (Jahan and Amundsen 2012). Fareed Zakaria argues that 50% of new democracies in the world today are neither confirmed dictatorships nor full democracies, but rather stand somewhere in between. In these regimes citizens are allowed to exercise political rights but denied civil liberties; Zakaria calls these countries "illiberal democracy" (Zakaria 1997).

Linz and Stephan argue that transition to a substantive democracy is possible when all actors involved in the democratic process take it for granted that democracy is by far the best of any alternative form of government. Elections should not only routinely take place but also be fair and contested, guaranteed by institutional mechanisms, and not be overturned. Bangladesh, after holding four successful electoral turnovers, could not resolve the foundational challenge of holding free and fair national elections. Democratic development in Bangladesh stalled because political actors did not shift to democratic practices in words and deeds. The two main contenders the AL and BNP do not believe in the basic principle—democracy is a way of governing and being governed (McIver 1950). The first thought for any party that won an election in Bangladesh was to consider how to consolidate its power and keep it in office by any means necessary. The parties very often violated agreed-upon rules and norms of democratic competition (Jahan 2008) because the violators were not taken to task if they were aligned with incumbent government party. One senior MP of the ruling party stated in his interview that democracy cannot be institutionalized if rule of law, an independent judiciary, independent media and neutral civil society do not exist or work effectively.[12] The institutionalization of democracy requires a symbiotic contribution from all institutions, political and non-political. Weakness in one institution affects the whole system. Larry Diamond and Leonardo Morlino pointed to this in explaining that innumerable countries in the world today belong to the category of 'illiberal democracies' where lawlessness and abuse of power co-exist with competitive elections and popular participation (Diamond and Morlino 2004 quoted in Jahan 2008: 31).

Bangladesh has failed to consolidate its democracy after four successful electoral turnovers. Democratic consolidation calls for establishing other pillars of democracy—rule of law, accountability, non-partisan state administration, independent judiciary, protecting civil liberties and human rights, making space for political and civil opposition—not simply holding free and fair elections. Elections administered by NCGs in Bangladesh were to a degree participatory. However, none of the parliaments elected under this system paid any attention to strengthening these other pillars of democracy. In addition, the massive politicization of the administration weakened the building blocks of democracy (Jahan 2015). Diamond and Morlino argue that these are interlinked and "tend to move together either towards democratic improvement and deepening or toward decay" (Diamond and Morlino cited by Jahan 2008: 6). The survival of a democratic system requires the presence of some elements of political culture: a degree of restraint in one's partisanship; considerable trust and minimum suspicion in rival political actors; tolerance of opposition and criticism; and readiness to compromise, accommodate and cooperate (Hakim 2002: 106). Democracy can thrive in a culture of compromise, where agreed rules of the game are adhered to and there is impartial arbiter to impose sanction on those who breach the rules, and an impartial law-enforcing agency to treat government and opposition equally in the eyes of law (Jahan 2008).

The people of Bangladesh expected a strong and effective role from Parliament in conflict resolution and democratic consolidation of the country. A senior veteran ruling party MP has remarked that 'instead of appeasing tension, parliament often provokes tension' (Ali Ashraf 2017).[13] The current Deputy Speaker of the ruling party argues that: "Parliament should have been the platform where divergent views could be discussed; conflict could be resolved through consultation, compromise, and consensus among major stakeholders on any national issue." However, in Bangladesh Parliament this kind of culture is yet to develop (Fazle Rabbi Mia, MP 2016). This is putting it lightly. As a matter of fact, Bangladesh experienced a horrendous governance scenario for a long period centering on the issue of Fourteenth and Fifteenth Amendments. The lives of ordinary people were crippled in the face of all sorts of human-made catastrophe: political violence, extra-judicial killings, confrontational politics, human rights violations, bomb attacks, prolonged *hartals*, and unlimited nationwide blockades. This human rights situation is indicative of the nature and quality of democracy and disregard for the rule of law (Riaz 2015: 4). During this critical time, the Bangladeshi people did not notice any efforts from Parliament to intervene or quell the situation. On the contrary, the government adopted increasingly authoritarian measures to counteract the ensued backlash ranging from oppression of political opposition to arbitrary attacks on the media (Tim Meisburger asiafoundation.org/resources/pdfs/OccasionalPaperNo11FINAL.pdf). Globally, the level of democratization is measured in terms of political rights to vote and the extent to which civil liberties and fundamental freedoms are enjoyed. Our discussions in Chap. 2 illustrate that from 1991 onward political rights were granted and exercised (legitimate elections were held) but civil liberties were denied.

Where Bangladesh Stands

Granted that Bangladesh has seen some participatory elections and democratically elected governments in the last two decades, we must examine in more detail why it has failed to achieve the other pillars of democracy. This section, then, analyzes Bangladesh in reference to some key benchmarks—

civil liberties and human rights protection, rule of law, tolerance of dissent and opposition, independence of judiciary, and neutrality of the civil service. Before we turn to that, let us look briefly at how democracies have been measured and categorized by analysts and experts.

Democracy Type

Levels of democracy vary across the world. There are indices to measure the worldwide variation of democracy in different time periods (Bollen 1986, 1990; Banks 1996; Beetham 1994). Bollen (1980) first systematically developed democracy indices covering 1960–1965 and later updated in 1993. Humana (1983, 1987, 1992) offered human rights ratings. Similarly, Gurr (1990) and Jaggers and Gurr (1995) made democracy scores by regime ratings. But the democracy index prepared by Freedom House on the basis of regime ratings have been the most commonly used since 1972. According to democratic scores reflected in these indices, the level of democracy is measured in 'third world' countries (Kurzman 1998 in Jeff Haynes, p. 39). Liberal regimes are differentiated from illiberal regimes by using Freedom House's ratings. The ratings are based on the criteria of political rights and civil liberties allowed to the citizens (Jeff Haynes 2001: 40).

Today based on the level of political rights and restrictions on civil liberties, democracy is denominated in several subtypes that includes inter alia: facade/pseudo-democracy, electoral democracy, hybrid democracy, illiberal democracy/minimal democracy, flawed democracy, liberal/full democracy, and so on. Jeff Haynes offered a simple—if not simplistic—tripartite democratic typology of relevance to 'third world' countries. These are: (1) 'facade' democracy; (2), 'electoral' democracy; and (3) 'full' democracy (Jeff Haynes 2001: 36). Diamond (1999) has offered a similar classification using the terms, pseudo, electoral, and liberal democracy. Of late, some critics like Fareed Zakaria designate many third world democracies as 'illiberal democracy,' calling it a 'growth industry.' According to Freedom House, 122 of the world's 193 countries claim to be democratic and can be classified as electoral democracies (Freedom House 2006 Report). In order to ascertain which typology Bangladesh's democracy falls into here it is worth describing the characterization of different democracies in terms their nature and quality of governance.

Facade Democracies

Facade democracies pretend to be democratic. Ruling parties get elected through elections that are regular but heavily controlled by state apparatus and the armed forces. Elections are intended to impress external observers, put on, as Whitehead puts it, 'for the English to look at'; called by Bayart 'fig leaf' elections (*para os ingleses ver* [Portuguese]) (Whitehead 1993: 316; Bayart 1993: xii–xiii in Haynes). In a pseudo-democracy formally legal opposition parties do not have any real opportunity to compete for state power. The ruling party exercises omnipotent power across the political system; uses coercion, patronage, controls the media, and denies civil and political liberty to opponents (Kemal Osden and Ihsan Yilmaz journals.sagepub.com/doi/abs/10.1177/097492841006700204).

Illiberal Democracies

There are regimes that can neither be called a full-fledged democracy nor a straight non-democracy; they oscillate in between and are recently identified as illiberal democracies based on the application of two criteria—degree of democracy and degree of illiberalism. Previously the countries which were elected through democratic procedure yet did not allow the citizens their civil rights were designated as 'semi-democratic,' quasi-democratic or authoritarian; they are now claimed to be democratic. Some political commentators, however, describe these democracies by a new catchphrase 'illiberal democracy' to depict their nature and quality of democracy (Zakaria 1997; Bell et al. 1995). In these regimes the democratic sphere is squeezed and societal control is established by a hegemonic party system which punishes dissenting views using methods of coercion (Emmerson 1995; Means 1996; Fukuyama 1995; in Haynes: 2001: 37) such as "vote-buying, legal fine-tuning, ethnic affirmative action, co-option, emergency laws and restrictions on the right to organize, debate and voice options" (Jeff Haynes 2001: 37). They justify their abridgement of civil liberties and point to the shortcomings of the western perceptions of human rights (Bell 2000; Foot 1997; Mcsherry 1998; Robinson 1996). This democracy is on the rise in the East Asian countries (Haynes 2001: 36–41). East Asian countries like Malaysia and Singapore have created their own style of democratization unlke of Western liberal democracy what they call Asian democracy, and 'Asian forms of human rights (Haynes 2001:37).

Electoral Democracies

There are large numbers of countries in the third world today which are designated as 'electoral democracies.' They manifest certain features that seem to be democratic but which, unlike consolidated democracies, are not embedded. Philippe Schimitter (1992) called these democracies unconsolidated or electoral democracies principally because there is no consensus among important political actors that democracy is 'the only game in town.' These regimes miss out *all* important liberal aspects of democracy that can transform a polity into a consolidated democracy (Almond 1996; Lijphart 1968; Finer 1974; O'Donnell 1994). Electoral democracies restrict civil liberties, do not extend *as much* minority rights than full democracies, show inadequate social tolerance, and provide little opportunity for citizens to participate in politics except for exercising voting rights at election times (Jeff Haynes 2001).

Full/Liberal Democracy

Full democracy is one that fulfills all necessary political and civil liberty requirements. It is totally different from all other forms. It is not symbolic or metaphoric or irregular; it goes beyond compliance to a few formal democratic rules and regulations of electoral democracy. Its real emphasis is on sustained democracy (Diamond and Plattner 2001 cited in Jahan 2008) stressing individual freedoms, representation of interests via elected public representatives, and political participation (Haynes 2001: 10). The characteristics distinguishing full-democracy are the presence of a "high degree of equity, justice, civil liberties and human rights" (Haynes 2001: 10). Diamond and Morlino emphasize three substantive qualities of liberal democracy: freedom, equality, and responsiveness (Diamond and Morlino 2004, cited in Jahan 2008). However, it is unlikely that third world countries will have all three qualities at any given time. Exceptions include Dominica, Barbados, and the Marshall Islands, all of which achieved such a position in 1999. In addition, four other third-world countries—São Tomé and Príncipe, South Africa, and Uruguay—came close to achieving this position at the end of the 1990s (Haynes 2001: 10).

In this section we shall assess Bangladesh's democratic standing against recognized benchmarks such as rule of law, fundamental human rights, civil liberties, independence of judiciary, and neutrality of civil service. The term 'rule of law' is embedded as a principle in the Constitution of Bangladesh. Its Preamble states 'rule of law' as one of the objectives to be attained. In *Anwar Hussain Chowdhury v. Bangladesh* (1989) 18 CLC (AD), the rule of law was declared by the Supreme Court of Bangladesh as one of the basic features of the Constitution. According to Articles 7 and 31, any state action and legislation must be justified with reference to the laws. And, any action of the state would be void if it contravenes fundamental rights guaranteed in the Constitution (Nazir Ahmed http://

www.parisvisionnews.com/articles/3052-politicisation-of-the-supreme-court-of-bangladeshnazir-ahmedbarrister-at-law-.html).

Rule of Law

Articles 31–47(a) of the Bangladesh Constitution guarantees fundamental rights and civil liberties for all citizens that include equality before law, equal protection of law, protection of right to life and property, freedom of movement and assembly, freedom of thought and conscience, and speech. Nobody is to suffer harm in person or property without due process of law. Over the years these constitutional protections of citizens have been flouted with the passage of draconian legislations. In this regard Wade remarks if the laws are wide enough to be able to justify dictatorship and tyranny without breaching legal principle then they evidently fail to establish or uphold rule of law (Wade 1971). Various global surveys score Bangladesh's performance on enforcement of the rule of law very lowly. Amnesty International held as recently as 2015 that the human rights situation in Bangladesh has declined continually and, most alarmingly, it is the state that is largely responsible (www.amnesty.at). European Parliament in its September 2014 session adopted a very detailed resolution expressing its grave concern over human rights violations in Bangladesh (2015 EPRS | European Parliamentary Research Service Author: Jacques Lecarte).

In 2014, the World Justice Project portrayed a grim law and order situation in Bangladesh. In its Rule of Law Index, Bangladesh is ranked 92 out of 99 countries in the world. In some parameters Bangladesh's position stands below Afghanistan, Pakistan, Nepal, and other South Asian countries (See Khan, M. R. Prothim Alo, July 8, 2014). It is hardly surprising then that when interviewed MPs were asked how they rate and describe the democracy of Bangladesh, one ruling party MP called it "a party democracy"[14] while another party stalwart rated it as a "partially liberal democracy."[15] The chart below depicts the situation of law and order in Bangladesh in comparison with other South Asian countries (Fig. 10.1).

Extra-Judicial Killings and Torture

The doctrine of the rule of law emphasizes that no man or woman is punishable unless he or she distinctly breaches the law and is found guilty beyond doubt. This principle is both honored and breached in Bangladesh.

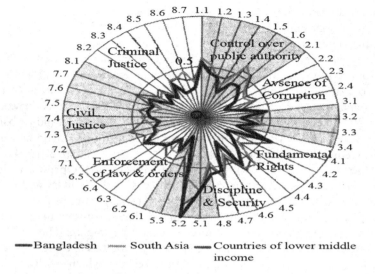

Fig. 10.1 Law and order situation in Bangladesh and other South Asian countries

For years, domestic and international human rights organizations have documented state-sponsored human rights violations including abductions, extra-judicial killings, enforced disappearance, and torture by the Bangladeshi security forces. The RAB—an elite counterterrorism squad—and the Bangladeshi police are both alleged to have been involved in human rights violations by international watchdogs such as the Human Rights Watch.

Extra-judicial killings have been used since the early 1970s by the state security forces in Bangladesh to counteract terrorists, hooligans, and outlaws, though no regime has ever admitted that fact. The issue of extra-judicial killings carried out by the RAB has been a matter of concern since it was first established. It was created in March 2004 as a "composite force comprising elite members from the military (army, air force, and navy), the police, and members of Bangladesh's various law enforcement groups" with the stated intention of launching war against terrorism (www.hrw.org/report/2011/05/10/crossfire/continued-human-rights-abuses-bangladeshs-rapid-action-battalion). The RAB initially gained public confidence because of its success in cracking down on outlaws and criminals, but soon courted controversy because of the methods they used. When the AL was in opposition it strongly condemned extra-judicial killings by the RAB but on assuming power used the elite force in the same manner. As a matter of fact, since its creation successive governments have used the RAB "not only to fight crime, but often as an in-house death squad, leaving a string of extrajudicial killings—often referred to as 'crossfire' deaths, torture, disappearances, and arbitrary arrests in their wake" (www.hrw.org/news/2017/01/19/after-narayanganj-verdict-bangladesh-should-disband-rab). As such, the RAB carried on its operations with little or no accountability, seemingly absolved from human rights violations (Riaz 2015: 4).

In October 2002, the BNP-led government launched 'Operation Clean Heart' to counteract the outlaws in assistance with the military and police forces. This operation temporarily improved law and order in Bangladesh. Nevertheless, human rights groups claimed that forty-four people were killed due to the excessive use of force during the campaign (Jahan 2008: 24). The government also constituted speedy tribunals and set up special law enforcement forces—the Rapid Action Teams—which, with the help of the Bangladesh Rifles (later renamed Border Guards Bangladesh [BGB]), cracked down on hoodlums in 'Operation Spider Web.' Rapid Action Teams could control the situation only to the extent where hooligans were not affiliated with political stalwarts (Jahan 2015). This view was corroborated in a statement from the cabinet secretary who complained in a seminar in 2003 that the RAB and Rapid Action Teams could not discharge their functions impartially and effectively due to the interventions of political leaders (Jahan 2002). Not only the RAB, but the Bangladeshi police forces have also been accused of routinely making unlawful arrests and torturing detained individuals to obtain confessions. Deaths in police custody in recent years have also increased. For example, in 2006 some fifty-one prisoners are reported to have died in police custody (Fahim Quadir).

According to one estimate, 179 people lost their lives in extra-judicial killings in 2013 alone (https://www.hrw.org/world-report/2016/country-chapters/bangladesh). These deaths occurred during raids, arrests, and other law enforcement operations, which the government described as "crossfire killings," "gunfights," or "encounter killings." The government used these terms to denote exchanges of gunfire between RAB/police units and criminal gangs and the media sometimes used these terms to describe legitimate uses of the police force. According to the human rights group Odhikar,[16] between January and September, there were thirty-five disappearances allegedly involving security personnel, compared with fourteen in all of 2013. For the same period, the Bangladeshi human rights group Ain O Salish Kendra (ASK) estimated there were eighty disappearances, compared with fifty-three in all of 2013. On May 15, a group of men in a van attempted to kidnap ASK director Mohammed Noor Liton Khan as he was leaving his office.

A government spokesperson said there would be "zero tolerance" and that it would fully investigate all reports of extra-judicial killings by security forces. However, the statement proved hollow; the government never released any statistics on the total number of killings committed by security personnel, nor took comprehensive measures to investigate cases. ASK reported that between January and September 2015, 135 people were killed by security forces—ninety by the police, thirty-three by the RAB, and the rest by other security agencies including the BGB (https://www.hrw.org/world-report/2016/country-chapters/bangladesh). According to the Internal Inquiries Cell investigation, the number of incidents and guilty verdicts increased in 2016 compared to the previous three years. However, this did not result in convictions for the offenders. In a few instances, those found guilty received only administrative punishment (Country Reports on Human Rights Practices for 2014 United States Department of State • Bureau of Democracy, Human Rights and Labor).

A survey of newspapers between January and September by ASK in 2015 presented forty-three cases of individual enforced disappearance. Later, six were found dead; four released after their abduction; and five found in police custody. The destiny and locations of the other twenty-eight is unknown (https://www.amnesty.org/en/countries/asia-and-the-pacific/bangladesh/report-bangladesh/2015-16).

In 2014 RAB officers in Narayanganj abducted and killed seven individuals, including a prominent local politician, in broad daylight at the behest of a local strongman with AL connections. Of course, in this case the government forced the responsible RAB personnel to retire from service and be brought before trial (Country Reports on Human Rights Practices for 2014United States Department of State Bureau of Democracy, Human Rights and Labor). On January 16, 2017, in the Narayanganj District and Sessions Judge's Court, Judge Syed Enayet Hossain delivered a guilty verdict and sentenced to death twenty-six persons involved in the Narayanganj murders.[17]

Torture

The Constitution and law of the land prohibits torture and other cruel, inhuman, and humiliating treatment of detainees. The Torture and Custodial Death (Prevention) Act of 2013 prohibits torture in custody. The law made the provision for a minimum punishment of life imprisonment, with fines for law enforcement officers and security agencies or government officials for causing the death, torture, or inhuman treatment of detainees. The Act also made the offender liable for paying the victim's family 200,000 taka (US$2500) in compensation. No official can justify his/her action in causing death in custody, torture, or inhuman treatment in any circumstances, including state of war, internal political instability, state of emergency, or an order from a superior officer or public authority (Country Reports on Human Rights Practices for 2014United States Department of State • Bureau of Democracy, Human Rights and Labor). Local and international human rights organizations and the media reported that security forces, including the RAB and police, abused detainees both physically and mentally and inflicted torture during interrogations. Security forces used threats, beatings, and electric shock treatment. According to Odhikar, the security forces tortured ten persons to death of total twenty-three persons (http://www.state.gov/documents/organization/236846.pdf Country Reports on Human Rights Practices for 2014 United States Department of State • Bureau of Democracy, Human Rights and Labor). "The government rarely charged, convicted, or punished those responsible" (Country Reports on Human Rights Practices for 2014 United States Department of State • Bureau of Democracy, Human Rights and Labor).

Attacks on Civil Society

The government increased its attacks on CSOs and media critical of its activities in 2015. Freedom of speech came under increasing attack. Print and electronic media continued to face closure, and editors faced charges and detention. *Prothom Alo* and *The Daily Star*, two leading newspapers known for their critical stance, were on especial surveillance. Business enterprises were warned in October 2015 that they would be penalized if they advertised in these two newspapers.

The anti-corruption NGO Transparency International Bangladesh was threatened with de-registration in November for criticizing Parliament.

Forty-nine civil society activists were charged for contempt of court after they had criticized court trials as unfair. Authorities blocked social media messaging and other communications applications in November 2015. Odhikar faced regular harassment and its access to foreign funding was blocked. In August, after its publication of a report on extra-judicial killings, police warned Odhikar that activities tarnishing the reputation of the security forces would be considered acts of subversion. Criminal charges remain pending against its secretary, Adilur Rahman, and director, A.S.M. Nasiruddin Elan, for allegedly publishing false information (https://www.hrw.org/world-report/2016/country-chapters/bangladesh).

In 2011 Muhammad Ruhul Amin Khandaker, a university teacher, was convicted for a Facebook comment blaming the prime minister for a rise in deadly traffic accidents. The journalist Probir Sikdar was arrested for a Facebook post that alleged to have "tarnished the image" of a senior AL leader, a relative of Prime Minister Sheikh Hasina, and member of her cabinet. The crackdown on social media continues today. On August 2, 2016, a law lecturer at Rajshahi University was sacked for an allegedly disparaging post on Facebook in regard to the law minister's comment on terrorist attacks at Gulshan Holly Artisan Restaurant (The Star, August 2, 2016).

Political Violence

Bangladesh has witnessed confrontation and use of pervasive violence in politics since the early days of independence. However, after the introduction of the NCG, parliamentary elections in 1991 and 1996 took place in a relatively peaceful environment. However, the 2001 elections were overwhelmed by violent clashes between the AL and BNP before and after the election results. The Election Monitoring Working Group reported massive violence resulting in deaths and injuries between August and September. The post-election scenario was even worse; the supporters of the victorious alliance perpetrated an unprecedented rampage on the lives and properties of opponent political parties. The minority Hindu community, alleged to be AL supporters, was worst hit (Jahan 2008). The violence in politics took the most appalling and gruesome shape in its scale and nature, surpassing all previous records, following the Fifteenth Amendment in 2011. In the milieu of months-long general strikes and blockades, mass vandalism and a state of terror reined over the country.

Public and private properties were set on fire, crude petrol bombs were hurled at moving vehicles, and the terrorized public forced to stay home. The public lost its trust in politicians and the threat to personal security for political reasons increased to its highest ever (Arafat Kabir 2015; Jahan 2008). Despite gross dissimilarities in ideology and issues of democratic governance, one commonality is discernible between the AL and BNP—the use of terror tactics when in opposition. Both parties assumed it their responsibility to storm Parliament and bring the government down as soon as possible. The ruling party spends much of its time confronting the challenges of the opposition because its survival in power becomes crucial in the post-electoral stage (Hakim 2002).

Political violence between the AL and BNP left 908 people killed and 10,556 injured in the period of 2009–2014 (Islam 2015: 359–380). The "winner takes all" idea of the FPTP electoral system has become a literal practice in Bangladesh and given rise to extreme polarization and confrontation in politics. In this electoral system political parties are engaged in a power struggle for survival; the party that loses the election fears it will be vanquished and justifies seizing state power by means fair and foul "as the only way to survive in an insecure political and economic environment" (Islam 2015). Vengeance and violence were a feature not only of BNP–AL parliamentary contests; factionalism between the two major parties frequently ended in murder and violence. Initially lower-level party workers were the victims of political violence. However, as the abhorrence heightened over time between the AL and BNP, party stalwarts became targets of political violence. In May 2004, when his party were in opposition in Parliament, the veteran AL MP Ahsanullah Master was assassinated at a public meeting by a group of gunmen (Jahan 2008). Just three months later, on August 21, a grenade attack was launched at an AL rally in Dhaka in broad daylight. Party chief Sheikh Hasina narrowly escaped with her life and several presidium members and senior leaders were injured. This heinous attack killed twenty-three people, including senior AL leader Ivy Rahman, and maimed hundreds (Jahan 2008). S.M.A.S. Kibria, another AL MP and a former finance minister, was assassinated on January 27, 2005, while addressing a public meeting in his constituency in Sylhet (Fahim Quadir 2007). The wave of political violence did not just affect politicians; secular intellectuals and cultural activists also became victims of widespread bomb and grenade attacks from 1999 onwards.

Independence of Judiciary

The prime virtue of the rule of law as opposed to the French *droit administratif* system is that all cases come before ordinary courts and the same general laws are applied to all cases irrespective of the power, position, and status of the litigants (Dicey 1885). A large segment of the Bangladeshi population does not believe that equality before law is maintained for all citizens when they seek justice in the lower courts of the country, particularly for marginalized groups. Another key benchmark of democracy, the independence of the judiciary, is frequently questioned in Bangladesh.

Whether the judiciary in Bangladesh can act independently of the executive is a perennial issue that remains unresolved. Both the AL and BNP, when in opposition, pledged to make the judiciary independent by separating it from the executive branch of the government. But when they assumed state power the issue of an independent judiciary never received priority. A 1999 High Court Division ruling made it obligatory on the part of the government to make the judiciary independent. Neither the AL nor the BNP implemented the court order when in government. Finally, the Appellate Division of the Supreme Court in a landmark decision—*Ministry of Finance v. Masdar Hossain* (1999) DLR (AD)—unequivocally reaffirmed the High Court's decision.

> They argued that subordinate courts were part of the judiciary and therefore persons in judicial service could not be included within Bangladesh Civil Service Reorganization Order 1980 nor could be controlled as though they were a part of BCSs rules 1981. (www.assignment.point)

The Supreme Court ruling laid down twelve declarations for implementation (www.assignment.point). In essence, the case was decided on the issue of "how far the independence of judiciary is guaranteed by our Constitution and whether the provisions of the Constitution have been followed in practice"(http://www.bangladeshsupremecourtbar.com/Masdar_Hossain_Case.php). Nevertheless, both parties procrastinated in implementing the ruling. Eventually, NCG headed by Fakhruddin Ahmed took the momentous decision to separate the judiciary from the executive branch of government. This decision brought the lower courts under the control of the Supreme Court. However, the magistrates' courts, a part of the lower courts, remained under the executive branch and still successfully retains a number of important judicial functions within their jurisdiction, including summary trials, which Jahan apprehends can still "be used by a partisan government to intimidate political opponents and reward partisan supporters" (Jahan 2008: 20).

Despite this change, the judgment of lower courts is easily influenced by political pressure from the party in power since the executive still directly controls the career path of judges and magistrates—their appointments, transfers, and promotions. Political persecution is exerted by unnecessary harassment, arbitrary arrest, denial of bail, time in custody, and retention for long periods of time on flimsy legal grounds until bail is granted by the higher courts. Public prosecutors are appointed by governments based on party affiliation. These prosecutors cannot exercise their judgment dispassionately particularly when political opponents are on trial (Jahan 2008: 20). When the law is preferentially applied to exempt some and persecute others and impartial enforcement is not assured for all by independent judges, rule of law is broken (Dicey 1885).

The Supreme Court comprises the High Court Division and the Appellate Division. The Constitution provides that all other courts are subordinate to the High Court Division and act under its the direction and supervision (Article 109 of the Constitution). The judgment of the Supreme Court shall be binding on all courts subordinate to it (Article 111 of the Constitution). All authorities in Bangladesh, including the executive and judiciary, are required to act in aid of the Supreme Court (Article 112 of the Constitution). Supreme Court judges thus have special position, status, and prestige. They are neither civil servants nor ordinary employees (Nazir Ahmed http://www.parisvisionnews.com/articles/3052-politicisation-of-the-supreme-court-of-bangladeshnazir-ahmedbarrister-at-law-.html).

The Supreme Court has to some extent lost its reputation of independence and impartiality in recent years due to the controversial appointments of judges. The most conspicuous was the change that took effect with the passage of the Thirteenth Amendment which provided that the Chief Justice have the opportunity to assume the position of chief advisor of the interim, unelected NCG, as per Article 58(b) of the Constitution (Jahan 2015). The party in power tried to ensure that judges getting promotions to the Appellate Division were sympathetic to their regime and ideology. In such a circumstance the supersession of senior judges by their juniors was somewhat conspicuous. This led to several judges claiming to be victims of injustice. In spite of having advanced skills, expertise, experience, and seniority, several were superseded by junior judges simply to prevent him/her occupying the top ladder of the judiciary.[18] Put bluntly, judges in the Higher Court Division who were sympathetic to the regime were preferred to others for promotion to the Appellate Division or the position of Chief Justice. This situation has not only demoralized skilled and able judges but also expedited disastrous consequences for the judiciary (Nazir Ahmed http://www.parisvisionnews.com/articles/3052-politicisation-of-the-supreme-court-of-bangladeshnazir-ahmedbarrister-at-law-.html).

In recent years the qualifications of High Court judges has come into question. An investigative report appeared in *Prothom Alo* that revealed that of the seventeen judges appointed by the present government nine hold third-class degrees in LLB and thirteen obtained third-class awards in more than one public examinations in their life (Nazir Ahmed http://www.parisvisionnews.com/articles/3052-politicisation-of-the-supreme-court-of-bangladeshnazir-ahmedbarrister-at-law-.html). Two of the seventeen judges were involved in criminal activities. One was the prime suspect in a murder case at Rajshahi University where he received his education. The other was directly involved in vandalism at the Supreme Court premises; the news was published with a photograph in the national newspaper. Yet they have been subsequently appointed as judges in the Higher Court Division (Nazir Ahmed http://www.parisvisionnews.com/articles/3052-politicisation-of-the-supreme-court-of-bangladeshnazir-ahmedbarrister-at-law-.html). In a more recent case ten judges were appointed purely on political consideration on the dictates of government officials superseding almost 200 district judges. Advocate Abdul Matin Khasru, the former law minister under the last AL government and present law secretary, reacted angrily in the media:

> They [newly appointed Judges] have not been seen in the corridor of the Supreme Court. Despite being Law Secretary of the Ruling party I knew nothing and I have not been even consulted. They do not have skills to become upper division clerk, yet they are made Judges! (Nazir Ahmed, http://www.parisvisionnews.com/articles/3052-politicisation-of-the-supreme-court-of-bangladeshnazir-ahmedbarrister-at-law-.html)

NEUTRALITY OF CIVIL SERVICE

Another key benchmark of democracy is a neutral civil service. The BCS, grown on the legacy of the British ICS, traditionally recruits its staff via an independent agency (the PSC) on the basis of merit. An independent, impartial merit-based civil service is preferred to the spoils system since the latter has a propensity to degenerate into a system of patronage, nepotism, and corruption. Whereas having a credible recruitment process and a system of promotion based on merit through an impartial agency provides defense against such abuse, the civil service must still ensure it enforces of rule of law through characteristic impersonality and helps establish democracy by making peaceful and orderly political succession possible.[19] Articles 137–141 of the Constitution entrusted the Bangladesh Public Service Commission with the role of selecting the most competent persons for public service through competitive examinations and tests in a fair and transparent manner. However, since inception the PSC's operations and its credibility has been subject of controversy, reaching a peak in recent years. Barring a few exceptions, its chairmen and members have been appointed on partisan political lines since 1972, making the Commission an outfit that serves political interests, and a recruitment agency of candidates aligned to the ruling parties (TIB 2007: 8). The degree to which the country will have a competent, professional, honest, neutral, and fair public service rests on the independence, integrity, effectiveness, and credibility of this constitutional body (TIB 2007).

Presently, the Bangladesh Public Service Commission is charged with a host of allegations, including recruiting ruling party activists and supporters, leaking BCS examination question papers, and selecting by bribery. These charges have understandably contributed to a massive erosion of trust and credibility. It is alleged that the organization is manned in such a manner that staff known as supporting the ruling party are placed in the important and influential units of the PSC (such as Confidential and Recruitment Units). Analysts have argued that the recruitment process of the BCS is manipulated by accepting candidates who are known to be affiliated with the party in power (Khan et al. 1997: 5–8).

Moreover, the perception of a prevailing system of patronage within civil service management has ruined its character as a career service. A trend has been established that with change of party in power, many civil servants have their job terminated, are harassed, humiliated, or sidelined as an 'officer on special duty' (OSD) on the charge of having connections with previous government or opposition party. According to one count, in the AL regime between 2008 and 2013, approximately 350 officers were relegated to status of OSD (MazumderProthom 2013). Of course, this wasn't the first time. A similar number of civil servants suffered the same fate under the BNP-led government (2001–2006). The table below

Table 10.2 OSDs in the Bangladesh Secretariat

Position	Number
Secretary	2
Additional secretary	39
Joint secretary	107
Deputy secretary	116
Senior assistant secretary	32
Assistant secretary	47

Prothom Alo May 27, 2013

depicts the scenario of OSDs as on May 26, 2013. Each regime wants to rely on those officials who they consider close to their party ideology and manage state affairs via them. This situation leads to quick promotion of officials on party lines causing an oversized and inefficient national Secretariat (Obaidullah 2017) (Table 10.2).

Generally, selection to Secretariat posts is made on "professional expertise, diversity of experience, demonstrable leadership performance in public institutions, and a capacity to innovate and accept challenging assignments". But in Bangladesh, political allegiance outweighs everything else. In last eight years the AL government has given massive promotion to all level officials from Secretary down to the deputy secretary level numbering 2109 between the years 2009–2013. And large scale allegations have been made that comparatively better merit, efficient and senior officials have been superseded by junior and incompetent ones on political consideration. WB observes that "…nearly half of the staff who are reemployed after reaching their retirement age being rewarded for political ties, rather than in recognition of their skill and expertise" (WB 2002: 71). As such, the Secretariat has a head count double what it requires. The indiscriminate promotion and creation of supernumerary posts for additional secretary, joint secretary, and deputy secretary, and their appointments creates a chaotic situation in the national Secretariat (Ali Imam Mazumder, Prothom Alo, March 19, 2013).

Party in power distributes favor to their loyal; reward them rapid promotion and put them in strategic positions. In return beneficiaries of power help incumbent government stay in power through suppressing political opposition and protecting ruling party during general elections. Party patronage in the recruitment and career progression made civil service an extended wing of party in administration. It has seriously impinged on citizens' trust about civil service neutrality and their integrity. Of the whole cadre services police and administration are ones who greatly waned public trust.

> Their role becomes particularly controversial during the time of elections. Each Caretaker Government had to transfer a large number of officials in the civil and police administration to assure the opposition political parties that the administration in the headquarters as well as at the constituency level would remain neutral and would not influence the electoral process. (Jahan 2015: 20)

In recent years, the BCS has been widely criticized for discriminatory treatment of citizens biased in favor of the party in power and susceptible to political influence. The administration is allegedly busy with protecting the interests of government party supporters. In regard to the maintenance of law and order and dispensation of justice, police stations do not dare taking cases against persons close to the power structure and justice is being carried out at the face value of litigants, which has been a teasing illusion for the weaker section of the population. The Mayor of Narayangang City Corporation said in a recent television interview that the entire district administration was engaged in providing security and services to a government party MP who is allegedly at the root of all misdeeds at Narayangang City Corporation. Increased politicization of the bureaucracy and establishment of a patron–client relationship between politician and civil servant has reached such a height that it overtly contravenes the basic elements of rule of law and anonymity of bureaucracy and professionalism of the civil service (Obaidullah 2017).

The politicization of the BCS has been a concern since independence though its magnitude has varied from regime to regime. After the restoration of democracy in the 1990s the elected political regimes pledged to maintain neutrality of administration and equality of treatment since they vouched for establishing the rule of law. In practice, they did not do that. To put it bluntly, establishing the rule of law would constitute a big stumbling block in running a partisan administration. The neutrality of the civil bureaucracy and lower judiciary has been sacrificed at the altar of partisan interest: "Through a partisan administration and judicial system, successive elected governments have rewarded their supporters and oppressed their opponents" (Jahan 2015: 24) and successfully tightened their grip throughout the country in perpetuating state power.

Conclusion

Judged in the light of the legislative behavior of successive and present parliaments, the nature and intent of the laws enacted, the extent to which the human rights and civil liberties of citizens have been protected, we may conclude that democracy in Bangladesh may be accurately said to stand in between pseudo-democracy and illiberal/electoral democracy. The polity has manifestly suffered from the lack of an institutionalized parliament, a functional democracy, and the absence of strong institutions to ensure rule of law, accountability, and transparency in governance.

Notes

1. The third wave of democracy began in the mid-1970s and continued until about 1990 when the collapse of the Soviet Union brought a new dynamic to geopolitical relations. Just how many countries it can be fairly said made a successful transition to democracy from authoritarianism depends on what criteria is used for assessment. That said, it is plainly true that the number of democracies increased dramatically in just a few decades, most of which had electoral institutions with fragile political and civil rights granted to citizens. Many of these newer democracies are still not fully 'consolidated,' however, meaning that while they have electoral institutions in place, political democracy remains fragile. The reasons underlying this fragility included economic instability, continued elite dominance of politics, and the ongoing military interference in civilian affairs, among others (https://en.wikipedia.org/wiki/Third_Wave_Democracy).
2. In regard to the opposition's role in Parliament, an AL presidium member said "they don't know it." On the same issue, the present Deputy Speaker said that a "party that holds [presently JP] the cabinet minister position, cannot be called an opposition in the parliamentary democracy."
3. In most cases committees were allowed three days to send their report to the House. Several respondents argued that this timespan is not adequate for a detail examination of the bills. Unsurprisingly, a few of the ruling party MPs interviewed claimed it was.
4. The main objective of parliamentary oversight is to ensure that the executive complies with the will of Parliament and remains accountable for all policies and programs it formulates and executes. It is intended to: (a) improve the efficiency, economy, and effectiveness of government operations; (b) evaluate programs and performance; (c) detect and prevent poor administration, waste, abuse, arbitrary and capricious behavior, or illegal and unconstitutional conduct; (d) protect civil liberties and constitutional

rights; (e) inform the general public and ensure that executive policies reflect the public interest; (f) gather information to develop new legislative proposals or to amend existing statutes; (g) ensure administrative compliance with legislative intent; (h) investigate issue-based cases of irregularities and malfeasance; (i) prevent executive encroachment of legislative authority and prerogatives (Kaiser 2006, available at www.fas.org/spg/crs/misc/97-936). Paradoxically, he again mentioned that committee oversight suffers for not having the right person in the right committee, nor the appropriate training to match the mandate of the committee, nor the adequate support service from the Secretariat. He also blamed the inefficiency of committee functionaries.

5. One senior ruling party MP who served in the PAC held the view that sometimes members do not know what their exact job is or the mandate of the committee and the result they are to deliver. Sometimes meeting materials are served at such short notice that no one has enough time to go through and prepare points of queries or clarifications in the meeting.
6. Present ruling party MP and Deputy Speaker Advocate Fazle Rabbi Mia expressed this views to the author in a discussion in his office on December 10, 2016.
7. See the judgment in *State vs. Md. Abdul Gofur* (2006) 35 CLC (HCD).
8. This was the suggestion made by The Asia Foundation study in 1991.
9. Interview with the former chief whip was held on December 10, 2016. He held the view that Parliament as it is a quasi-institutionalized one. Real institutionalization needs the total galvanization of the Secretariat as an organization and change in mindset of senior management. However, in his view the circumstances in which Parliament can exercise its supremacy and become institutionalized does not exist. A strong Parliament needs a strong Parliament Secretariat. He held that the non-implementation of the PSA 1994 was chiefly to blame for the inefficiency of the Secretariat.
10. The Deputy speaker argued that even though the Act was made in 1994 the appropriate rules to give it effect had not yet been made.
11. This interviewee was recruited by the Secretariat in the 1990s and still remains there today at the level of senior assistant secretary.
12. Former chief whip Vice Principal Abdus Shahid, MP.
13. Ali Ashraf MP, who is current chairman of the Standing Committee on Government Assurance.
14. This remark was made by Professor Ali Asraf MP. The role of a political party in the governance process varies depending on the regime type. In liberal, socialist, and communist systems parties play significantly varying roles. In democracies people vote a party/alliance of parties to state power. However, after assuming state power, if the ruling party MPs become beholden to their party leadership/dictates instead of their larger

constituents' demands what type of democracy should that be classified as? (Luke Savage, Case for Party Democracy, https://www.jacobinmag.com/2016/09/jeremy-corbyn-labour-leadership-democracy-doug-saunders).

15. This term was used by Col. (Retired) Fauk Khan, presently chairman of the Defense Committee and one of the members of the AL presidium.
16. On October 10, 1994, Odhikar (a Bangla word that means 'rights') came into being with the aim to create wider monitoring and awareness-raising on the abuse of civil and political rights. The principal objectives of the organization are to raise the awareness of human rights and its various abuses.
17. Ruling AL activist and a former councilor of Narayanganj City Corporation Nur Hossain and three sacked RAB-11 officials—Lt. Col. Tarek Sayeed Mahmud, Major Arif Hossain, and Navy Lt. Cdr. M. Masud Rana were among the thirty-five accused.
18. If things had taken their course without political interference Justice Shah Abu Nayeem Mominur Rahman, not Justice Md. Muzammel Hossain would be Chief Justice today. Not only this, he would have been the Chief Justice before even Justice A.B.M. Khairul Haque. Justice Abu Nayeem was superseded for a second time on May 11, 2011 when Justice Md. Muzammel Hossain was appointed as the 20th Chief Justice of Bangladesh. The following day Justice Abu Nayeem resigned apparently in protest against this appointment. Having provided justice for fifteen years, Justice Abu Nayeem became himself a victim of injustice (Politicization of the Supreme Court of Bangladesh -The protector of the fundamental rights and ensure of the rule of law: Nazir Ahmed http://www.parisvisionnews.com/articles/3052-politicisation-of-the-supreme-court-of-bangladesh-nazir-ahmedbarrister-at-law-.html).
19. Public Administration Reform and Anti-Corruption in Asia and the Pacific Civil Service Reform, Asia-Pacific Regional Center, UNDP.

References

"Introduction" in L. Diamond and Marc F. Plattner (eds) (2001) The Global divergence of Democracies. The John Hopkins University Press, Baltimore

Fareed Zakaria (1997) "The Rise of Illiberal Democracy" Foreign Affairs, Vol. 76, No. 6, pp. 22–48, November–December, 1997

Patterson, Samuel (1995) 'Legislative Institutions and Institutionalization in the United'

Adam Przeworkski 'Minimalist Conception of Democracy: A Defense' in Ian Shapiro and Casiano Hecker- Gordon eds, Democracy's Value, Cambridge University Press, Cambridge

Ahmed, N. (1997) "Parliament –executive Relations in Bangladesh" Journal of Legislative Studies, 3 (4)

Ahmed, N. (2002) The Parliament of Bangladesh, Ashgate Publishing Limited, London

Ahmed, N. (2011) Parliament and democratic consolidation in Bangladesh, *Parliamentary Review, Parliamentary Review*, Spring 2011, Vol. 26, No. 2, pp. 53–68

Ahmed, N. In search of institutionalisation: Parliament in Bangladesh, The Journal of Legislative Studies ISSN: 1357-2334 (Print) 1743-9337 (Online) Journal homepage. http://www.tandfonline.com/loi/fjls20

Ali Ashraf (2017) Member of Bangladesh Parliament. Currently Chairman of the Public Undertaking Committee, Bangladesh Parliament

Almond, G. (1996) Comparative Politics A Development Approach, Little, Brown, Boston

Amnesty International (2015) https//www.amenesty.org

Arafat Kabir (2015) Democracy Departs from Bangladesh. http://thediplomat.com/2015/05/democracy-departs-from-Bangladesh

Bangladesh: World Report 2016: Bangladesh Human Rights Watch. https://www.hrw.org/world-report/2016/country-chapters/bangladesh

Banks, A. S. (1996) 'Cross-national time series data archive', Binghamton, NY: Center for Social Analysis, State University of New York

Jabine, T. B. and R. P. Claude (eds) Human Rights and Statistics: getting the Record Straight, Philadelphia, University of Pennsylvania Press, pp. 364–91

Bayart, F. J. (1993) The State in Africa, Harlow: Longman

Beetham, D. (1994) Prospects for Democracy: North, South, East West, Cambridge: Polity, pp. 55–73

Bell, D. A. (2000) East Meets West: Human Rights and Democracy in Asia, Princeton, NJ: Princeton University Press

Bell, D. A., Brown, D., Jayasuria, K., and Jones, D. M. (1995) Towards Illiberal Democracy in Pacific Asia, Basingstroke: Macmillan

Bollen, K. A. (1980) 'Issues in the Comparative Measurement of political democracy', American Sociological review, Vol. 45, pp. 370–90

Bollen, K. A. (1990) 'Political Democracy Conceptual and Measurement Traps', Studies in Comparative International Development, Vol. 25, pp. 7–24

Bollen, K. A. (1986) 'Political Rights and Political Liberties in Nations; an Evaluation of Human Rights Measures 1954–1964', Human Rights Quarterly, Vol. 8, pp. 567–91

Bratton and van de Walle (1997) Democratic Experience in Africa, Cambridge: Cambridge University Press

Country Reports on Human Rights Practices for 2014 United States Department of State • Bureau of Democracy, Human Rights and Labor

Diamond, L. (1999) Developing Democracy; toward consolidation, Baltimore and London: Johns Hopkins University Press

Dicey, A. V. (1885) Introduction to the law of the Constitution, Macmillan, London

Elkit, J. and Renolds, A. (2000) The Impacts of Election Administration on the Legitimacy of Emerging Democracies: A New Research Agenda, Working Paper, Notre Dame, Ind.: Kellogg Institutes for International Studies, University of Notre Dame

Elklit, J. (1994) 'Is the Degree of Electoral Democracy Measurable Experiences from Bulgaria, Kenya, Latvia, Mongolia, and Nepal' in D. Beetham (ed) Defining and Measuring Democracy, London, Sage, pp. 89–111

Emmerson, D. K. (1995) 'Singapore and the "Asian Values" debate', Journal of Democracy, Vol. 6, No. 4, pp. 95–105

Fahim Quadir (2007) Bangladesh: Countries at the Crossroad. Survey of Democratic Governance, Freedom House. http://www.fredomhouse.org

Fazle Rabbi Mia (2016) Member of Parliament, and Currently Deputy Speaker of the Bangladesh Parliament

Finer, S. E. (1974) Comparative Government: An Introduction to the Study of Politics. Harmondsworth : Penguin

Foot, R. (1997) 'Human Rights, Democracy and Development: the debate in East Asia', Democratization, Vol. 4, pp. 139–53

Freedom House (2006) Freedom in the World 2006:Selected data from Freedom House's Annual Global Survey of Political Rights and Civil Liberties

Fukuyama, F. (1995) 'Confucianism ism and Democracy', Journal of Democracy, Vol. 6, No. 2, pp. 20–33

G. Copeland and Patterson, S. (1995) 'Parliament in The Twenty First Century' in G. Copeland and S. Patterson (eds) Parliament in the Modern Worlh, Michigan University Press, Ann Arbour, pp. 1–12

Gurr, T. R. (1990) 'Polity II : Political Stuctures and Regime Change', 18001986 (Computer File), Boulder: center for comparative politics (producer), 1989, Ann Arbor: Mi.: Interuniversity Consortium for Political and Social Research

Hakim, A. (2002) "Parliamentary Politics in Bangladesh in the 1990s: Consensus and Conflict" pp. 103–132 in (Chowdhury M. H (ed.) Thirty Years of Bangladesh Politics, University Press Limited, Dhaka

Hasanuzzaman, A. M. (2007) 'Role of Parliamentary committees in Bangladesh' (Ahmed, N. & Obaidullah ATM (eds.) The Working of Parliamentary Committees in Westminster Systems: Lesson for Bangladesh, University Press Limited, Dhaka

Haynes, J. (ed) (2001) Democracy and Political Change in Third World, Routledge, London. https://www.hrw.org/world-report/2016/country-chapters/bangladesh. Unknown https://www.amnesty.org/en/countries/asia-and-the-pacific/bangladesh/report-bangladesh/2015-16

Humana (1983) World Human Rights Guide, London: Hutchinson

Humana (1987) World Human Rights Guide, London: pan
Humana (1992) World Human rights Guide, 3rd edn, New York, Oxford University Press
Huntington, S. P. (1991) 'Democracy's Third Wave', Journal of Democracy 2(2), pp. 12–34
Islam M. M. (2015) Electoral violence in Bangladesh: Does a Confrontational Bipolar Political System Matter? pp. 359–380. Published online: 21 Oct 2015
J. Liaz and Alfred Stephan, 'Towards Consolidated Democracy', Journal of Democracy, Vol. 7, No. 2, pp. 14–33
Jacques Lecarte. (2015) EPRS | European Parliamentary Research Service
Jaggers, K. and Gurr, T. R. (1995) 'Tracking Democracy's Third Wave with Polity III data', Journal of Peace Research, 12: 469–82
Jahan R. "Bangladesh in 2002: Imperiled Democracy", Asian Survey, Vol. XLIII, No. I, pp. 222–229
Jahan, R. (2008) The Challenges of Institutionalization of Democracy, ISAS Working Paper No. 39, March 6
Jahan, R. (2015) 'The Parliament of Bangladesh: Representation and Accountability', The Journal of Legislative Studies, 21:2, 250–269
Jahan, R. and Amundsen, I. (2012) The Parliament of Bangladesh: Representation and Accountability, CPD-CMI Working Paper 2. Dhaka
Kaiser, F. M. (2006) Available at www.fas.org/spg/crs/misc/97-936.pdf)
Kemal Osden and Ihsan Yilmaz. 'An Attempt at Pseudo—Democracy and Technical Liberalization in Turkey: An Analysis of OIsmet Inou 's Decision to Transition to Multi Party Political System', European Journal of Economics and Political Studies. www.journals.sagepub.com/doi/abs/10.1177/097492841006700204
Khan, M. M., Rahman, H. and Zafarullah, Habib. (1997) Civil Service Systems: Bangladesh
Kurzman, C. (1998) 'Waves of Democratization', Sttudies in Comparative International Development, Vol. 33, pp. 42–64
Larry Diamond and Leonardo Morlino. (2004) 'The Quality of Democracy: an Overview' Journal of Democracy, Vol. 15, No. 4, pp. 20–31
Lijphart, A. (1968) 'Typolgies of Democratic System' Comparative Political Studies: 1: 3–44
Luke Savage, Case for Party Democracy. https://www.jacobinmag.com/2016/09/jeremy-corbyn-labour-leadership-democracy-doug-saunders
Mainwaring, S. (1988) 'Political Parties and Democratization in Brazil and the Southern cone', Comparative Politics
Mainwaring, S., O'Donnell, G., and Valenzuela, J. (1992) 'Introduction' in Mainwaring, S., O'Donnell, G., and Valenzuela, J. (eds) Issues in Democratic Consolidation: The New South American Democracies in Comparative Perspectives, Notre Dame, Ind.: University of Notre Dame Press

Mazumder, A. I. "*Goder Upor Bishfora*" in Prothom Alo, (Bangla Daily) March 19, 2013
McSherry, J. P. (1998) "Emergence of Guardian Democracy", NCLA Reoprt on the Americas, Vol. 32, No. 3, pp. 16–25
McIver, R. M (1950) Web of Government Macmillan Company, Toronto.
Means, G. P. (1996) 'Soft Authoritarianism in Maysia and Singapore', Journal of Democracy, Vol. 7, No. 4, pp. 103–17
Nazir Ahmed, "Politicization of the Supreme Court of Bangladesh -The protector of the fundamental Rights and Ensurer of the Rule of Law". http://www.parisvisionnews.com/articles/3052-politicisation-of-the-supreme-court-of-bangladeshnazir-ahmedbarrister-at-law-.html
Obaidullah, A. T. M. (2017) "Civil Service Reforms and Development of Professionalism: A Case Study of Bangladesh", in Rumki Basu Shamsur Rahman (eds) Governance in South Asia Rutledge, India
O'Donnell, G. (1994) 'Delegative democracy', Journal of Democracy, Vol. 5, No. 1, pp. 55–69
Odhikar (human rights organization) Dhaka
Patterson, S. and G. Copeland. (1994) 'Parliaments in the Twenty-First Century', p. 4
PROGATI (2011) Bangladesh: Promoting Governance, Accountability and Transparency: Assessing Parliament Capacity to Conduct Public Expenditure Oversight, DAI/Asia Foundation: Dhaka
Riaz, A. (2015) How Did We Arrive Here? Prothoma Prokashan: Dhaka
Riaz, A. (2017) "Astonishing Interpretation of Article 70" A Bangla article published in Prothom Alo, August, 23, Wednesday
Robinson (1996) Promoting Polyarchy. Globalization, US Intervention and Hegemony, Cambridge, Cambridge University Press
Schimitter, P. (1992) 'Interest System and Consolidation of Democracies' in G. Marks and L. Diamond (eds.) Re-examining Democracy, London: Sage: 156–81
Secretary, Ministry of Finance v Masdar Hossain (1999) 52 DLR (AD). http://www.bangladeshsupremecourtbar.com/Masdar_Hossain_Case.php
States, *The Journal of Legislative Studies*, Vol. 1, No. 4, p. 14
Tim Meisburger, Strengthening Democracy in Bangladesh (The Asia Foundation). asiafoundation.org/resources/pdfs/OccasionalPaperNo11FINAL.pdf
Transparency International Bangladesh (2007) Bangladesh Public Service Commission: A Diagnostic Study (draft) Dhaka
Wade, H. W. R. (1971) Administrative Law, Oxford Clarendon Press
White, G. (1998) 'Constructing Development al Democratic State'. M. Robinson and White, G. (eds) The Democratic Developmental State, Political and Institutional Design, Oxford University Press

Whitehead, L. (1993) 'The Alternative "Liberal Democracy", A Latin American Perspective' in D. Held (ed) Prospect for Democracy, Cambridge, Polity, pp. 312–29

World Bank (2002) Taming Leviathan, Reforming governance in Bangladesh, March 2002, Dhaka

CHAPTER 11

Concluding Observations and Recommendations

The preceding chapters reveal a complex situation relating to democracy and the institutionalization of parliament in Bangladesh. The people of Bangladesh bear democracy in their hearts and dreamed in a liberal democratic state to be built after independence. It inspired them to fight a liberation war against Pakistan and, two decades later, to launch restore democracy after a mass uprising against civil and military autocracy. The dream of democracy, however, remains just that—a dream. The democratic journey in Bangladesh has always been extremely hazardous. In essence, the history of democratization has extended really only to the struggle to hold parliamentary elections in a free, fair, and participatory environment. After four successful electoral turnover tests under NCGs after 1991 many assumed that Bangladesh had overcome the foundational challenge of democracy. The scrapping of the NCG system by the Fifteenth Amendment, however, did much to undo this minimal progress in democratic development. Consequent to this unwelcome amendment, Bangladesh witnessed its worst parliamentary election ever in 2014 where not only majority parties including the BNP boycotted but also 154 candidates were elected unopposed. This type of democratic failure was not new in Bangladesh. Indeed, the pro-democratic rule in legislation, constitutional amendment, and conflict resolution anticipated of successive popularly elected governments and parliaments since 1991 has not been forthcoming.

Popularly elected governments in Bangladesh since 1991 have concentrated more on clinging to power than strengthening the pillars of democracy. They have consistently paid little or no attention to establishing the rule of law, guaranteeing the independence of the judiciary, ensuring a neutral bureaucracy, protecting the civil liberties and human rights of Bangladeshi citizens, and creating and safeguarding space for political opposition in the media and in civil life. Without this lifeblood of democracy, the sustainability of a truly democratic system is impossible. The process of governance under legitimately elected regimes was essentially no different from the autocratic regimes. In 2012, The Asia Foundation published an occasional paper on strengthening democracy in Bangladesh. Its author observed that once a government is elected there are few checks on its power "as the opposition is neutered by institutional design, and ordinary voters lack effective accountability mechanisms" (Tim Meisburger, The Asia Foundation, asiafoundation.org/resources/pdfs/OccasionalPaperNo11FINAL.pdf). Parliament made no use of the resources and power vested in it by legal enactments in the post-restoration period. Institutional and operational reforms carried out under the persuasion of the development community made no impression in the operational mode of Parliament particularly in restraining the overbearing power of the executive. It remained a constitutional ritualistic body for rubber-stamping executive decisions. The entrenched culture of parliamentary boycott crippled the House and left ruling parties a blank check to take their own course of action as they liked. The treasury bench, on the other hand, instead of adopting constructive measures to resolve political conflicts by accommodation and consensus with the opposition in session, preferred a standoff in the House. Amid arch-rivalry, factionalism, and mimetic standoffs between government and opposition, the consolidation of democracy and institutionalization of Parliament lost its way. Democracy remained an empty word as Parliament continued to be as subservient as it was under autocratic regimes.

Having observed the inner working of popularly elected governments and parliaments in the post-restoration period it is no exaggeration to say that democratic consolidation and institutionalization of Parliament is impeded not by a lack of resources and authority of the House but by the high-handedness of the chief executive. As a modern independent state Bangladesh yet remains hostage to the philosophy and practices of its the British viceregal system—a colonial legacy of executive power refusing to be held accountable by Parliament. The nature and authority of the prime minster in Bangladesh and the level of discretion he/she uses, irrespective of regime, differs little from the viceregal leaders of the colonial era. Let us revisit briefly the underlying reasons for the failure of parliamentary institutionalization and democratic consolidation in Bangladesh to identify the root causes and address how they may be remedied going forward.

First, post-restoration parliaments failed to restrain an omnipotent executive. At every turn of nationalist movement in Bangladesh since the 1950s political leaders agreed in principle that the viceregal system was one of the root causes hindering an accountable democratic system. However, upon assuming state power, the same leaders fell back on the old system and proceeded to assume all (de facto) powers and render other organs of government subordinate to the chief executive (Jahan archive, the daily star, starnet). So long as Bangladesh continues with this viceregal tradition its democratically elected governments will continue to implement autocratic rule. The Constitution grants the prime minister so much power that it in effect converts him/her into an authoritarian ruler. In fact, under the present constitutional system and for all practical purposes the prime minister has become such a hegemon in the entire government structure and political party that every member, be they on the backbench or front bench works merely his/her shadow. The concentration of the pivotal positions of head of government, Leader of the House, and chairperson of the party allows the prime minister to be the source of all power. His/her will prevails over any institution in any case of crisis and in formulating any new policy. The parliamentary system that has been in existence without interruption for over two decades can at best be termed a prime ministerial system (Stigtitz 2007).

Second, modern democratic government is expectedly a deliberative government where people would believe that decisions taken are reasoned and reached through deliberation and dialogue. The system itself is based on the belief that everyone has the right to participate in the management of public affairs(Legislative Debates And Democratic Deliberations In Parliamentary System SYSTEMS https://www.uio.no/english/research/interfaculty-research-areas/democracy/news-and-events/events/seminars/2011/papers-yale-2011/Yale-Rasch.pdf). The cardinal feature distinguishing democracy from other forms of government is the belief in and practice of solving any difference "first and foremost through dialogue." Parliament is the forum where every member has a right to make his/her voice heard be they in opposition or government. The House will listen; because the ability to listen is sometimes more important than our ability to speak. A democratic system can sustain the ability to build a genuine partnership between the treasury and opposition benches (http://www.ipu.org/idd/dialogue.htm). In this the Bangladesh Parliament is seriously lagging; since independence it has essentially served as a party echo chamber. Article 70 conditions an MP to be more a representative of their party than of their constituents since as long as they are a member of the House they are under compulsion to follow the party line. Any statement made by an MP against their party, or a vote against the whips, or even a decision to abstain from voting in the House, will inevitably lead to their being forced to vacate their seat (GOB Constitution Article 70). In this culture of fear and partisanship a vibrant and deliberative Parliament is too much to expect. Shuronjit Sen Gupta said in 1972 while the Constitution was in the making that Article 70 had such undemocratic overtones that no democratic system in the world, except for Ayub Khan's democracy, could retain such a provision (Riaz 2015, August 13). Moreover, almost every analyst who has studied democracy in Bangladesh has drawn the conclusion that Article 70 has obstructed its growth (Riaz 2015, August 13).

Third, weak parliament and volatile democracy has been rendered weaker by the improper role of the major opposition. The opposition is the integral part of parliament in the Westminster model. It is expected to rectify the lapses of the majority party through constructive criticism and through debate reach consensus with the government on policies in the national interest. When the opposition's criticism is based on objective fact and information and is given to improve the performance of the government and rectify its mistakes, the treasury bench cannot fail to take it into account. However, if the opposition is engaged merely in discrediting the government on trifling grounds and hatching conspiracies to oust the regime from power, the majority party will ignore them. On the other hand, the governing party itself must likewise eschew the idea that opposition itself is subversive.

The functional effectiveness of parliament is dependent on the reciprocity between the opposition and government. This kind of situation is missing in Bangladesh. In each parliament since 1991, the major opposition party or alliance has considered it their primary role to storm the government, while the government has cynically concluded that suppressing any kind of dissent is their chief concern. Making Parliament effective and consolidating democracy is the responsibility of both the ruling party and the opposition bench. Mutual accusation does not bring solutions. The treasury bench has shown no spirit of compromise nor willingness to keep opposition members in the House; rather, it has blamed the opposition as 'unwilling and indifferent' to playing their constitutional role. The opposition benches have retaliated by attacking the treasury for its non-cooperation and resistance to creating and safeguarding a space for that constitutional role to take effect. Much of parliamentary democracy in Bangladesh then has been buried in the skirmishes between treasury and opposition benches.

Consistent opposition boycotting in the Westminster system inevitably leads to unchecked government rule since ruling party members get a free ride in the House and become increasingly used to facing no opposition, thus leading to a breakdown in the accountability system (Jahan and Amundsen 2012: 63). Parliamentary conflict can be functional if it does not exceed its limits, but too much of it is entirely dysfunctional and makes parliament ineffective. A considerable degree of trust and respect for rival political actors and tolerance of opposition and criticism are essential in a parliamentary culture. The philosopher Bertrand Russell said 'I should say, love is wise, hatred is foolish.... if we are to live together and not die together, we must learn a kind of charity and a kind of tolerance, which is absolutely vital to the continuation of human life on this planet'.[1] Political parties frequently defend boycotting as a part of parliamentary culture as a form of protest. While that may be true, its sheer scale in Bangladesh from the mid-1990s on suggests that this practice needs to be reconsidered in for the sake of both parliament and constituents. As we've mentioned, it seems that the one things that unites the AL and the BNP is their tactics in opposition—boycotts, *hartals*, extra-parliamentary activities, and so on—and their apparent disregard for the consequences of these tactics. Tactics that are adopted, as Dilara Chowdhury has observed, "not exactly to make the executive behave, but to fulfill its own agenda"(Chowdhury 2013) (http://www.thedailystar.net/news/culture-of-parliament-boycott-in-bangladesh). The allegations of partisan house management by the Speaker, frequently given as justification for opposition boycotts, needs to be properly looked into. The election of the Speaker in Bangladesh Parliament differs from the British and Indian systems. The House elects the Speaker exclusively from ruling party/alliance, which has had played a significant role in the partisan character of parliament in Bangladesh (Jahan 2015).

Fourth, post-restoration Bangladeshi politics has been and continues to be dominated by conflict, coercion, and confrontation, all of which are detrimental to democratic development. Fair democratic competition in the electoral process transformed into fierce conflict and violence in a game of winner takes all. No party wants to concede defeat, since it results not only in a loss of power but vulnerability to personal security with the threat of harassment, humiliation, torture, unwarranted arrest, and enforced disappearance looming large. Grabbing state power by any means necessary is the only way to survive in such an environment. The high personal stakes in politics lead parties to exploit opportunities to reduce the probability of losing an election, even if such opportunities involve illegal or unethical tactics.

> For a politician's party lose an election not only implies some loss of control over important aspects of public policy – as must, almost by definition, be true in all democracies – but, often, also the loss of an important source of his her personal income, as well the income of clients situations. (Stigtitz 2007: 11)

Based on these four root causes for democratic and parliamentary failure in Bangladesh, it remains for me to offer the following seven recommendations to policy-makers in the present government to consider in working to build a new future for our country.

First, a true constitutional government has to be established in place of the viceregal system that is the British colonial legacy. Power must be limited within the framework of the Constitution and laws of the land in a real sense, not just on paper. Government functional legitimacy has to be judged not on its expediency and desirability but rather on the basis of how power is adopted in the interests of the people, maintenance of individual liberty, and safeguarding of the inalienable rights of citizens (Thomas Paine, 1791 available at https://en.wikipedia.org/wiki/Rights_of_Man). A government can claim to be a constitutional one only when the whole administration of public affairs is wisely conducted in strict conformity to the principles and objectives of its constitution. If the constitution of a country grants the government so wide a power base that it can justify tyranny and dictatorship without breaching its legal principles then neither those principles nor the constitution itself are a fit legal basis for what Paine and others define as a truly constitutional government.

Under constitutionalism two types of limitations are imposed on the government: power is proscribed and procedure is prescribed (William G. Andrews 1968: 13). Against these restrictions the behavior of the Bangladesh government, as reflected in the scale of constitutional amendments made and laws enacted (see Table 2.2 in Chap. 2), do not conform to the basic spirit of constitutional government. The fact is that Bangladesh has a Constitution that establishes a 'government by constitution' not a 'constitutional government.' To establish a democracy that guarantees civil liberties and fundamental human rights, the country is in dire need of real constitutional government.

To realize such a government, checks and balances on the executive power have to be established to counteract the emergence of authoritarianism. Checks and balances can be established by strengthening vertical and horizontal checks on the executive. In a formal legal sense, Bangladesh does have provision for checks and balances but it is relatively weak compared to current systems in place in functioning presidential governments in which there is an organic separation of power which differs from the personal union that is often found in the parliamentary form of government.[2] The Bangladesh Parliament as it stands needs to be aroused with the spirit of supremacy and with a disposition to assert its authority on the executive in accordance with existing legal provisions that authorize them to do so.

Third, elections to Parliament, as the first step to establishing democracy, must be fair, participatory, and credible guaranteeing a level playing field for all contestants. The peaceful transfer of power has to be ensured by an agreed mechanism across all political parties. For that matter, a national consensus among the major power contenders has to be forged as soon as possible.

Fourth, the fear of defeat and its consequence is the root of confrontation in politics and seemingly used as the *raison d'être* for adopting fraud and violence in elections. It has to be ensured by the victorious party that the losing parties shall not be subject to reprisals or suffer any harassment, torture, or imprisonment without warrant of law. Put bluntly, the opposition must be protected and, by extension, dissent in the political, civil, and public spheres safeguarded. Democracy can endure when it can reduce the stakes of politics (Przeworski 1991; Mainwaring and Shugart 1997; de Figueiredo and Weingast 1997; Weingast 2005). A first step to reducing the stakes in politics is ensure a House and wider political discourse that is free from vengeance and personal vendetta.

Fifth, a neutral merit-based civil service as the machine of government has to be established in place of the present patron–client system. The evidence suggests that state bureaucracy in Bangladesh is in the thrall of partisan interests. Confrontational politics between the AL and BNP emanating from the fear of losing elections has led both parties to build a clientelism between government and civil bureaucracy in order to maintain reciprocal interests. A patrimonial government maintains patron–client relations with the civil service rank and file linked to the regime by providing resources and other forms of support to protect them during crisis, for example, rescuing alleged criminals from justice to serve the interests of the regime. Legally convicted criminals under 'due process of law' get impunity on political grounds. Political parties are scared of prosecuting the perpetrators of electoral violence in apprehension of losing their future back up. Civil bureaucracy is now used as tool to manipulate elections in favor of the regime (Islam 2015). All parties that have formed a government since 1991 have discriminated against civil servants seen as political enemies in the processes of recruitment, promotion, and placements. The government uses this clientele group not only for carrying out day-to-day administration and law and order but also for suppressing political opposition and manipulating results in parliamentary elections to ensure they stay in power (Obaidullah 2016). It is hardly necessary to mention that a non-partisan civil service is crucial to sustaining a democratic transition in peaceful and orderly political succession (Public Administration Reform and Anti-Corruption in Asia and the Pacific Civil service Reform, Asia-Pacific Regional Center, UNDP). A professional bureaucracy possesses the capacity to constrain the executive from the flagrant and the excess use of power. A partisan bureaucracy cannot; too many civil servants are indebted to their political patrons for their position and will expect further favor and patronage in their future career.

Sixth, a significant component of institutionalizing Parliament is transforming the Secretariat. As the body that provides the main support service to MPs and committees it must be managed and staffed by its own professional staff, not deputed ministry officials. The current weakness of the Secretariat can be recovered by the adoption of a well-conceived HRD. Crucially, this is not just about training; it's about recruiting the right people and ensuring the body is independent and efficient. As we have seen, the massive training programs that have been conducted at home and abroad have had little effect and this will continue to be the case with the present staffing policy in place. Until the Secretariat stands on its own feet and removes mercenary influence of senior ministry officials from its ranks, capacity development programs will only go so far.

Last but not the least, if politics is considered a game, there should be rules. All actors involved in this game of politics have to abide by the rules set for it. In the context of Bangladesh politics, there is a plethora of rules.

But only rarely are they followed because their violation is not penalized. If Parliament is to work and democracy to thrive in Bangladesh there should be an impartial referee/arbiter to apply these laws equally to all, the powerful and powerless alike, in every aspect of government and society. If Bangladesh is to realize its potential as a modern democracy and bring to bear the dream of 1971, there is no alternative in the years ahead to establishing truly constitutional government and enforcing rule of law. These are the first of many steps this country must take to turn our dream to reality.

Notes

1. Lord Russell made this remark from the life he lived and lesson he learned for our future descendants in an interview with BBC in 1959.
2. 'Personal union' is the terminology used by W. F. Willoughby in describing the nature of the separation of power in parliamentary system as opposed to the presidential system. In a parliamentary system executive members are chosen from the members of parliament and remain parliament members. There is a union between members of the cabinet and MPs. They act as separate organs yet originate from one source. This is why Willoughby called this system an 'organic separation and personal union'.

References

International Day of Democracy 2012 Dialogue and inclusiveness—central to democracy. http://www.ipu.org/idd/dialogue.htm

Chowdhury, D. (2013) *The Daily Star*, "Culture of Parliamentary Boycott in Bangladesh". http://www.thedailystar.net/news/culture-of-parliament-boycott-in-bangladesh

De Figueirdo, R. and B. Weingast (1997) "Rationality and Fear: Political Opportunism and Ethnic Conflict" in Jack Snyder and Barbara Walter (eds) Military Interventions in Civil Wars. New York: Columbia University Press

GOB Constitution of the People's Republic of Bangladesh constitution

Islam, M. M. (2015) "Electoral violence in Bangladesh: Does a Confrontational Bipolar Political System Matter?" pp. 359–380 | Published online: 21 Oct 2015

Jahan, R. (2004) "Why Are We Still Continuing With a 'Viceregal' Political System?" *The Daily Star*, 31 January 2004 (Jahan archive, the daily star, starnet)

Jahan, R. (2015) The Parliament of Bangladesh: Representation and Accountability, The Journal of Legislative Studies, 21:2, 250–269, https://doi.org/10.1080/13572334.2014.975470

Jahan, R. and Amundsen, I. (2012) The Parliament of Bangladesh: Representation and Accountability, CPD-CMI Working Paper 2. Dhaka

Mainwaring, S. and Shugart, M. (1997) 'Presidentialism and Democracy in Latin America: Rethinking the Term of the Debate' in S. Mainwaring and S. Shugart (eds) Presidentialism and Democracy in Latin America, Cambridge: Cambridge University Press, pp. 12–54

Obaidullah, A. T. M. (2016) "Civil Service Reforms and Development of Professionalism" in Rumki Basu and M. Shamsur Rahman (eds) Studies in South Asian Governance, Routeledge, London

Przeworski, A. (1991) Democracy and the Market. Cambridge University Press, New York

Riaz, A. (2015) How Did We Arrive Here? Prothoma Prokashan: Dhaka

Stigtitz, E. H. (2007) Political Competition and the Stability of Parliamentary Democracy: The People's Republic of Bangladesh, Dhaka: UNDP SPD Project

Thomas Paine (1791) Rights of Man available at https://en.wikipedia.org/wiki/Rights_of_Man

Tim Meisburger, Strengthening Democracy in Bangladesh (The Asia Foundation). asiafoundation.org/resources/pdfs/OccasionalPaperNo11FINAL.pdf

UNDP, Public Administration Reform and Anti-Corruption in Asia and the Pacific Civil service Reform, Asia-Pacific Regional Center

Weingast, B. (2005) "Self- Enforcing Constitutions: With an Application to Democratic Stability in America's First Century." Typescript. Stanford University

William G. Andrews (1968) Constitution and Constitutionalism, Third Edition, Princeton: D. Van Nostrand

Annex 1

The chronology of constitutional amendments when parliaments had enjoyed super-majority before and after restoration of democracy is shown in this section.

Super-Majority in the Parliament and Constitutional Amendments

Parliaments	Election year	Ruling party coalition	Number of seats belonging to the ruling party (coalition)	Constitutional amendments
First parliament	1973	Awami League (AL) Sheikh Mujibur Rahman	293	First Amendment Act, on 15 July 1973: Section 47A is inserted, which permitted trial and punishment of any individual accused of 'genocide, crimes against humanity or war crimes and other crimes under international law'. Article 47A specified inapplicability of certain fundamental rights in those cases Second Amendment: Article 33 was amended for preventative detention, and Part IXA was inserted conferring authority on to deal with emergency state and providing for postponement of enforcement of the fundamental rights during emergency Fourth Amendment scrapped the democratic system and introduced one-party BAKSAL system. This Act (i) amended Articles 11, 66, 67, 72, 74, 76, 80, 88, 95, 98, 109, 116, 117, 119, 122, 123, 141A, 147 and 148 of the Constitution; (ii) was alternated by Articles 44, 70, 102, 115 and 124 of the Constitution; (iii) amended Part III of the Constitution out of existence; (iv) altered the Third and Fourth Schedule; (v) absolute the term of the first Jatiya Sangsad; (vi) ended unique supplies relating to the office of the President and its serving; (vii) inserted a new part, i.e. part VIA in the Constitution and (viii) inserted Articles 73A and 116A in the Constitution

Second parliament	1979	Bangladesh Nationalist Party (BNP) Ziaur Rahman	207	Fifth amendment changed the fundamental principles of state policy and restored multi-party democracy. The phrase 'Bismillah ar-Rahman ar-Rahim' was added before the preface of the Constitution. The idiom 'historic struggle for national liberation' in the introduction was swapped by 'a historic war for national independence'. Essential principles of state policy were ended as 'absolute trust and faith in the Almighty Allah, nationalism, democracy and socialism meaning economic and social justice'
	1981			Sixth Amendment was approved on condition that, inter alia, if the Vice President is elected as President, he shall be believed to have left his office on the date on which he enters upon the office of President
Third parliament	1986	Jatiya Party (JP) H.M. Ershad	153	Seventh Amendment: 11 November 1986. It revised Article 96 of the constitution, and Fourth Schedule to the constitution validated all ML Orders, announcements, proclamation of the Chief Martial Law Administrator Martial Law Regulations, ordinances and other laws prepared during the period between 24 March 1982 and 11 November 1986

(continued)

(continued)

Parliaments	Election year	Ruling party coalition	Number of seats belonging to the ruling party (coalition)	Constitutional amendments
Fourth parliament	1988	Jatiya Party (JP) H.M. Ershad	251	Eighth Amendment: amended Article 100 of the Constitution and thereby setting up six permanent Benches of the High Court Division exterior the capital and authorizing the President to fix by noticing the territorial jurisdiction of the permanent Benches 'Islam' was made the state religion of Bangladesh This Act also revised (i) the word 'Bengali' into 'Bangla' and 'Dacca' into 'Dhaka' in Article 5 of the Constitution, (ii) Article 30 of the Constitution by eliminating acceptance of any title, honors, award, or medal from any foreign state by any citizen of Bangladesh without the prior approval of the President
	1989			Ninth Amendment Act 1989. This amendment presented for the direct voting of the Vice-President; it limited a person in holding the office of the President for two successive terms of five years each; it also provided that a Vice-President might be chosen in case of a vacancy, but the selection must be permitted by the Jatiya Sangsad
	1990			Tenth Amendment Act 1990 revised, among others, Article 65 of the Constitution, stated for reservation of thirty seats for next ten years in the Jatiya Sangsad entirely for women members, who will be elected by the members of the Sangsad

ANNEX 1   327

Fifth parliament	1991	Bangladesh Nationalist Party (BNP) Khaleda Zia	158	Eleventh Amendment Act 1991 approved all actions taken by the caretaker government headed by Justice Shahabuddin Ahmed. It also approves the appointment of Chief Justice Shahabuddin Ahmed as the Vice President who afterward becomes Acting President upon Ershad's resignation. In addition, the Act also established and made possible the return of Acting President Shahabuddin Ahmed to his preceding place as the Chief Justice of Bangladesh Twelfth Amendment: Act 1991 re-established the parliamentary system of government; the Prime Minister became the executive head; the cabinet led by the Prime Minister became liable to the Jatiya Sangsad; the post of the Vice-President was brought to an end; the President was compulsorily to be voted by the members of the Jatiya Sangsad
Sixth parliament	1996	Bangladesh Nationalist Party (BNP) Khaleda Zia		Thirteenth Amendment: Act 1996 offered for a non-party caretaker government which stand-in as an acting government and would provide all potential aid and assistance to the Election Commission for holding the general election of members of the parliament. The caretaker government, consists of the Chief Adviser and not more than ten other advisers, would be communally accountable to the President and would stand on charge on the date on which the Prime Minister entered upon his office after the charter of the new Sangsad
Seventh parliament	1996	Awami League Grand Alliance	179	Scrapped Ordinance No 50 of 1975 titled Indemnity Ordinance on 12 November 1996

(*continued*)

(continued)

Parliaments	Election year	Ruling party coalition	Number of seats belonging to the ruling party (coalition)	Constitutional amendments
Eighth parliament	2001	BNP Grand Alliance	216	Fourteenth Amendment: Act 1994 made the provisions for reservation of 45 seats for women on a comparative demonstration basis for the next ten years; increase in the retirement time of Supreme Court Judges from 65 to 67 years; and put on view of portrayal of the President and the Prime Minister in all government, semi-government and autonomous offices and diplomatic missions out of the country
Ninth parliament	2009	AL Grand Alliance	262	Fifteenth amendment of the constitution scrapped the NCG in 2011 and revert to holding parliamentary elections under party government
Tenth parliament	2014	AL Grand Alliance	245	–

Source: Author prepared from the archive

Annex 2

ANNEX 2

Organogram of The Bangladesh Parliament & Parliament Secretariat

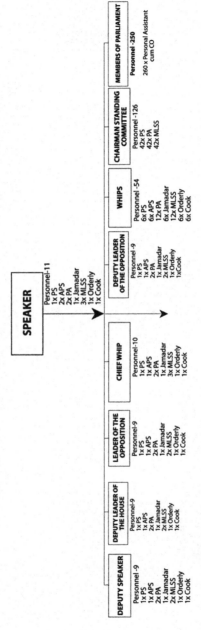

ANNEX 2 331

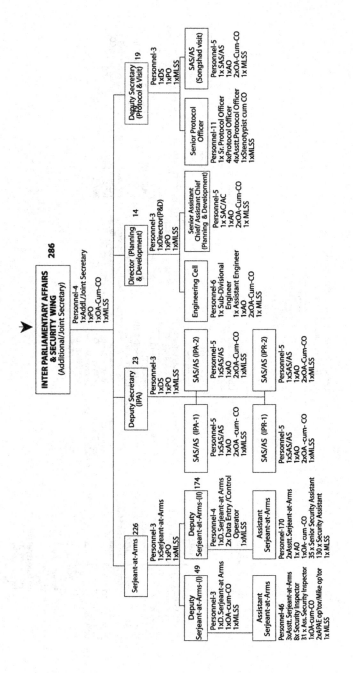

ANNEX 2

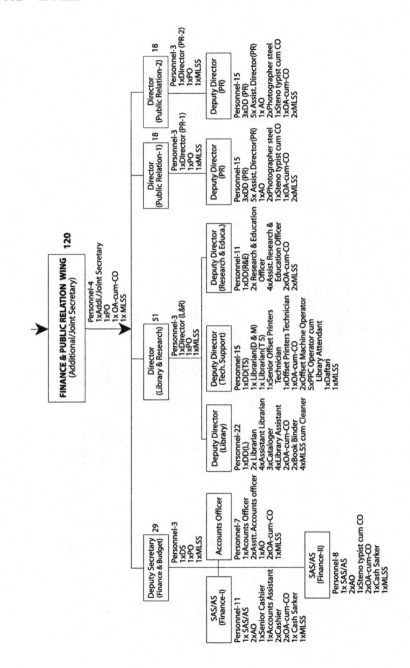

ANNEX 2 333

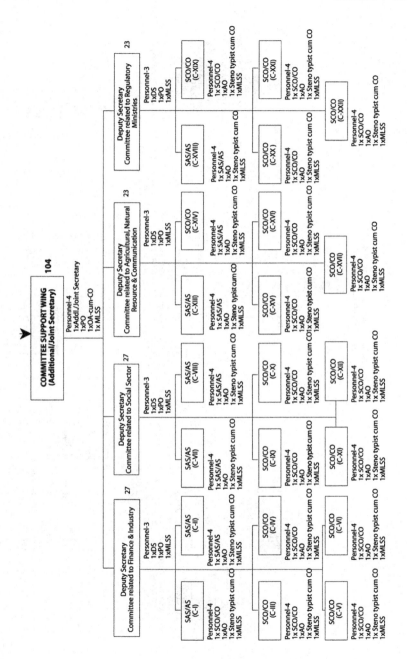

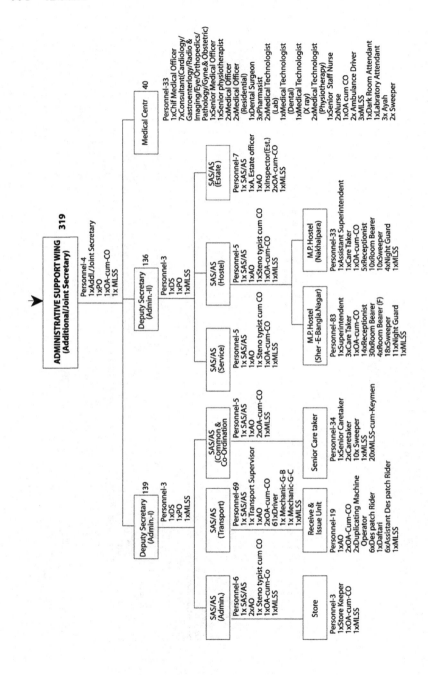

ANNEX 2 335

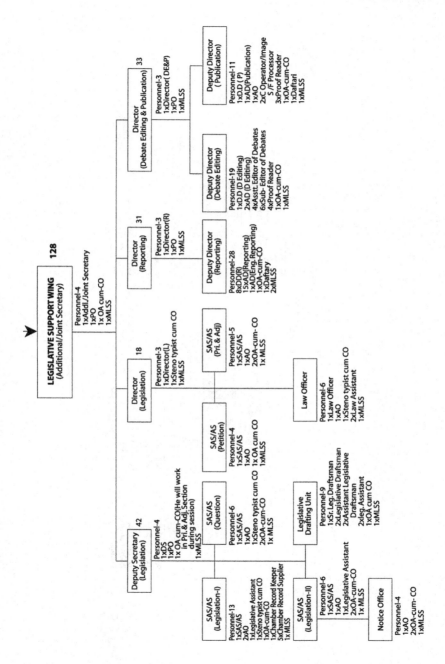

336 ANNEX 2

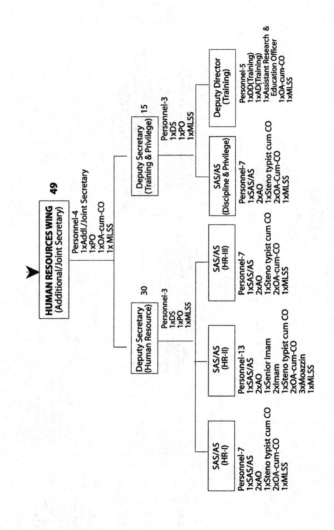

ANNEX 2   337

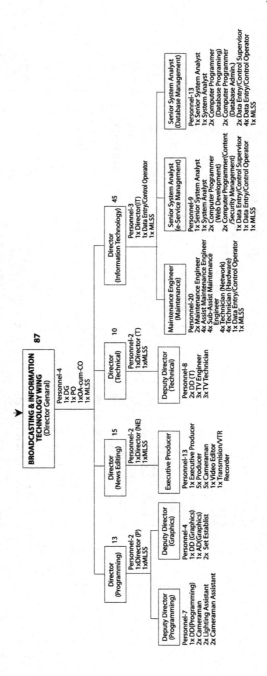

SUMMARY OF MANPOWER

Class-I

SL No.	Name of Posts	No of Posts
1.	Secretary	1
2.	Additional Secretary	2
3.	Joint Secretary	4
4.	Director General	1
5.	Serjeant at Arms	1
6.	Deputy Secretary	12
7.	Director	11
8.	Senior Assistant Secretary	10
9.	Deputy Director	24
10.	Senior Committee Officer	6
11.	Assistant Secretary	19
12.	Assistant Director	31
13.	Others Class-1 Officers	86
	Total=	**208**

Class-II

SL No.	Name of Posts	No of Posts
1.	Administrative Officer	62
2.	Personal Officer	27
3.	Security Inspector	8
4.	Others Class-2 Officers	34
	Total=	**131**

Class-III

SL No.	Name of Posts	No of Posts
1.	Medical Technologist	6
2.	Sub Editor of Debates	6
3.	Caretaker	6
4.	Steno typist cum Computer Operator	37
5.	Assistant Security Inspector	31
6.	Senior Security Assistant	35
7.	Office Assistant cum Computer Operator	78
8.	Receptionist	19
9.	Security Assistant	130
10.	Driver	61
11.	Others Class-3 Staffs	108
	Total=	**517**

Class-IV

SL No.	Name of Posts	No of Posts
1.	MLSS	112
2.	MLSS (Key man)	20
3.	Room Bearer	44
4.	Others Class-4 Staffs	70
	Total=	**246**

Grand Total = 1102

CPSIA information can be obtained
at www.ICGtesting.com
Printed in the USA
LVOW13*2007170718
584093LV00016B/433/P